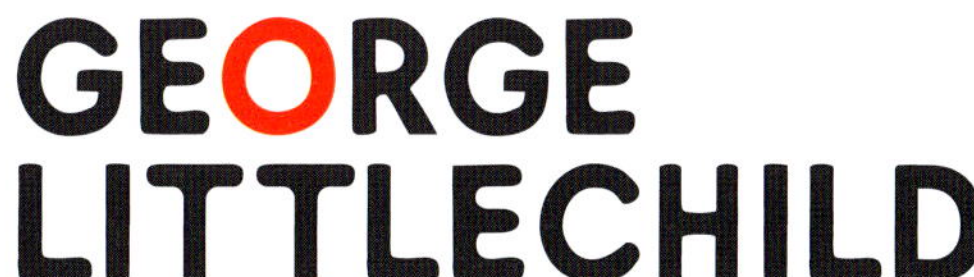
GEORGE
LITTLECHILD

GEORGE LITTLECHILD

THE SPIRIT GIGGLES WITHIN

FOREWORD BY **RYAN RICE**

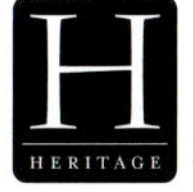

VICTORIA · VANCOUVER · CALGARY

::

For all of my parents:
Rachel Littlechild and James Ernest Price,
Frederick Olthuis and Winnie Prins

::

CONTENTS

NEVER AGAIN

Never Again

mixed media

44" x 30" :: 1993

FOREWORD

George Littlechild wears many hats. He is neither a doctor nor a lawyer nor an Indian chief. However, Littlechild's art satisfies his relentless curiosity and his desire to ground himself wholeheartedly in contemporary culture and society by transforming himself into a historian, humanitarian, philosopher and visionary. He rummages through archives (personal and public), intuitively listens to stories, and is witness to and an active participant in Aboriginal-Canadian history as it unfolds and is revealed daily. His canvases, coated with vibrant colours, lure us to a jovial place, instantly dazzling our eyes and warming our hearts. I remember that feeling sometime in the early 1990s when I first came across one of Littlechild's works reprinted on a postcard at the Montreal Museum of Fine Arts store. Quickly, I bought the "souvenir" and admired its beauty. The image, which embodied a strong Native presence and pride, made an impact on my own journey in the arts from that moment on.

George Littlechild is an amazing colourist—a magician who has the ability to create a rainbow. His colours defy darkness; when you close your eyes, you can imagine his kaleidoscopic palette lighting your path. He uses colour to represent the beauty and spirit of Native people, similar to the late Ojibway artist Arthur Shilling. Littlechild's canvases, covered in pinks, blues and golds, are layered deep with meaning, unfolding matters to be acknowledged and understood from a significant, peaceful and sensitive insight. He employs bold brushstrokes as a unique form of power to resist, disarm and remember a tumultuous history of colonial injustices. In many of his works, Littlechild creates collages from haunting archival images of his ancestors as a means to resuscitate their breath and grant a respectful presence for those who came before us.

In the mixed-media painting *Never Again* (1993), a hand-tinted/coloured, collaged photograph of George's late mother, Rachel Littlechild, bravely represents the spirit stolen from Native children who were taken into custody of the national residential school project. *Never Again* is compelling and addresses the generations of Native children robbed of their innocence through the government's effort and policy to "kill the Indian." The work recognizes the endurance of Native people in the face of oppression and forceful transition disguised as progress. It is also representative of the power Littlechild's art wields by recouping a profound and honest depiction of past experiences that allows us all to move forward—remembering, respecting and honouring life.

Littlechild's creative generosity is supported by his multidisciplinary approach to his work by being versatile in executing his stirring visions. He has successfully conveyed the breadth of his unique talent and personal aesthetic beyond the canvas. I recall the glaring presence that his chine-collé etching *Coup Stick Marks for Pauline* (1996) commanded as it hung in the Donald Cameron Hall dining room overlooking hundreds of visitors to the Banff Centre. Whether working in printmaking, public art or installation practices, George pushed as well as rounded out his abilities to disseminate and share a masterful blend of tradition and modernism to exist with sensitivity and honesty.

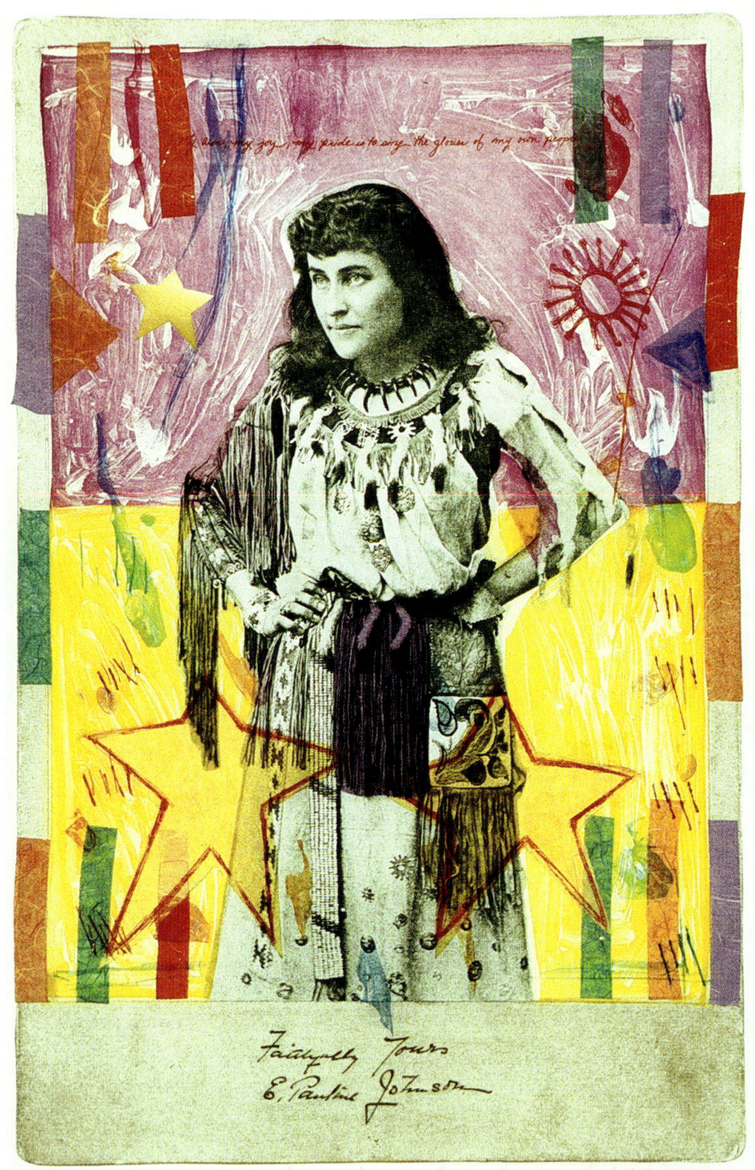

Coup Stick Marks for Pauline

chine-collé etching :: 47.75" x 31.5" :: 1996

Littlechild's own life experience is emblematic and common to Native history of the 20th century. His placement within the foster home system from infancy to adulthood barred his relationship to his immediate family and home. His circumstances as a victim of what is referred to as the "Sixties Scoop" steered him on a path to recover what was missing and instilled in him a desire to belong. Many of his works, such as *Big Sister, Little Brother Price* (1996) and *Me Chasing Mother* (1989), document his experience of alienation and the inner turmoil infiltrating his spirit. Through creativity, Littlechild found himself on a path of recovery that led to empowerment—confronting his upbringing and losses and reclaiming his Plains Cree identity.

Art became an integral form of healing Littlechild's memories of his past and played an integral role in overcoming an unclear state of grief. Similar to the condolence ceremony of the Haudenosaunee (Iroquois), Littlechild's art practice helped him address loss and the emotional disruption with the intent to clear his mind and reduce his pain. His paintings have helped him to metaphorically "wipe away the tears" and restore his heart to its rightful place.

The restorative process allows people to move forward and locate beauty, solace and happiness. The burden of Littlechild's experience is freed and transformed though his creativity and joyfulness, yet laid bare for us to understand. Many of his paintings embody both frivolous whimsy and acute gravity, which Littlechild masterfully reconciles.

Through his exploration of the human spirit, Littlechild criticizes the powerlessness imposed upon him by society. In *I Could Do Nothing as I Was a Boy* (2003), he presents emotional anguish in the overlaying text on a photograph of his older brother and his mother. The stark sepia-toned image reflects a nostalgia that

Littlechild holds on to dearly, while the poem embodies the fragility of his fragmented maternal relationship.

In the First Nations art collective Nation to Nation exhibition *Native Love*, Littlechild and collaborator Aaron Rice presented an art book titled *Since You've Gone Away*, which sifts through the complications of love and relationships. Littlechild's rendered photographs of his birth parents and Rice's flowing words reimagined the obstacles and circumstances of longing, evident among an interracial couple's relationship in 1950s rural Alberta. The subject matter reunited the artist with his parents, whose destiny was unattainable due to the many challenging circumstances they faced. Littlechild's brave attempt to reunite his parents has granted him a sense of their love that he can carry forth.

Iconic images like buffalos, teepees and horses bind Littlechild to his Plains Cree culture and identity. Gold and silver stars chart the course of his career, indicative of the good boy and son he works hard to be and proudly emanates. Through each of these symbols, Littlechild signifies elements of home, survival, movement and brilliance in the face of the suppression he meets head on.

Following on the heels of his previous illustrated works, *What's the Most Beautiful Thing You Know about Horses?* with Richard Van Camp, and his own *This Land Is My Land, George Littlechild: The Spirit Giggles Within* is a beautifully presented survey of his profound work that will inspire compassion and incite contemplation. Littlechild is very generous and shares an informed, sensitive and sincere perspective that encompasses the beauty he carries within. By combining and manipulating senses of naïveté steeped in knowledge, he challenges, defies and demands that attention be given to the unbridled legacy of Aboriginal peoples' endurance and struggles that are critical to a historical, social, political and cultural ecosystem in North America.

Ryan Rice
2012

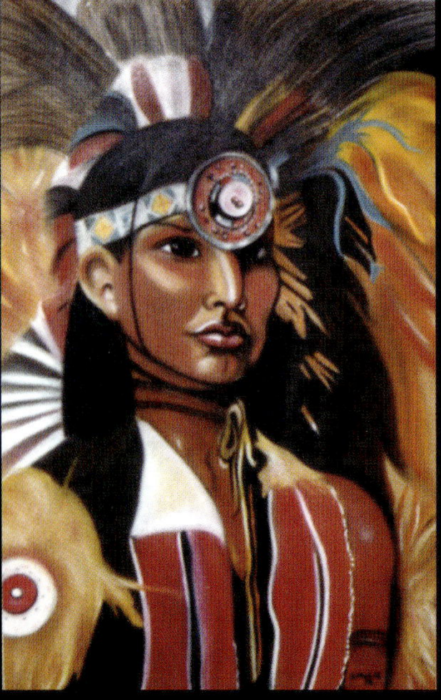

Untitled

pastel on paper :: 22" x 15" :: 1979

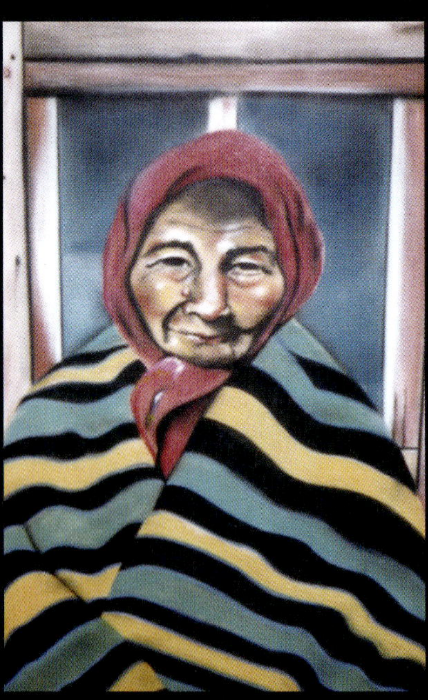

Untitled

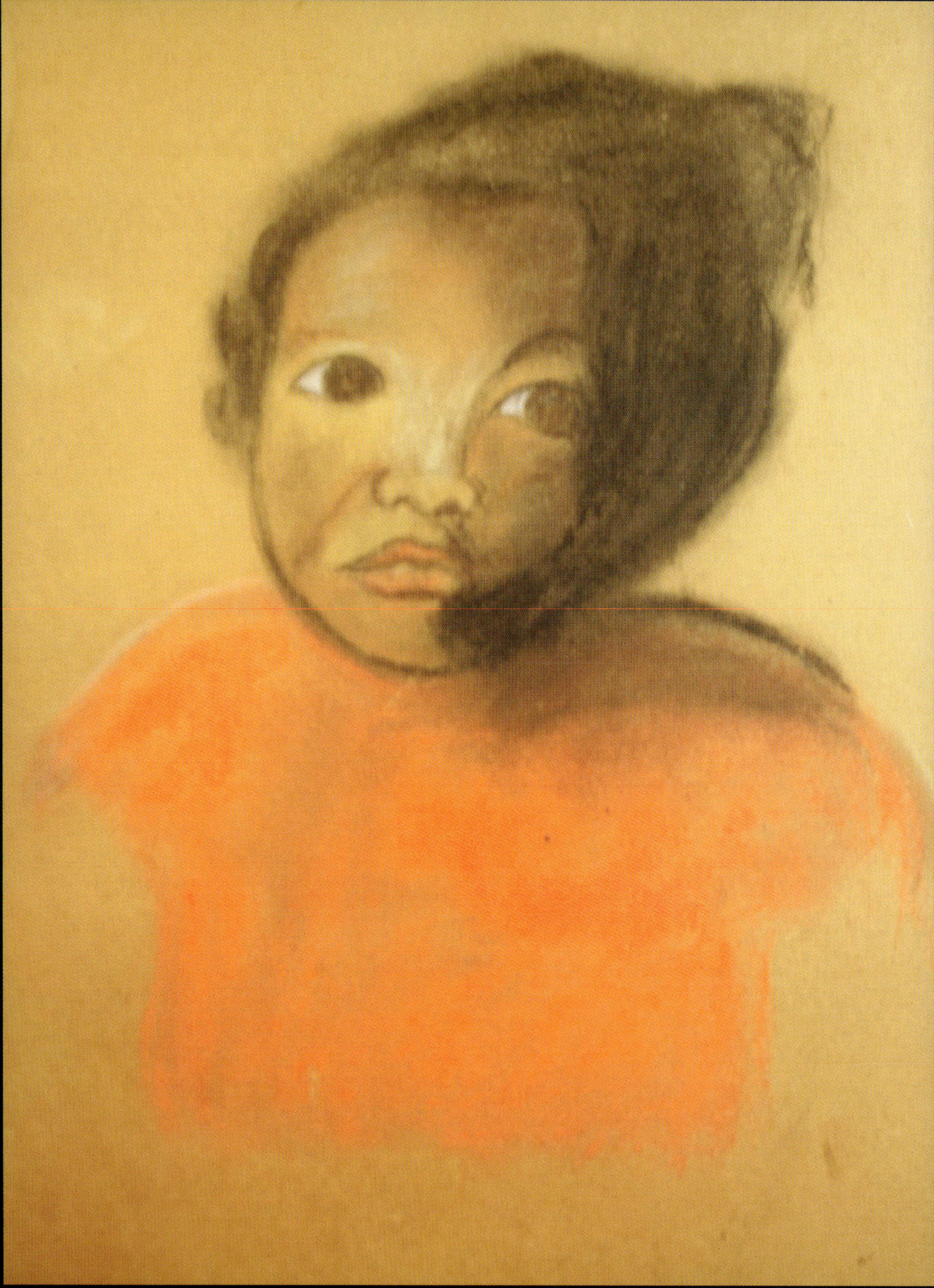

A painting I did in 1972 at age 13.

INTRODUCTION

Life. I am inspired by life. First Nations, history, people, situations, places, whimsy, transformation, spiritualism, culture: the combination of all these things is the recipe that initiates my art. As humans, we are fraught with complexity. Political and social occurrences, child's play and the spirit of fun, and cause and effect trigger great intrigue within my mind and come forth from my fingertips.

I rely on my intuition. Rarely do I sketch before I begin my work; I draw directly onto the paper or canvas and then let the creation begin. I let balance and colour inform me, and it is a meditation and a science. I live with images, thoughts and ideas in my head, sometimes for days, weeks and years. Other times, these images compel immediate action. My art, like science, relies on equations, experiments, formulas and an outcome. All things are weighed and thought out as I listen to the chatter within and let my instincts guide me.

My foster mother, Winnie, said that when I arrived at her home at the age of four, I was already drawing. She was instrumental in seizing and nurturing my young talent. By the time I was in Grade 3 or 4, Winnie had sought out an art teacher for me. Every Wednesday after school, I would sit in a room in the basement of an old Victorian home in Edmonton's Highlands neighbourhood. For 50 cents a lesson, my teacher, Miss Ethel Field, taught elderly women and children the basics of painting. Miss Field had been a professor at the University of Alberta, but when modern art started to dominate the scene, she retired. Her forte was painting portraits of First Nations and Inuit people. She was my first role model and mentor.

My second great art adventure was obtaining a Bachelor of Fine Arts from the Nova Scotia College of Art & Design. I had to prove to others as a First Nations man that I had the intelligence and drive to pursue and complete a degree program. It was a goal of mine—I did what, at one time, I thought was impossible. In fact, for many years I tried to resist my calling as an artist but the voice was too strong. Post-secondary education added the right information and skills to help create the artist I would become. It was a good foundation that informed me about art and art history. It was an important period of my life and has remained with me since.

As a youth, I did not realize that I was biracial, half Plains Cree and half white. I had not been told that my late father, James E. Price (1913–1966), was white or that my late mother, Rachel Littlechild (1929–1965), was of the Plains Cree First Nation. All I knew was that I was Indian. I was raised in foster care, a victim of the Sixties Scoop, and I was labelled "Indian" by those around me. As a child, I fought racism and had a true understanding of "the other," not equalling or belonging. I embraced my situation and found a way to speak out against racism and ignorance through my art. My foster parents were Dutch–Canadian, and I am lucky to have been placed in such a loving home where I was accepted without reservation and encouraged to explore my First Nations heritage. It was only when I turned 17 that I learned of my white blood. It was then that I started an 11-year sojourn to learn about my personal family history and to connect with my birth family, thus creating a new identity. I am a blend of many things.

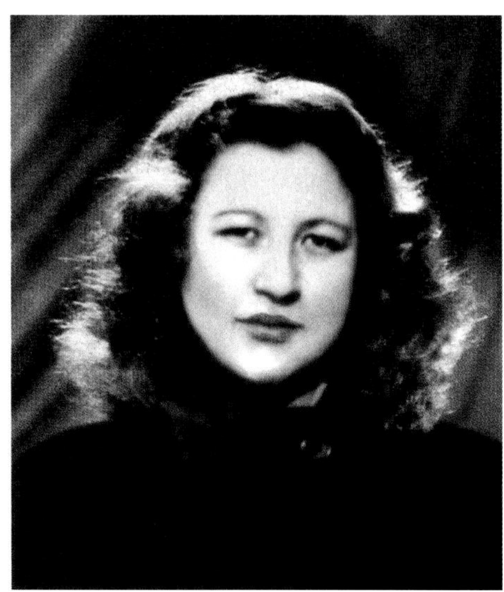

My mother, Rachel Littlechild, at age 19 in 1948.

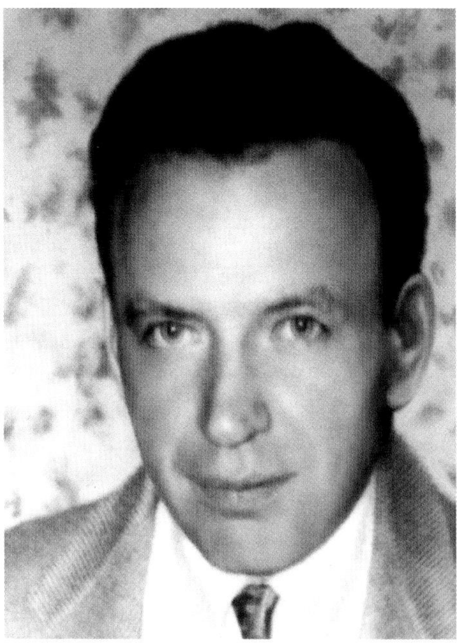

My father, James Ernest Price, at age 45 in 1958.

In my search to reconnect with my biological family, I found myself at many archives—researching people and dates, towns and censuses—and I placed ads in newspapers with requests, hoping to reconnect with family members. I became an avid detective in the process. Amazingly, some interesting and supernatural situations occurred while I was seeking my family. Without these events, I may have never even found or met certain family members, including my sister Marilyn. My motto was to never give up. I didn't, and now I have a huge extended family. I even discovered that I stem from some famous Alberta chiefs, such as Maskepetoon.

Over time I began to address First Nations history, and eventually mixed-race politics and realities in my art. First Nations history, since European settlers arrived, has been an uneven affair. Elements of this unfairness have created fodder and resources for my inspiration, fuelling me to create images that tell that story of repression. It is a story of survival, loss and reconstruction after enduring disease, reserve systems, residential schools and the Sixties Scoop. First Nations peoples have persevered, despite being dominated by the federal government's Department of Indian and Northern Affairs (now called Aboriginal Affairs and Northern Development).

In First Nations cultures, there is no word for art because art was in every aspect of life. In spiritual practice, adornment and how a person conducted themself, art was life itself. Art plays an important role in culture, and it is essential that artists create a diorama for dialogue about issues that affect humanity. The artist or visionary has an acute awareness and understanding that allows him or her to stand up and raise awareness or make social change about things and events that the public does not or cannot address. The artist's stance is strong and full of insight, creativity and commitment. Being an artist means being political. The artist becomes the medium to translate issues and a conduit to create change and provoke thought.

Over the years, I have been called on to conduct art workshops and residencies in schools and at conferences and art-related events. These opportunities have given me great joy as I witness art being created in youth and adults who may never have had such an experience. To see the happiness that art creates within these gatherings and the people who are part of these workshops is beautiful. As a full-time artist and part-time educator, my art practice has provided me with ample projects over the years. I am always amazed at the varied art-related situations of which I have been a part and continue to participate in.

In my work, I am committed to righting the wrongs that First Nations peoples have endured by creating art that focuses on cultural, social and political injustices. As an artist, an educator and a cultural worker, my goal is a better world. It is my job to show the pride, strength and beauty of First Nations people and cultures, and contribute to the betterment of mankind.

Art is my best friend. It has never let me down through tough and good times. We have remained united. I thank the Creator daily for this gift, the gift of art.

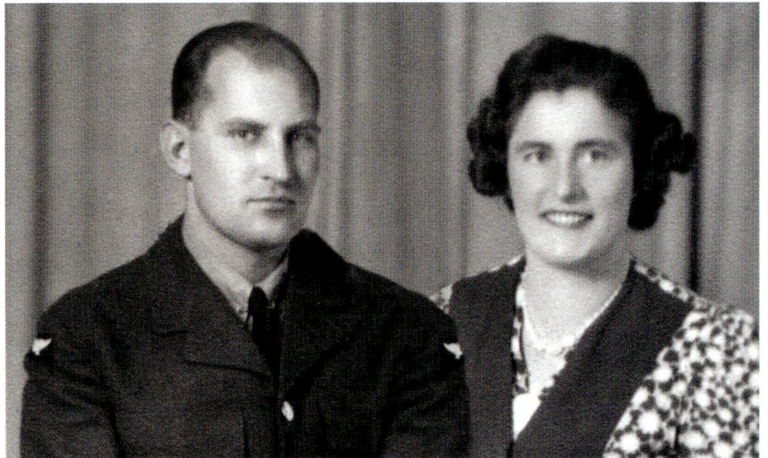

My foster parents, Fred and Winnie Olthuis.

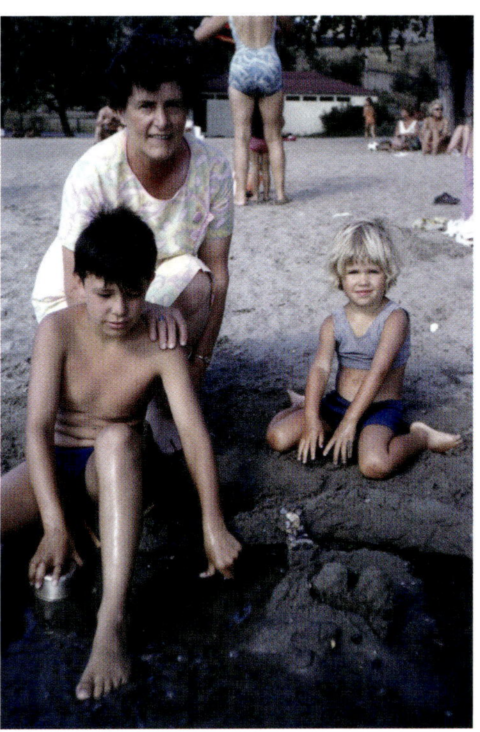

My foster mother, Winnie, with her granddaughter Adrianne and me. I am about 12 here.

PART 1 1986–1989

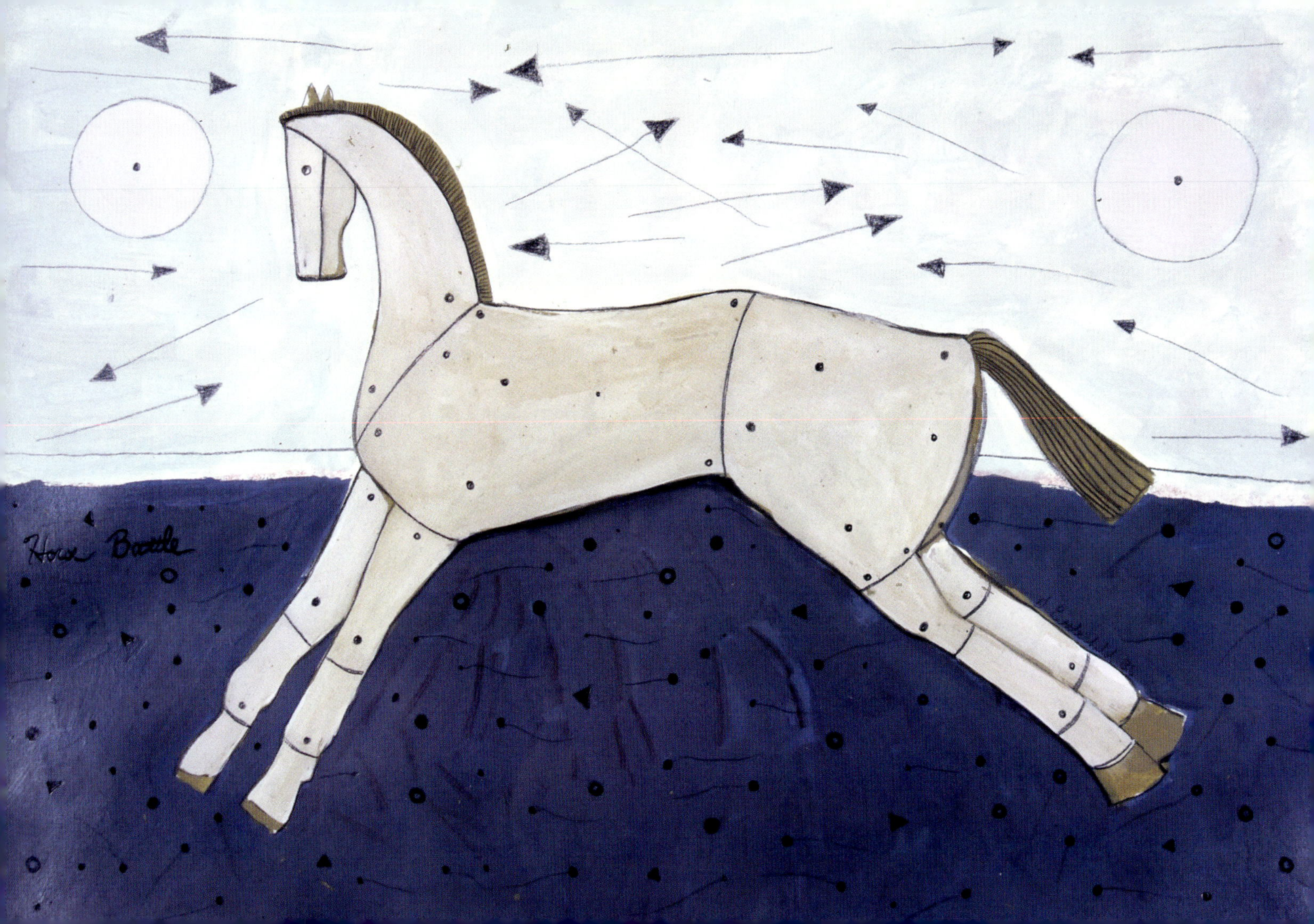

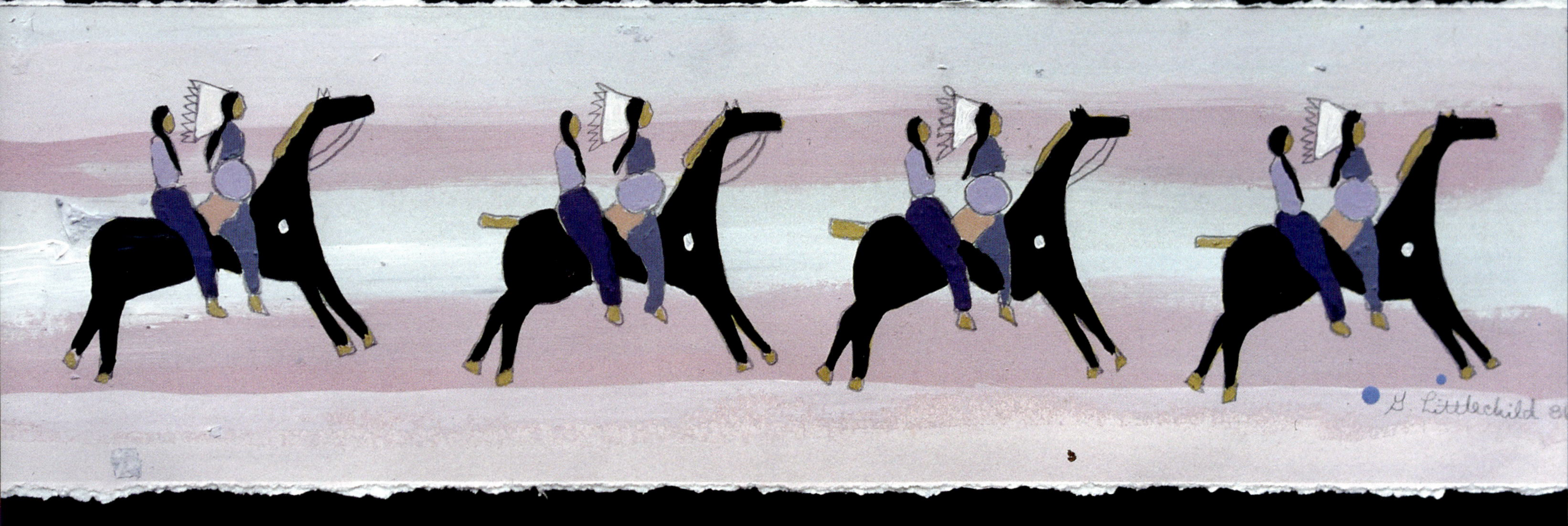

Spot on Horse Blanket acrylic on paper :: 5" x 16" :: 1986

My ancestors, the Plains Cree, were horse people. They were of one of many nations who used horses for warfare and as a mode of transportation, taking them from one hunting or gathering place to another. Horses were revered by the sacred societies of the great Plains

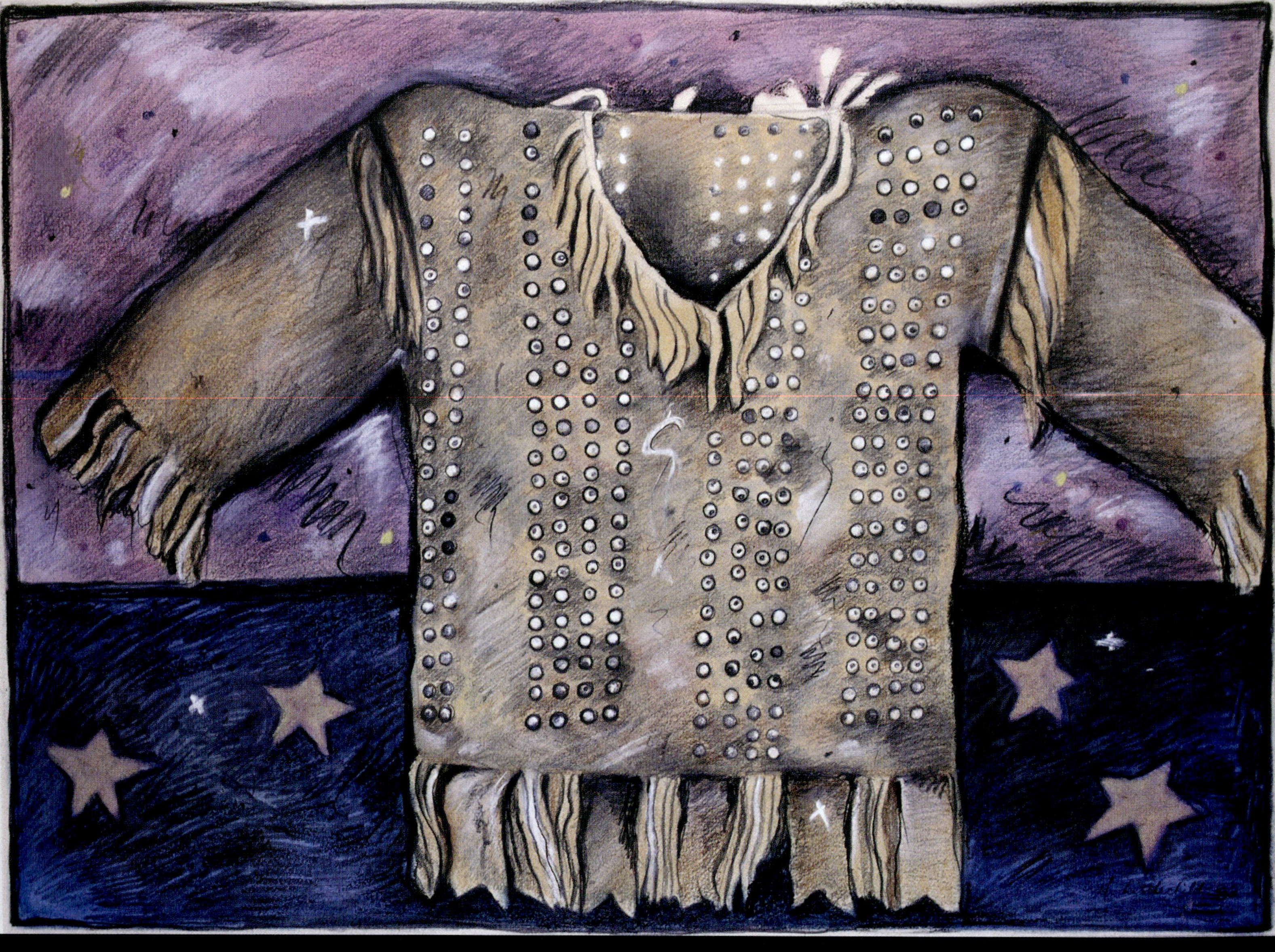

Ghost Spirit pencil on paper :: 17.5" x 25" :: 1986

Regalia was used not only to adorn the individual who wore it, but also in ceremonial practices. One's energy would be enmeshed in the embellished animal skins, which created a storyboard of family connections or symbols. Women of the tribe quilled, beaded and sometimes painted motifs on the regalia with ground pigment and bear grease.

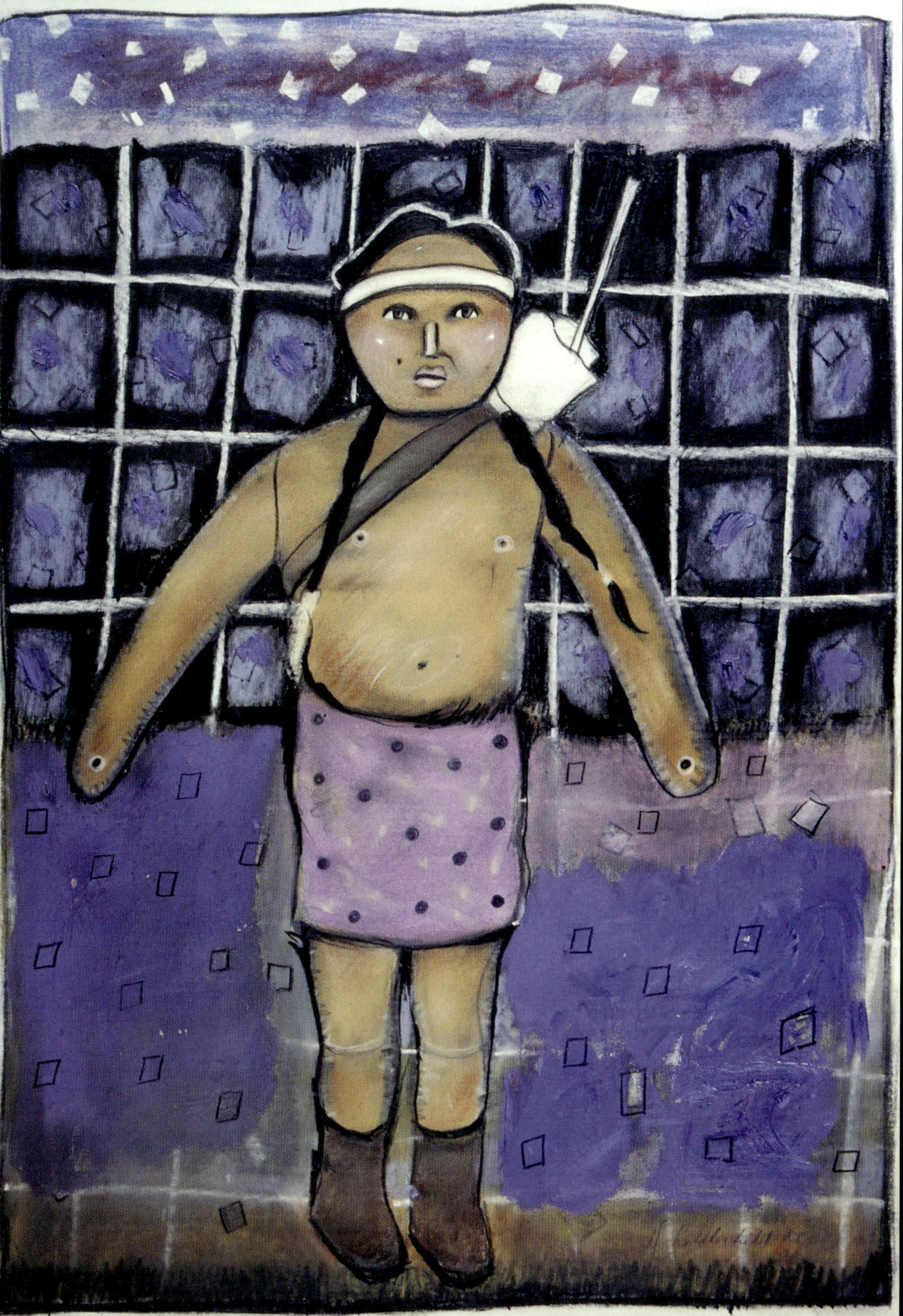

Transitional Man

pencil on paper/mixed media
24" x 18" :: 1986

A traditional warrior posed on top of squares, which represent modern society. This is a self-portrait of the person I had become in the 28 years I had lived—my position and place in society and time, in transition and flux, moulded and shaped. Without undergoing the ceremonies of my First Nation that would have initiated me into manhood, I learned, listened and determined my journey on my own.

Winter Count

mixed media :: 23" x 17.5"
1986

Teachings of the past spoke of great deeds in the life of the tribe. Tribal historians were informants who kept records of events such as births, deaths, raids, losses and gains. These events were recorded and painted onto hides and used as a way to look back—pictographic reminders. These earlier paintings foreshadow the historian and record keeper I would become.

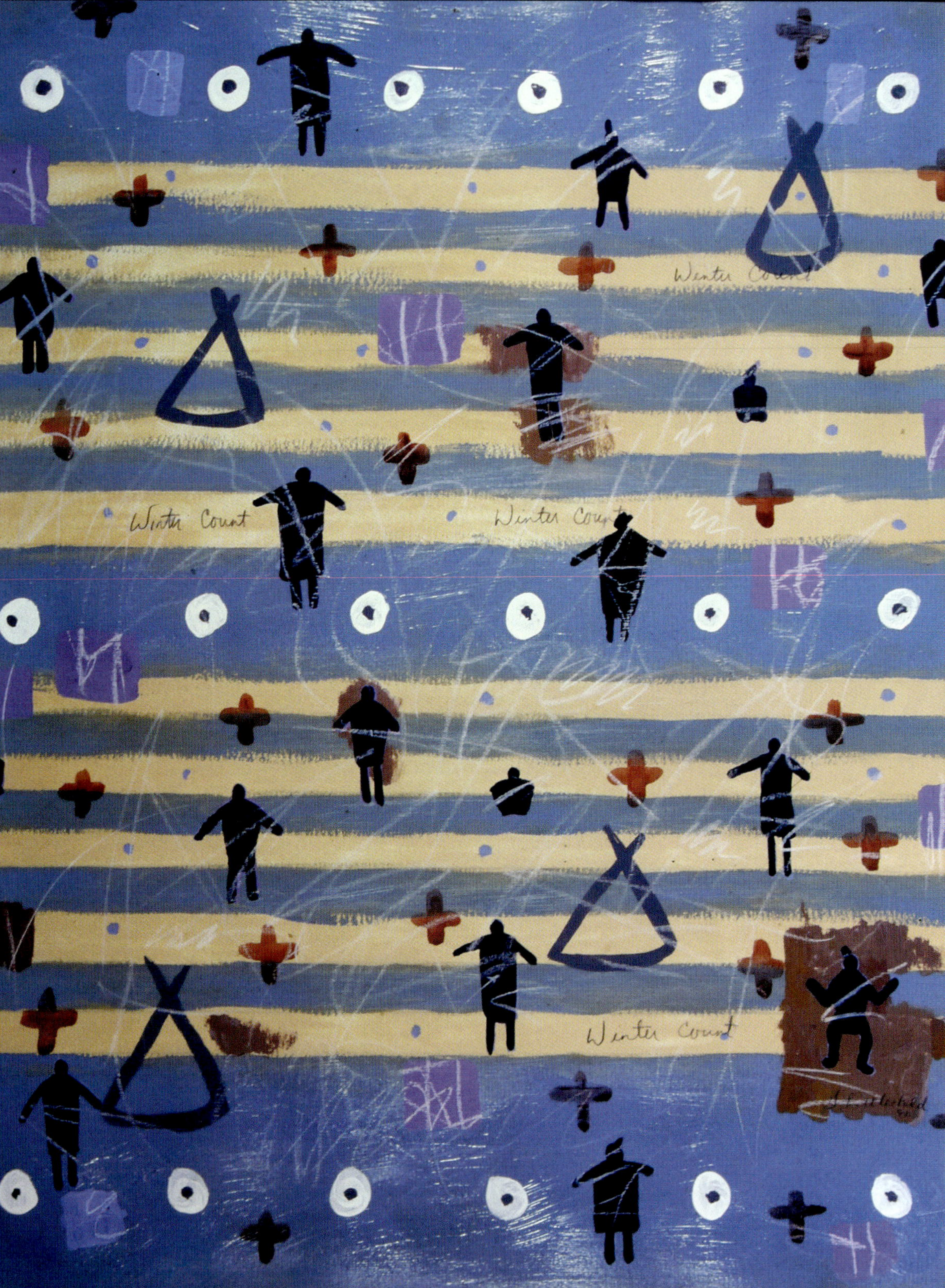

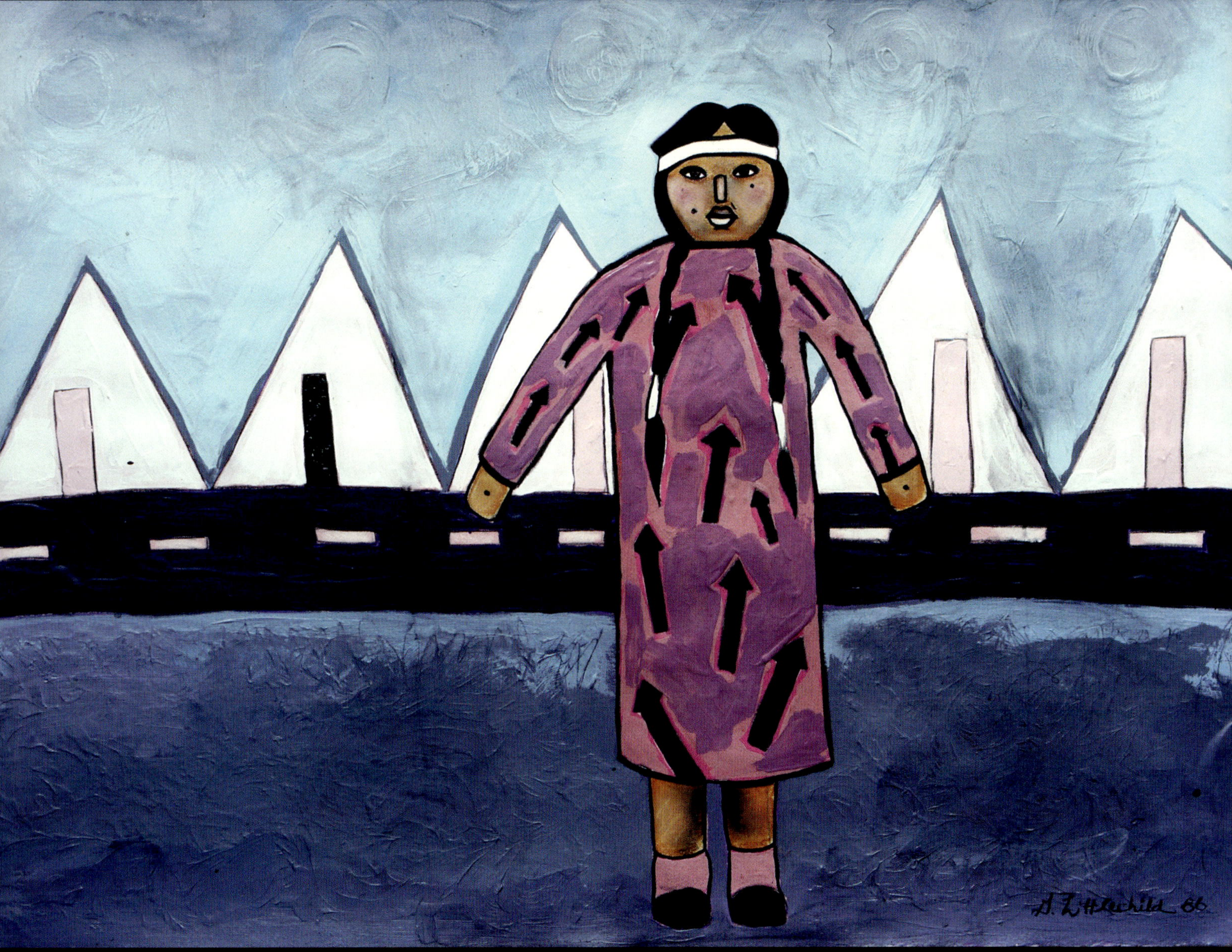

The Enfranchised Indian acrylic on paper :: 22" x 30" :: 1986

My late mother, Rachel Littlechild (1929–1965), was one of the many First Nations women and men who lost their "Indian status" rights through enfranchisement. An enfranchised Indian was one who was no longer considered "Indian." Enfranchisement for women often happened when they married non-status men and were no longer recognized by the (then) Department of Indian Affairs as "Indian"—they ceased to be "Indian" in the government's eyes and in the eyes of the chiefs and councils of many First Nations in Canada. Their names were struck from government records and an enfranchisement document was issued.

In 1985, after a long fight by a group of enfranchised First Nations women, enfranchised women, children and men regained their Indian status and rights. Some bands accepted their people back as band members; however, some bands did not.

The arrows on my mother's dress represent reversal of her enfranchisement, had she lived. The highway represents how she could have gone in any direction, and the five teepees represent her children. I am the one with the black door.

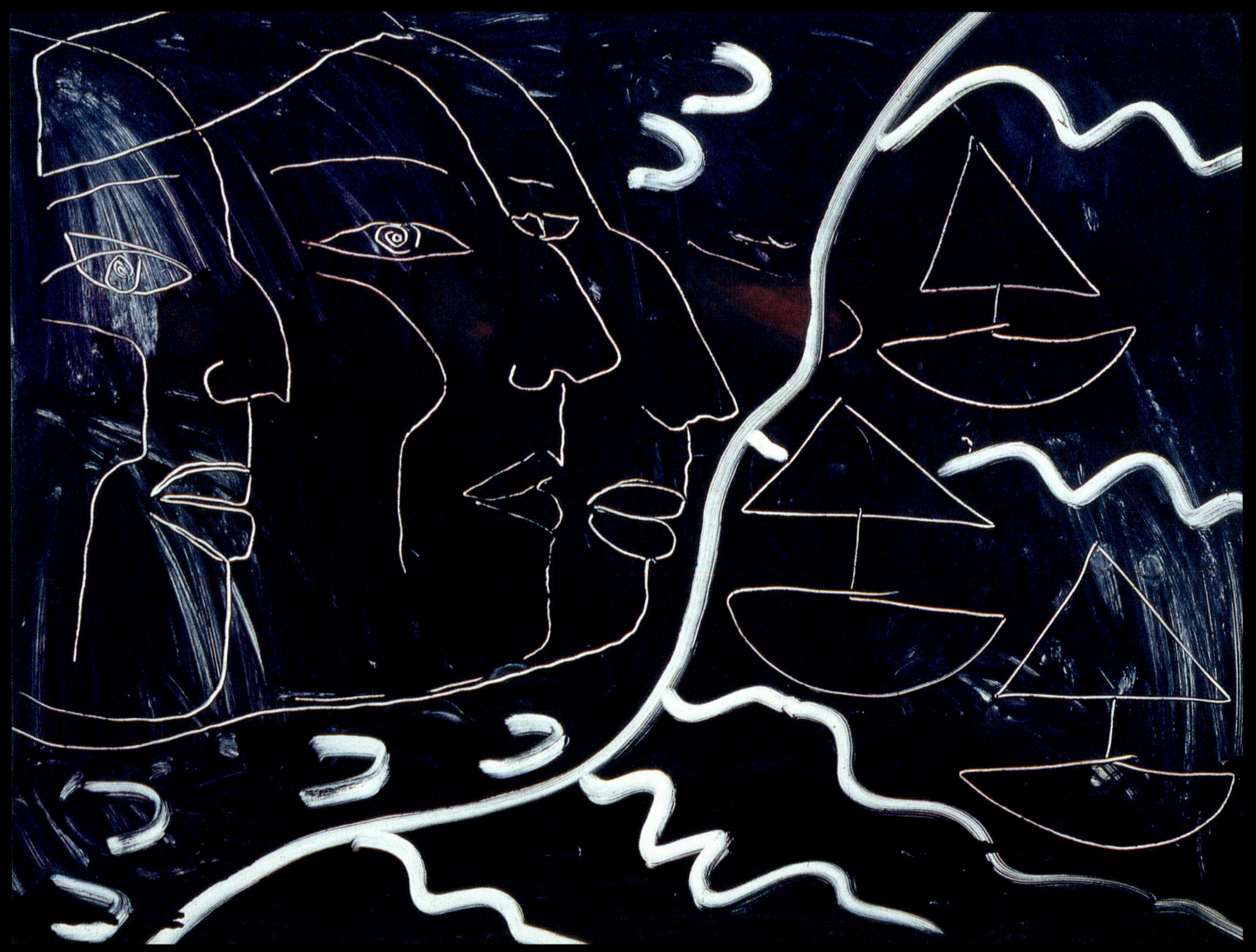

Eastern Indians Beware monotype print :: 17.5" x 23.5" :: 1987

While at art college in Halifax, Nova Scotia, I was a printmaking major, creating a variety of prints via different processes. The experience and the art I made were very fresh and spontaneous. The art captured different social and political aspects of First Nations history in Canada. This piece in particular depicted the Beothuk tribe from Newfoundland, who were wiped out by the European settlers. I found the title fitting for this piece.

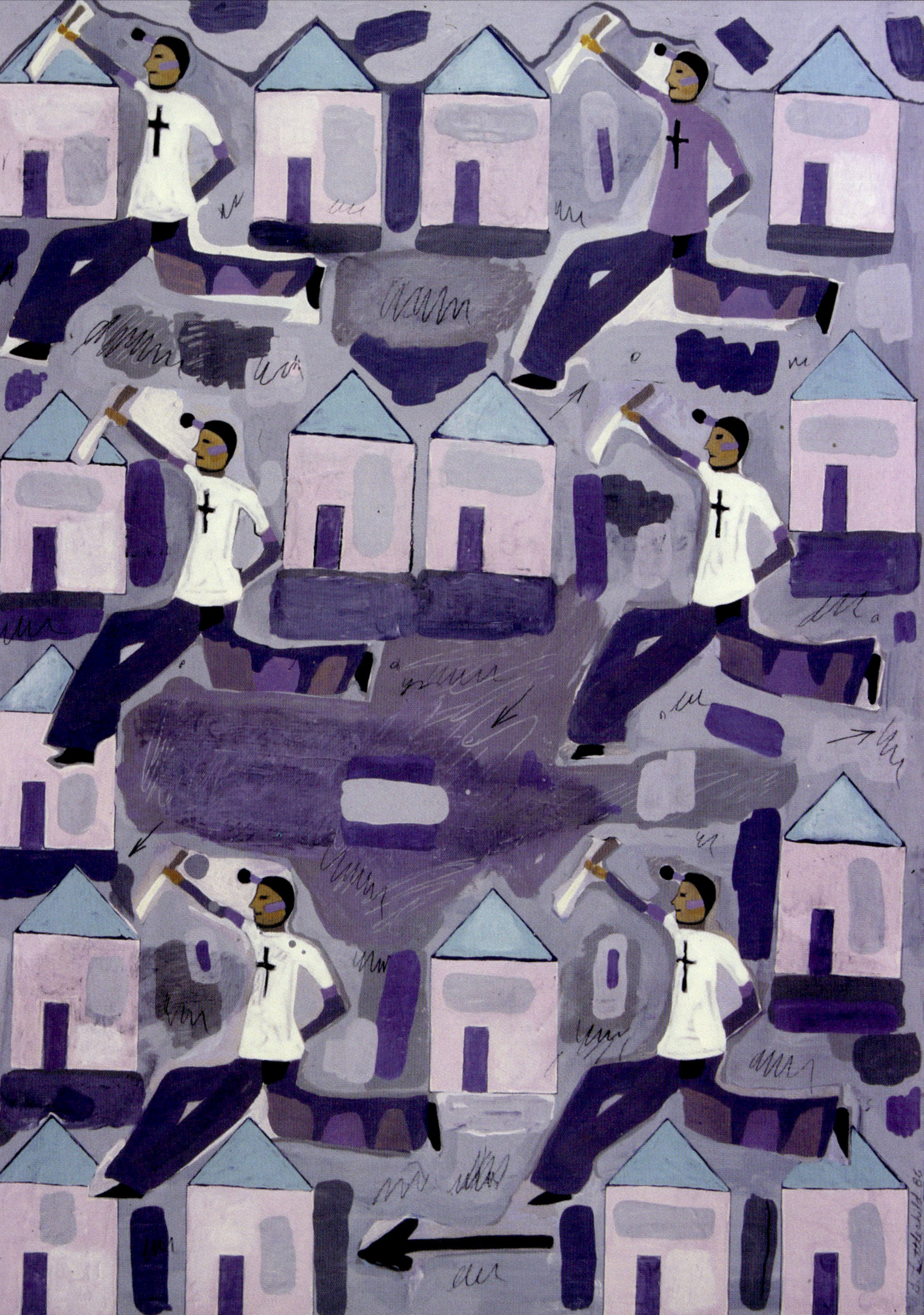

I Looked Out My Teepee One Day and All I Saw Was This

acrylic on paper :: 30" x 22" :: 1987

I can only imagine what it was like to live during the time of my ancestors, a time of great change when incoming missionaries were trying to indoctrinate them into Christianity and the Canadian government was developing reserve systems. The warriors in this piece, forced to relocate and live on small parcels of land, must have become angry or docile. I placed knives in their hands to represent their anger. The box-style Indian Affairs–issued houses replaced their nomadic, traditional home, the teepee.

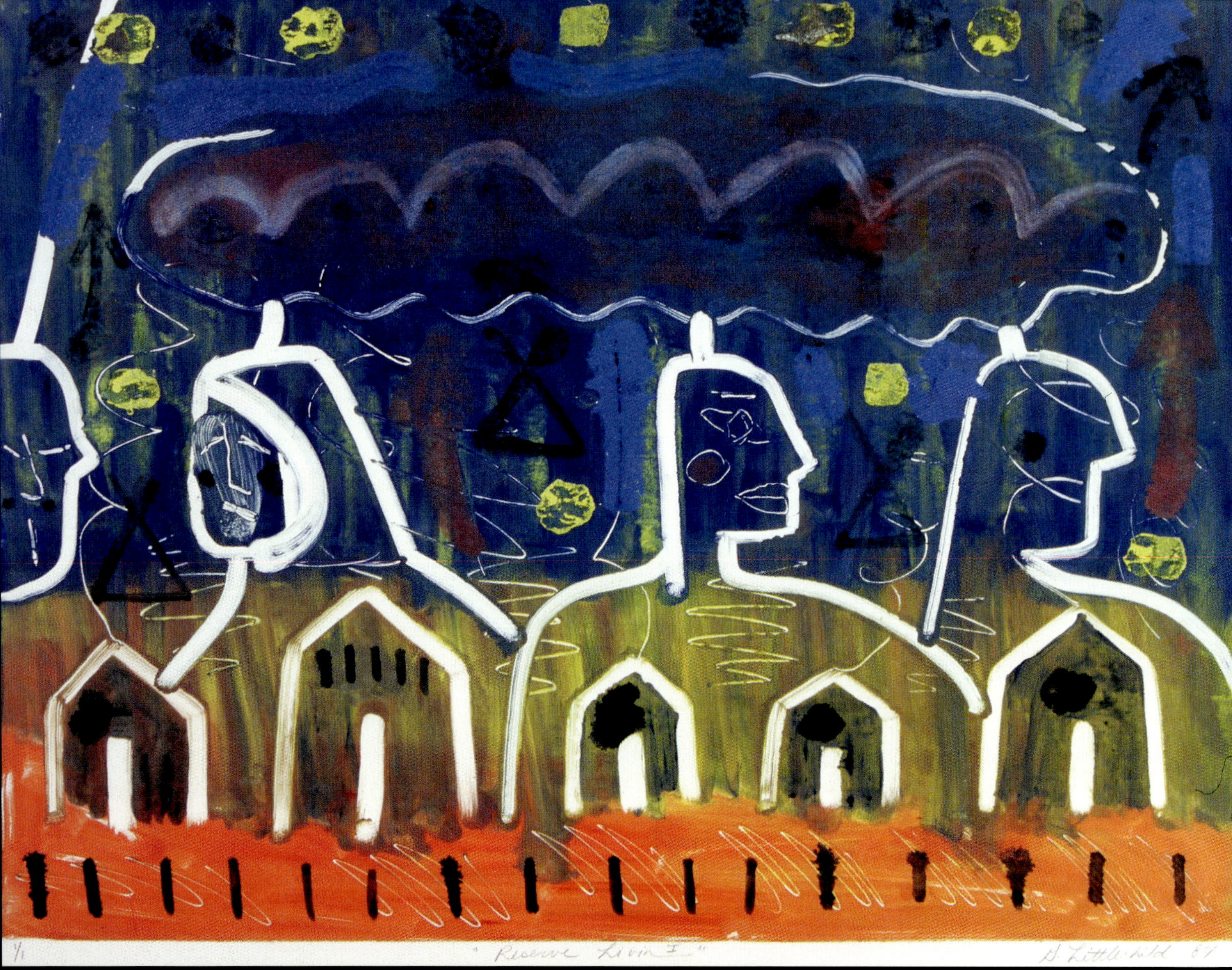

Reserve Housing 1 monotype :: 17.5" x 23.5" :: 1987

In the late 1980s, my colour palette began to expand. I was in my final years at the Nova Scotia College of Art & Design, where I majored in printmaking and studied under Ed Porter, a great instructor who influenced my process and creative art-making style.

In 1984, while taking art and design at Red Deer College, I began to realize that I could use art as a political and social tool to create change—to speak about issues, especially First Nations issues. I had a vision that I needed to share in order to let people know about First Nations history, facts and realities. *Reserve Housing 1* does just that. It speaks of a time when the Department of Indian Affairs forced Native peoples to live on reserves, captives on their own land. They were not free; they were controlled by the government who held jurisdiction over their lives and affairs.

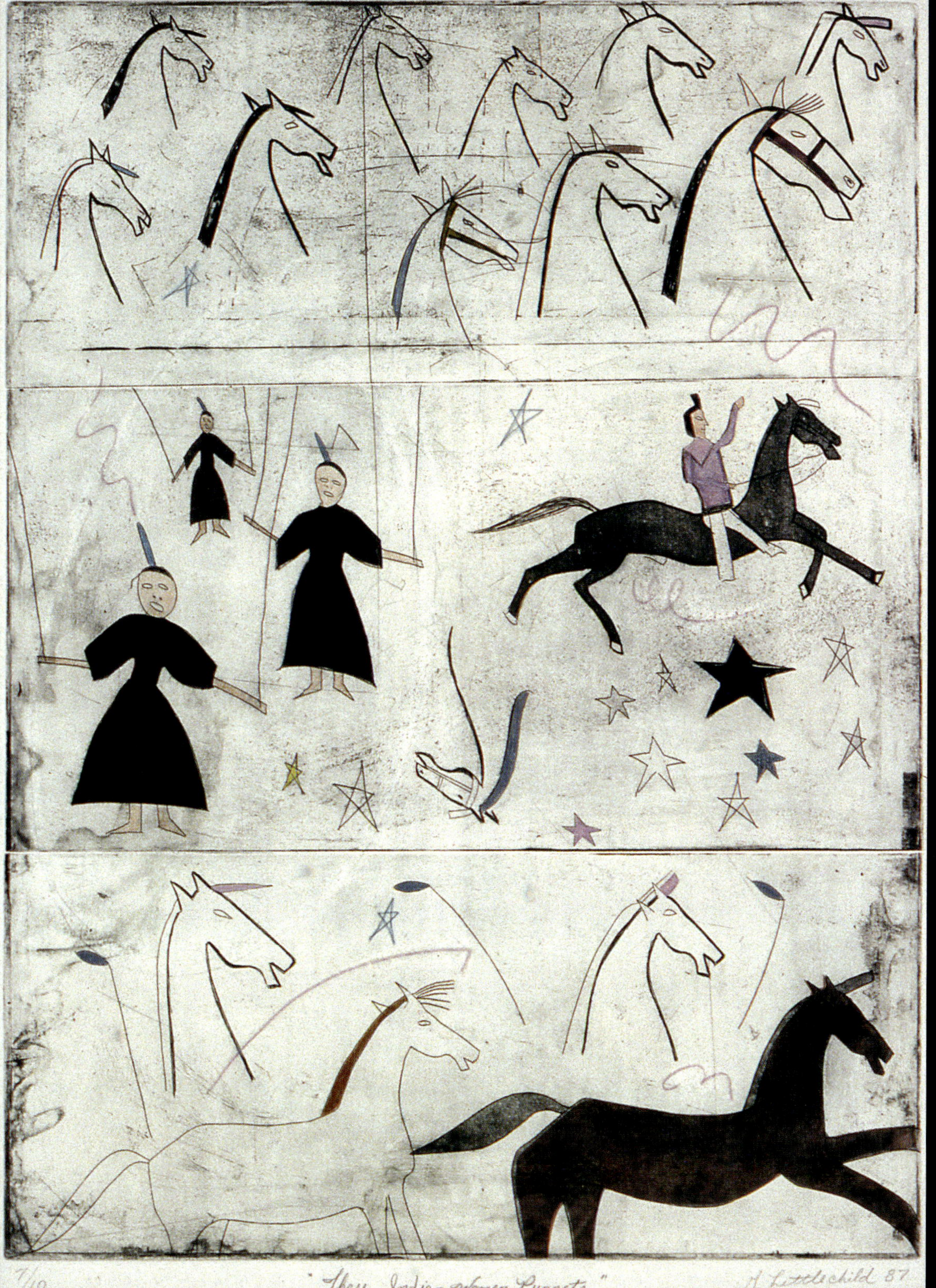

Three Indian Women Puppets

chine-collé collage/intaglio
30" x 22" :: 1987

In many cultures, women are dominated by men. Laws and teachings have put women in "their place" for centuries. In this mindset, women have become marginalized and sometimes powerless; they have maintained their identities under strict circumstances. In this piece, the women are puppets dominated by a man who prances away while they are confined to honour his manhood by taking care of him and their offspring.

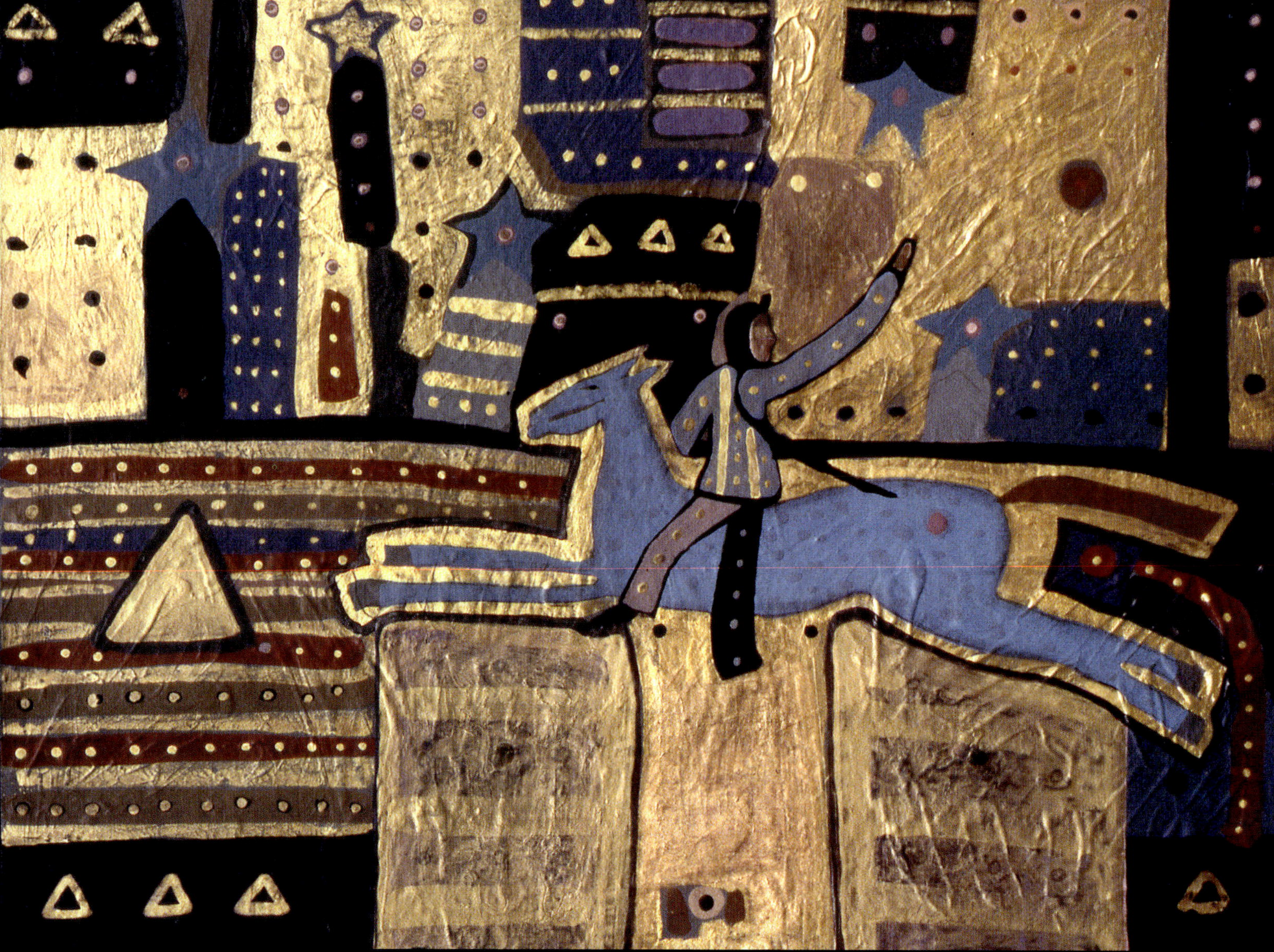

Look Back to the Land That Was Once Yours acrylic on paper :: 22" x 30" :: 1987

In the mid- to late 1980s, my artwork shifted from a muted pastel palette to a more vibrant one. The colours' vivid quality and intensity created a statement itself, as I was becoming a more confident individual; under the right advice and as a willing student, what I learned affected my art, creating a positive shift.

A young warrior sits on a turquoise horse in mid-flight, searching for identity, looking for the old ways. He imparts his teaching, culture and wisdom, represented by the gold underneath his horse. The warrior creates a mythic dust. In front of him, a triangle represents a traditional teepee, symbolizing his desire to return to a previous time. A cityscape illuminates the background, indicating change has occurred. However, it is never too late to learn your culture and language, unless these practices no longer exist within your nation.

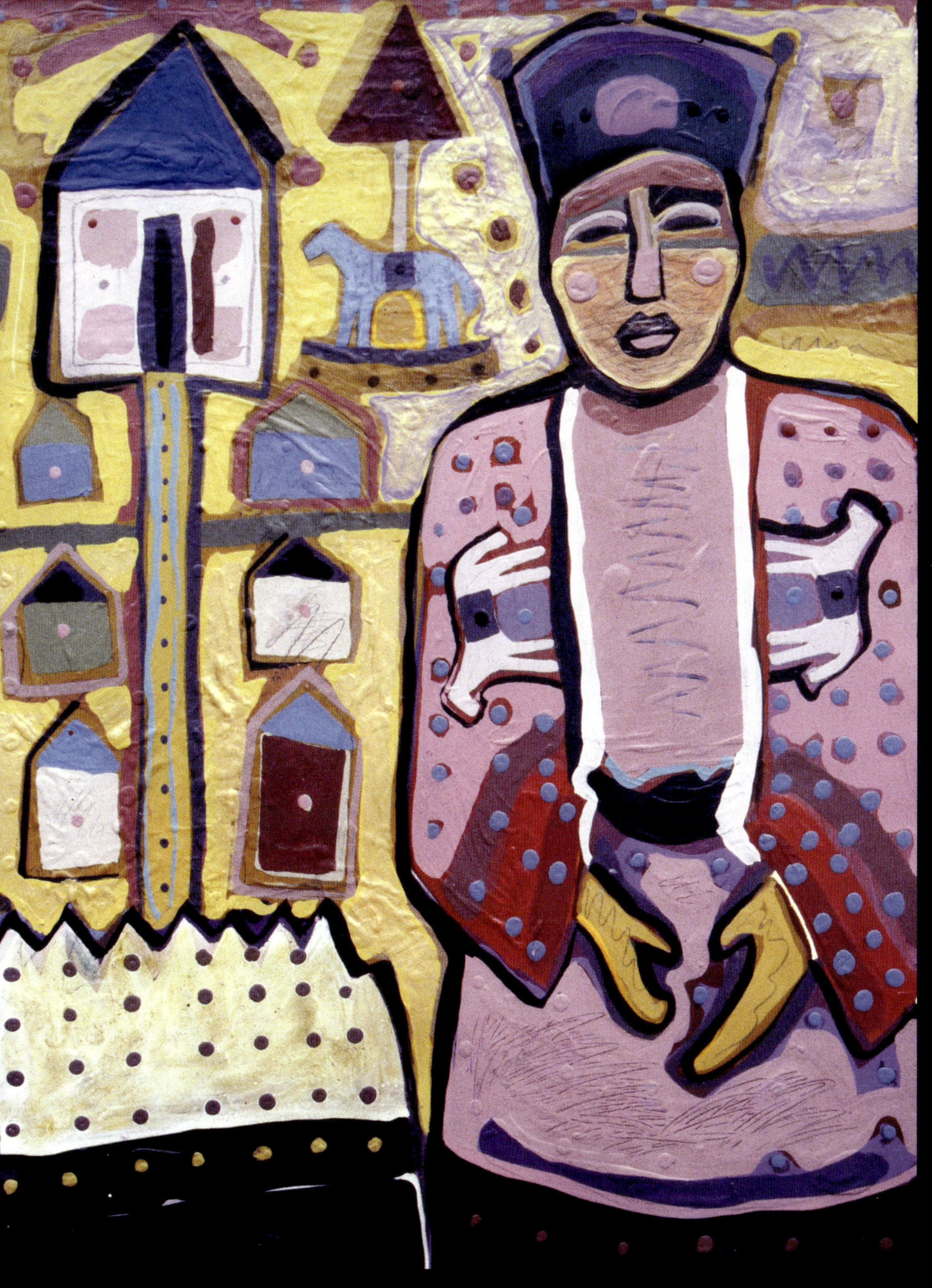

South American Shooting Gallery

acrylic on paper :: 30" x 22" :: 1988

In the late 1980s, Native cultures in South America were being repressed; people were being shot for practising their traditional knowledge and culture. A regime of fear had taken over, forcibly quietening the people. Those who were insubordinate were shot if they challenged the systems or governments that silenced their voices and identity.

She Was an Indian Princess . . . She Loved to Drink . . . She Died

oil pastel on paper :: 40" x 26" :: 1988

This is a homage piece dedicated to my mother, whose life was greatly affected by the Ermineskin Indian Residential School in Hobbema, Alberta. The artwork is to be read clockwise from the top left.

Four phases of my mother's life are depicted in this work. She was a young, vibrant woman who graduated from residential school in 1945. She ventured to the city of Edmonton after working at the Hobbema hospital for a time. In Edmonton, she met Joe Smith, married, had a good life and bore one son. Joe died young in 1956. She later met my father, James Price (1913–1966), and lived in a common-law union and bore four more children, all by 1962. Her life was fraught with abuse, including an addiction to alcohol. She began to lose her spirit to this disease, as seen in the bottom right image where she is shrinking and loses her face. The final image tells of her demise and the end of her life at age 37. She was so young, so full of promise.

This story is not unique; it happened to many people in the First Nations community and beyond.

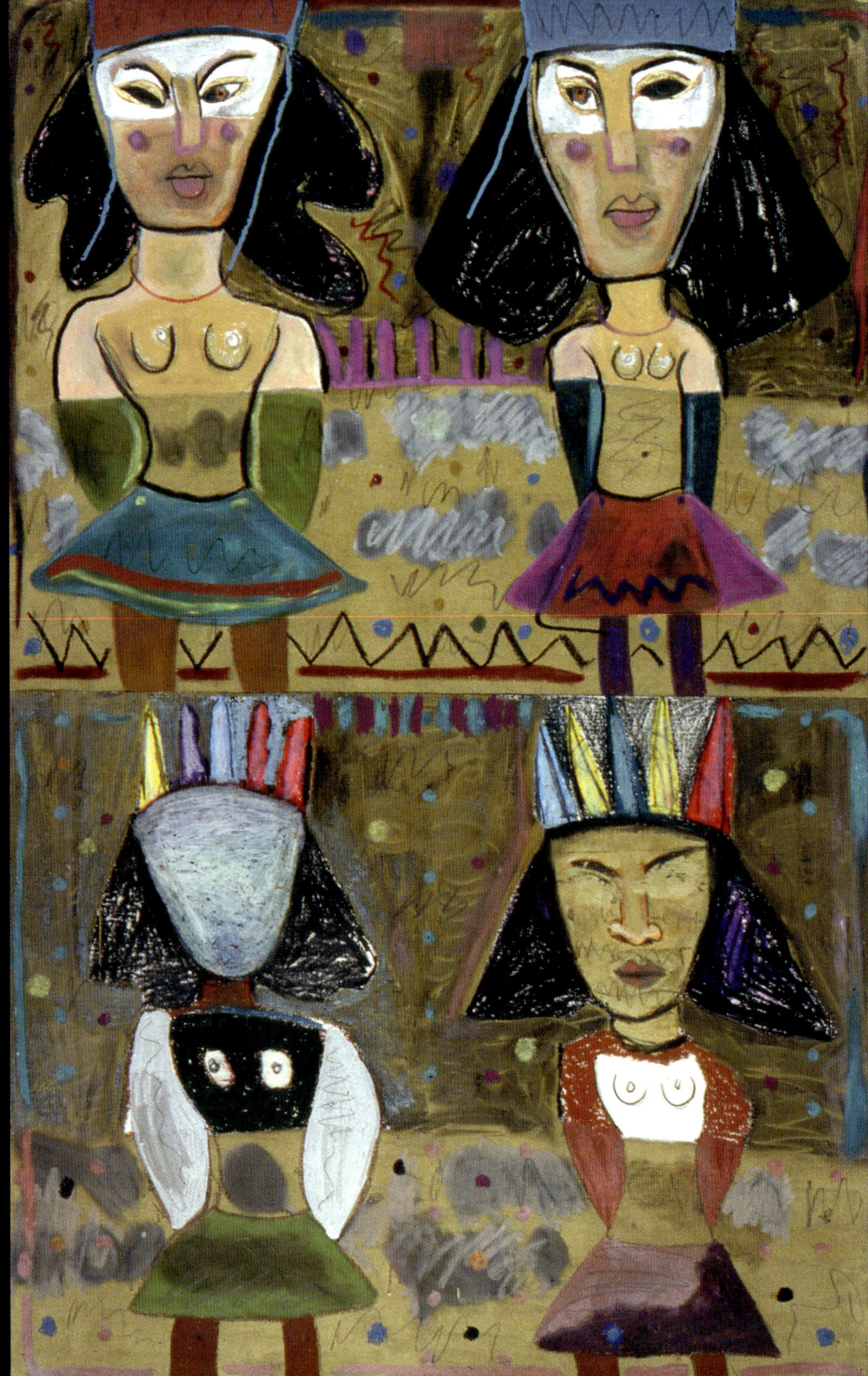

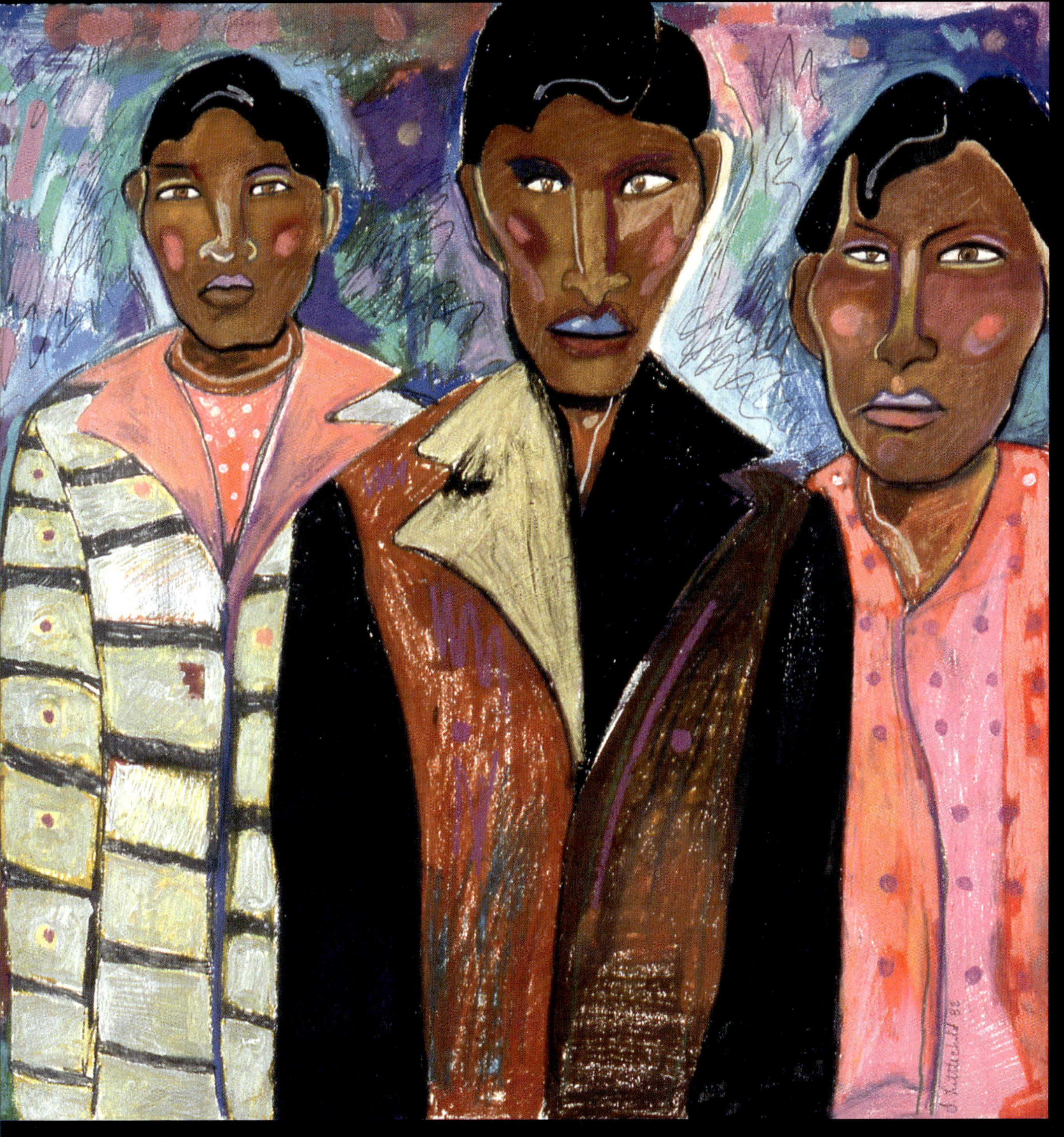

Three Cree Boarding School Boys

oil pastel on paper :: 30" x 30" :: 1988

In my late teens and early 20s, I began to search for photos of my parents, aunts, uncles, grandparents and extended family. Many relatives were very helpful. I remember the first time I held a picture of my late parents, James and Rachel. I was 18 or 19 at my Uncle Rene and Auntie Rachel (Ayiwastin) Littlechild's home on the Ermineskin Reserve. That day, I also met two aunties, sisters of my late mother. Mary Jane (Littlechild) Pietsch and Rosalie (Littlechild) Robson. One of them brought a photo of my parents. Fascinated, I stared at it, the first visual I had ever seen of them. I was so happy, intrigued and inspired to learn much more. I began scouring museums and archives. The Royal Alberta Museum archives, held in Edmonton, housed the photo collection where I did a lot of my research. The Oblate order had set up a mission in Hobbema. The Oblates' photos of Hobbema families, weddings and residential school children number in the hundreds. I would study these faces, all unknown. I began bringing the photos I had purchased to the four reserves in Hobbema and asked elders to identify the people in the photos. They were very kind, and I have great appreciation for those who sat with me for hours as I wrote the names on the backs of the photos. These unidentified people were no longer nameless.

That research led to the creation of this piece showing three nameless young Cree boys who were attendees at the residential school.

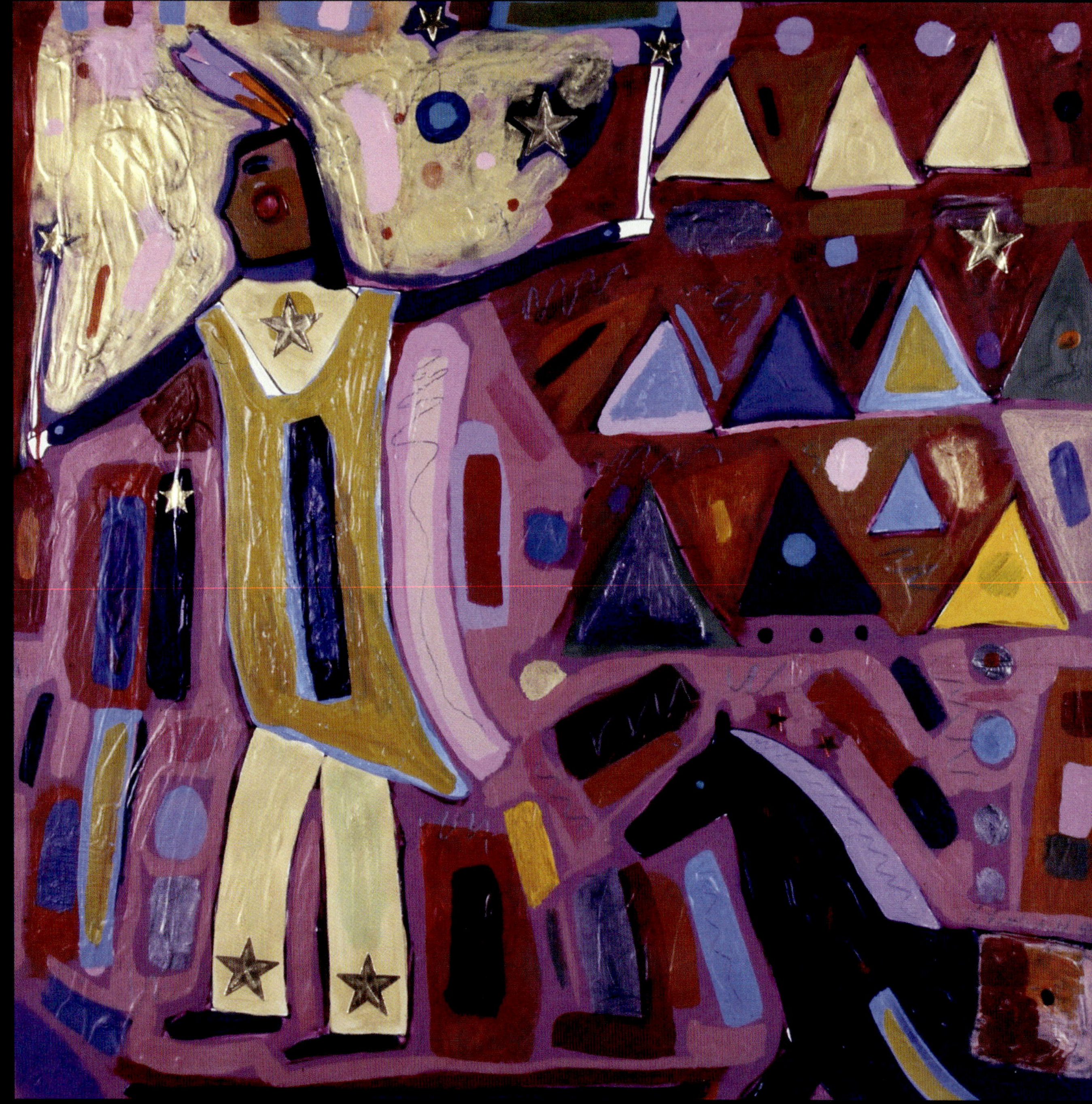

Forgotten Legends acrylic on paper :: 30" x 30" :: 1988

Elders, who are the historians within the tribe, have always shared their knowledge and teachings. These stories of past events, prowess and warfare would be told over and over, especially in the winter. I felt it was important to learn from elders, and those stories and lessons have stayed with me ever since.

The late Frank Turning Robe of the Siksika Nation at Gleichen, Alberta, shared advice at the Calgary Indian Centre (now the Aboriginal Friendship Centre of Calgary), where I worked as a young man. My uncle Rene Littlechild shared with me that his grandfather, or "Mosom," Chief Francis Bull, would gather all the young men and boys and sit them down in a circle while he shared teachings and stories with them.

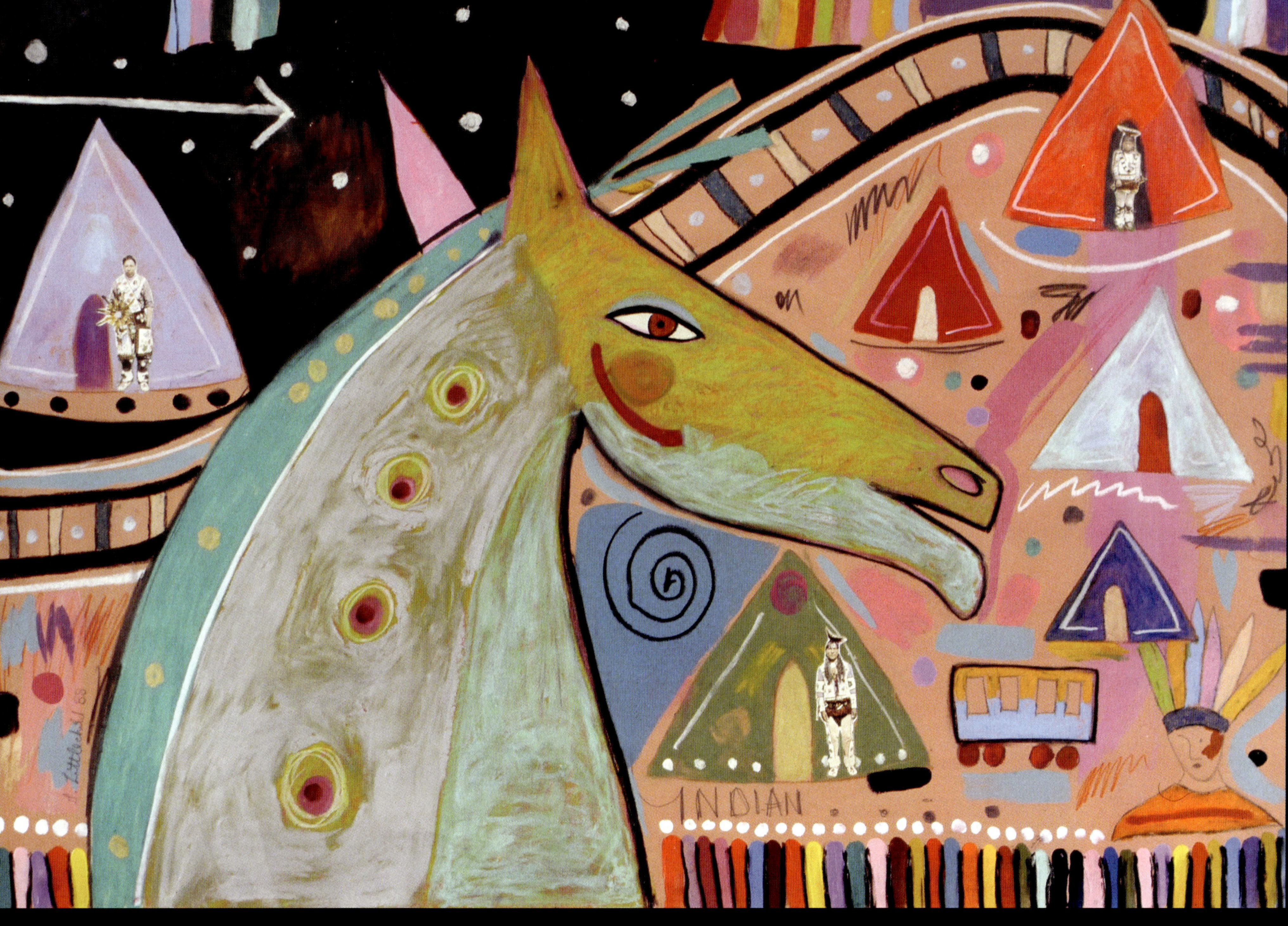

Dot the I in North American Indian mixed media :: 30.25" x 44.5" :: 1988

In school, our teacher would smack the board with her chalk brushes, and chalk dust would go flying in a puff of smoke. She usually did this in our penmanship class and would say, "Dot the I in North American Indian."

This painting speaks about the Canadian Pacific Railway that went through traditional First Nations homelands. Out of reverence, I have added a row of dotted I's to create a border and a dialogue around this issue.

Urban Indian Pain Dance 1

mixed media :: 44″ x 30″ :: 1988

In 1988, there were many First Nations individuals incarcerated in Canada's prisons. These men and women were imprisoned for crimes that were committed, I believe, due to the history and conditions experienced by their people and the abuses within their lives and those around them.

I looked at the lives of my four siblings and I realized we could have fallen into the penal system trap. However, we chose a different path. I created three large body portraits of my brothers and myself and titled the works *Urban Indian Pain Dance 1, 2, 3.*

In the first painting, I pay homage to my eldest brother, Jack, who chose to get a law degree. Jack has used his education to help First Nations bands become more self-reliant and sustainable. He is a mentor and guide for many.

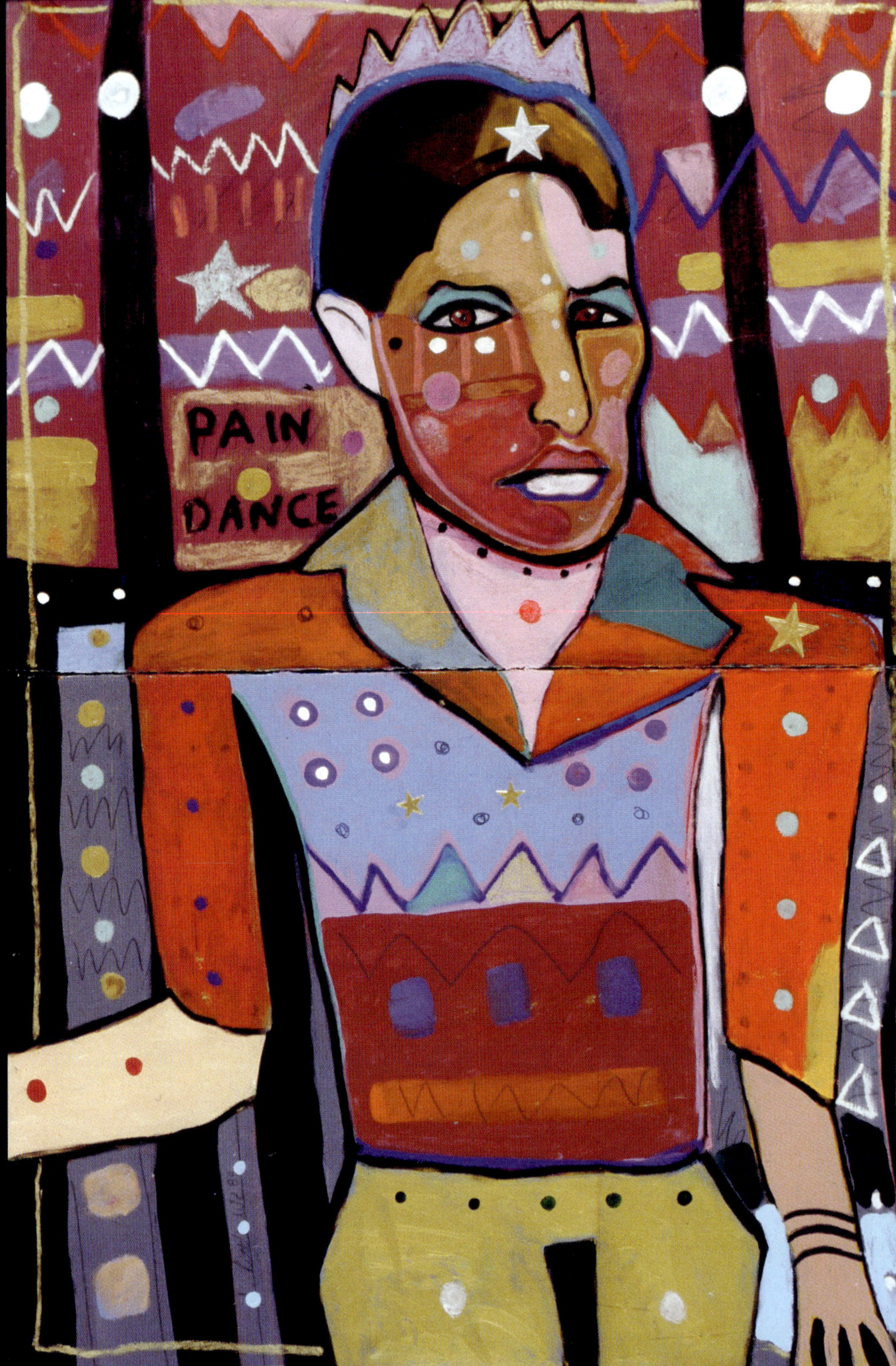

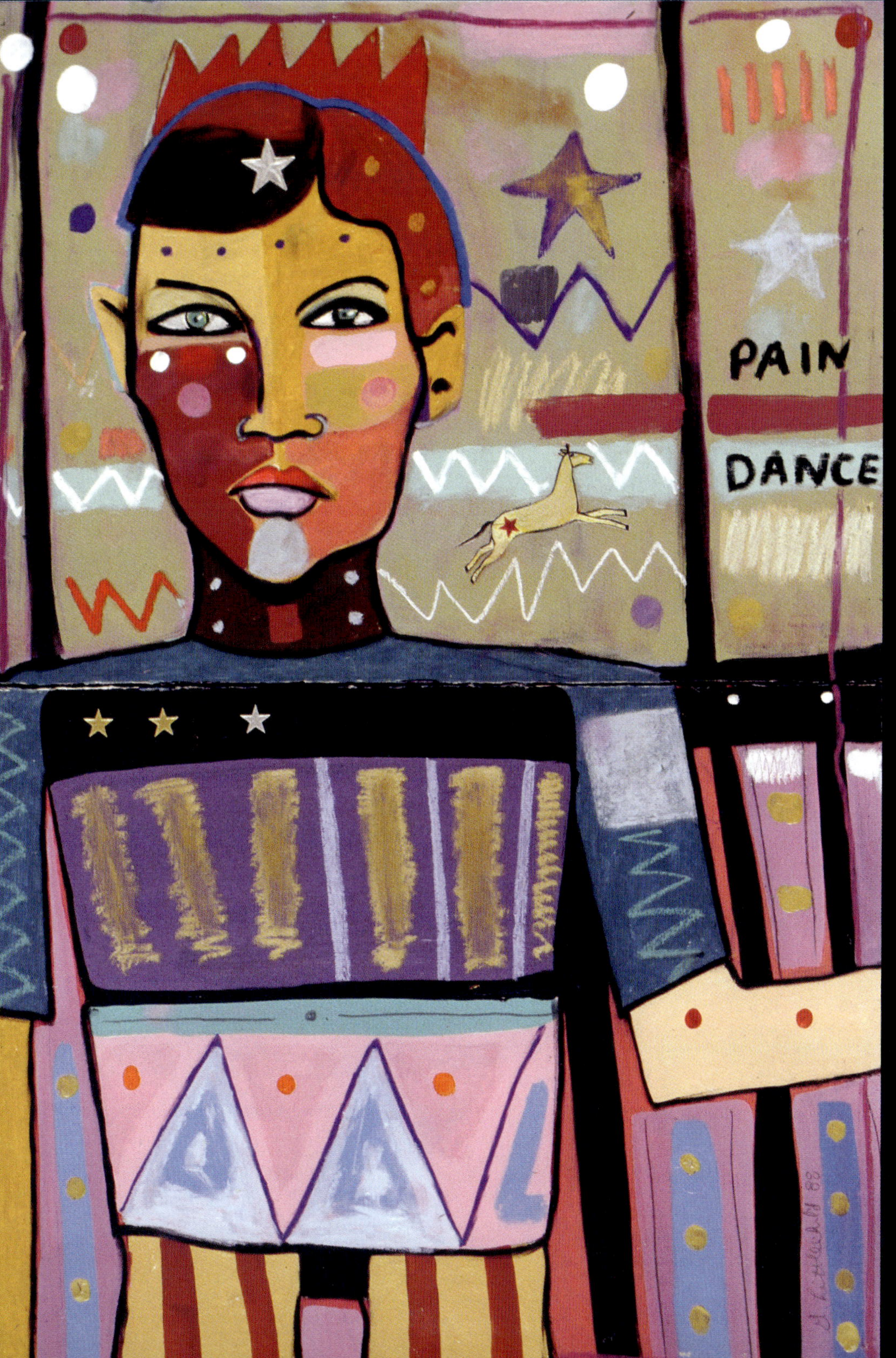

Urban Indian Pain Dance 3

mixed media :: 44" x 30" :: 1988

In this painting, I pay tribute to my younger brother, Raymond, who has dazzling green eyes, often seen in mixed-race people. He, like Jack, pursued education and obtained a business degree. I am very proud of both my brothers' accomplishments, as I am of my sisters'. Raymond works with First Nations business associations and helps to nurture business acumen and choices among his peers, associates and communities.

The black bars in each painting represent prison, which they both avoided through determination and education. The crowns in each portrait represent their successes.

Even Mrs. Horsechild Gets the Blues

mixed media :: 44" x 30" :: 1988

As a child, my eldest foster brother, Richard, had a collection of art books that I would page through. Fascinated by the artwork that filled their pages, I absorbed the subject matter and was especially attracted to the Egyptian imagery. Its narrative and storyboard resonated with me and that style found a place within these works. Paint, beads and crayons mixed together created an environment for Mrs. Horsechild, who every once in a while has a blue day. She reaches out for solace and tells her story and problems to anyone who is willing to listen (as seen by the purple mist coming out of her mouth). These paintings are a two-part series. Each transformative figure has dialogue between themselves and their troubles and woes. They were inspired by the term “even cowgirls get the blues.” Everyone needs a little help and advice sometime.

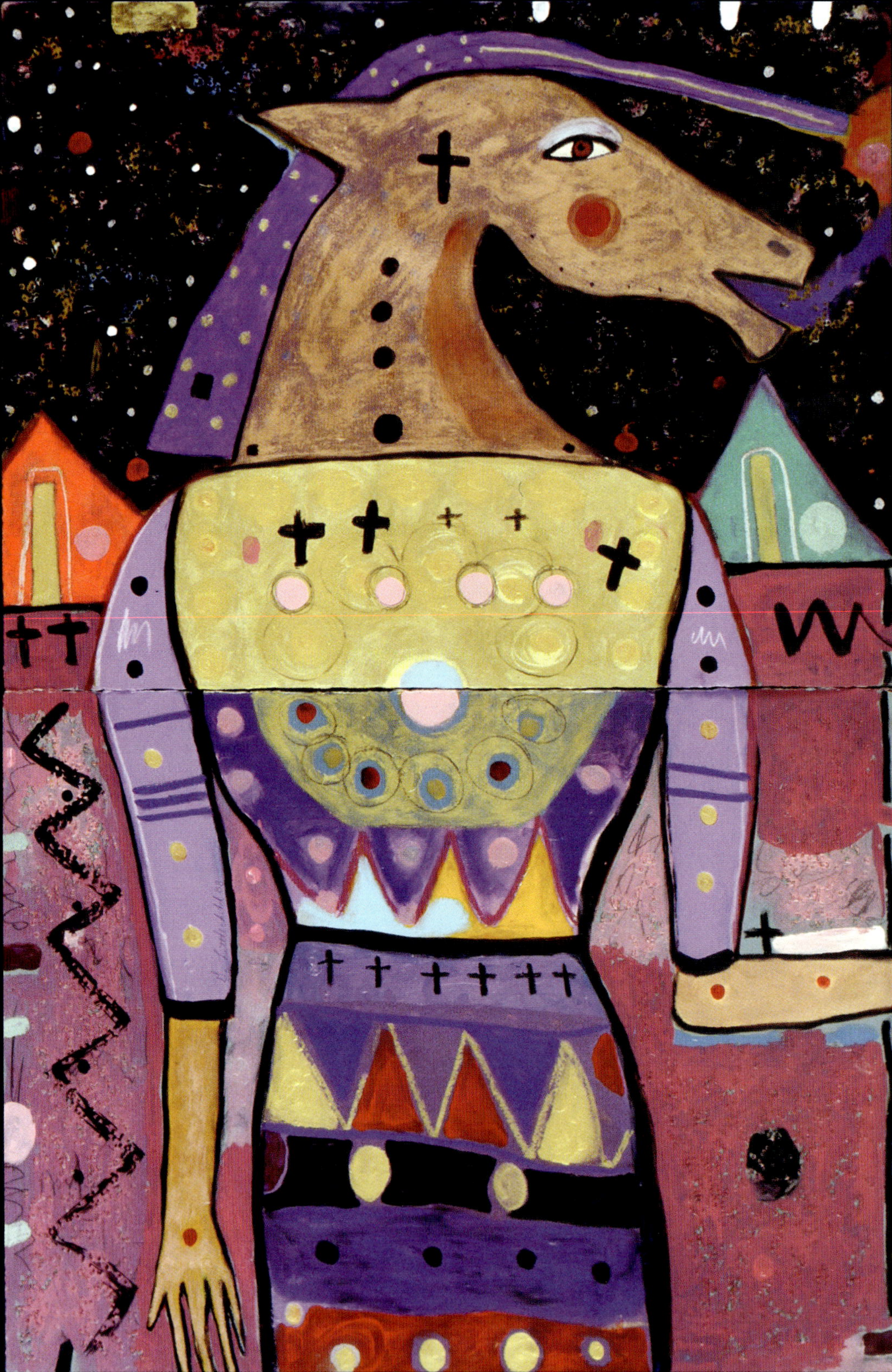

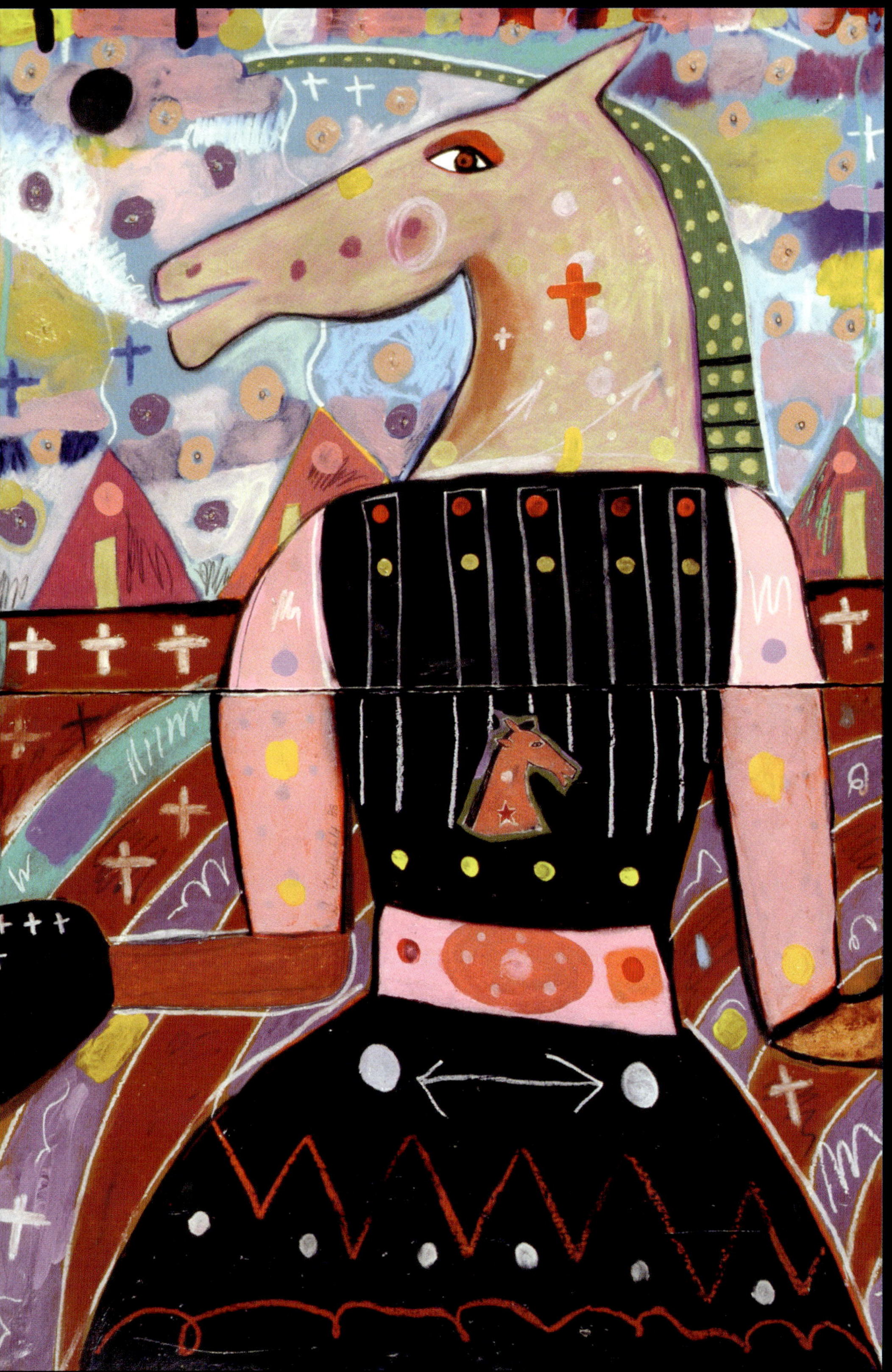

Mrs. Horsechild Gets the Blues

mixed media :: 44" x 30" :: 1988

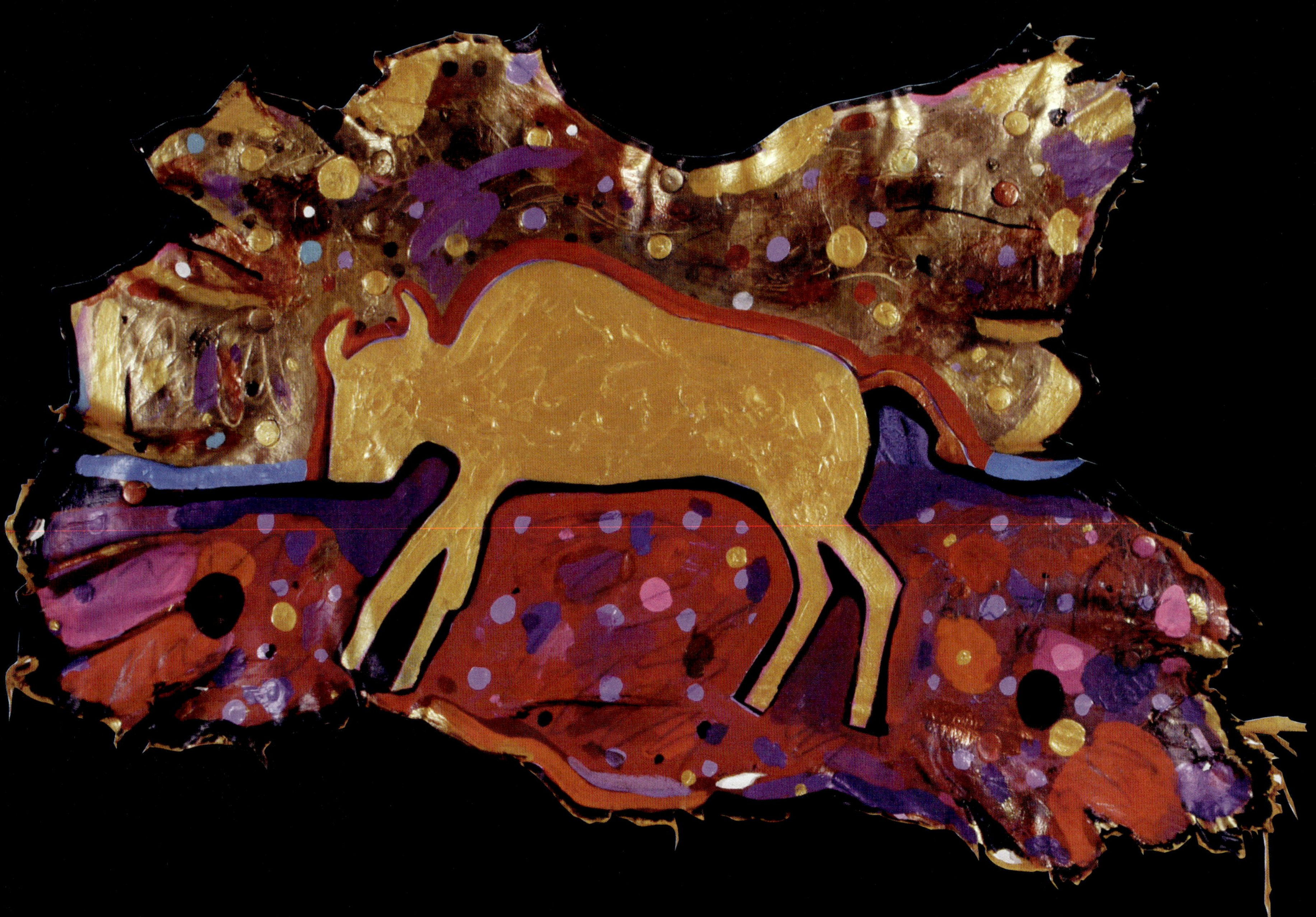

Modern Artifact 2 acrylic on deer skin :: 34" x 54" :: 1988

Drawers, shelves and cases were jam-packed at the George Gustav Heye Center in New York, a branch of the National Museum of the American Indian. "Indian artifacts," warriors' wear, war clubs, skins and so many items from Native American life filled the displays. I came back home with these images fresh in my mind and created a few deer hides, including *Modern Artifact 2*. When I think of how most of these items were collected and purchased, a bad feeling comes to mind. However, I feel better knowing sacred objects are being repatriated to First Nations to be used once again and that bones are being reburied in their proper places of rest.

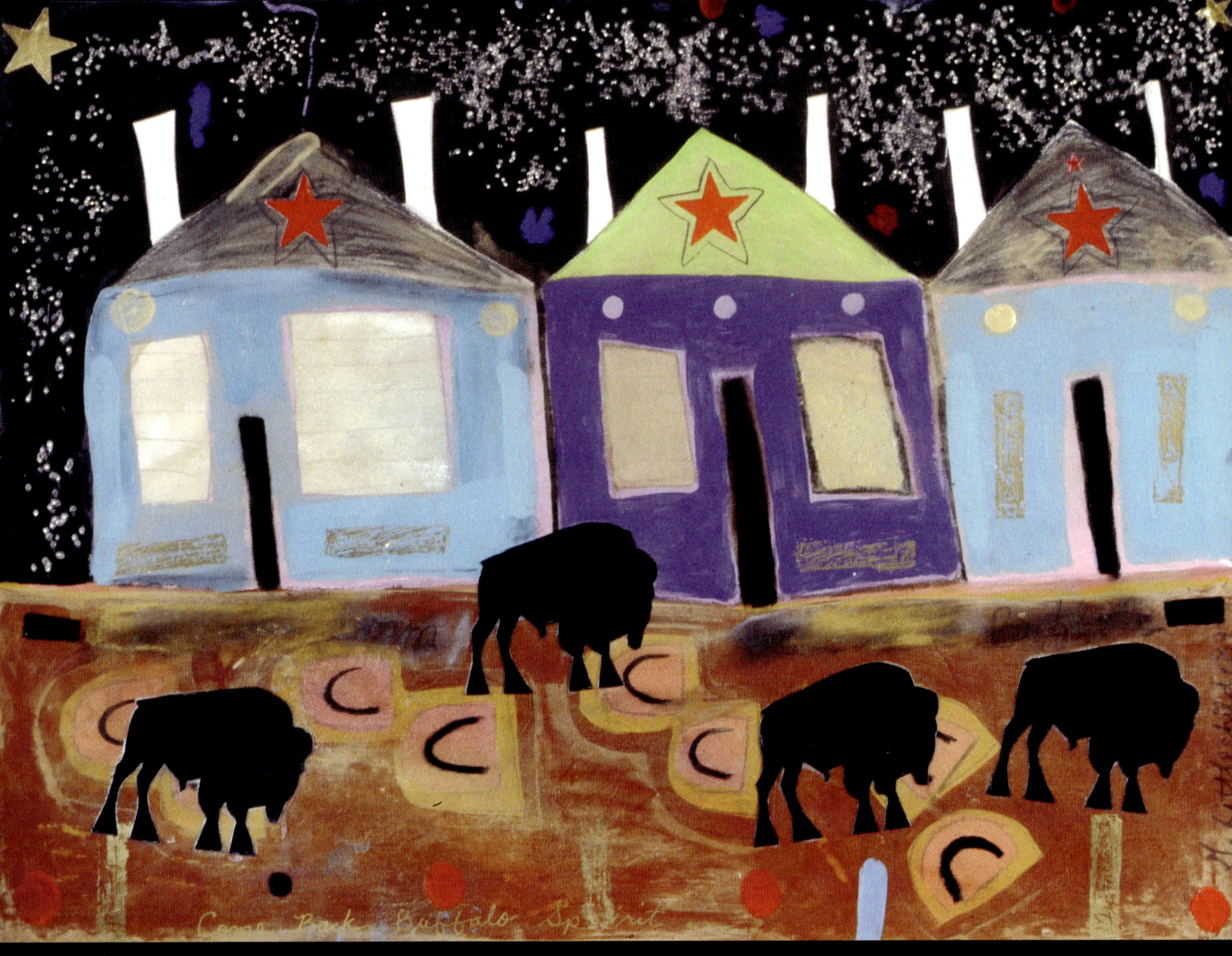

Four Buffalo Spirits mixed media :: 22" x 30" :: 1989

Thick acrylic paint, collaged stars and clear beads simulate the night sky and four beautiful buffalo spirits. Buffalo are emblems to the Plains First Nations, which include my Cree people. The buffalo clothed, fed and enhanced the lives of my ancestors. They were plentiful on the vast Great Plains of North America before the settlers arrived. Millions upon millions roamed the prairies; they were sought and hunted by First Nations peoples only when necessary. I thank you, Buffalo Spirits, for all you provided the ancestors.

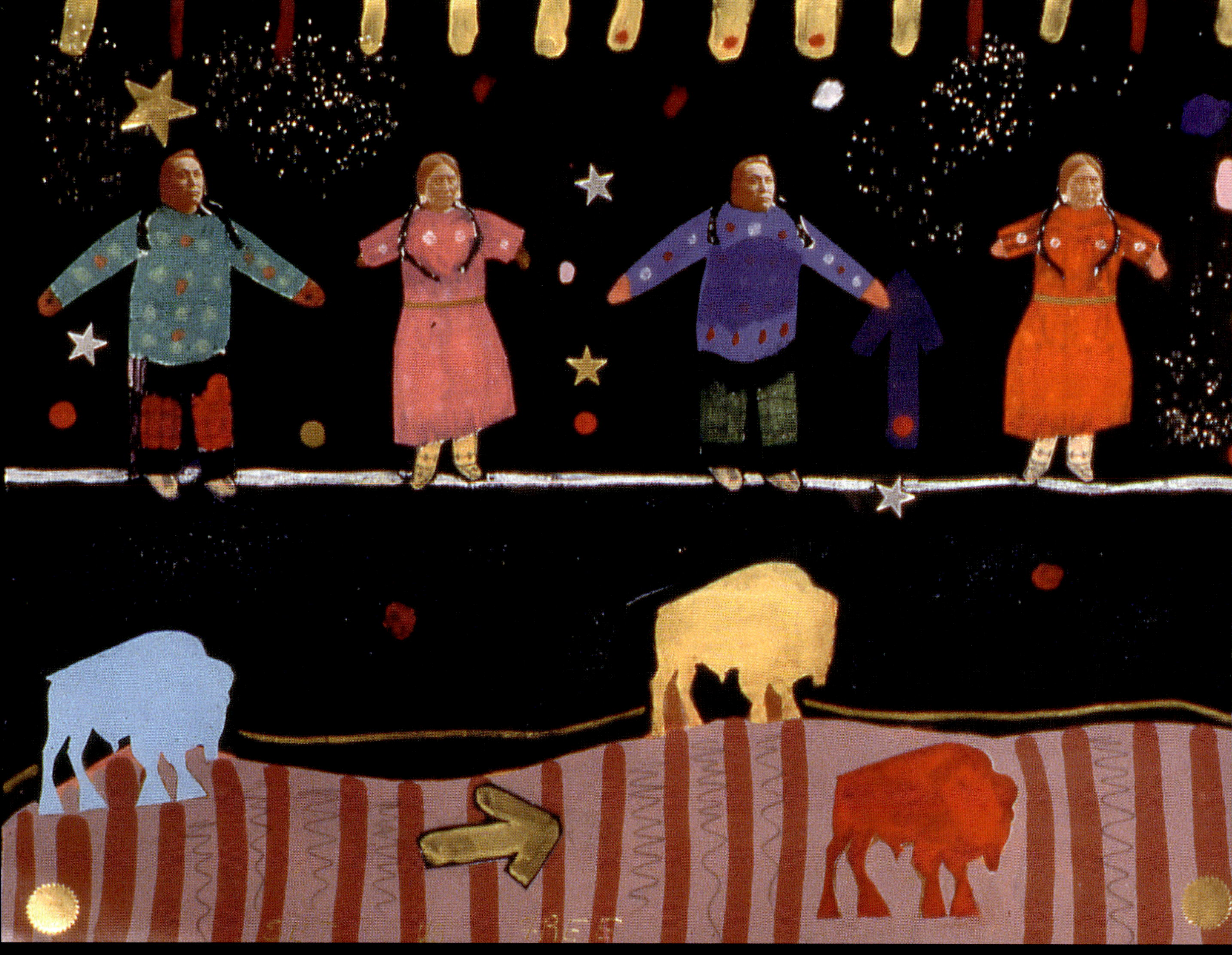

Walking Tightrope mixed media :: 22" x 60" :: 1989

Puppets, dolls and children's toys undergo a lot of use before being tossed, neglected or rejected. From time to time, these images appear in my artwork, used as a metaphor for First Nations peoples and their relationships with government and settler mentality. On the tightrope are four people. Once they fall off the tightrope, they are suspended, floating aimlessly and ungrounded. They have been uprooted from their traditional cultural ways into a new way of living that is far from what they were used to. I added the text, "Come back Buffalo Spirit & set us free, for we are trapped . . . " to articulate their desperation, calling upon the old ways to help them regain strength and connection to their true spirit and their cultural identity and land.

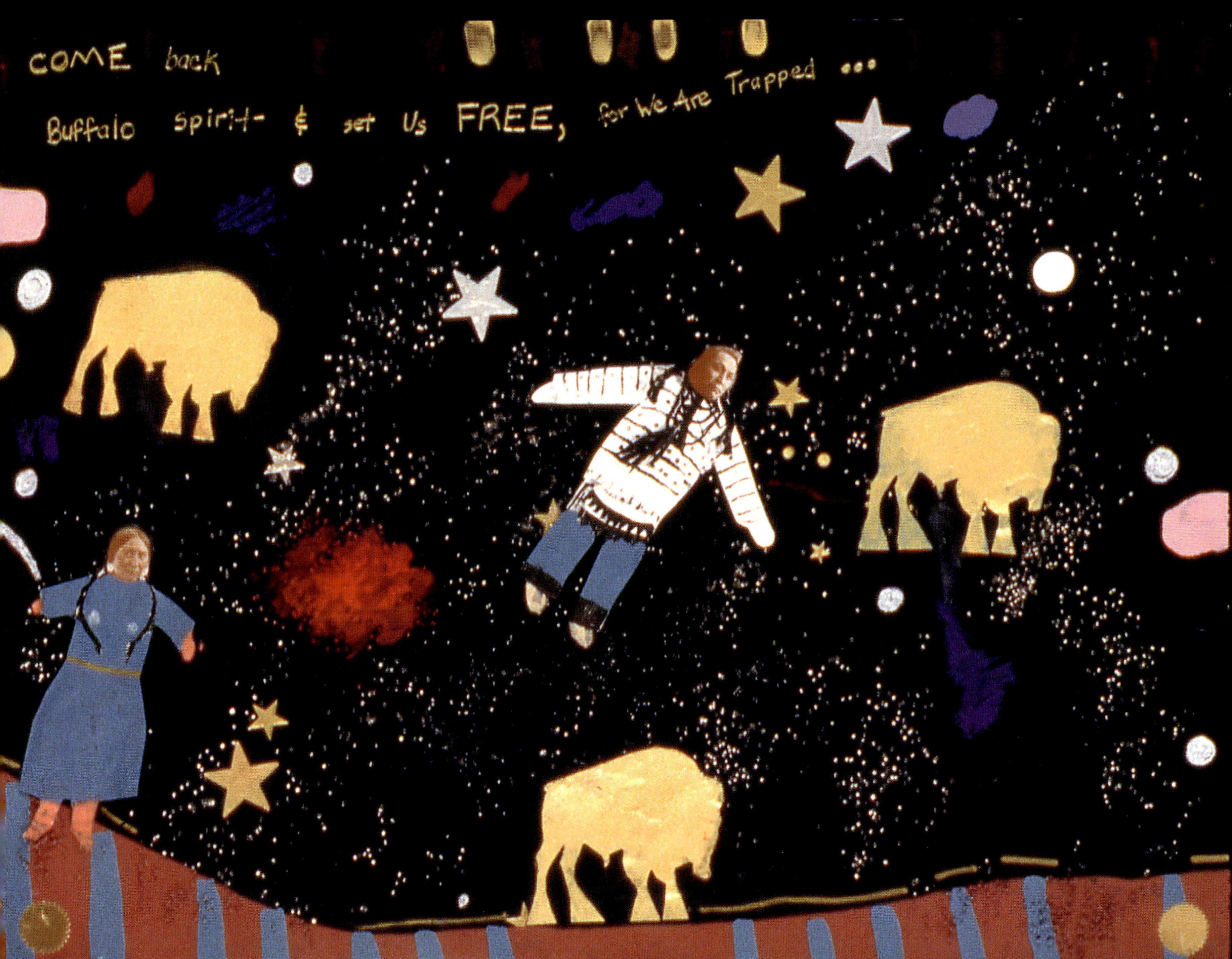
COME back
Buffalo spirit- & set Us FREE, for We Are Trapped ...

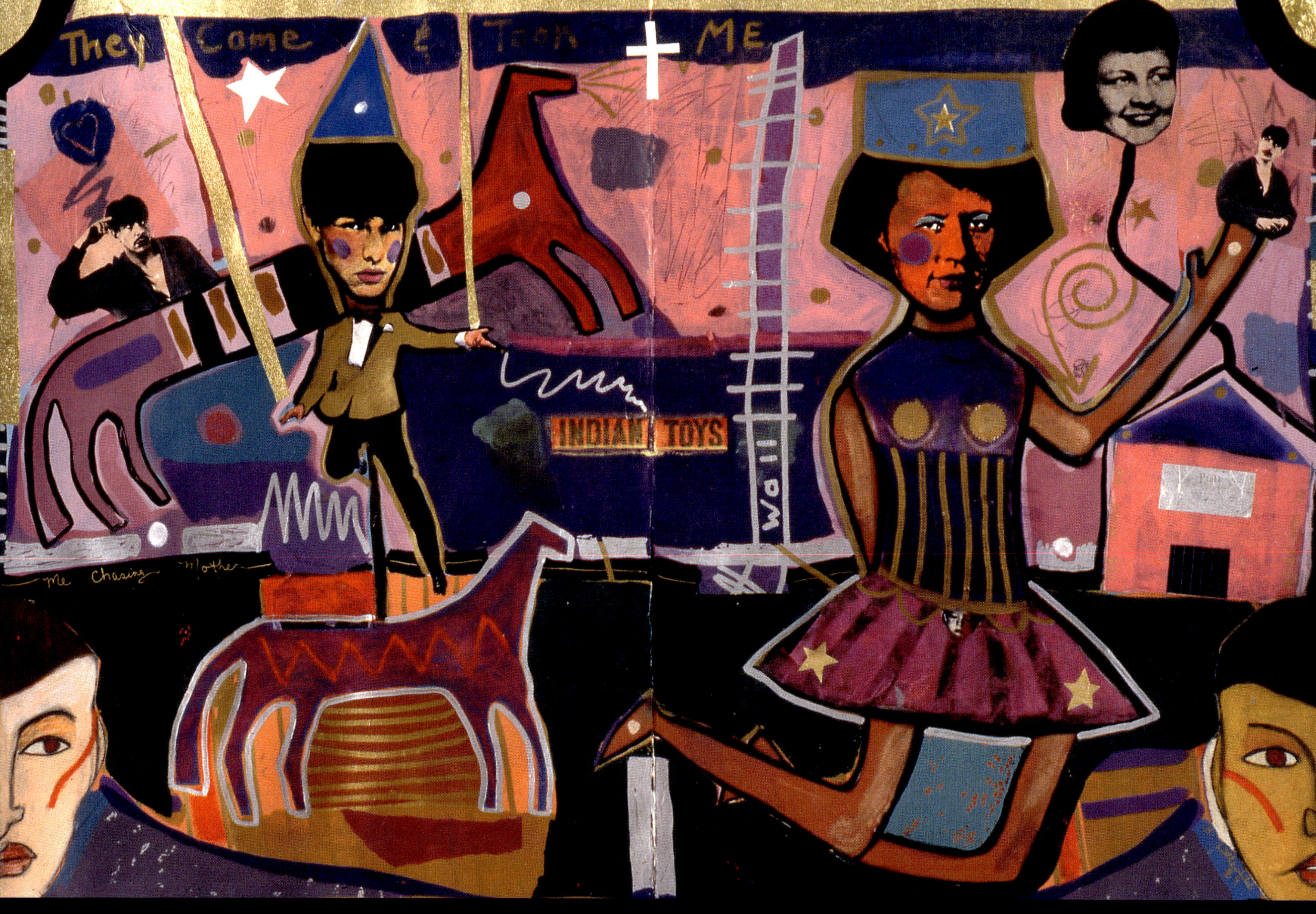

Me Chasing Mother mixed media :: 30" x 44" :: 1989

"They came & took me" is written in the sky, and I am riding on the back of a horse pointing, questioning and asking the question, "What is love?" The dashing, suited puppet (me) chases after Mother, who floats away. I cannot catch her. Horse Spirit supports me and keeps me grounded, and a wall separates me from Mother. I again appear in Mother's outstretched hand, staring at her happy face, thinking, "How could you leave us to welfare? Why did alcohol become more important than

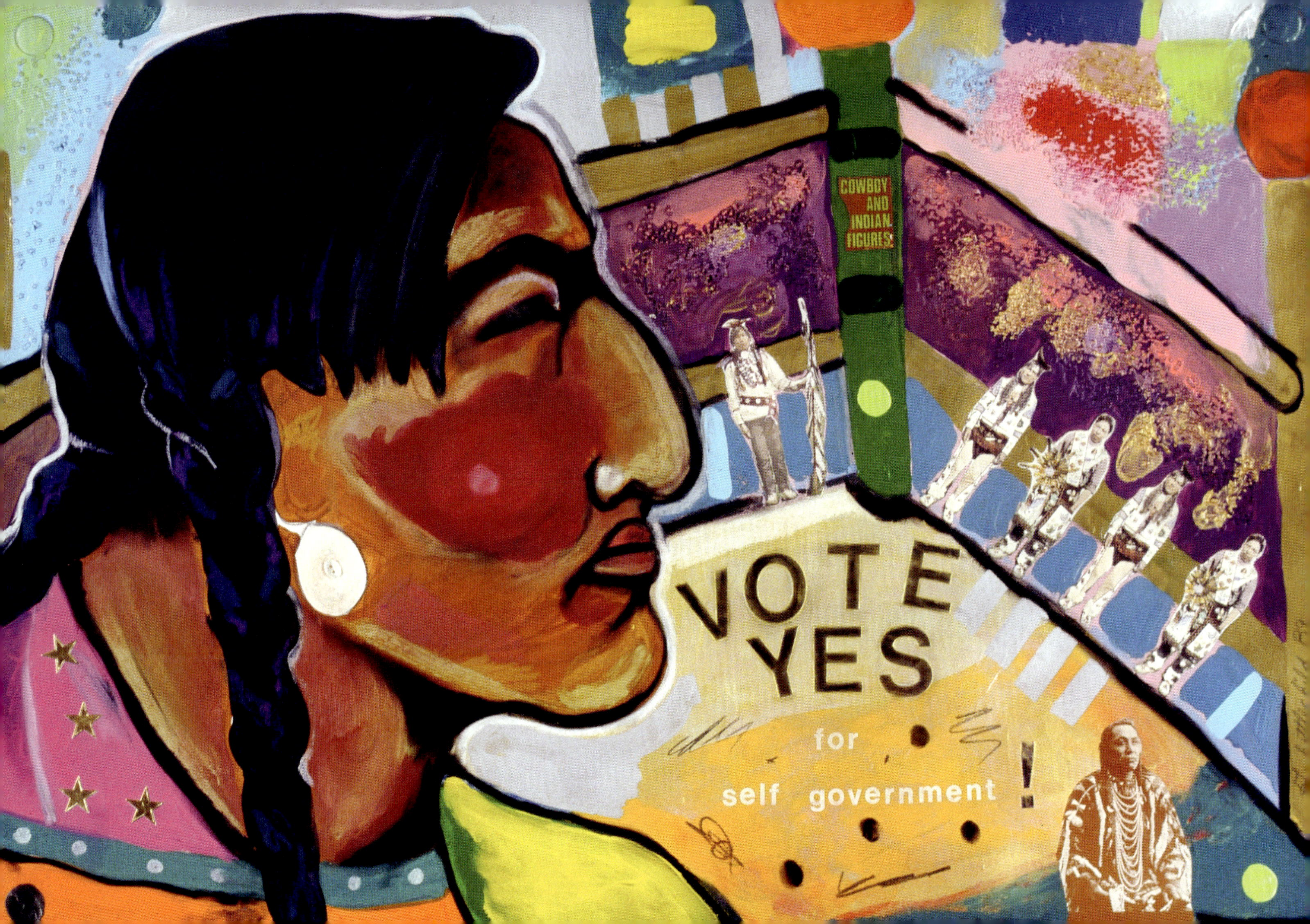
COWBOY AND INDIAN FIGURES
VOTE YES
for
self government !

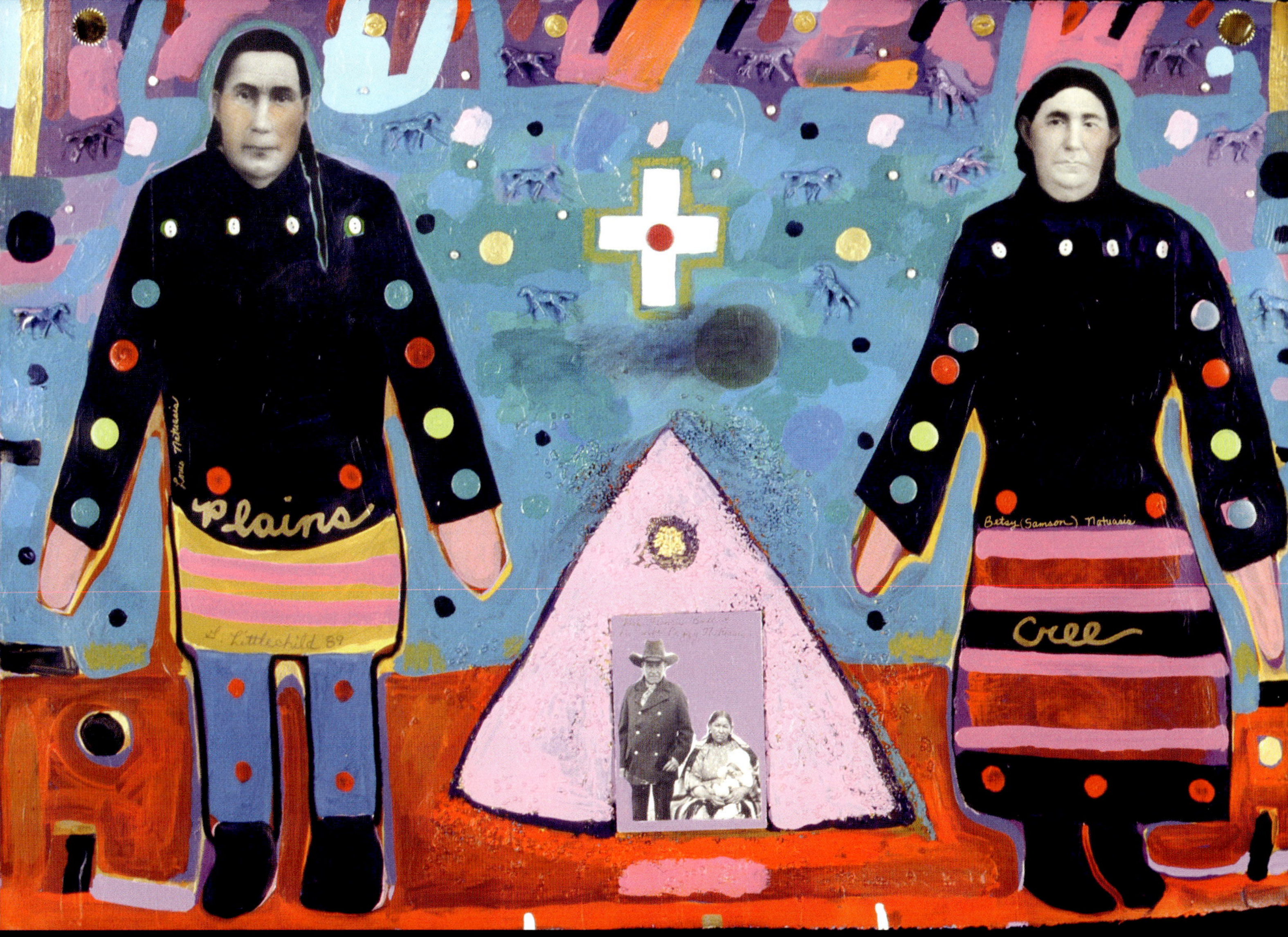

Plains Cree Ancestors mixed media :: 30" x 44" :: 1989

This homage to an amazing couple, Louis Natuasis and Betsy Samson, my great-great-grandparents, tells a little bit of their plight and story. Both were born before the reserve system was developed and implemented. They were raised in a traditional setting, lived in teepees, roamed freely and followed their food sources. Having been initiated into sacred ceremonies, societies and teachings, which ended abruptly, they and their extended families were forced to live on reserves and rely on the government for rations, homes and a parcel of land. No longer nomadic, they had to adapt to a new way of life. The way of life they knew was changed forever.

Louis Natuasis is on the left side of the painting, while Betsy stands on the right. The cross between them represents the Europeans' arrival and their Christian beliefs and teachings. In the teepee is a picture of their daughter, Peggy, and her husband, Chief Francis Bull, holding one of their many children, representing the future. Peggy and Chief Francis wear European clothes. Much was lost; an era ended, but not all was taken and teachings from the past, to some extent, are still practised.

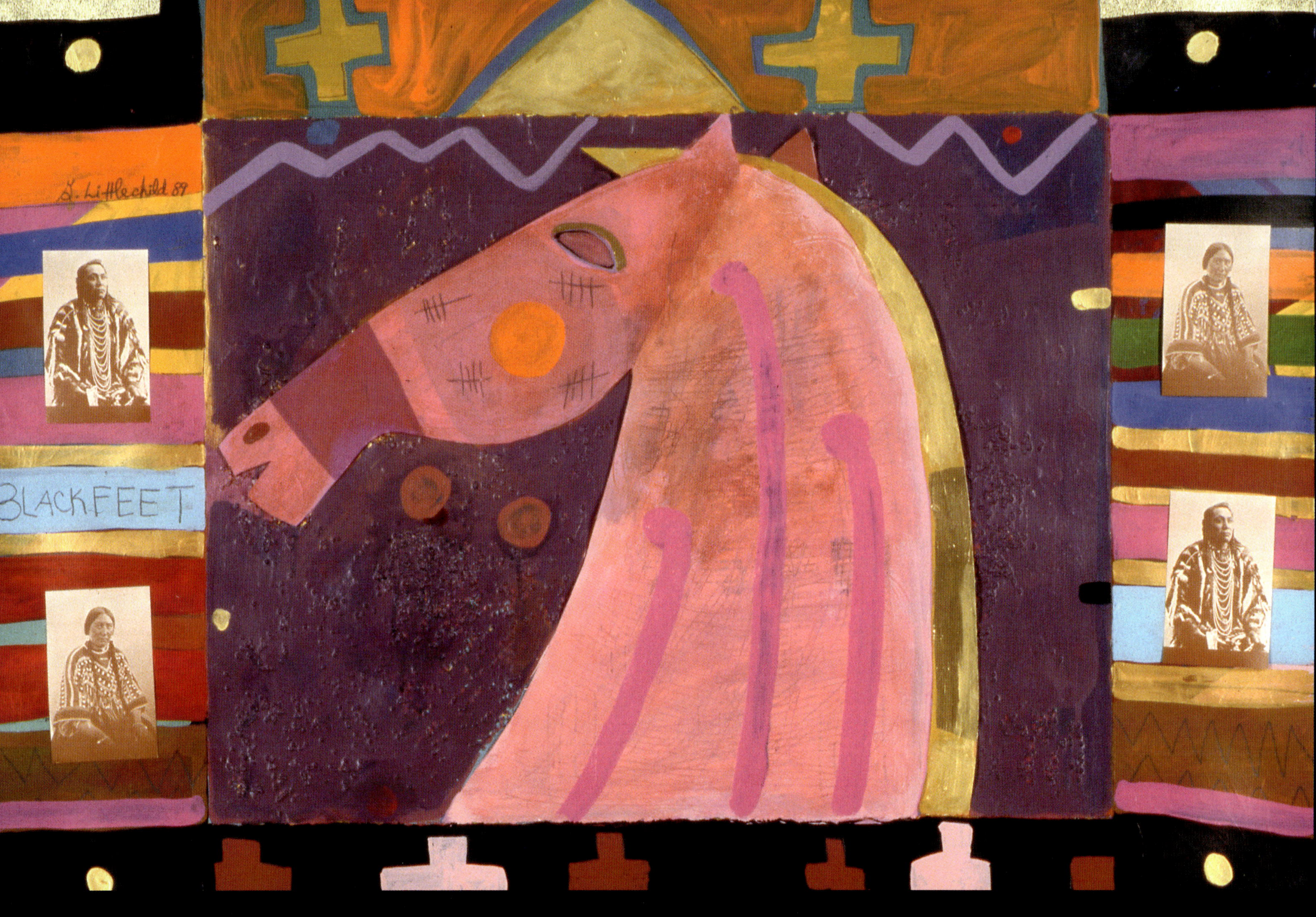

Blackfoot Horse Blanket mixed media :: 30" x 44" :: 1989

Over the course of my life I have travelled often for pleasure and work. I bought these sepia photographs of strong-featured Blackfoot people while on a trip to Montana, where I have cousins and where my father's mother, Sarah (Dunn) Price, lived after her divorce from my grandfather. I was attracted to the striking appearance of the Blackfoot people in these images, and I wanted to incorporate them into my art. I envisioned their hunting parties roaming over the Sweet Grass Hills up to what is now Glacier National Park in Montana, where they would have made camps in the Rocky Mountains, to north of Waterton Lakes National Park in Alberta. In homage, I created a Blackfoot horse blanket.

Plains Cree Ancestral Blanket 4

mixed media :: 44" x 30" :: 1989

Kokum, my grandmother Bella (Bull) Littlechild holding my mother, Hobbema, Alberta, 1929.

When I was creating this series, I was deep in exploration, learning about my ancestry and culture. These images provided a connection to those who had gone before and a visual recollection, which created pride within me.

When I began my search, I met some wonderful people and relatives along the way. It was through these relatives, like Auntie Louisa (Littlechild) Wildcat, that I found these amazing photos of our family, including this one of my mother being held by her mother, Bella. My mother was born on February 9, 1929; you can see in the photo that all the snow has melted and she is not wearing a coat, so she could be three or four months old in this photo. The sod homes are very telling of that era, and I love the way Kokum's hand holds my mother, who is wrapped securely in her moss bag.

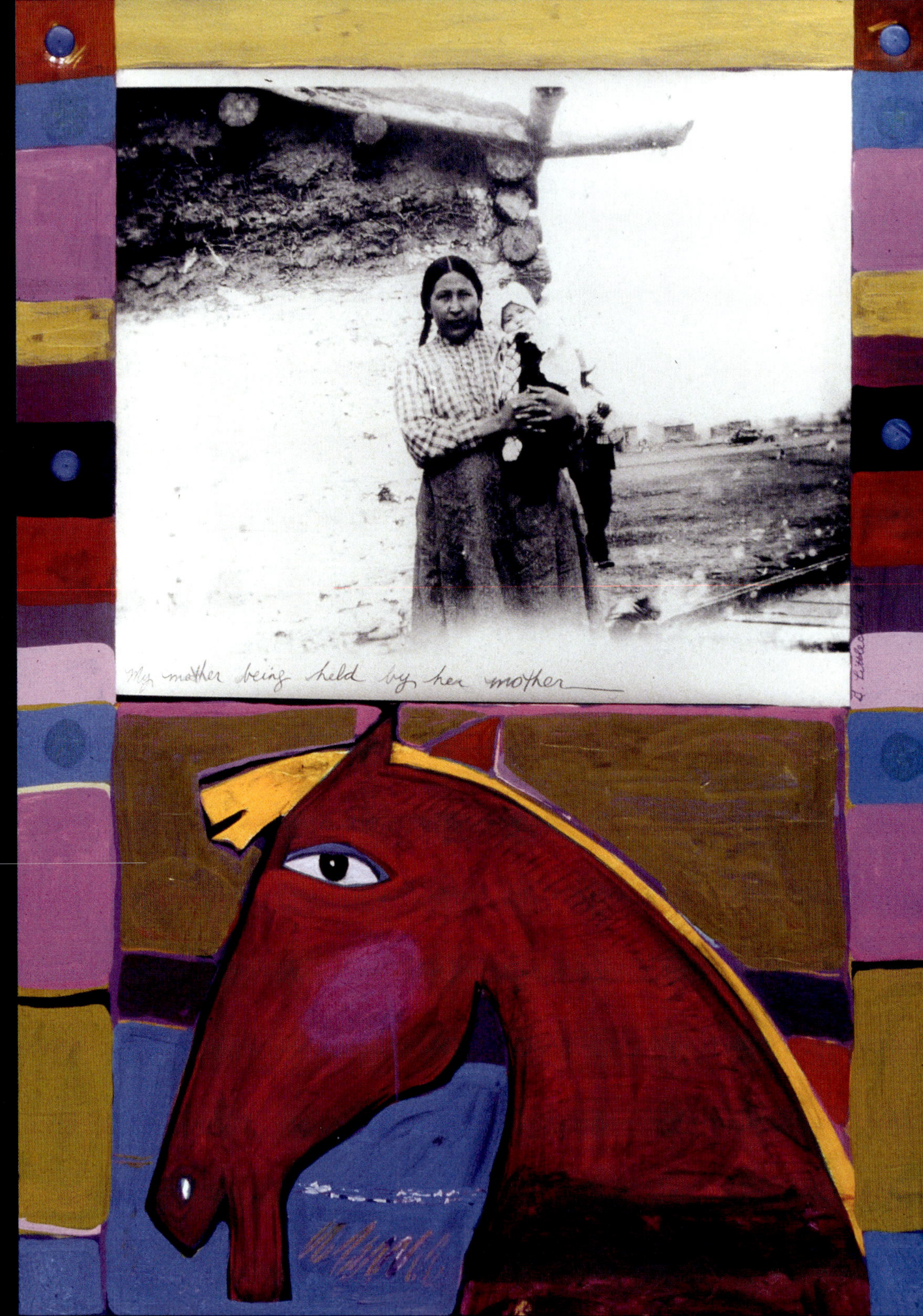

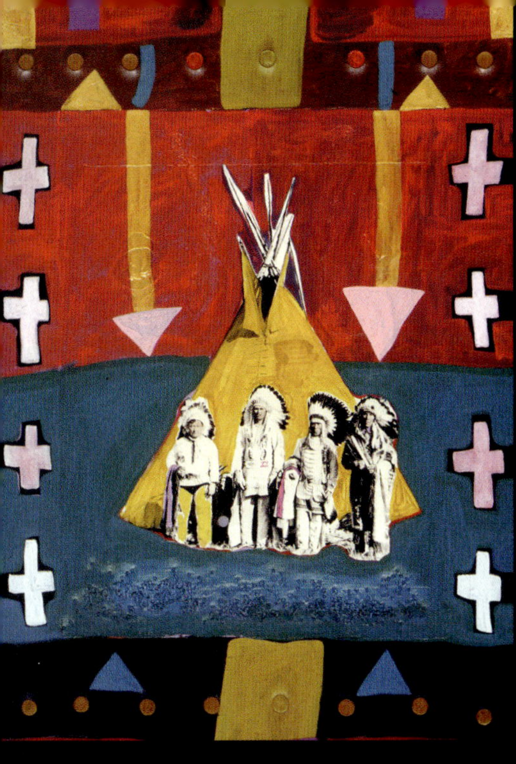

Plains Cree Ancestral Blanket 2

mixed media
44" x 30" :: 1989

A gathering of the four chiefs at a Plains Cree sun dance, Hobbema, Alberta. L-R Chief Francis Bull, Chief John Bear, Chief Joe Samson, Chief Panee Ermineskin, ca. 1930.

Plains Cree Ancestral Blanket 3

mixed media
44" x 30" :: 1989

Edward Littlechild and Bella Bull, my mother's parents, Hobbema, Alberta, 1915.

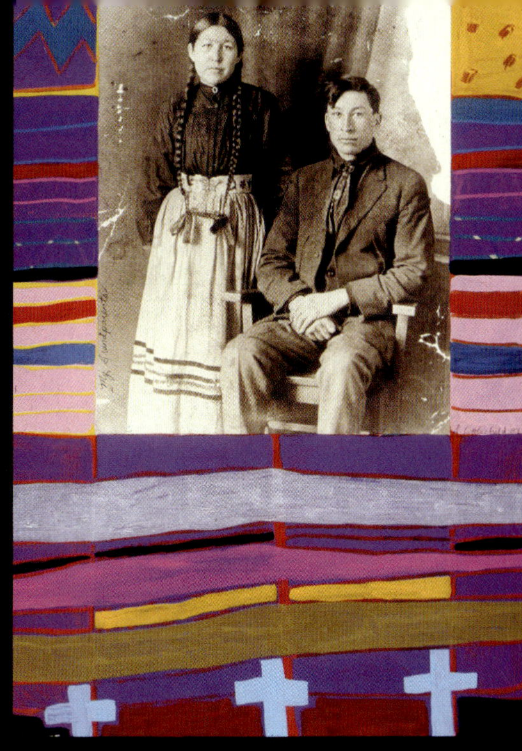

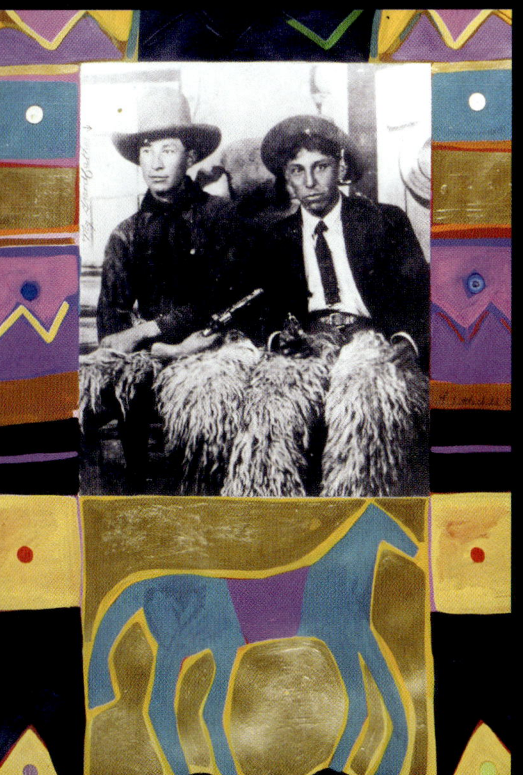

Plains Cree Ancestral Blanket 5

mixed media
44″ x 30″ :: 1989

Edward Littlechild (left) and his brother-in-law, Cyprien Laroque, Hobbema, Alberta, 1910.

Plains Cree Ancestral Blanket 6

mixed media
44″ x 30″ :: 1989

Ada (Littlechild) Buffalo holds her little baby wrapped in a moss bag. She is standing beside her grandmother Betsy (Samson) Natuasis.

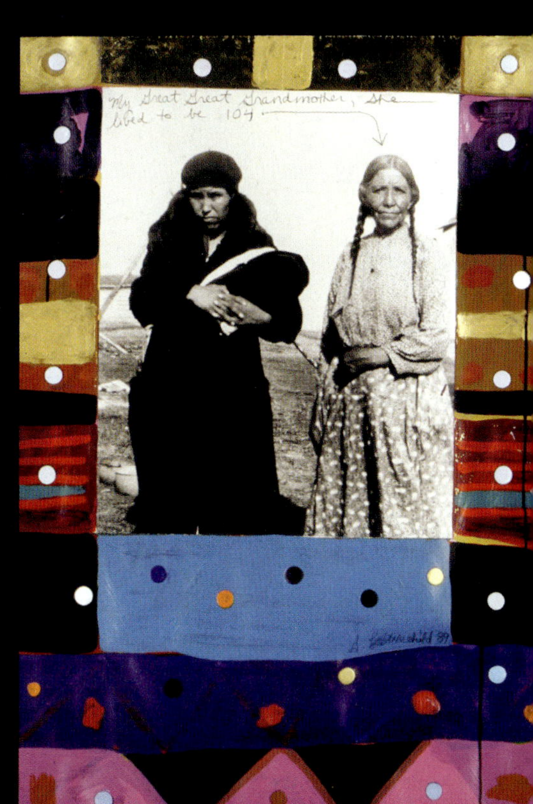

In Memory of the Sioux Indians

mixed media :: 44" x 30" :: 1989

A transformative horse figure stands transfixed by the many who perished at the Battle of the Little Bighorn, June 26, 1876. General George Armstrong Custer and the Seventh Cavalry of the United States Army were ordered by President Grant to round up hostile Indians, who were to be placed on reservations. Many Indians had been allocated to reservations; however, many resisted, famously Chief Sitting Bull and his Lakota band. This era was known as the Indian Wars.

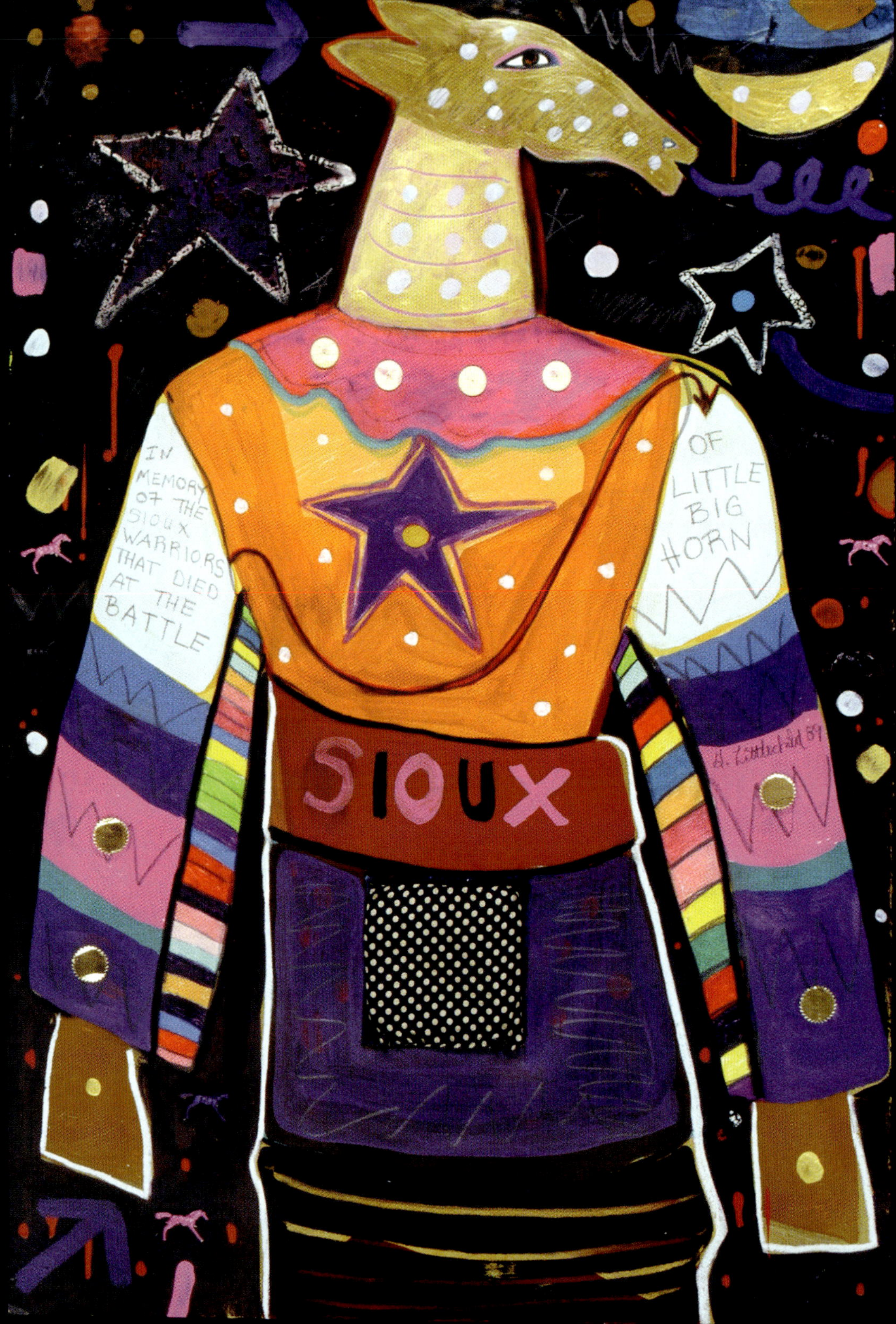

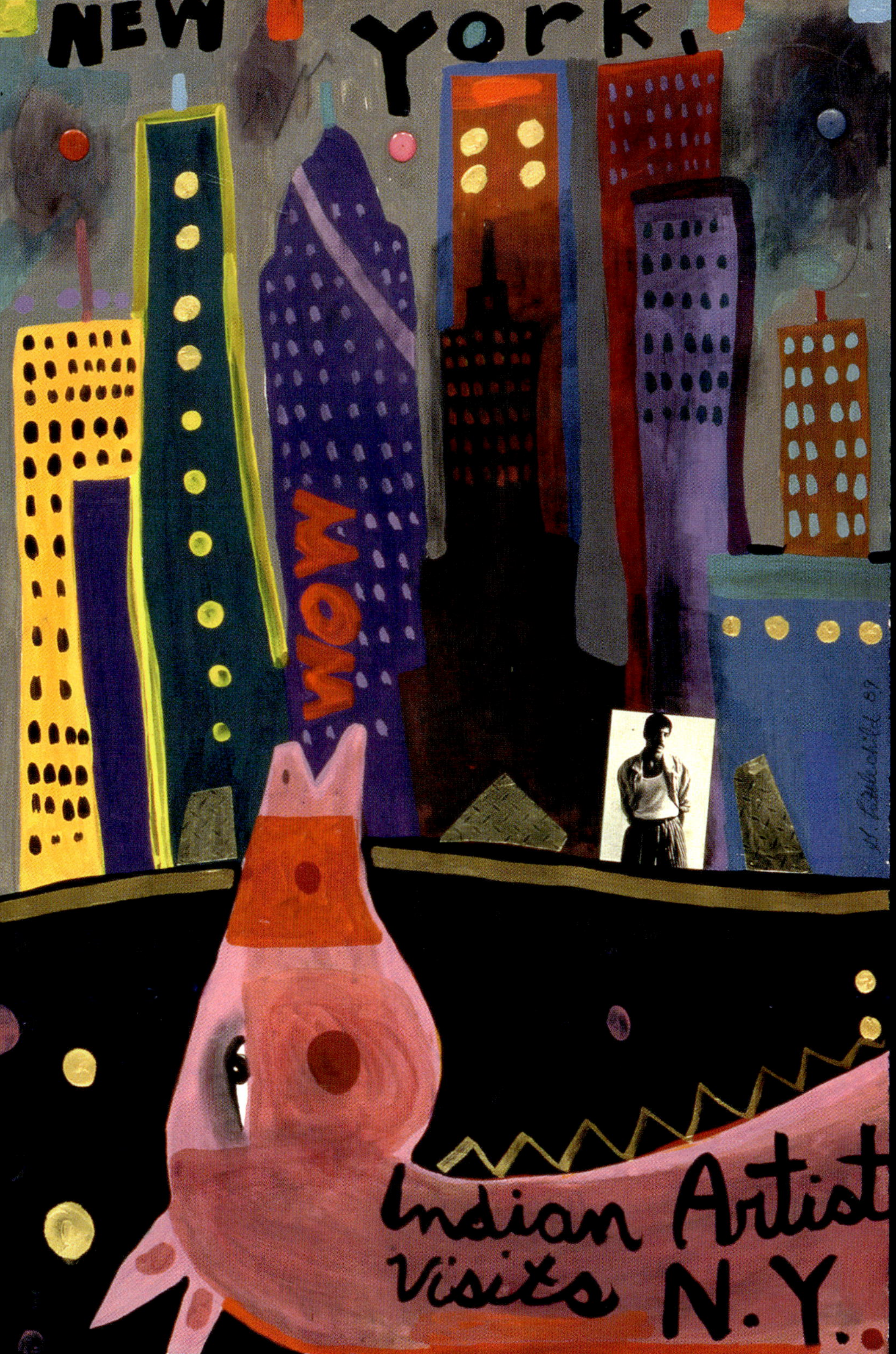

Indian Artist Visits New York, New York

mixed media :: 44″ x 30″ :: 1989

In 1988, while I attended the Banff Centre (once known as the Banff School of Fine Arts) for an independent study program, a group of students and I went on a trip to New York to visit galleries like MoMA (Museum of Modern Art) and artists' studios. We met painter Eric Fischl and other famous artists. We were encouraged to ask questions about their art and careers. It was a fascinating trip, and I was open and raw and somewhat naive. I saw art that touched me to the core. In New York, the tall buildings, smells and crowded streets made me respectful of life itself, as seen in this painting. I absorbed many ideas and experiences during that 10-day trip. It was like the floodgates of creativity opened and I began a new approach to making art. German artist Anselm Kiefer affected me the most; his style and approach fascinated me. A photograph of me is collaged onto Manhattan's cityscape, which made me feel ever so small, while a pink horse mouths the word MOM, which, when turned upside down, reads WOW. The pink horse is my alter ego, and the colour represents half red man, half white man.

Red Horse in a Sea of White Horses

mixed media :: 44" x 30" :: 1989

Racism has existed since dawn's early light, and so has human beings' ignorance and misunderstanding of one another. People make comments like, "Why does that man wear a turban?" or, "I like the powwow dancers' costumes." I always respond, "Ask the man why he wears a turban," or, "Costumes are worn at Halloween; what the powwow dancers are wearing is called regalia." *Red Horse in a Sea of White Horses* speaks about the alienation and isolation felt by the red horse, which is alone in a sea of white horses. The red horse is misunderstood and judged for being different, and is looked down upon, which the black arrow symbolizes.

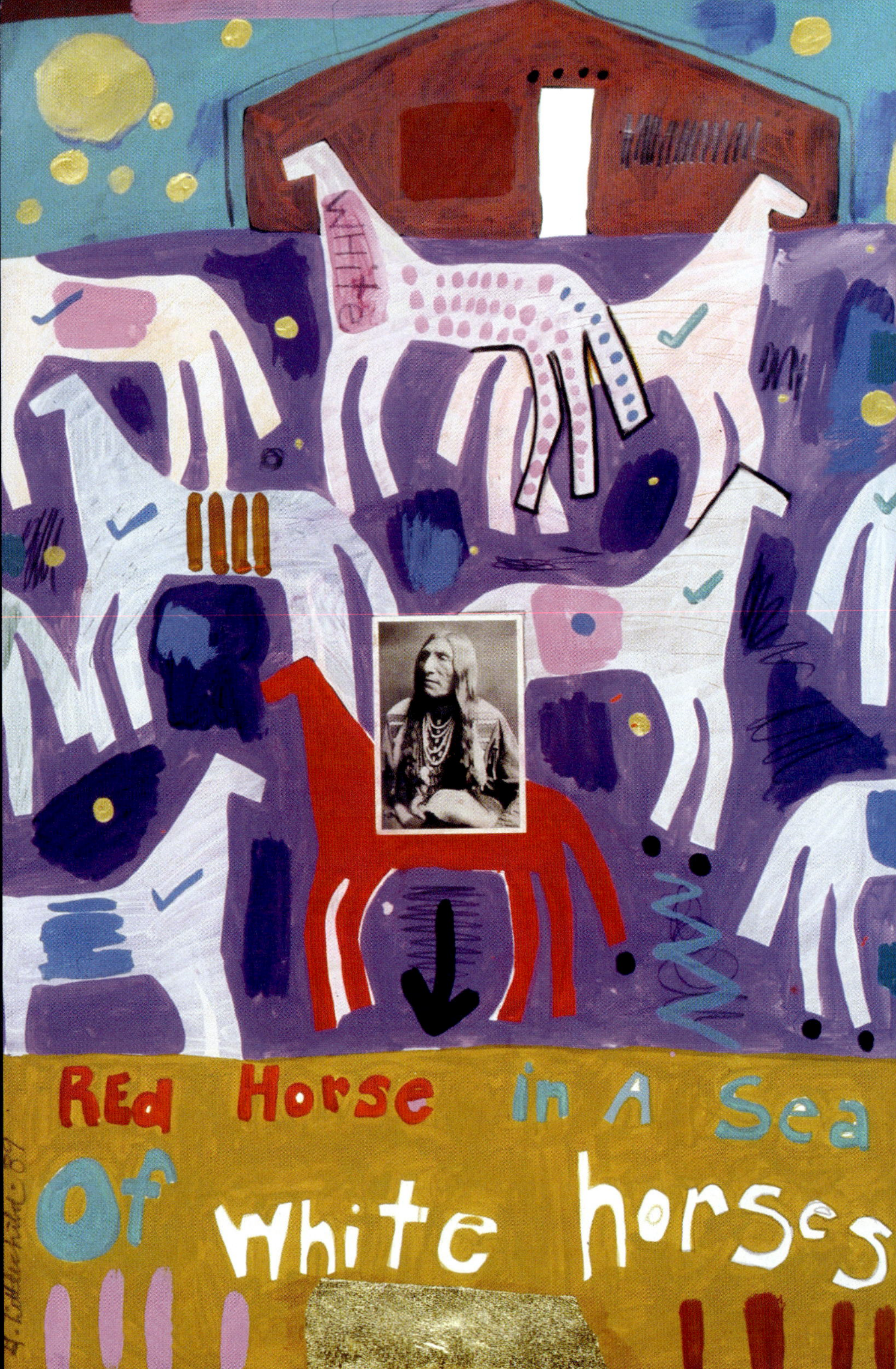

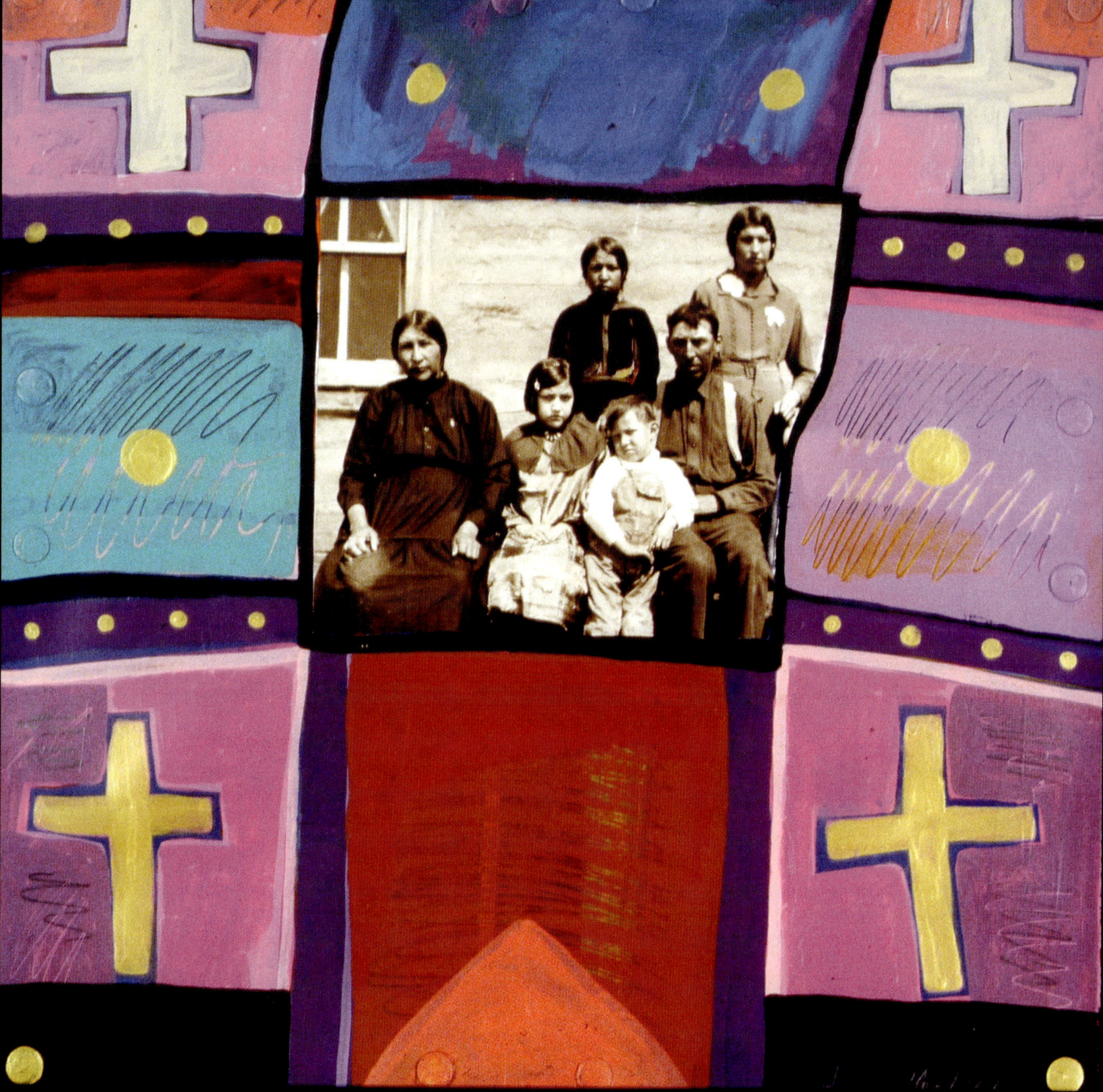

Convert to Catholicism 1 mixed media :: 30" x 30" :: 1989

Missions and missionaries have been part of the Canadian landscape for many, many years. The first missionaries to arrive on the Canadian prairies were French Catholics, led by Father Thibault. Others would soon follow. Reverends Rundle and McDougall came to preach the gospel to the poor, low savages, to convince them to change their ways. These missionaries were successful and counted many souls to add to their missions and churches and religions. In this painting, four crosses create a border, representing Christianity. Inside is a photo of Catholic converts of the Hobbema Oblate Mission. In the photo is a Plains Cree family, Cyprien and Marie Louise (Littlechild) Laroque and their children, who are my close relations.

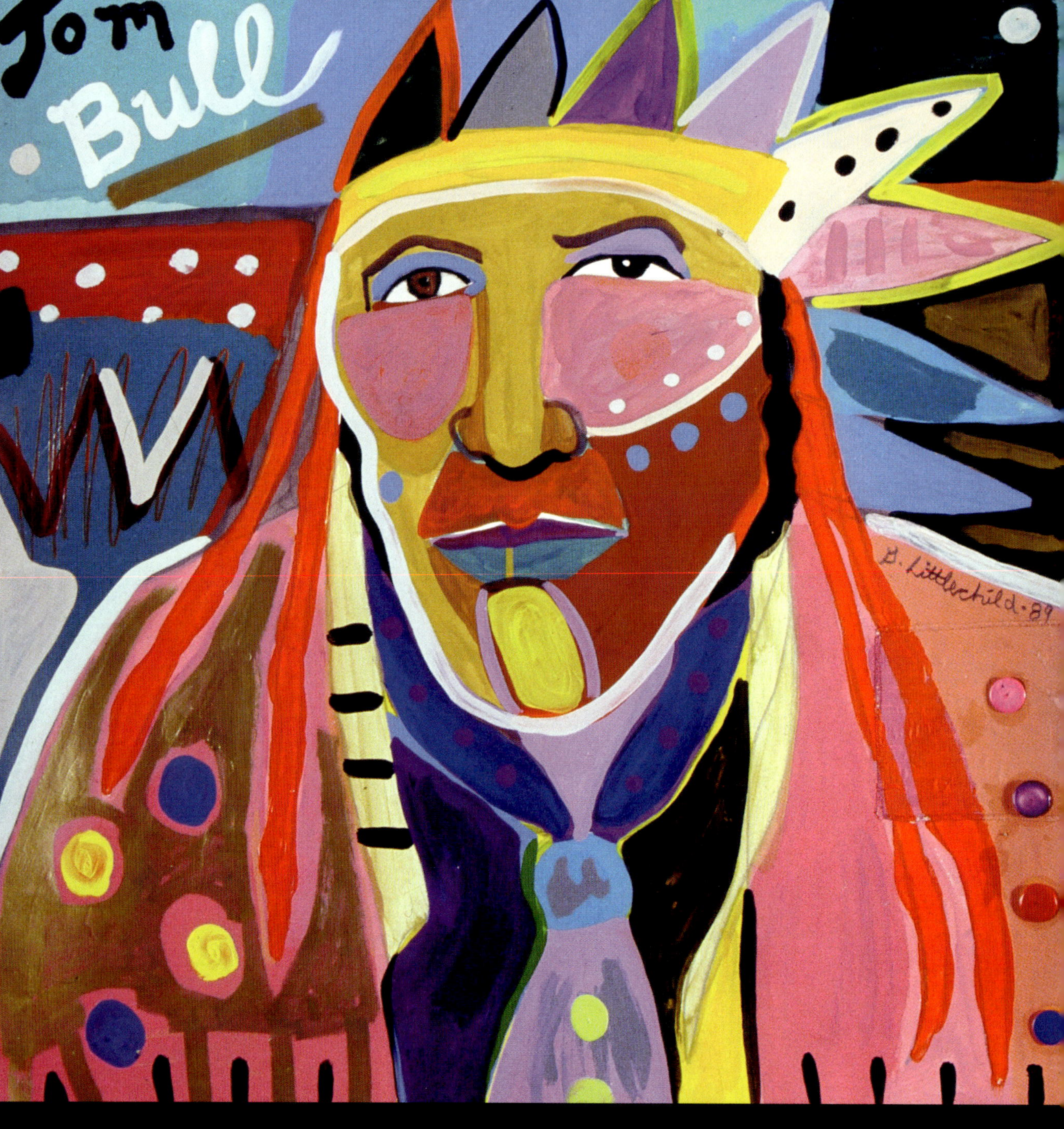

Tom Bull acrylic on paper :: 30" x 30" :: 1989

Tom Bull was the brother of my great-grandfather Chief Francis Bull. Their parents were Chief Louis Bull and Marianne Sikahk (Sikak). Their paternal grandparents were Chief Noah Muddy Bull "Askig Mutus" and Barbe.

Tom must have had a kind, gentle spirit, as his First Nations name is "good man." He was painted by Nicholas de Grandmaison, a portrait artist who painted First Nations people of Alberta.

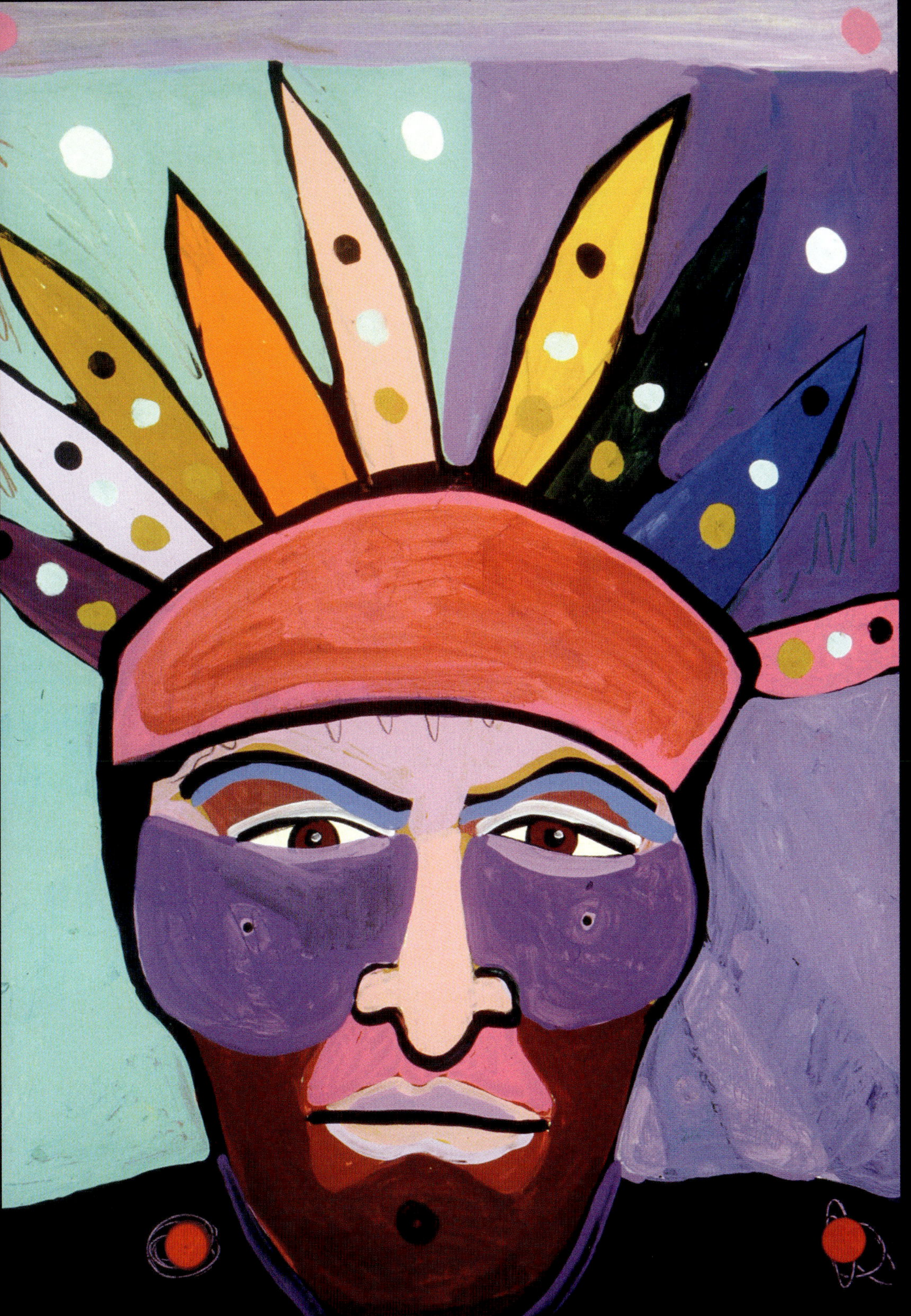

Hollywood Indians on Display 1

acrylic on paper :: 30" x 22" :: 1989

From time to time, I paint a series based on a theme or issue. It is my hope that people will come to learn or share in my observations on what I've witnessed and learned during my stay on Earth. This painting is one of a four-part series. This is a retort to old westerns, where cowboys and Indians created stereotypes through warfare and retreat. The Indians were always the "bad guys" who were hunted and killed. All the actors who played Indians were Italian, standing in stoic poses and communicating in guttural grunts that were a mish-mash of Indian languages. I wonder if any Native Americans actually could understand any of these grunts. Today, Hollywood is much more aware and astute when casting for Native roles. No longer does an Italian American stand in as a stoic chief.

PART 2 1990–1999

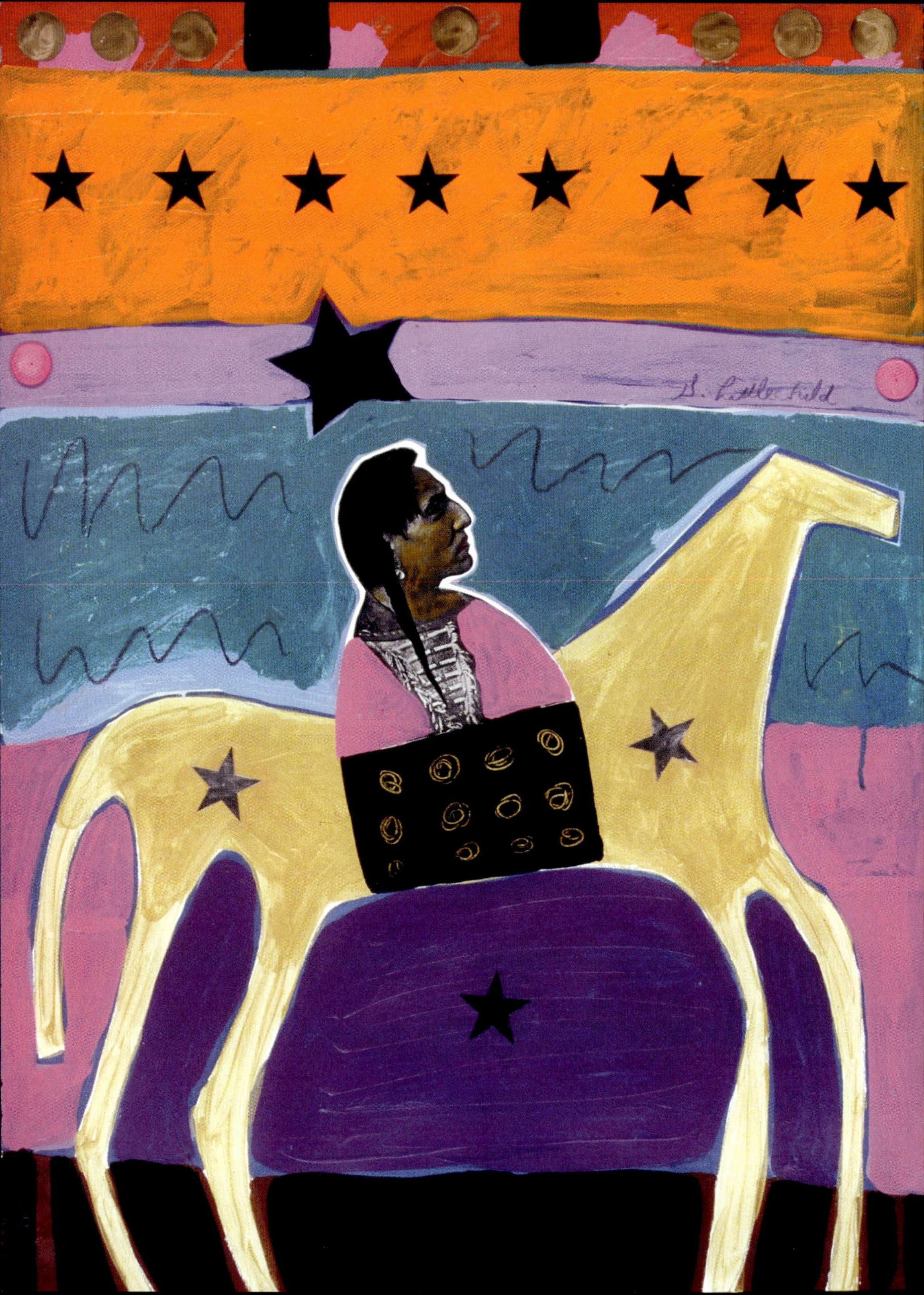

Sioux Warrior 7

mixed media on paper
30" x 22" :: 1990

A horse and rider roam through a colourful sunset landscape. Stars begin to appear and surround the man and horse in their quieter moments of the day. This man was photographed by Edward S. Curtis. I painted eight Sioux (Lakota) warriors in this series.

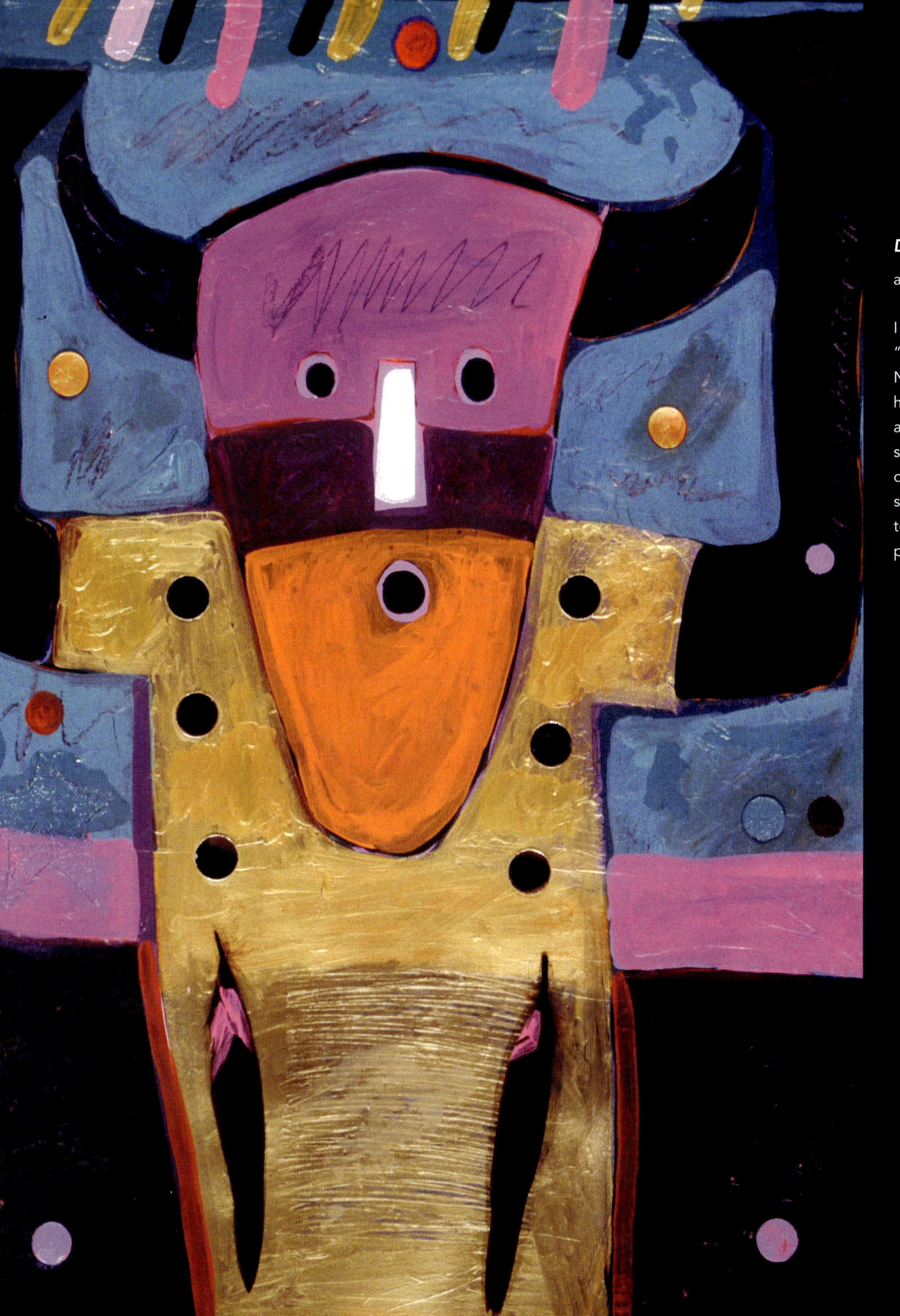

Dancing Buffalo 2

acrylic on paper :: 30" x 22" :: 1990

I like to have fun and at times have a "silly" perspective on life. Like many First Nations people, I have used humour to help heal past wounds. Can you imagine a buffalo dancing in a gold, mirrored skirt, its face painted pink, purple and orange? I like to make light of the heavy sometimes, but in the end, I pay homage to the millions of sacred buffalo who perished as a way of life came to an end.

Mohawk Warrior

acrylic on paper :: 50" x 38" :: 1990

Many Mohawk men came west with the fur trade's coureurs de bois. These men often intermarried with local Cree or Metis peoples, and their family names still exist in Alberta. Their descendants acknowledge their Mohawk ancestors.

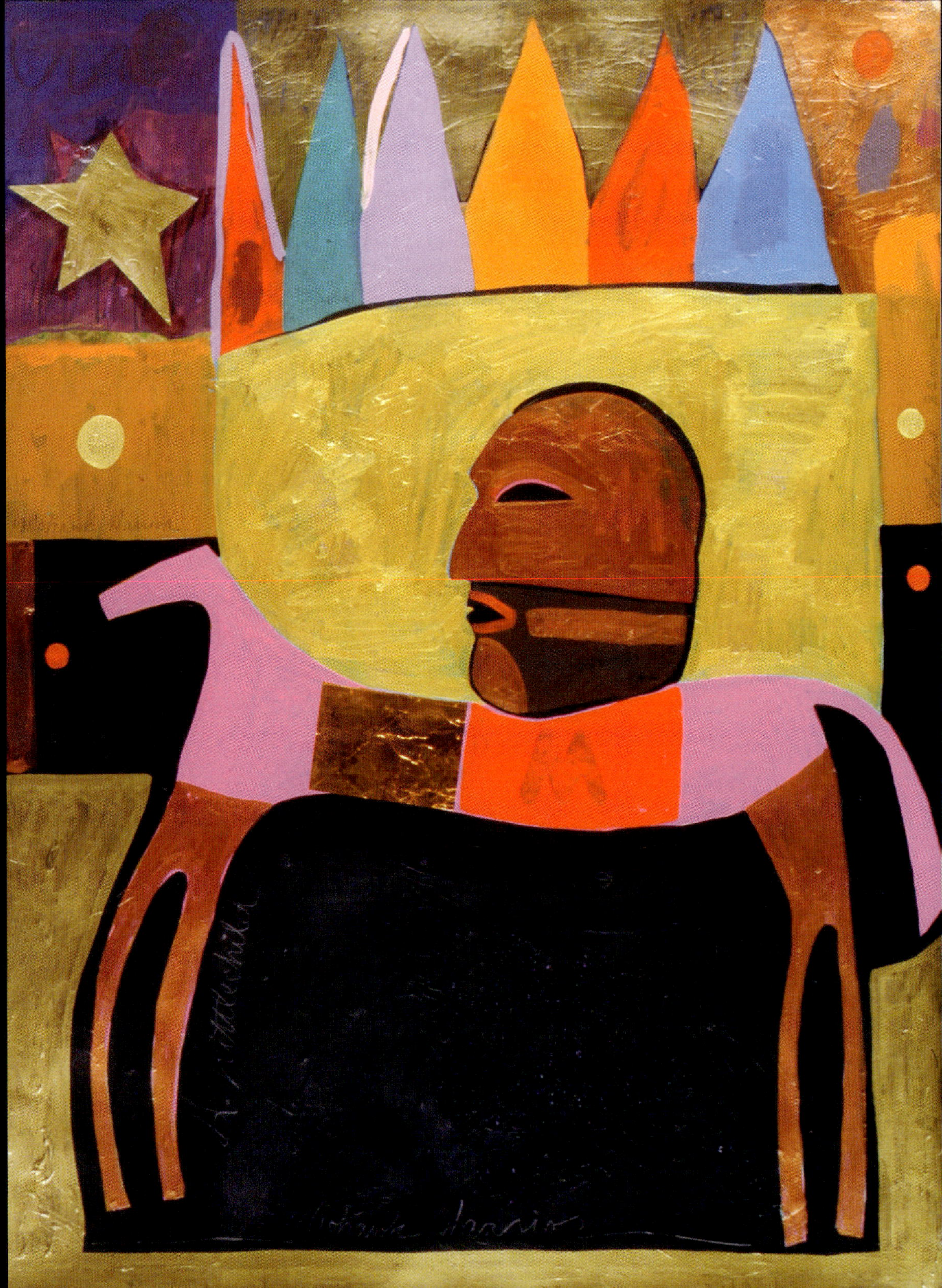

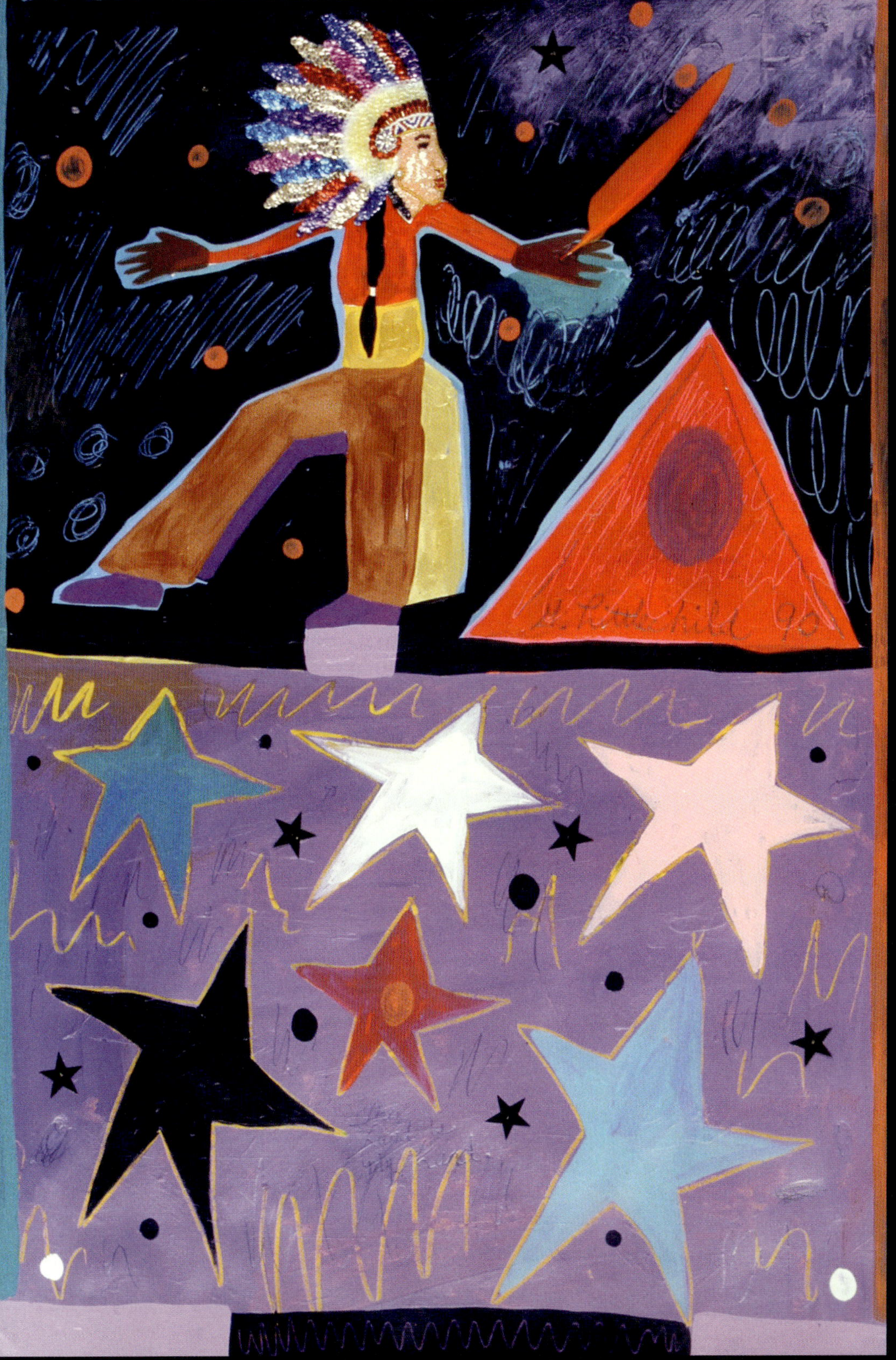

This Land Is My Land

mixed media :: 44" x 30" :: 1990

This First Nations man holds a feather as he conducts the song "This Land Is My Land," which I heard over and over as a boy. In reality, it was his ancestors' territory, which was only used temporarily as each generation passed through. We really don't own the land we live on. The concept of land ownership came with European settlers. Their quest to dominate the land by owning it was something First Nations people had never heard of; this was not their way.

Dancing Raven Spirit

mixed media :: 44" x 30" :: 1990

A fun, whimsical painting in honour of Raven and his trickster ways. He is dancing and wearing a turtle neckpiece in honour of the land, Turtle Island (as it is known by First Nations people), where he believes he is the ruler and king. Oh, that tricky Raven . . .

My art is often used commercially. This particular painting was used on a poster and T-shirt for the Bumbershoot Festival in Seattle, Washington. From time to time, I still see people wearing this T-shirt, all these years later.

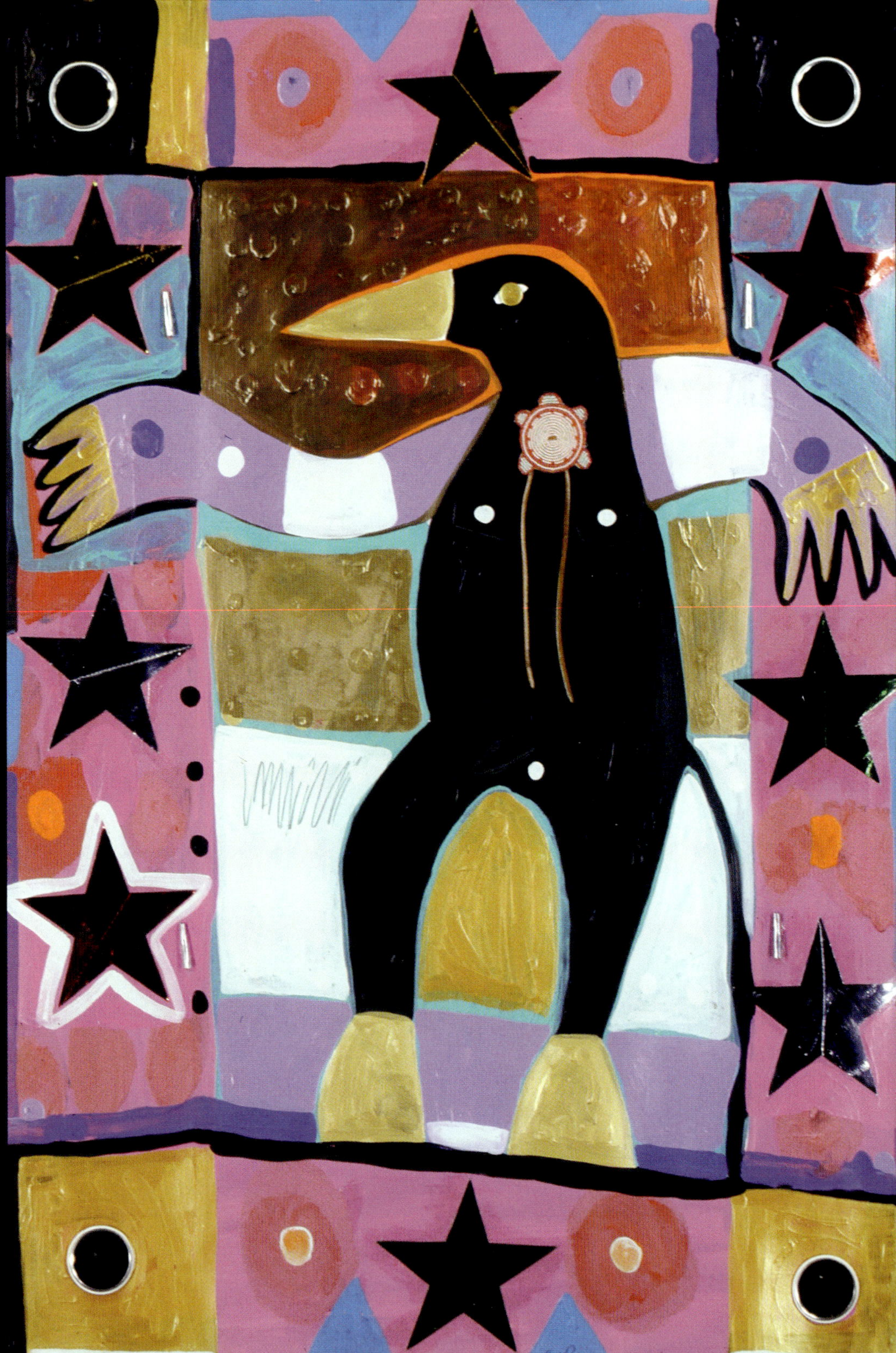

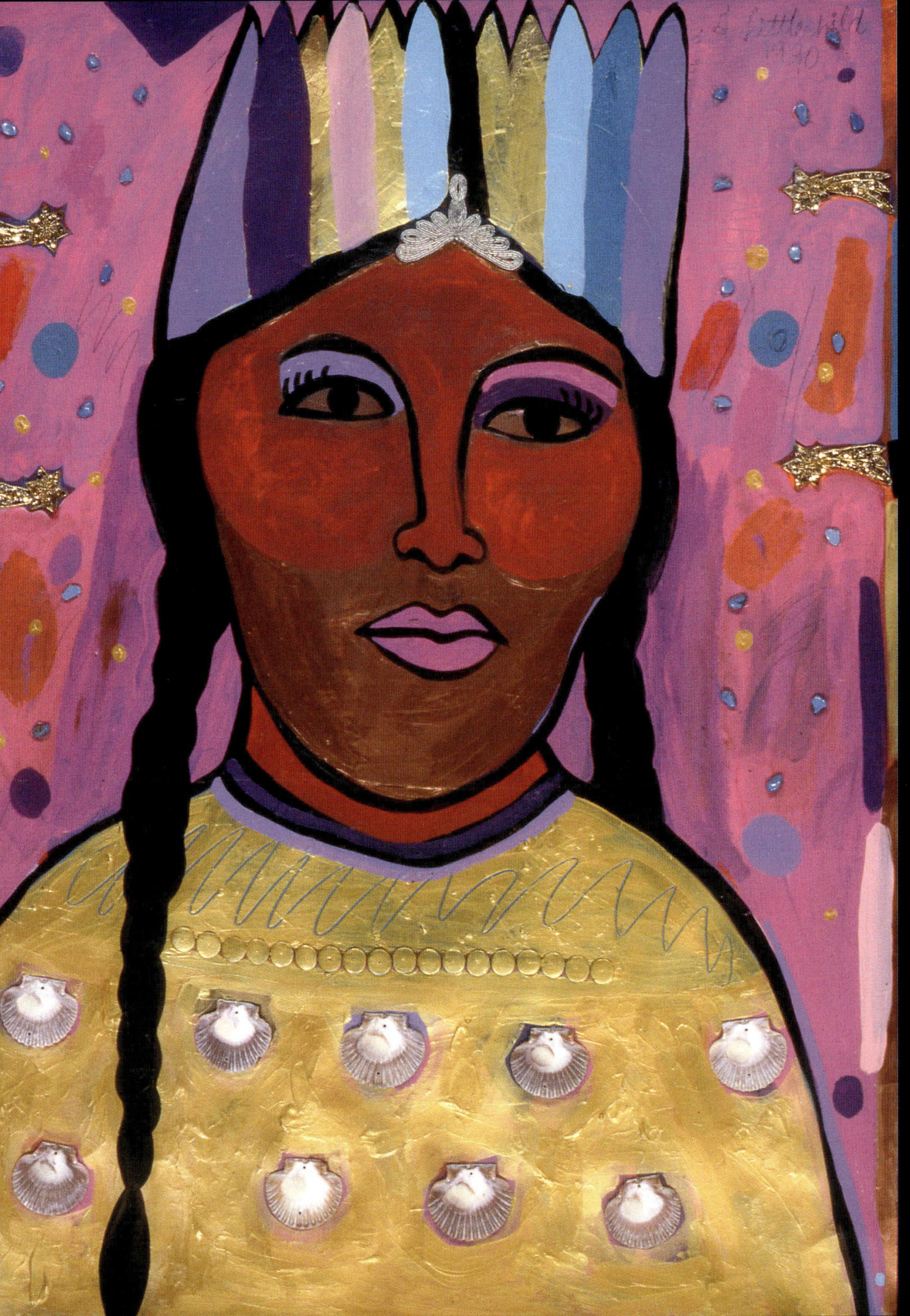

Winner of the Miss Hobbema Princess Pageant

mixed media :: 50" x 38" :: 1990

I created this painting to honour all First Nations women, but especially the women of the four bands of Hobbema. Author W.P. Kinsella had an image of a white drag queen on the cover of his short-story collection *The Miss Hobbema Pageant* (Harper Collins, 1989), which I found very distasteful. He is an amazing writer, but enough with the stereotyping of First Nations peoples! I wanted to promote the beauty, wisdom, pride and dignity of the Cree people of Hobbema.

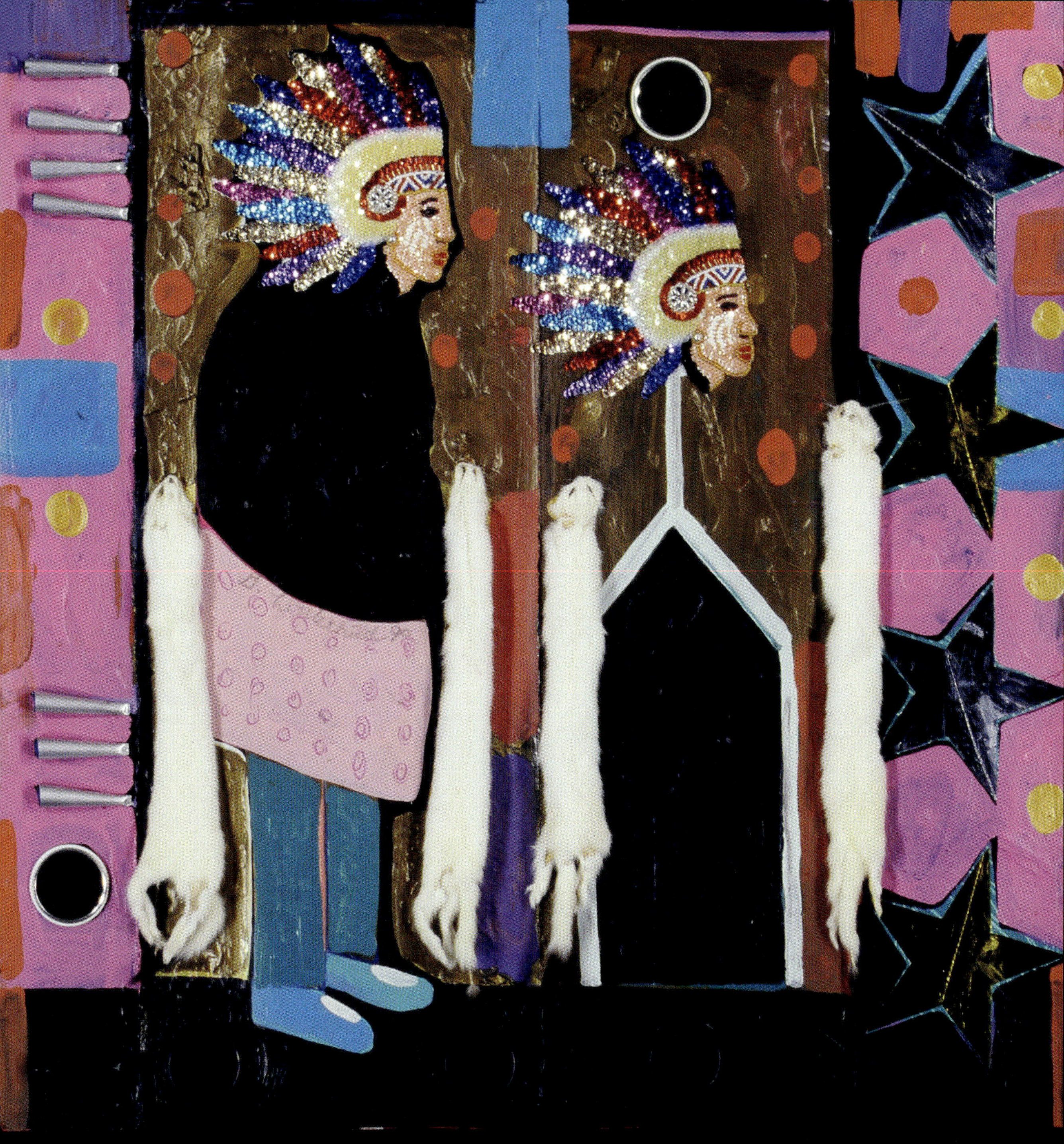

Mortuary Houses mixed media :: 30" x 30" :: 1991

In the old days, graves were covered in house-shaped structures and surrounded by white picket fences. I have seen photographs of these graveyards in archives. Tremendous reverence was given to those who passed. In this particular painting, a chief has passed. On the left is the chief alive and well, and on the right is the grave house that protects his earthly remains. I bought the sequined head-dressed faces and collaged them into the painting, along with little mirrors, ermine skins, metallic stars and tin bugle beads, and mixed with acrylic paint.

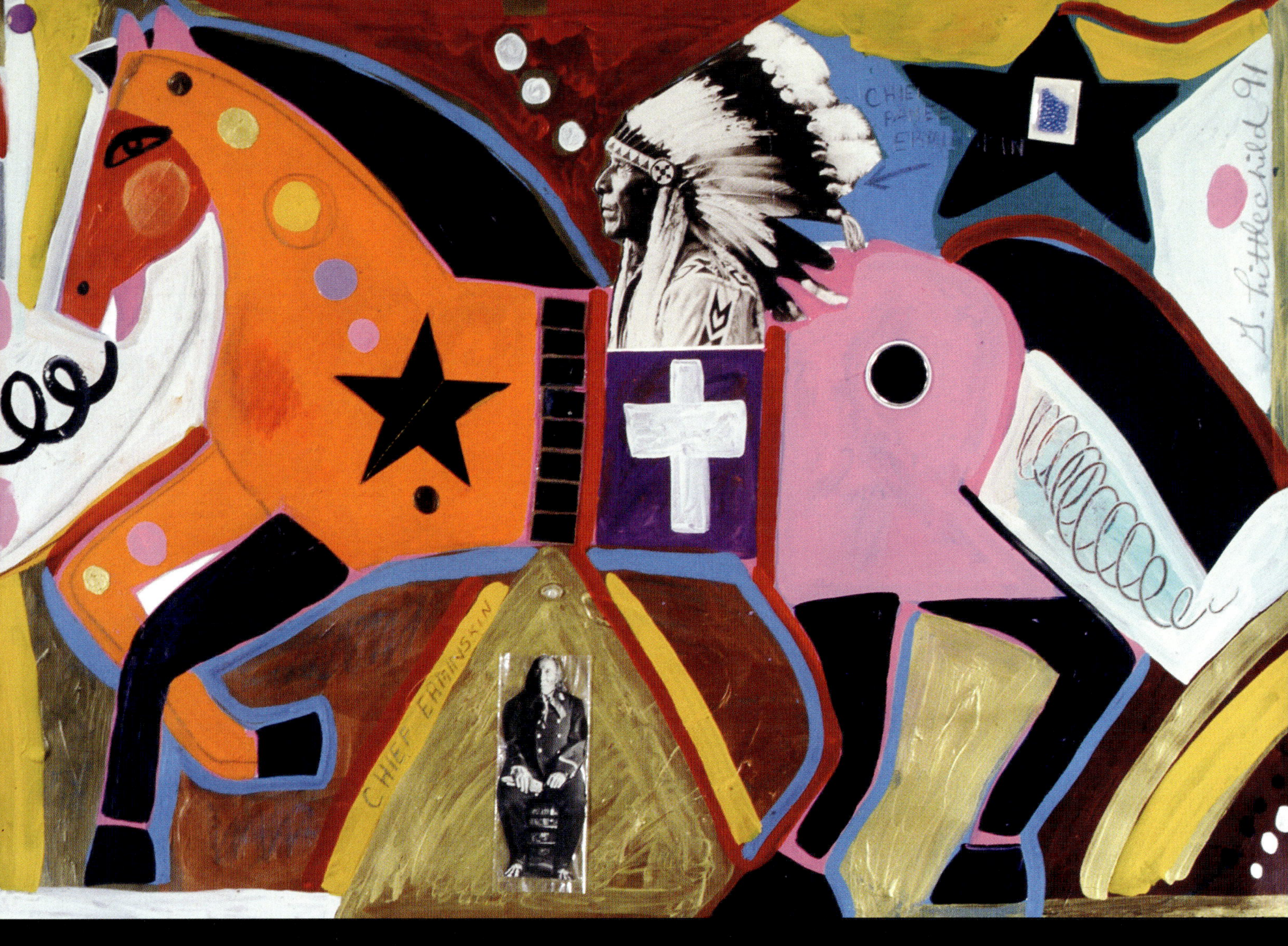

Tribal Leaders mixed media :: 30" x 44" :: 1991

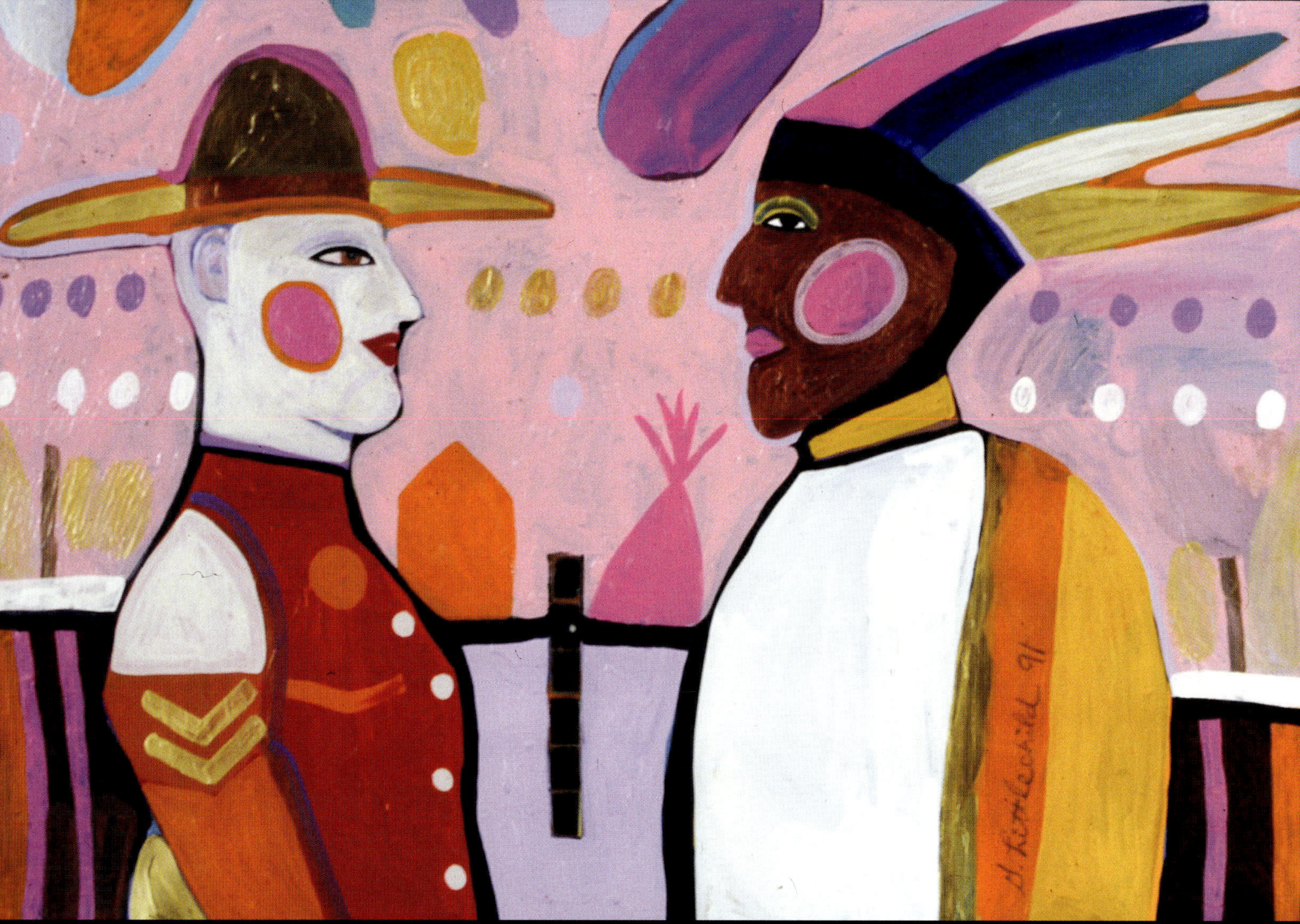

Mountie and Indian Chief acrylic on paper :: 30" x 44" :: 1991

A row of small mirrors separates the Mountie and Indian chief. The inspiration for this painting was a postcard that depicted the Mountie in his red serge and the chief wearing his regalia. It was a beautiful image; however, in the photo the chief was shorter. With artistic licence, I made the chief in my painting the same height as the Mountie.

I created a scenario. What did they know about each other? Could they see past stereotypes and the history they knew about others? Did they come in peace? Was this photo staged or an actual gathering? And what do you know about the First Nations–Mountie relationships in Canada's history?

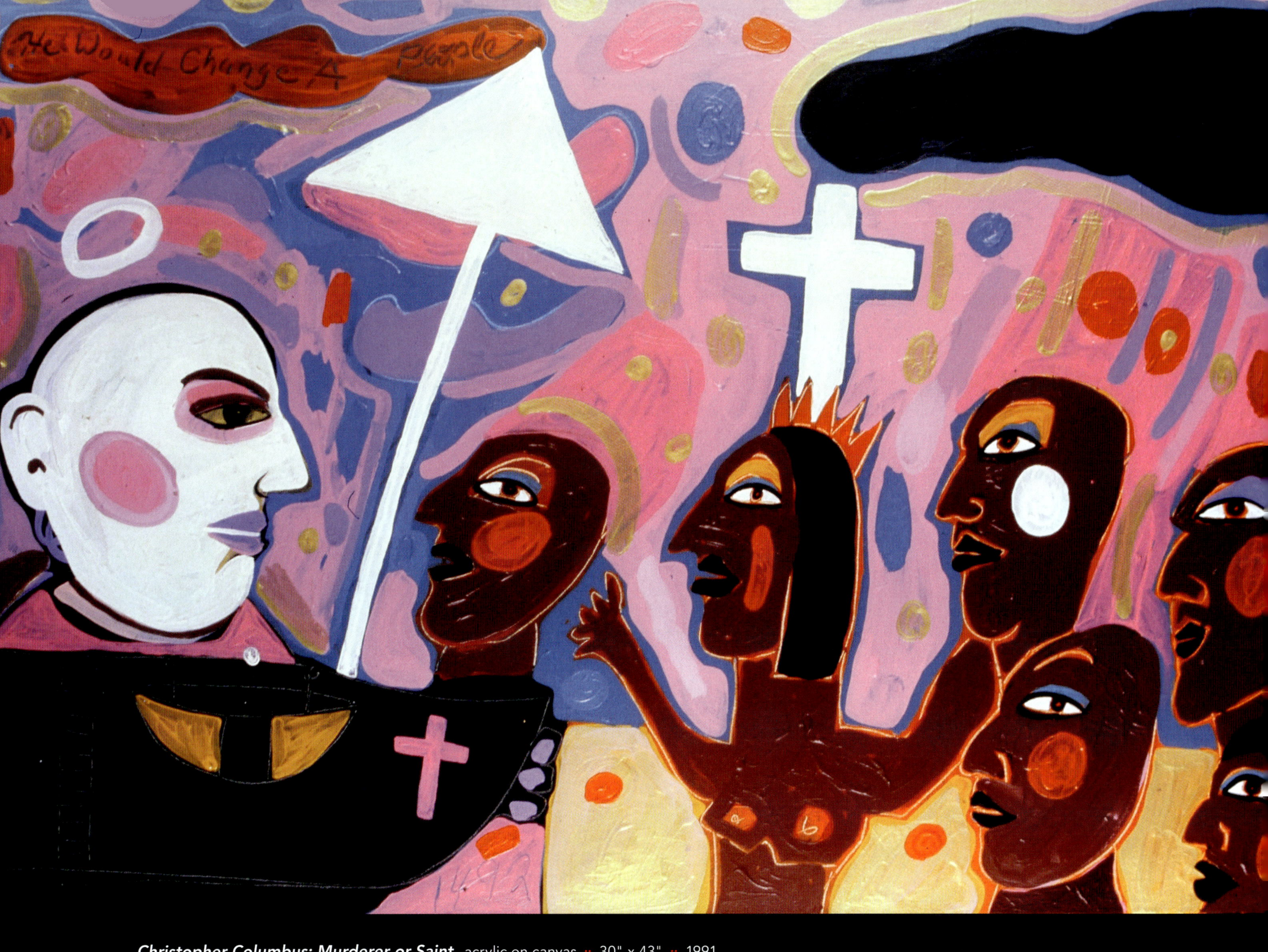

Christopher Columbus: Murderer or Saint acrylic on canvas :: 30" x 43" :: 1991

Who was Columbus but a man on a quest? Some say Columbus discovered South America; however, it was already inhabited by peoples with rich cultures. As a result of Columbus's arrival, these rich cultures were devastated and people died off by the millions. The lives and cultures he touched would never be the same; slavery and disease overcame them. Did the First Peoples see him as a ghost spirit? Was he to be respected and revered like a god? There are so many unknowns.

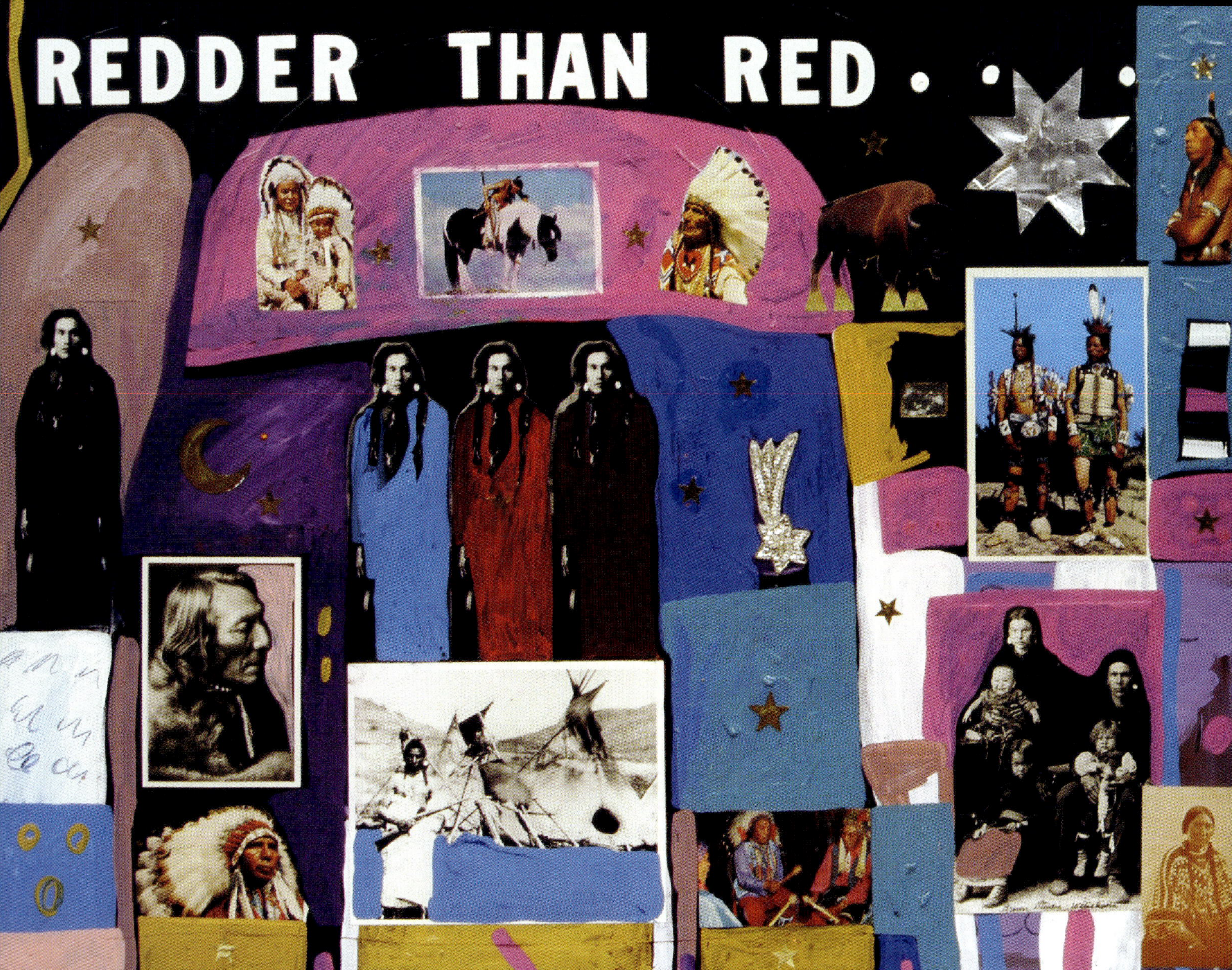

Redder Than Red mixed media on canvas :: 30" x 40" :: 1991

I find it troublesome how postcards portray iconic Native Americans and their landscape—creating a perception of what the "red man" was like. Did the photographers search for individuals who would maintain the stereotypes of "chief and squaw," "mythic rider on horseback," "warriors with spears" and "traditional teepee?" Yes, these were aspects of Plains First Nations life; however, the media played these ideas up. The title of this painting speaks to the idea that the people in those postcards are representative of the "red noble savage," thus "redder than red."

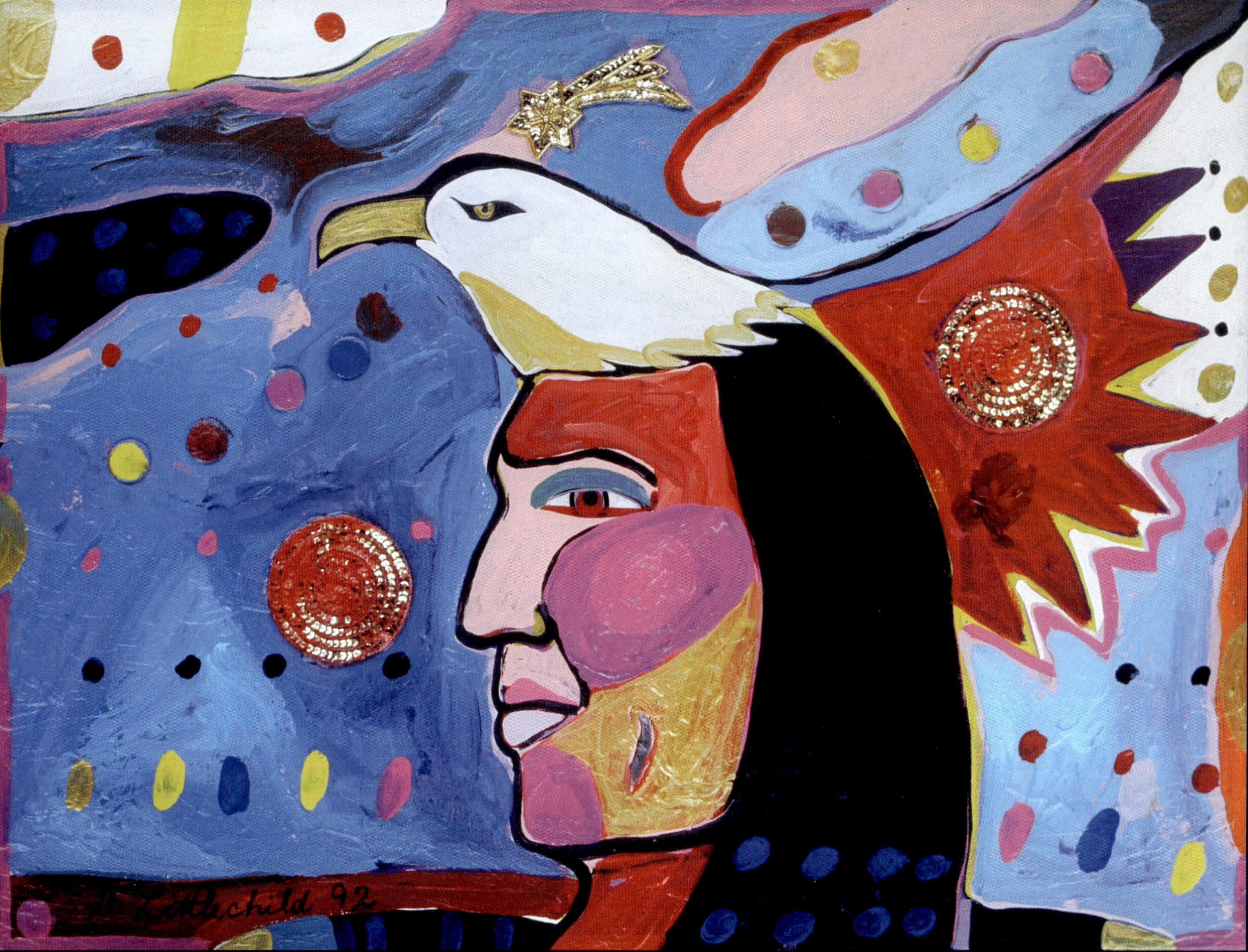

Eagle Man Dancer mixed media on canvas :: 22" x 30" :: 1992

I have a fascination with human-animal transformations. In this painting, the subject is in mid-swing, performing a dance, a ritual. Wearing an Eagle headdress, the man morphs into the Eagle. He imbues the Eagle spirit, and for that moment in time, becomes one with it. Vivid colours add to the stage and its brilliance, setting the tone for this sacred occurrence.

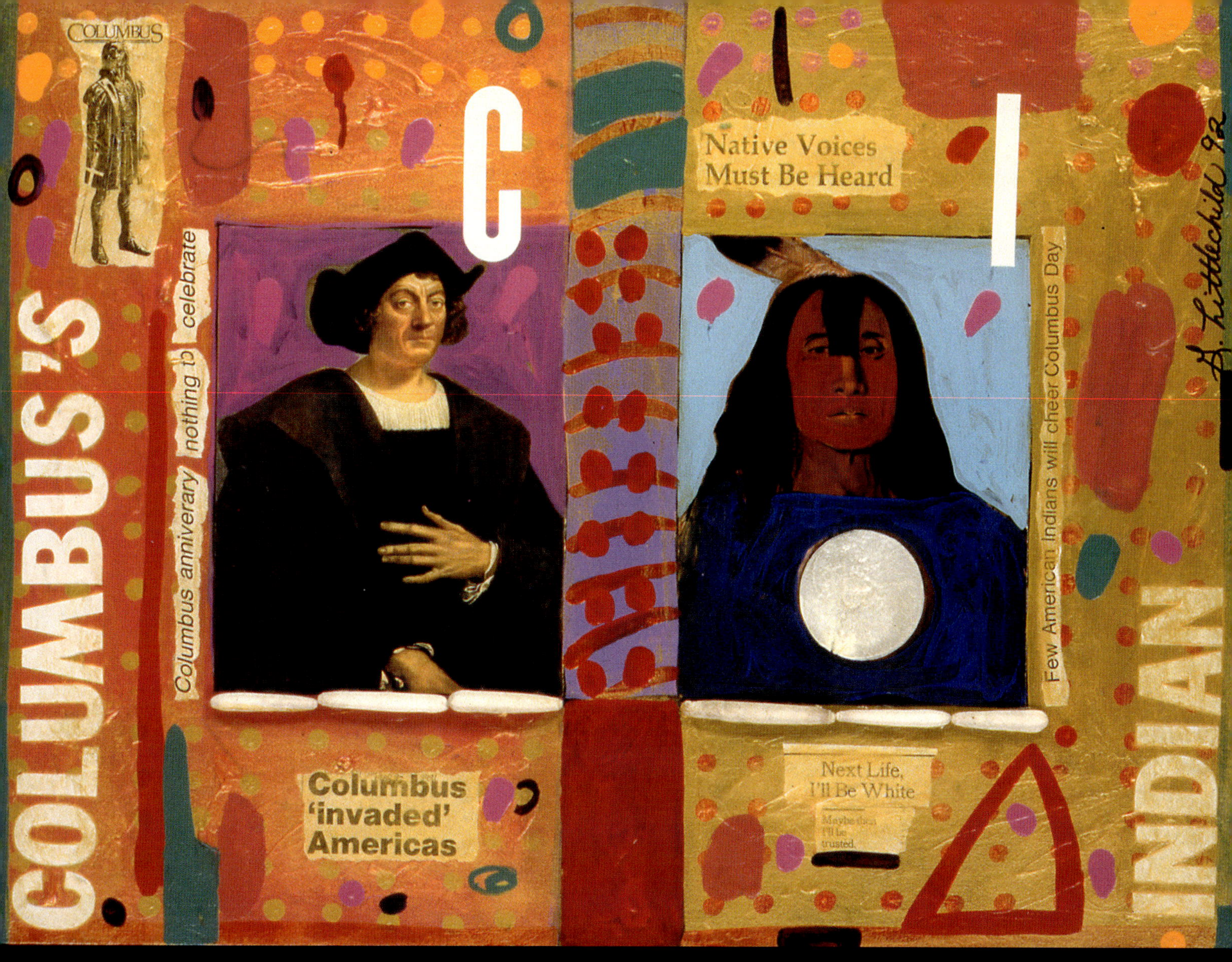

Columbus's Red Indian mixed media on canvas :: 22" x 30" :: 1992

The year 1992 was a time of remembrance for Aboriginal Peoples in the Americas, marking 500 years since Columbus's invasion. I collaged newspaper headlines onto my canvas along with two portraits, one of Columbus, one of a First Nations man. The headlines, "Columbus 'invaded' Americas," "Nothing to celebrate," "Next Life I'll Be White, Maybe Then I'll Be Trusted," "Natives Voices Must Be Heard" and "Few Native American Indians will cheer Columbus Day" evoke the climate in 1992. It is hard to fathom the

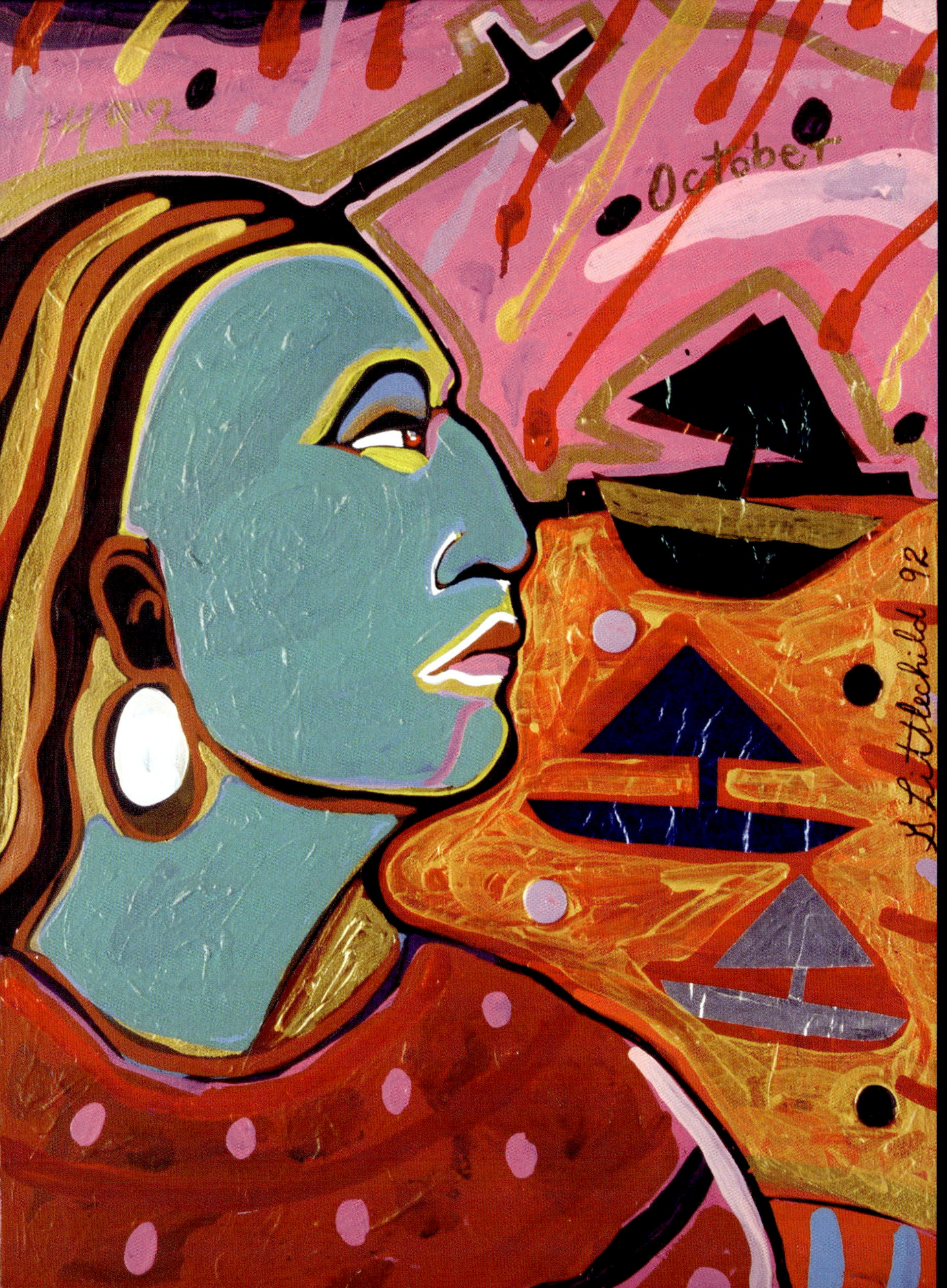

October, 500 Years Ago

acrylic on canvas
30" x 22" :: 1992

This man of the Taíno tribe lived in Hispaniola, the island now divided into modern-day Haiti and the Dominican Republic. He stares into the bay's red water, which represents the bloodshed of his people and all the First Peoples who suffered at the hands of Columbus and from colonization. The gold atop the bloodstained sea represents the gold Columbus discovered and took back to Spain. The iconic three ships brought the beginning of the end to an era. Christianity is seen piercing the man's skull like a lobotomy and dulling his senses. A genocide that wiped out millions placed a deep sorrow and wound into the consciousness of the First Peoples.

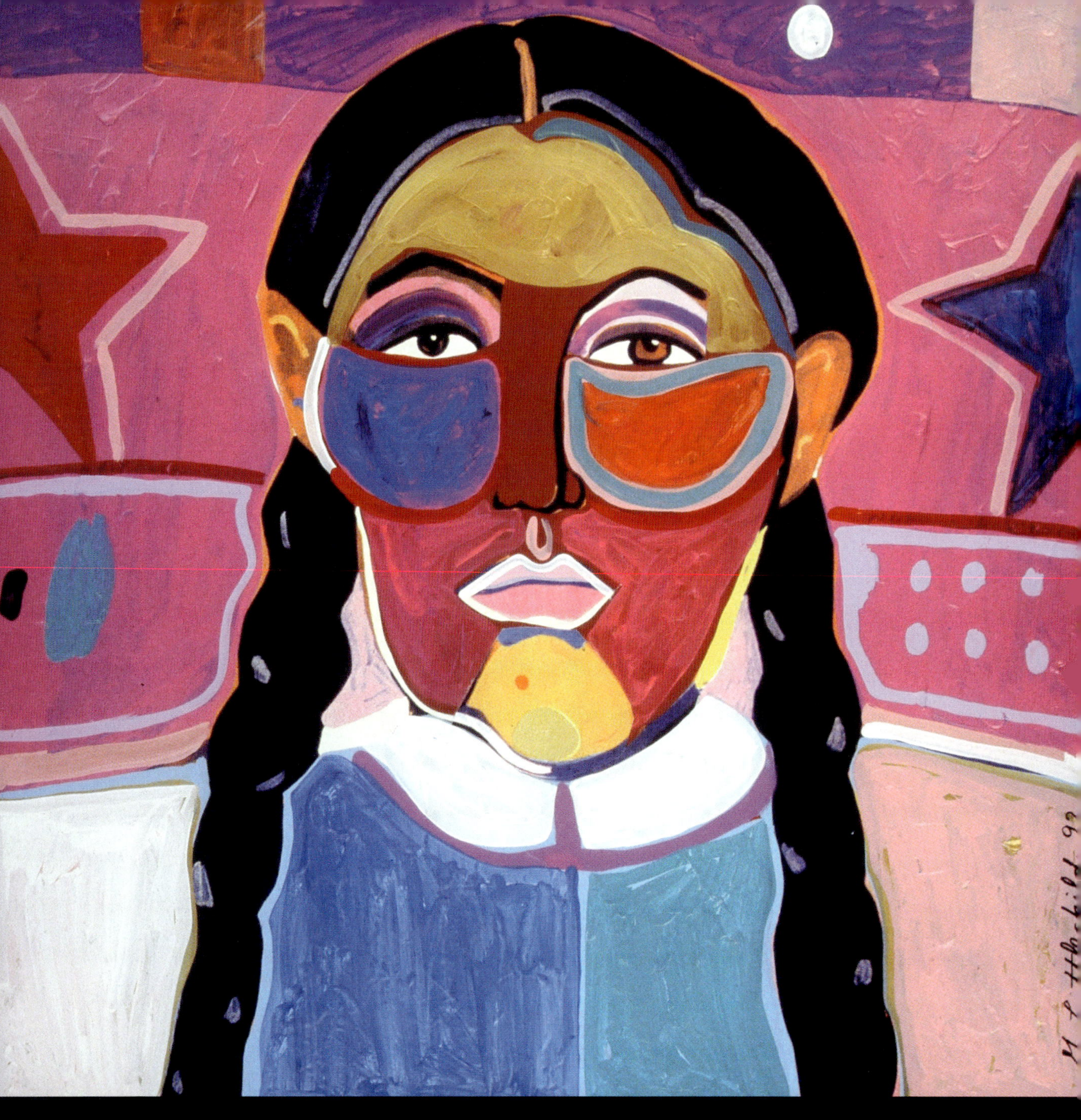

She Came to Me as an Angel in the Night acrylic on paper :: 30" x 30" :: 1992

This painting conveys ancestral dreams, messages, memories of another time—living by mountain meadows, camping by glacier-fed lakes, roaming freely on great grassy plains, watching the birth of spring and seeing wintertime encroach and steal away the warm, long days of summer. You, my beloved ancestors, lived as

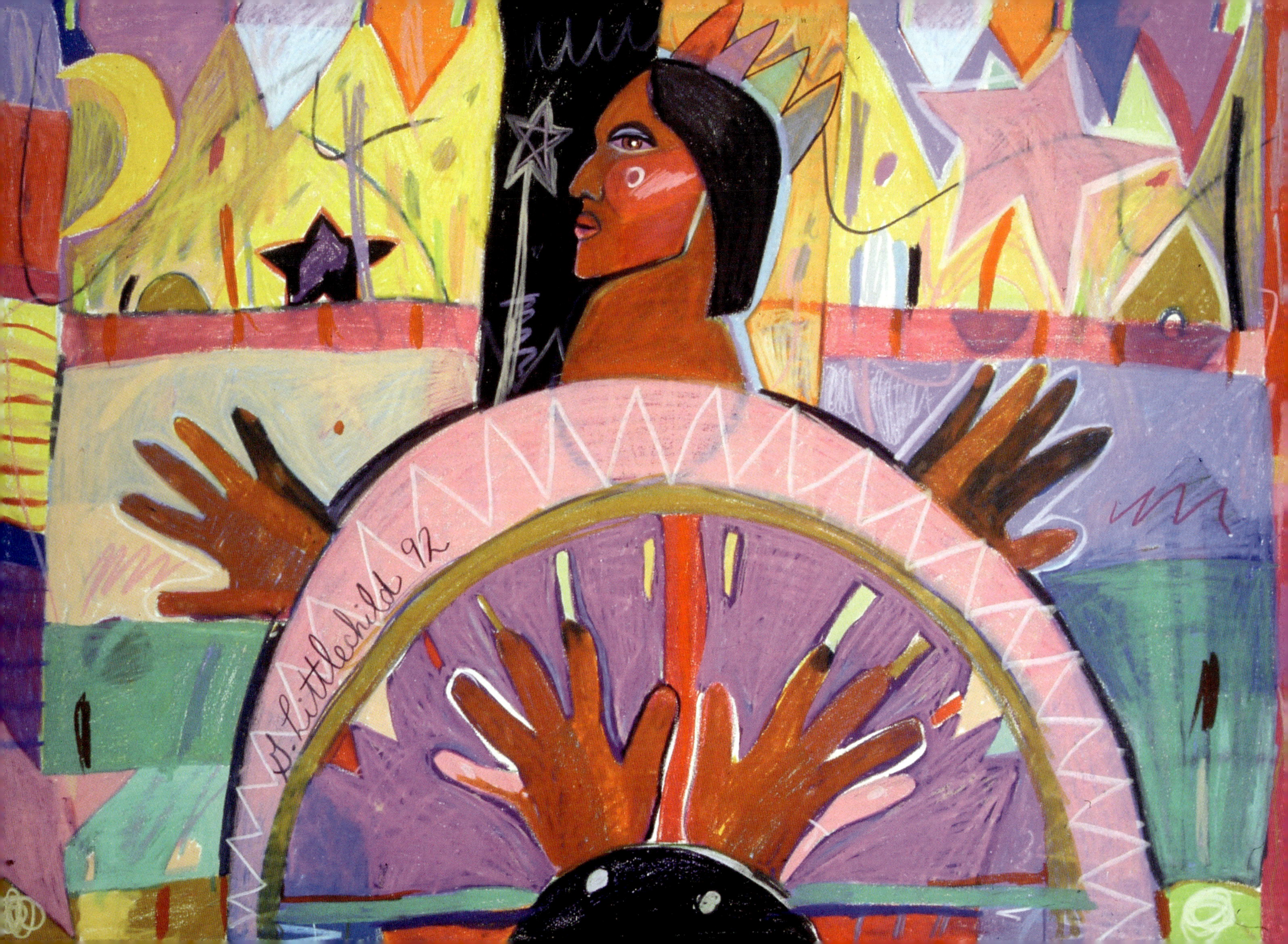
G. Littlechild 92

Portrait of Peggy Bull

mixed media on paper
25" x 22" :: 1993

The first time I ever saw a photo of my great-grandmother Peggy I was struck by her poise and Cree beauty, so elegant and self-assured, a strong, determined, hard-working woman. She married her cousin, Chief Francis Bull of the Louis Bull Band in Hobbema. Together they had nine children. Her parents were Louis Natuasis and Betsy Samson of the Samson Band in Hobbema. Peggy lived to be 90 and left behind many descendants.

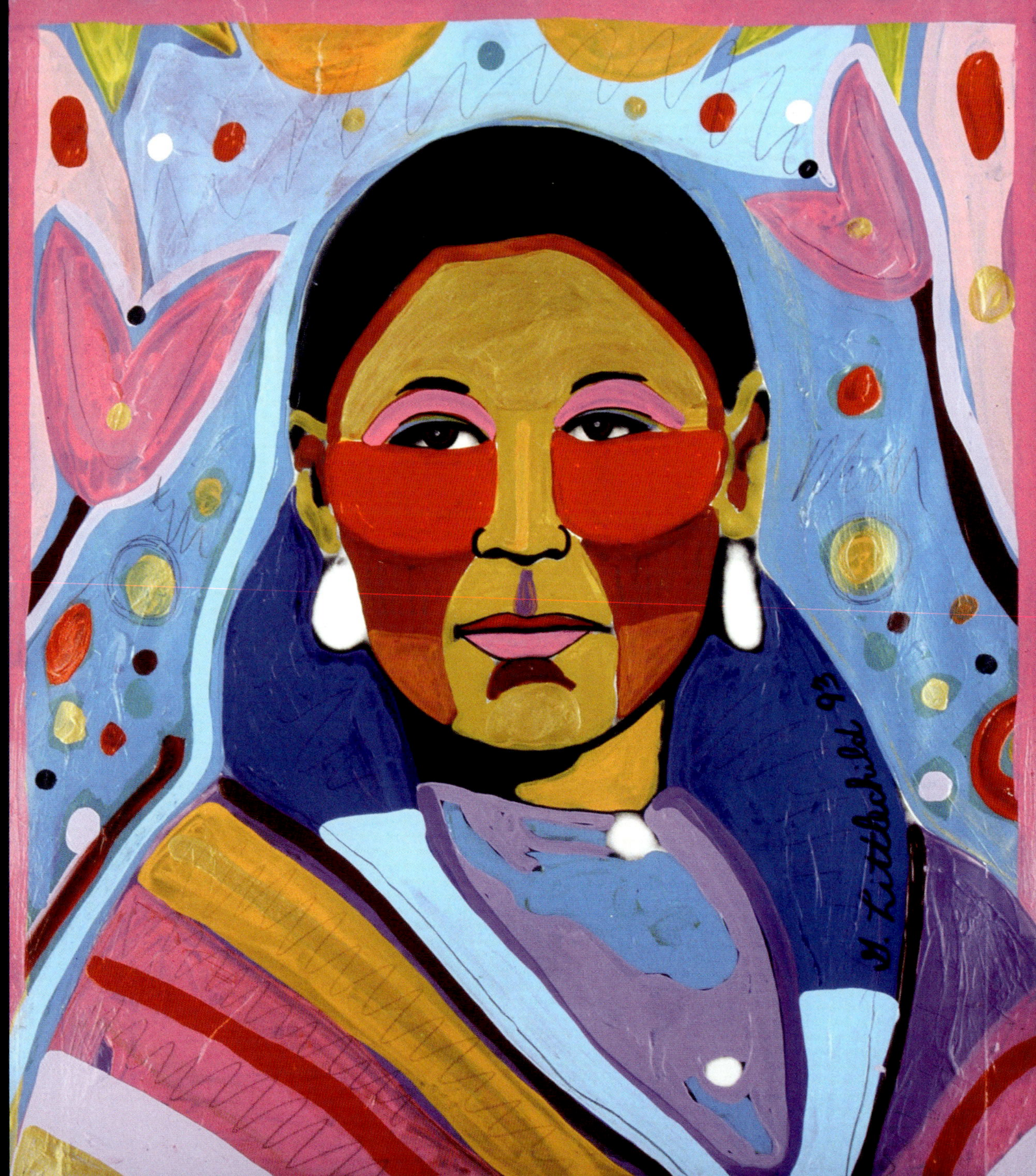

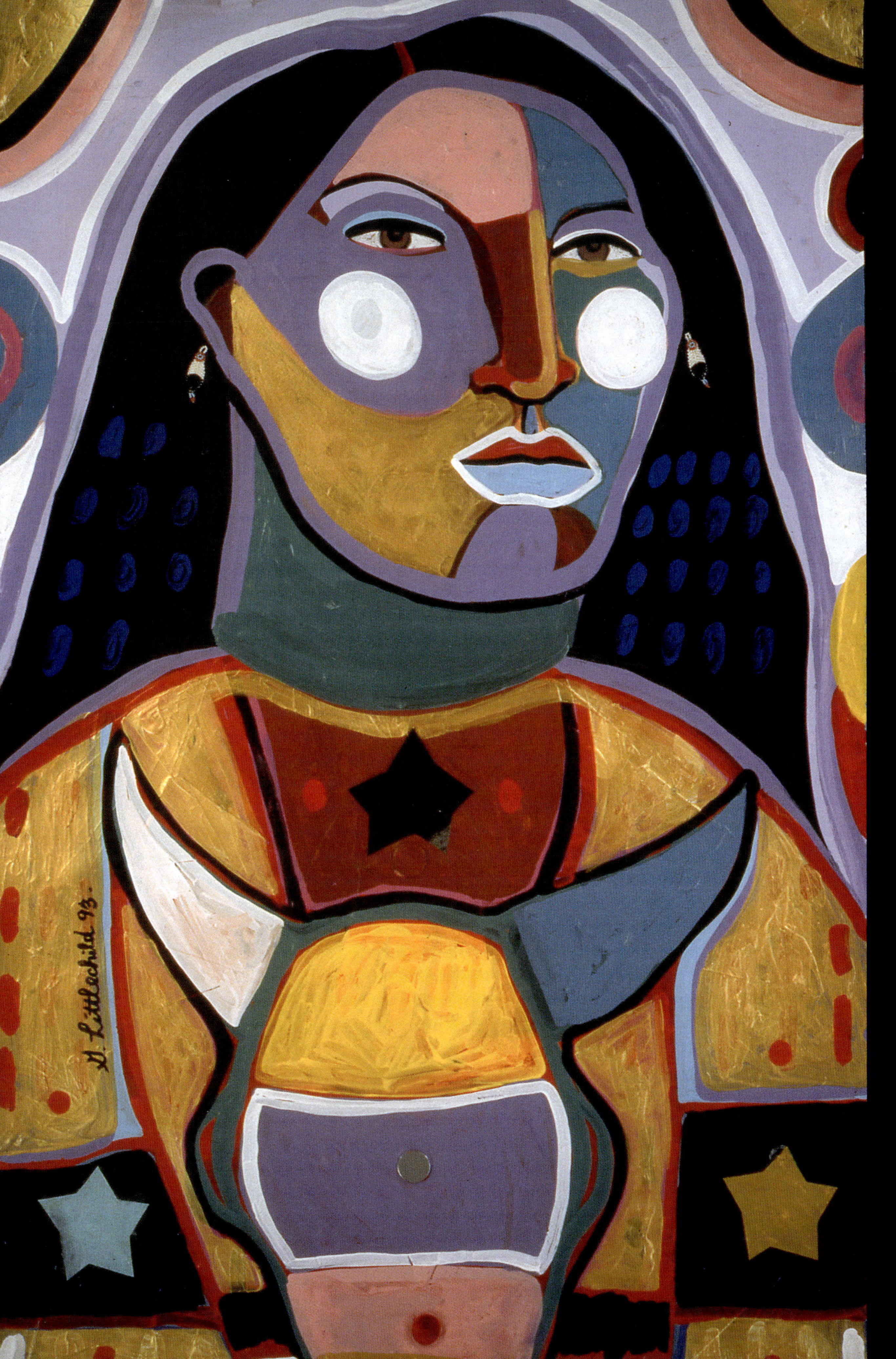

She Can See through Your Very Soul

acrylic on paper :: 30" x 22" :: 1993

Years ago, while living in Vancouver, I painted in my kitchen prior to getting a studio. I began working on a portrait of a woman, which I had tacked onto the kitchen door in its beginning stages. I had my back to the portrait doing chores when I felt a strong presence in the room. I turned around to see the woman in the portrait staring at me, looking right into my soul. I realized it was my late mother, Rachel (1929–1965). It was her spirit looking into mine. I knew that this portrait needed to transform her into the traditional Plains Cree woman she was meant to be but could not become because of residential school. I painted her with long, flowing black hair and traditional clothing showing her tribal connection to the buffalo, as she is part of the Star Nation. This was healing for both her and me.

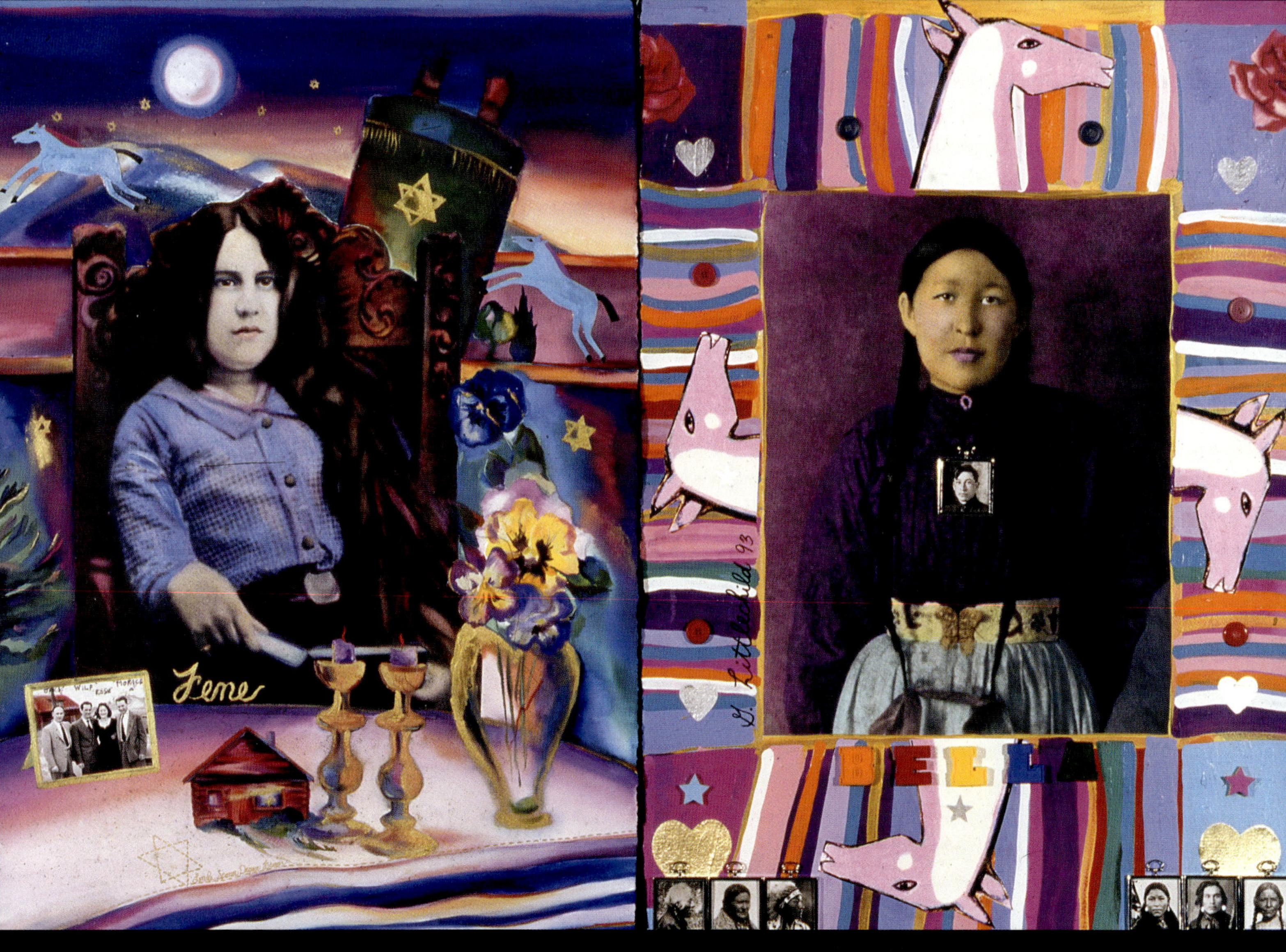

Persecute Us Not 2 mixed media :: 44" x 60" :: 1993

My dear friend Linda Frimer and I painted portraits of our grandmothers Bella and Fene, whose people had suffered persecution and genocide. Side by side in her studio, Linda and I painted these great women, offering each other a gift that we collaged into the portraits. Linda gave me a rose, which I cut in half and collaged onto the left and right top of the painting. I offered her a blue horse. We added our grandmothers' names and photos of their families. The two paintings were placed side by side in one frame and shown in several exhibitions—including one at the Consulate General of Canada Los Angeles. These women grace the cover of the book *In Honour of Our Grandmothers* (Theytus Books,

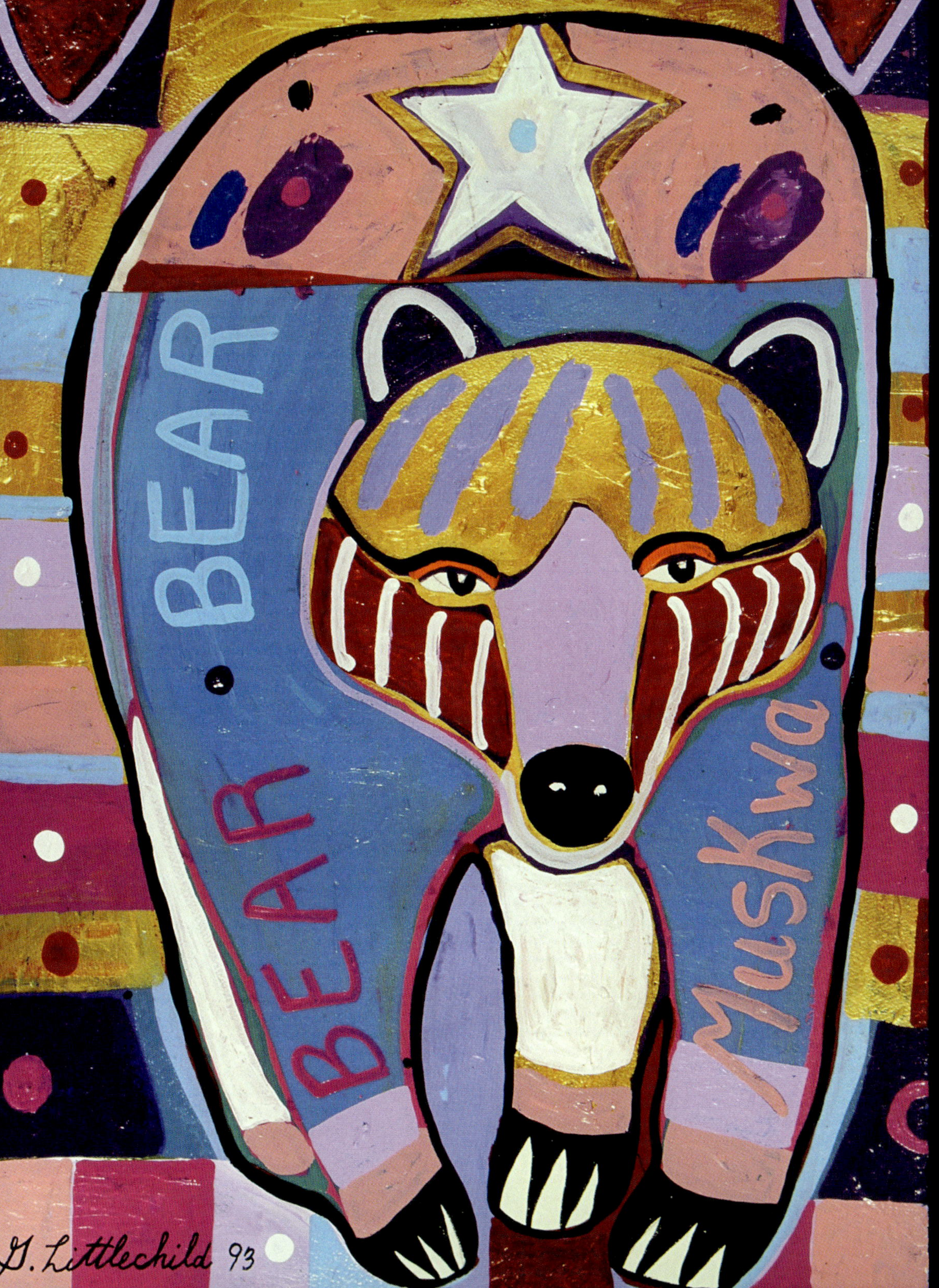

Muskwa Bear

acrylic on paper
30" x 22" :: 1993

A stylized, abstract bear honours his tenacious, curious and strong spirit. Much respect is given to this great creature of the forest and his abilities in First Nations cultures, stories and ceremonies. The Cree word for bear is Muskwa.

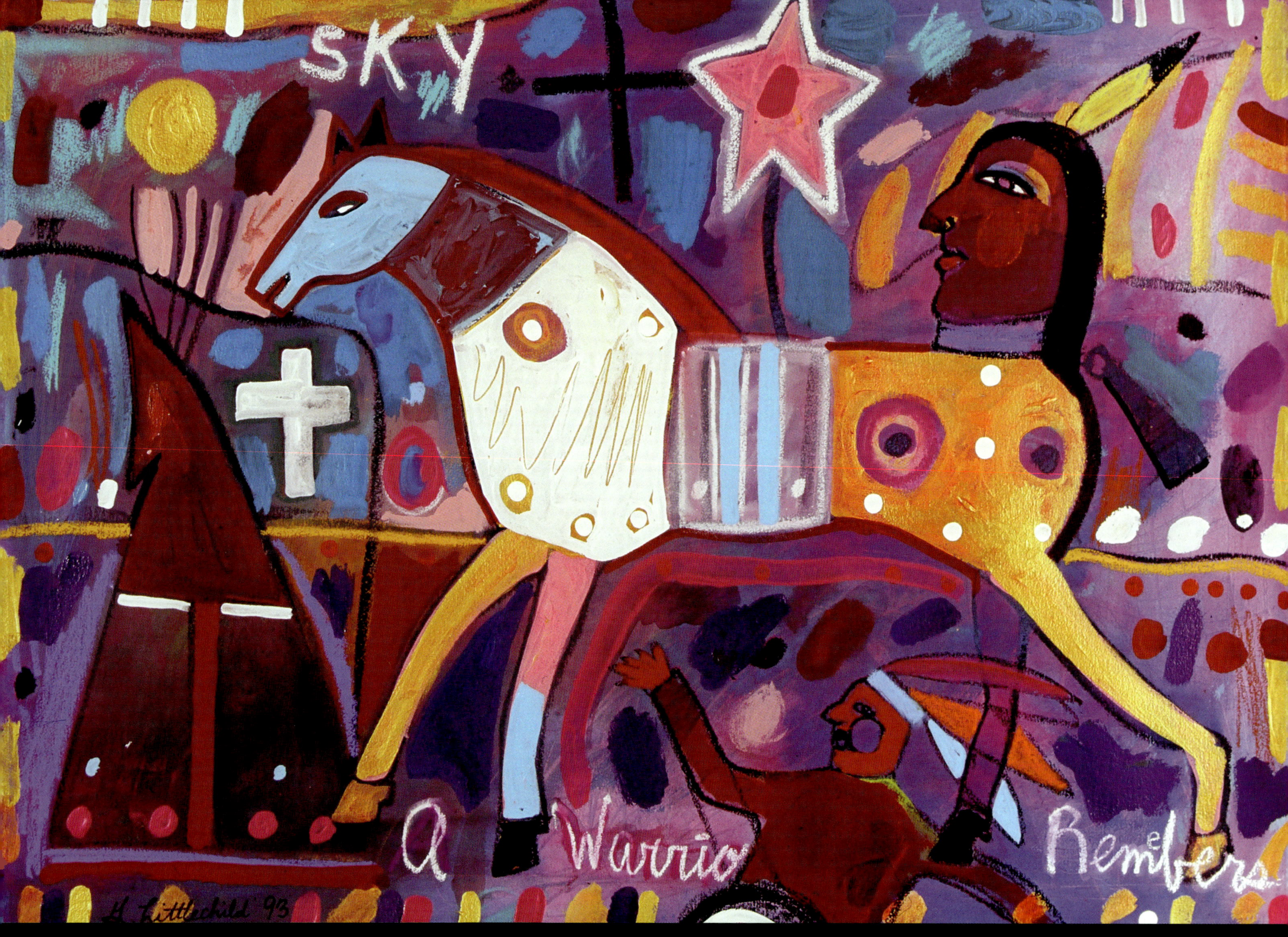

A Warrior Remembers mixed media :: 30" x 44" :: 1993

I revere these men whose prowess, wit and stamina helped them in times of warfare. To survive these battles over and over again, to live to the next day and grow another year older took great skill, courage and understanding. Elders and men of the tribe trained this warrior from a small boy to adulthood; they imparted great, powerful skills that would save and protect his tribe during times of war or hunting. In many of my paintings, a warrior returns home to his teepee and recounts the exploits of the day.

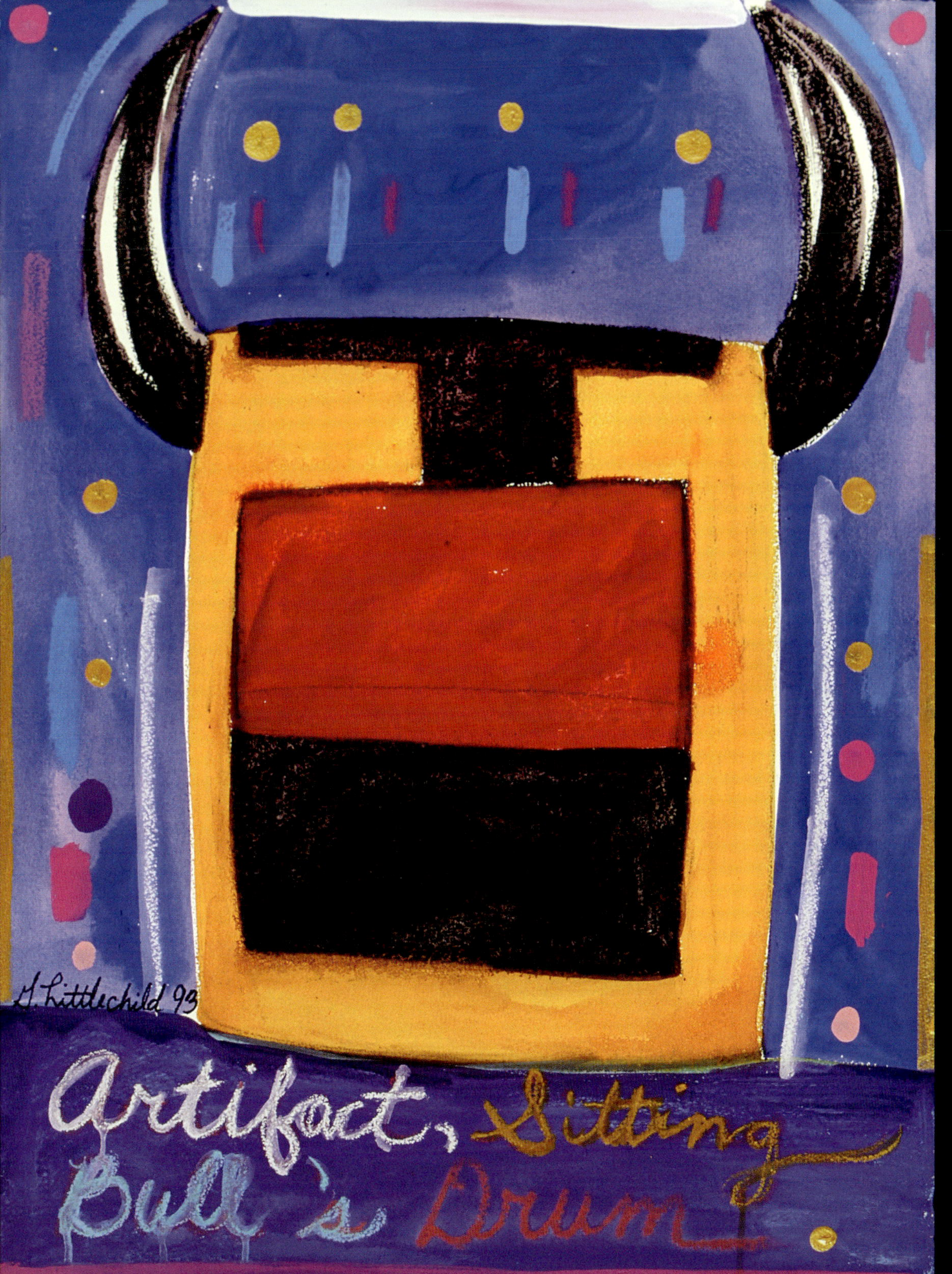

Artifact, Sitting Bull's Drum

mixed media on paper
30" x 22" :: 1993

Sacred objects, ceremonial rattles, drums, warfare items, ancestors' bones and scores of photographs of the proud, stoic Indian are housed in museums—often obtained by illegal means or because someone sold their sacred objects due to Christianity or to obtain the white man's currency. This is how I first became aware of Lakota chief Sitting Bull's drum. I saw it in a magazine and later found out it belongs to the Smithsonian Museum in Washington. Why were his clothes and sacred possessions in museums? Were they collected because of his persona, to own a part of him and his culture and legacy? His family should have his items.

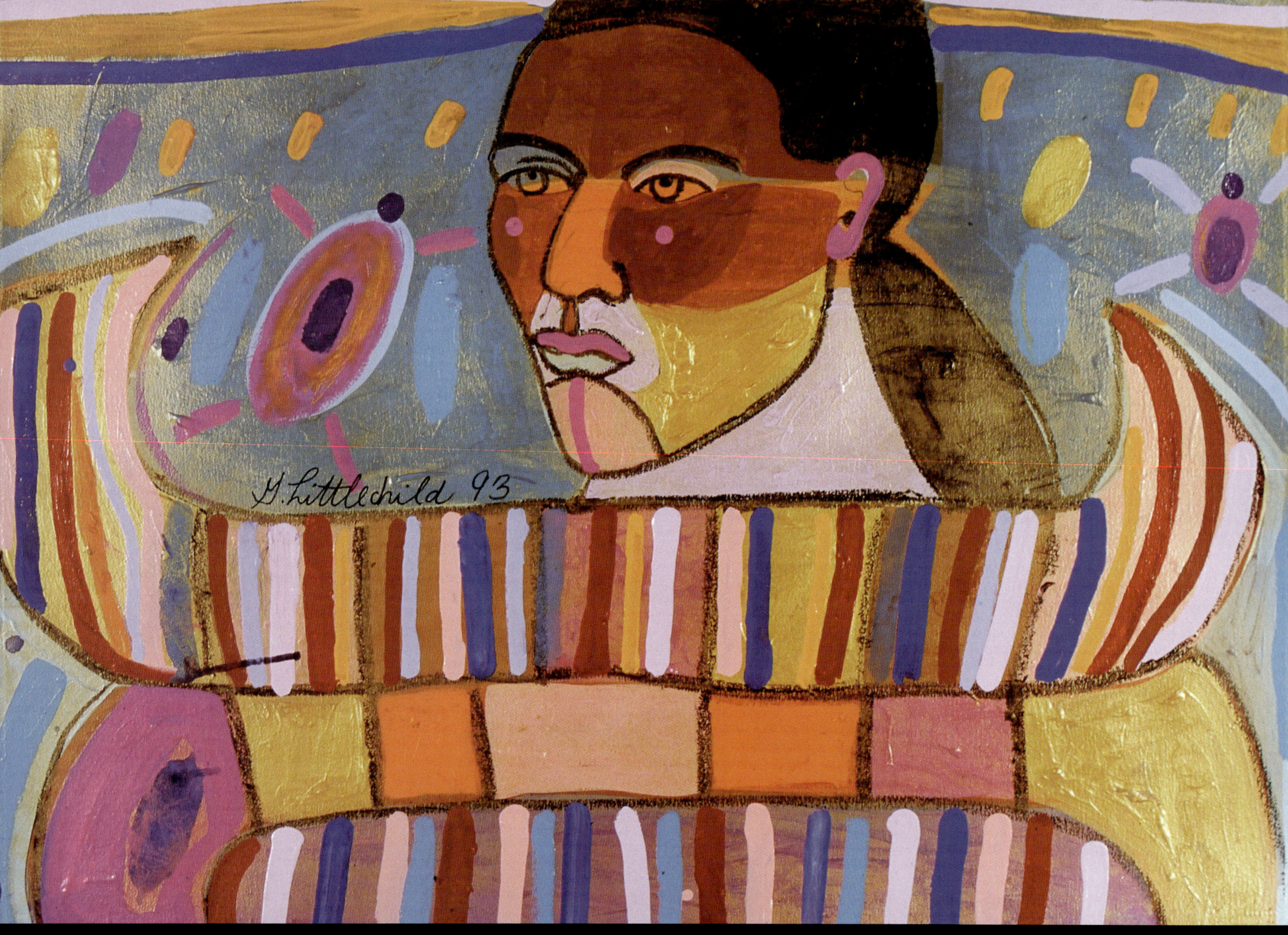

Jumbo Bell's Grandson mixed media :: 30" x 44" :: 1993

Chief Jumbo Bell of the Mamalilikulla tribe of Village Island, BC, was an honourable man and orator. He gave many potlatches and was the master of ceremonies at the big potlatch bust in 1921 when he and his people were stopped from practising their culture. That same strong spirit exists in his maternal grandson, John Powell, who is a carrier of oral tradition, names and events of days long past. His traditional name, Pah Noot Yah Dahss (great giver of oolichan-grease potlatches), was given to him at his grandfather's last potlatch in 1976.

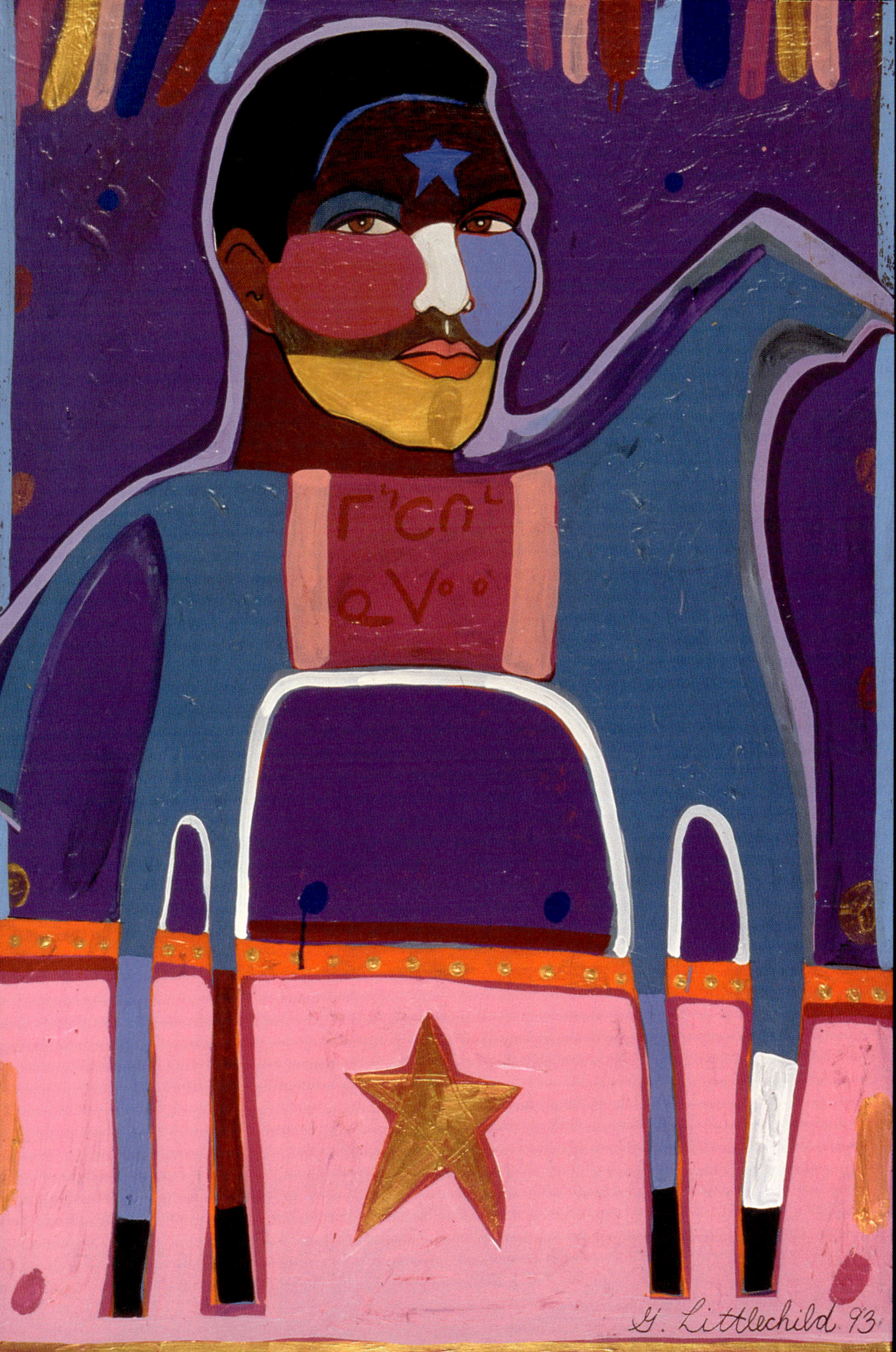

The Artist, the House, the Star

mixed media :: 44" x 30" :: 1993

This is a transformative self-portrait. I am proudly riding a gorgeous turquoise horse in a field of pink and purple and red, magical and transcendent—nothing like the world we inhabit. A gold star, gold dots and prayer flags act as borders and the blue star on my forehead represents hope. The high cheeks, raven-black hair and yellow chin attest to the character of the imaginary world I live in when I paint. I realize the gift of art that I possess is very special.

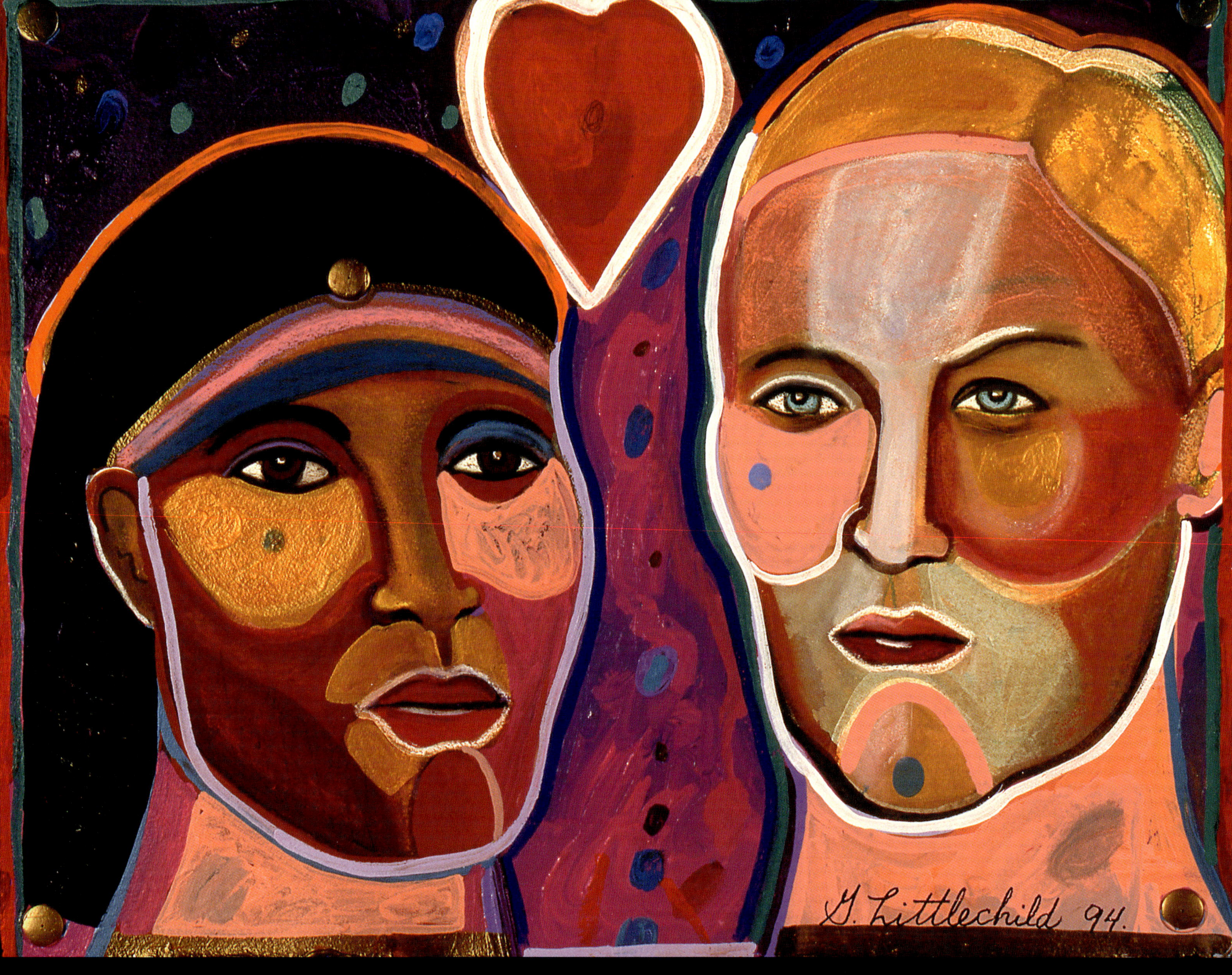

Love is Colour Blind mixed media :: 22" x 30" :: 1994

A Germanic-looking man and a dark-skinned First Nations woman meet and engage in a relationship based on their love for one another. In the 1940s and '50s, these relationships were looked upon with disdain. Likewise, those who were in mixed-race relationships were judged harshly, as was the case for my father and mother. However, love conquers and commitment bridged the gap between the two races.

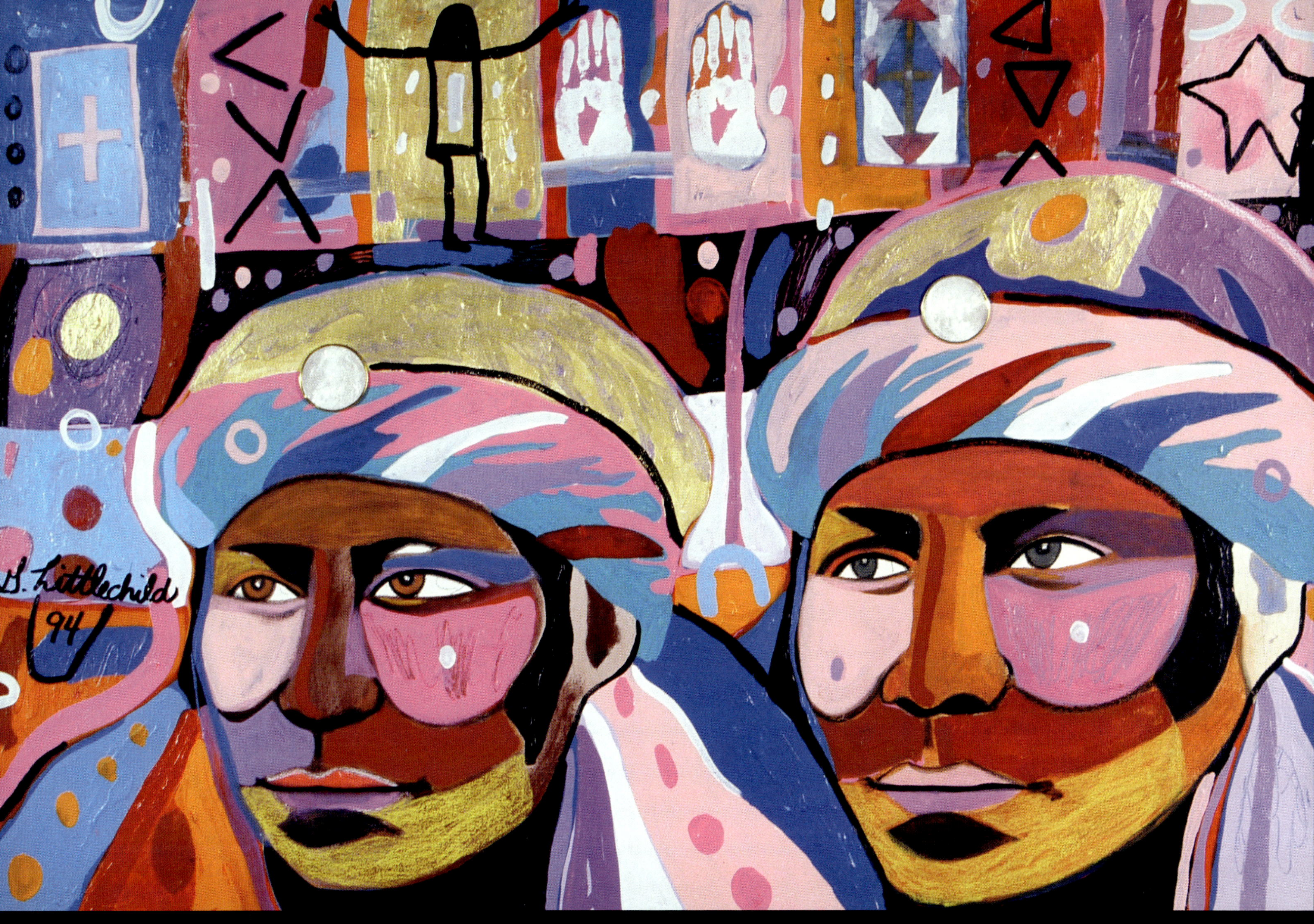

The Spirit of Two mixed media on paper :: 41" x 60" :: 1994

In First Nations communities, gay, lesbian and transgendered people were often seen as visionaries, seers, healers, teachers and artists, and they often held prominent and elevated positions within the tribe. After the arrival of European settlers, who brought their religious views and beliefs to this new land, the First Peoples were indoctrinated by force: missionaries, residential schools and the reserve system. Religion became part of the psyche of the First Peoples. No longer did gay, lesbian and transgendered people hold respected positions; they were seen as evil and inferior.

Not All Indians Look Alike

mixed media collage :: 44" x 30" :: 1994

It is such a crazy idea to think that all people from a particular race look alike. Yes, there are similar facial traits, hair colour and physical resemblances; however, each person is unique. I used humour within this piece, as the repeated face (I used my great-grandmother Peggy's face) is a way to laugh at these notions. Ignorance is ripe in some; however, raising awareness about these beliefs will help reshape people's ideas and beliefs.

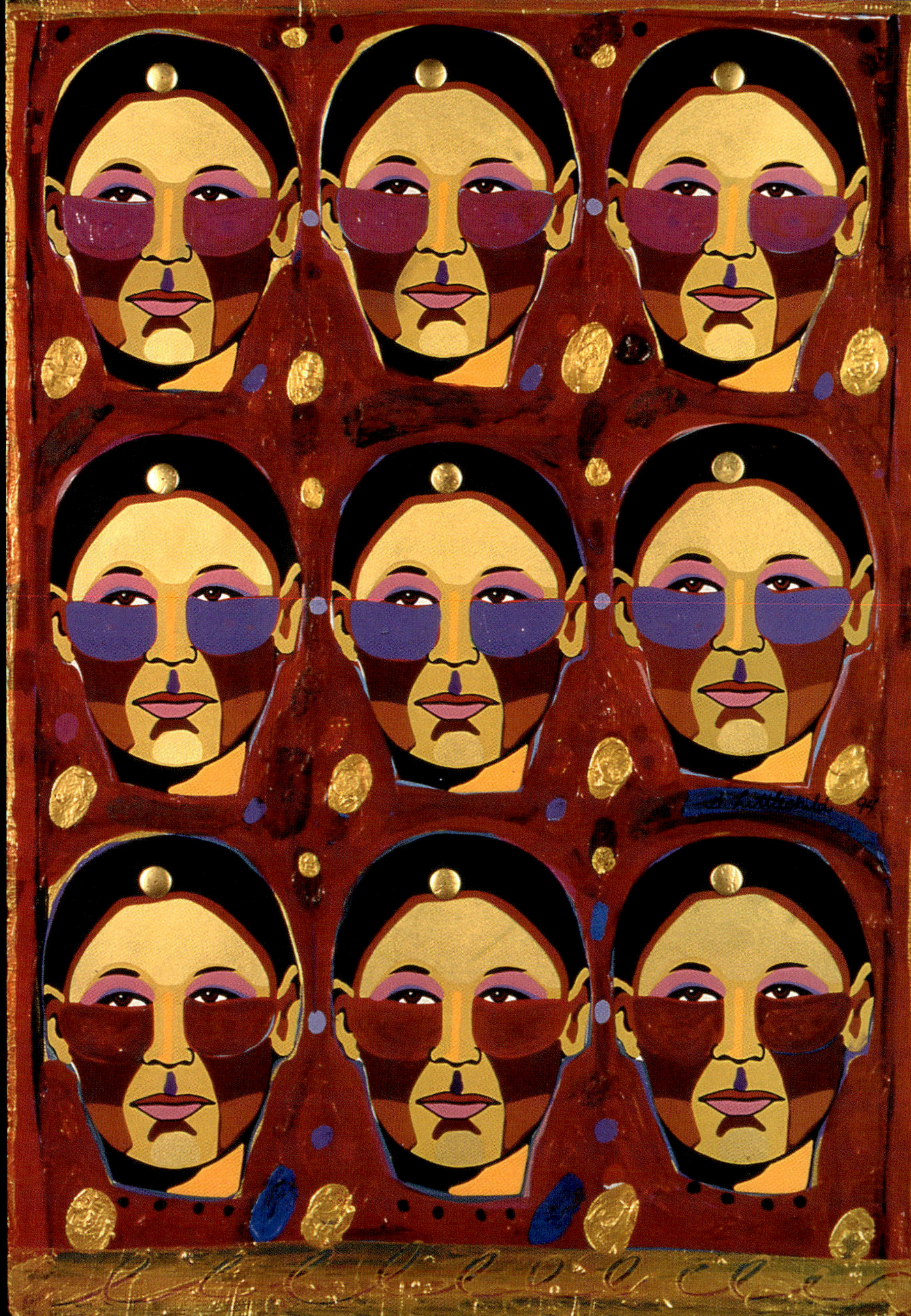

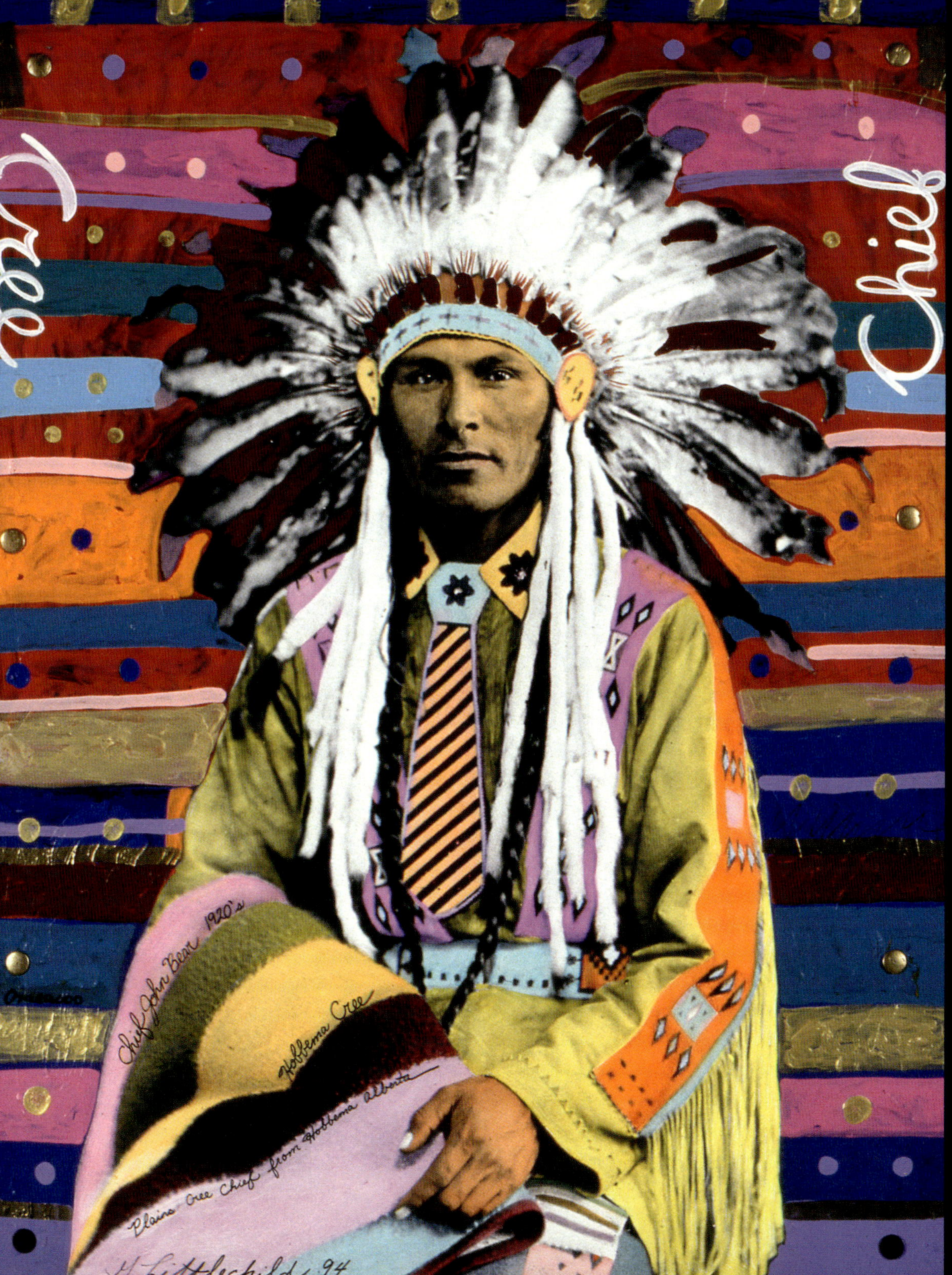

Omeasoo Cree Chief, Chief John Bear

mixed media
52" x 40" :: 1994

The tall, handsome man in this archive photograph is Plains Cree chief John Bear of the Montana Band near Hobbema, *ca.* 1925. The Montana Band was once Chief Bobtail's reserve before he became enfranchised and left his reserve. The Montana Crees, who were deported back to Canada in the late 1800s, were given this reserve as their new home and refuge. Chief John Bear married Mary Ermineskin, daughter of Chief Panee Ermineskin and Suzanne Panychat of the Ermineskin Reserve. Omeasoo means "pretty" in Cree.

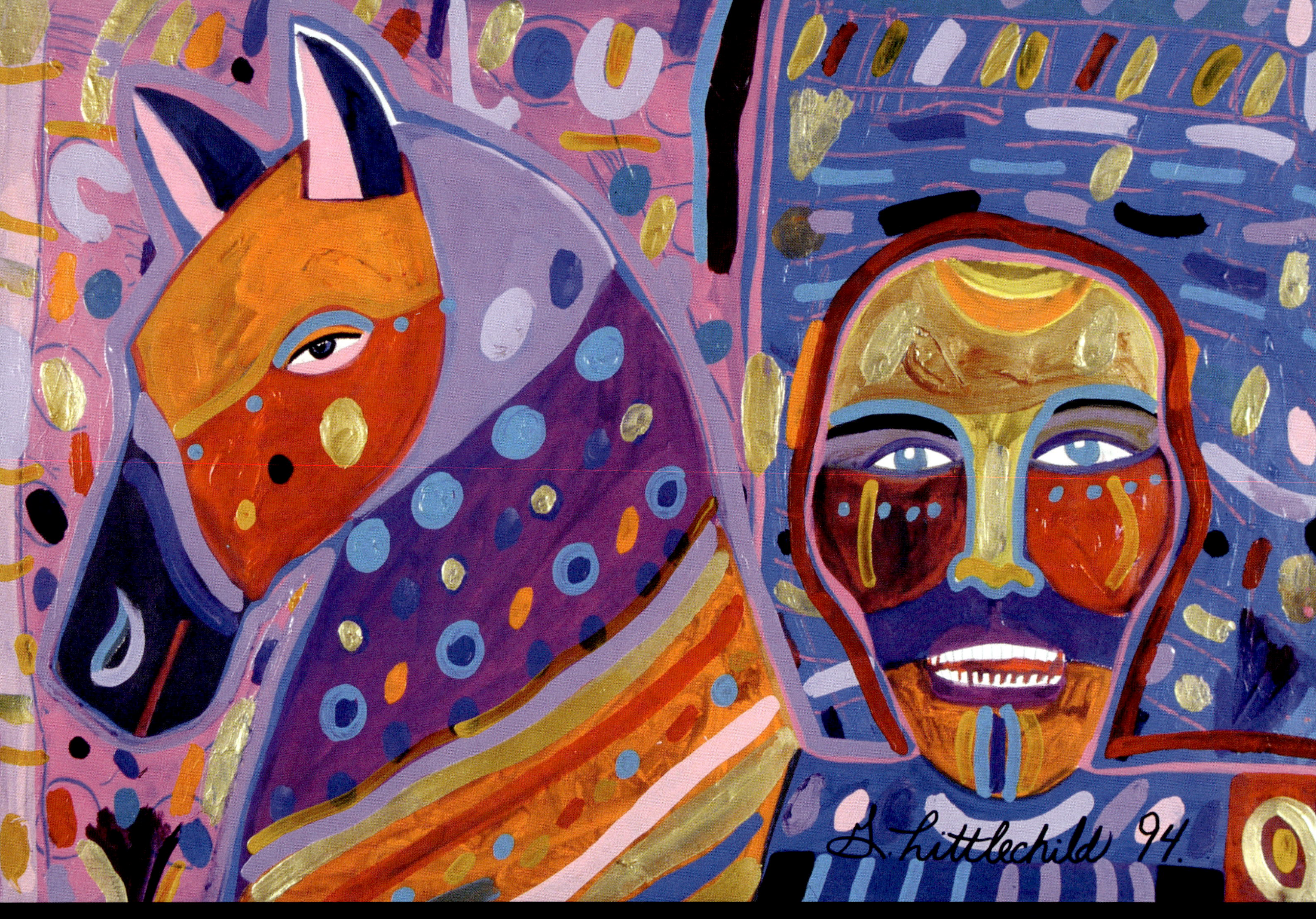

In Relationship to Horse mixed media :: 31.5" x 48" :: 1994

A bodiless, abstracted man rides a purple, red, orange, gold and pink horse, his guide and connection to the spirit world.

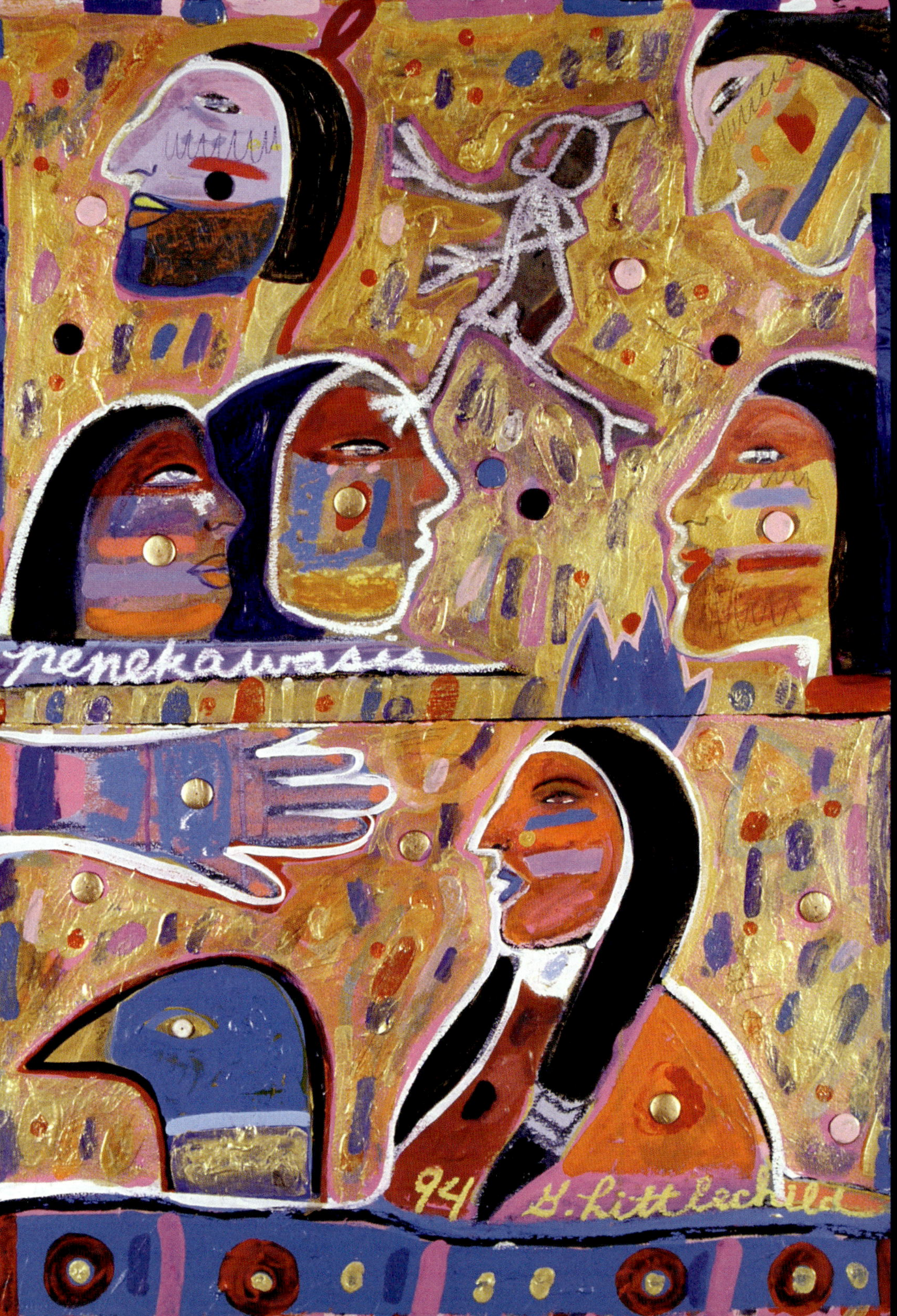

Nenekawasis

mixed media :: 44" x 30" :: 1994

This painting tells how my great-grandfather Alexandre Littlechild got his Indian name, Nenekawasis, which means swift or quick child in Plains Cree. Great-grandfather was a quick runner; in fact, each time he went hunting he would have a new pair of moccasins made, as he ran so fast he burned holes in them. They say he could club the deer with ease and grab running rabbits by their ears. He was also known for his kindness. His name was transferred to me at a powwow on the Ermineskin Reserve in Hobbema. My relations Pat and Marvin Littlechild wanted to honour me for my art career by giving me his name. I am proud to carry it.

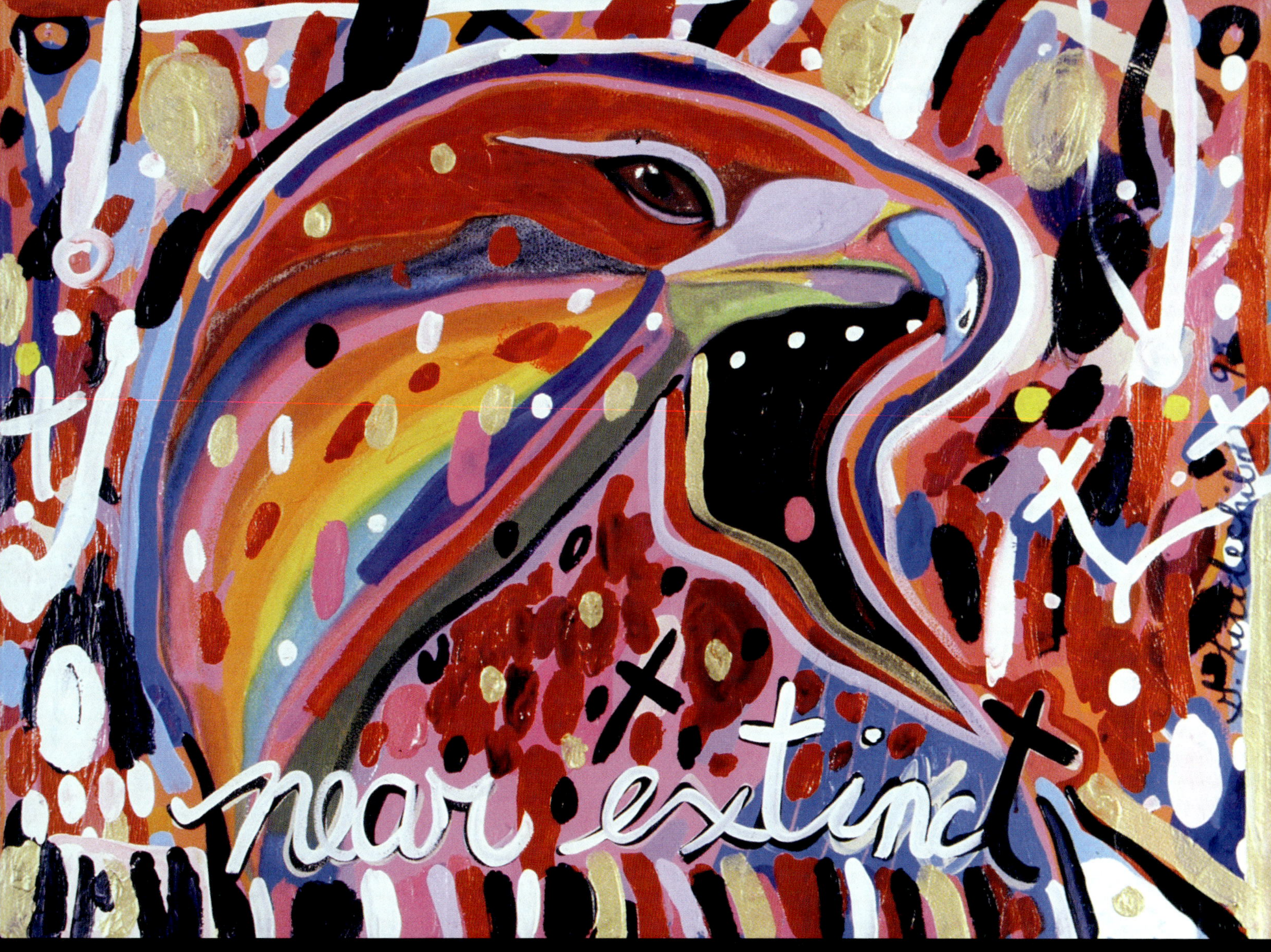

Near Extinct acrylic on paper :: 30" x 44" :: 1995

Winged, two-legged and four-legged creatures are all being affected by humankind and some are nearing extinction within our lifetime. How many hundreds of animal species have vanished from the face of the earth? Some are making a comeback; however, only when it is almost too late does humankind make great efforts to restore and protect through conservation and awareness. Let's just hope that all animal species continue and thrive.

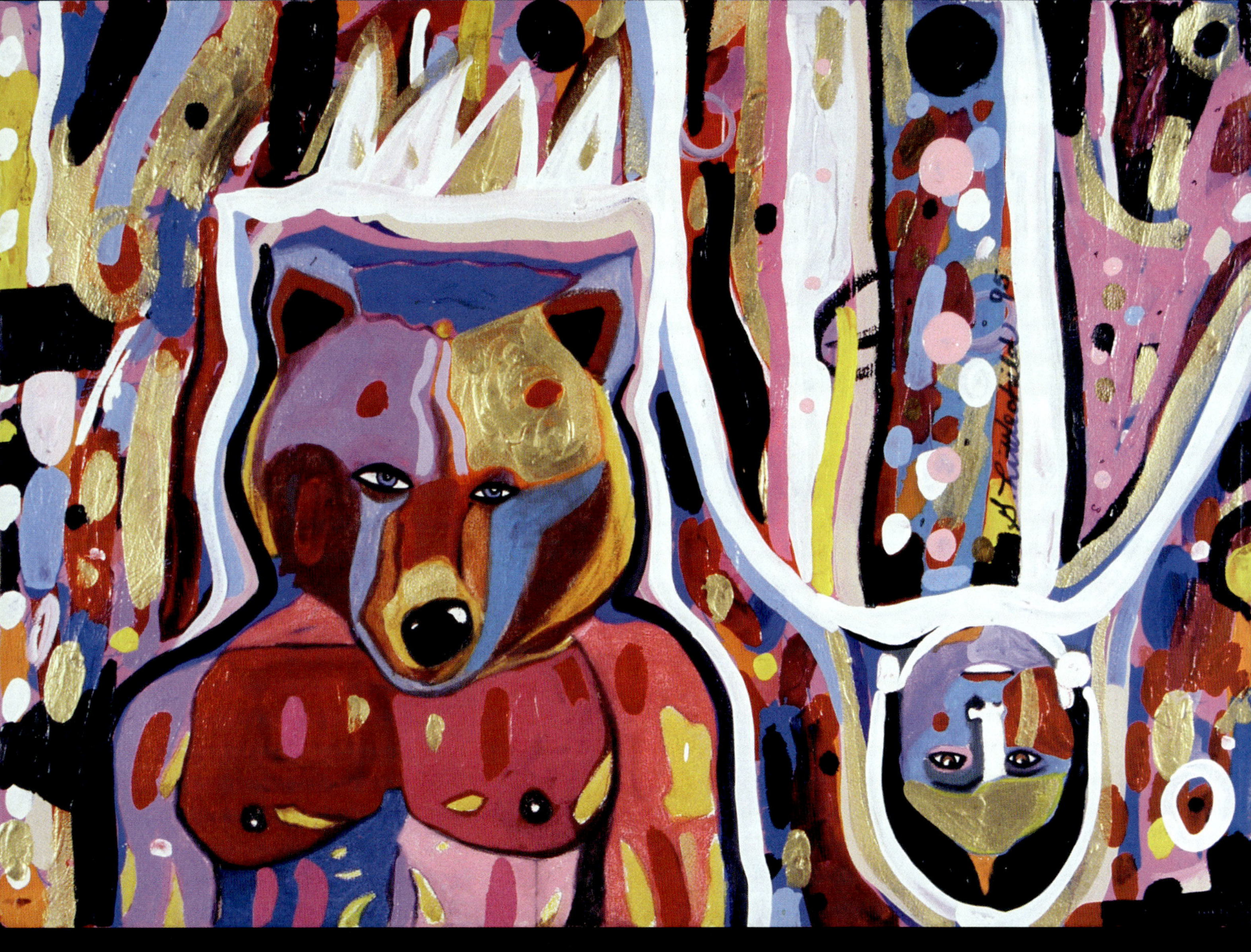

Reality in the Dream Time mixed media :: 30" x 44" :: 1995

Dream time, flip time, which time is real time? Some say in certain cultures that daytime is the dream time and nighttime, when we sleep, is the real time. When awake, we sometimes say that a dream was so real, so vivid, that it was like we were really there.

Chief Papasteyo/Papaschas 2

mixed media :: 44" x 30" :: 1995

Chief Papasteyo was a famous Alberta war chief whose Indian name was Woodpecker. His band made their home on the south side of Edmonton on their allotted reserve. The chief and council were swindled out of their reserve lands, and the members were disbanded and disappeared. My great-great-grandparents Pierre DeCoyne Cardinal and Agnes Letendre Batoche were members of the Papasteyo Band.

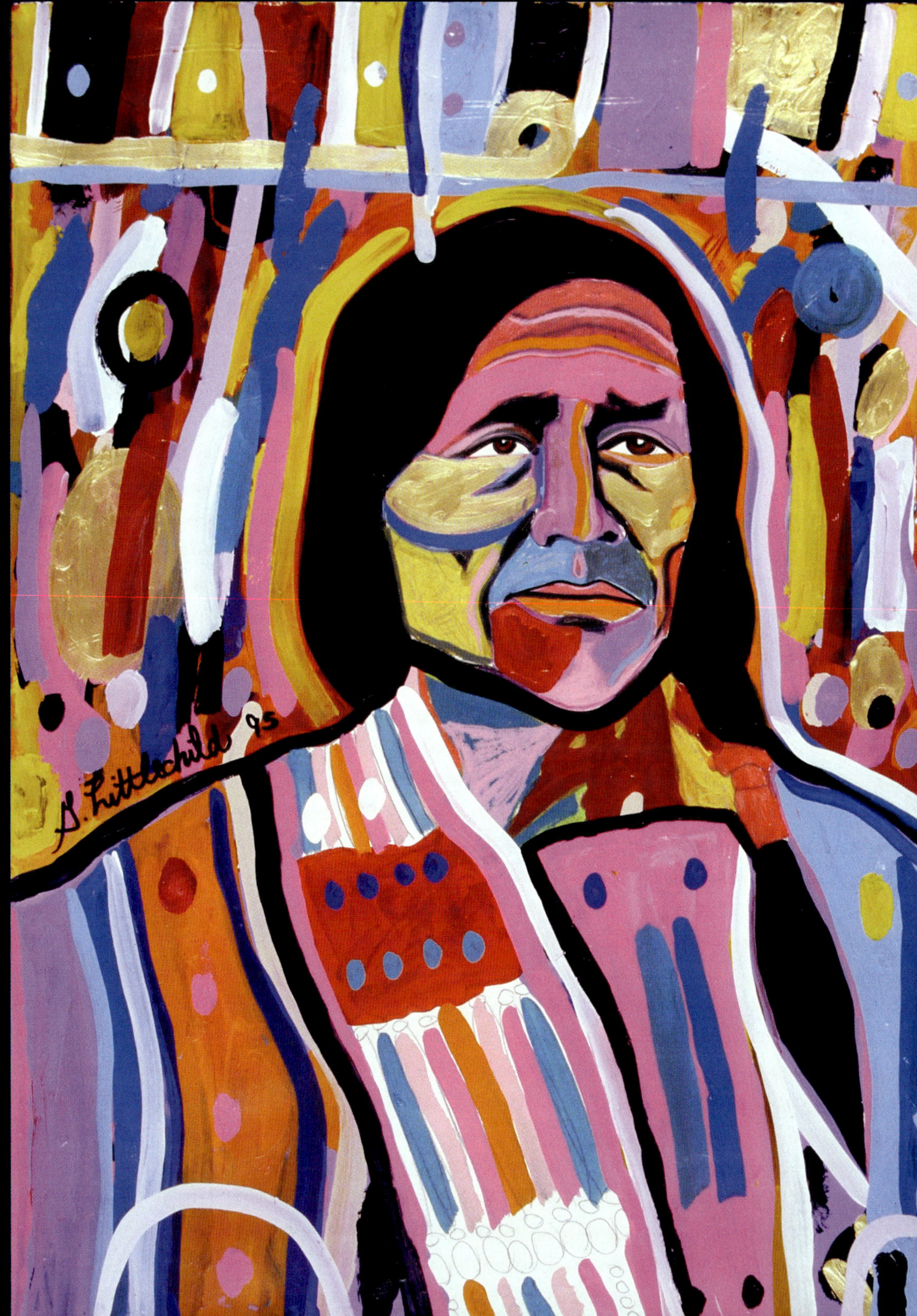

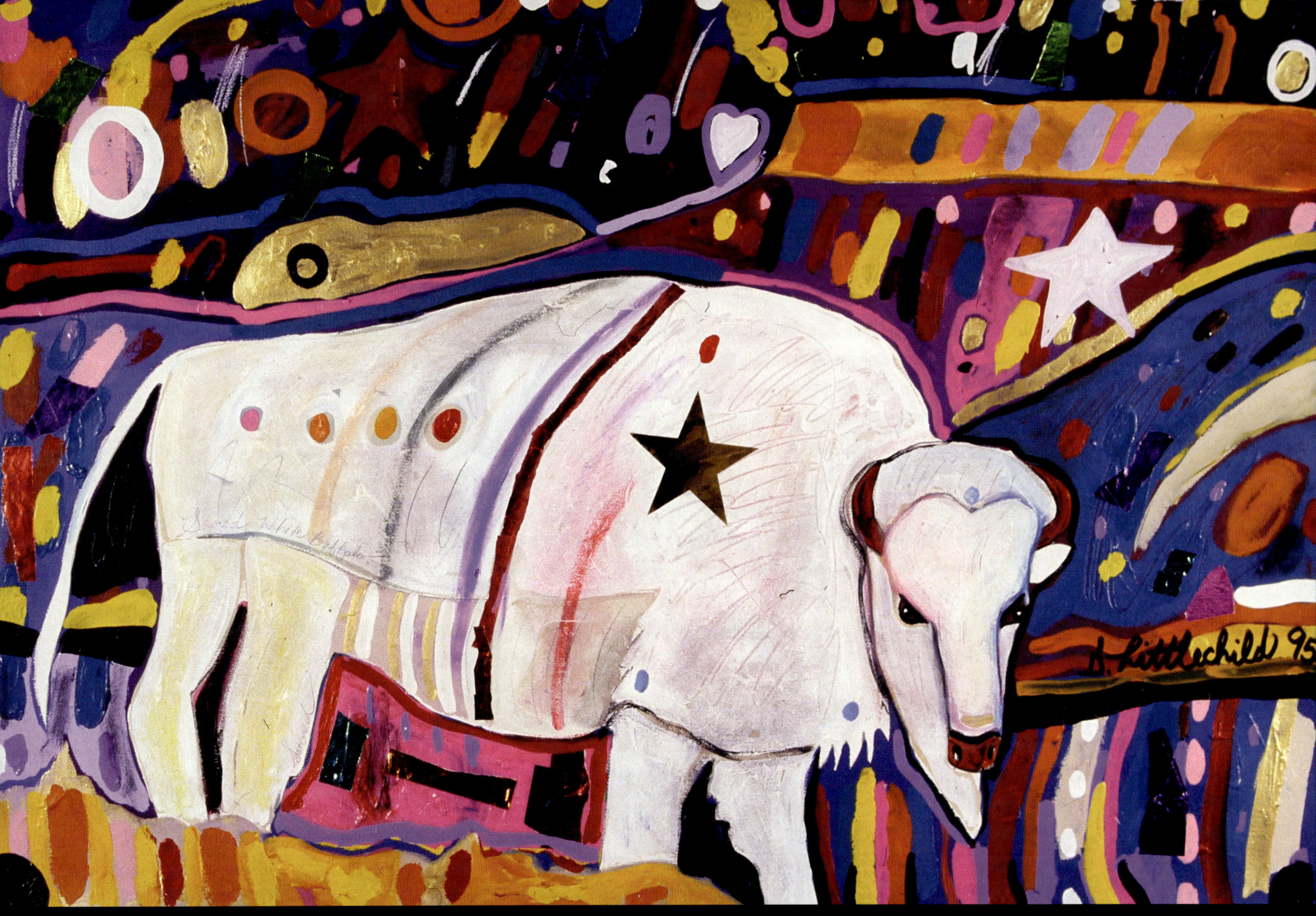

Sacred White Buffalo 2 mixed media :: 41" x 60" :: 1995

A gorgeous, luminous landscape creates a dazzling environment to emphasize the special importance of the Sacred White Buffalo. It was foretold that a White Buffalo calf would be born. The birth would be significant, announcing a great change for mankind and a time of spiritual resurgence. It is now that time—time to gain knowledge and understanding and help stop the destruction of our Mother Earth. It is up to each one of us to help to heal our Mother Earth so that we humans can live in harmony upon her for many generations.

Her First Communion

hand-coloured photo/
mixed media
30" x 22" :: 1996

The text handwritten across her gown reads “Communion. 1st Communion.” My mother wore this dress to celebrate her first communion while attending Ermineskin Indian Residential School. Each student in that photo had the same stoic, non-expressive face. One of mother’s brothers, Ross, also celebrated his first communion that day. Oh, how the Catholic religion changed, damaged and destroyed little souls who were forced into a religion unlike that of their ancestors. As First Nations people, we are still healing from the residential school experience and will be for years to come, but much healing is underway and great changes have occurred.

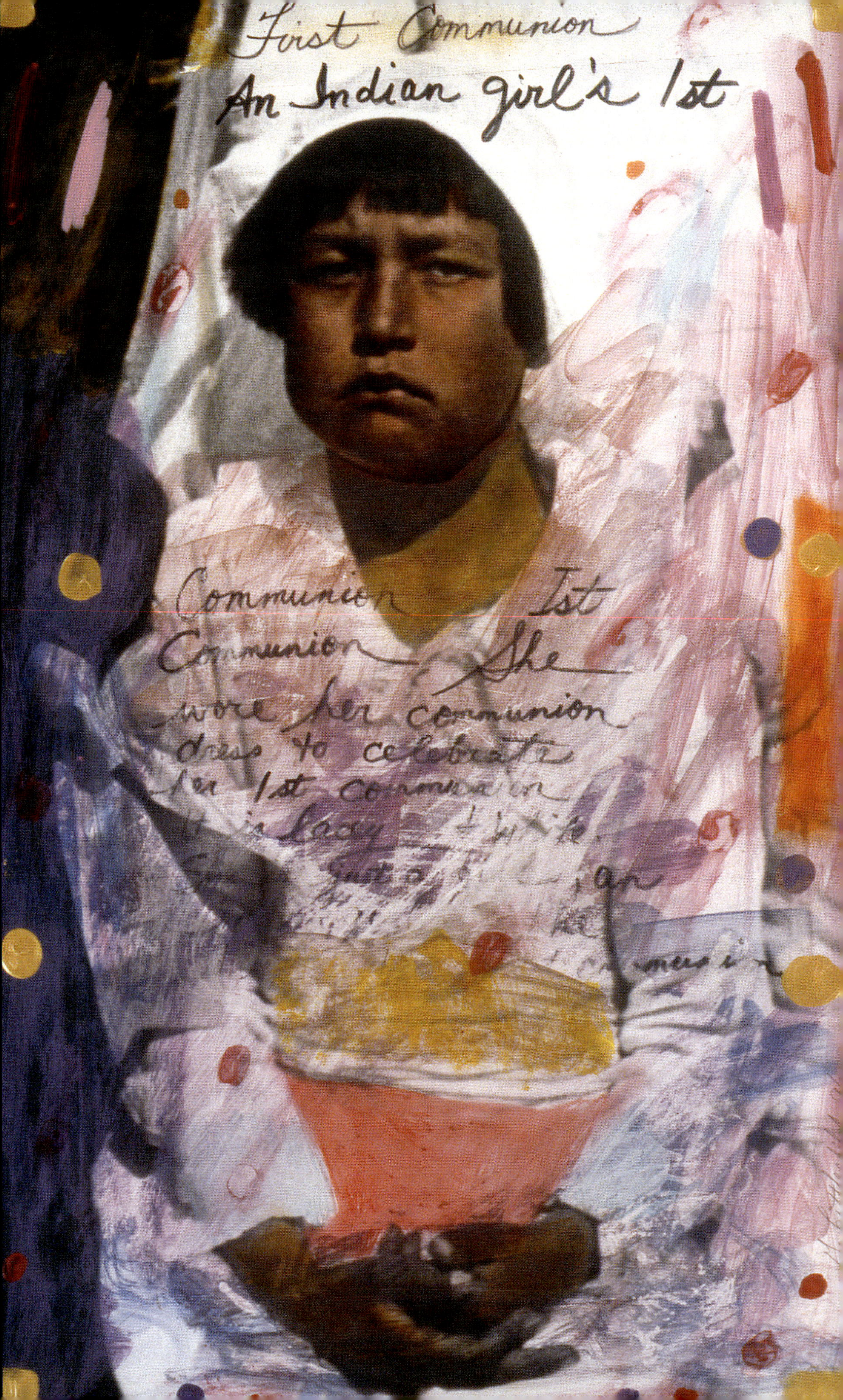

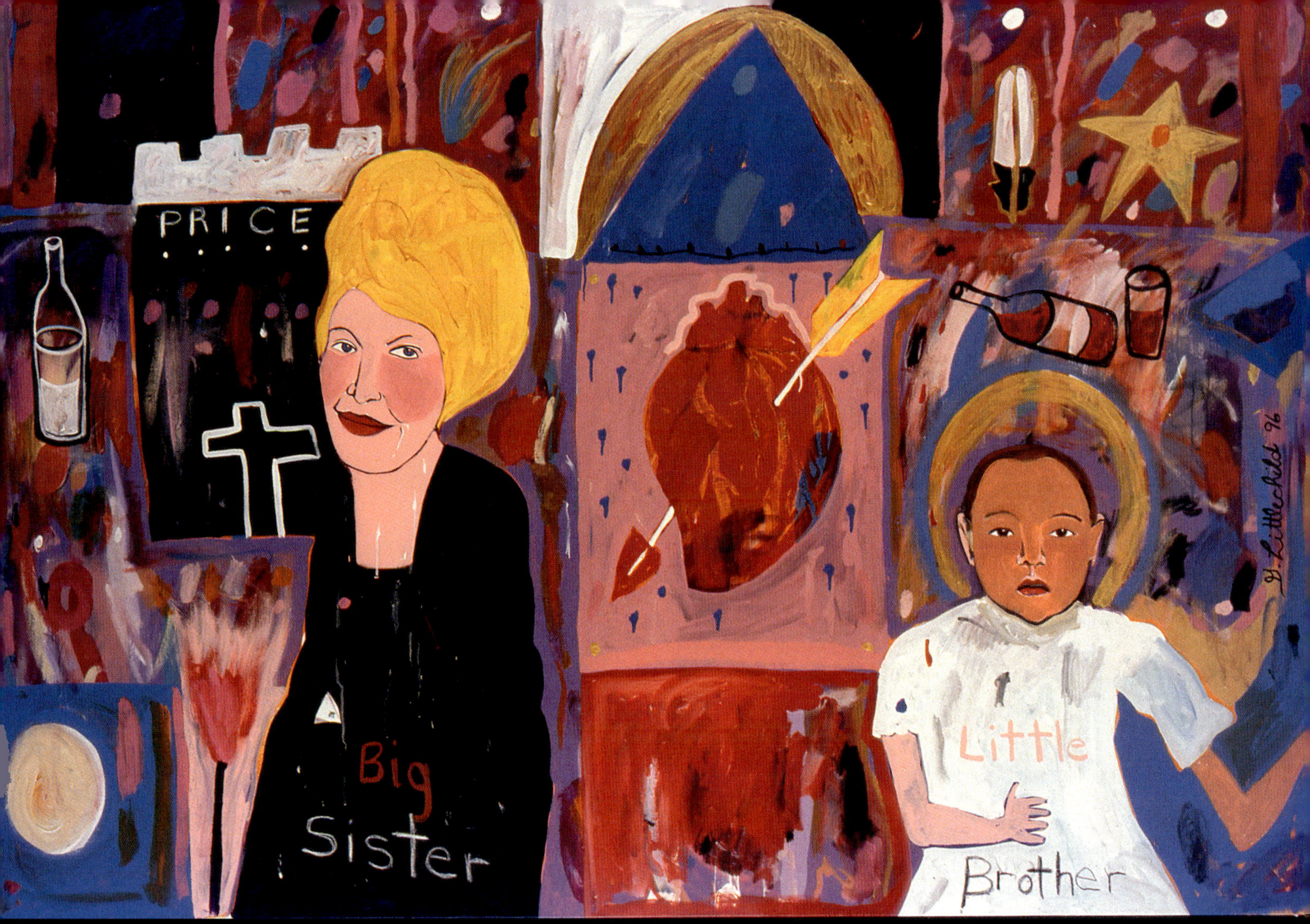

Big Sister, Little Brother Price mixed media :: 5' x 7'6" :: 1996

This is the story of my half-sister Evelyn Isobele Price and her half-brother (me), two of James E. Price's five children. The surname Price is Welsh; however, two other male Price descendants and I had our Y-DNA tests done. The test results came back: we were mostly Irish with small amounts of Scottish and English blood, as well as being [illegible] percent African, 1 percent Chinese and a few other ancestries, but there was not one drop of Welsh blood.

After 11 years of searching for my family, I found two full sisters, one half-sister, one full brother, one half-brother and numerous cousins, aunts and uncles. The last sibling I found was my half-sister, Evelyn. My Auntie Rosalie (Tillie), who had met her a few times years ago, described her as very pretty. I determinedly located Evelyn in Edmonton with help from phone books and her mother, whom I had also located. We had lengthy discussions about our father and his alcoholism, which ended a healthy family unit and is seen in the painting as the pierced heart inside the house we never lived in. Alcohol is about to be poured over my white baby dress. It is a dramatic stage for a traumatic storyline: sister Evelyn, so poised and classy, wears black evening attire beside the old Price castle in Wales and a half-drunk bottle. It shows how alcohol wrought havoc in our lives and eventually took the main player, our father (1913–1966). You can see the damage alcohol does when someone is addicted—a slave to it.

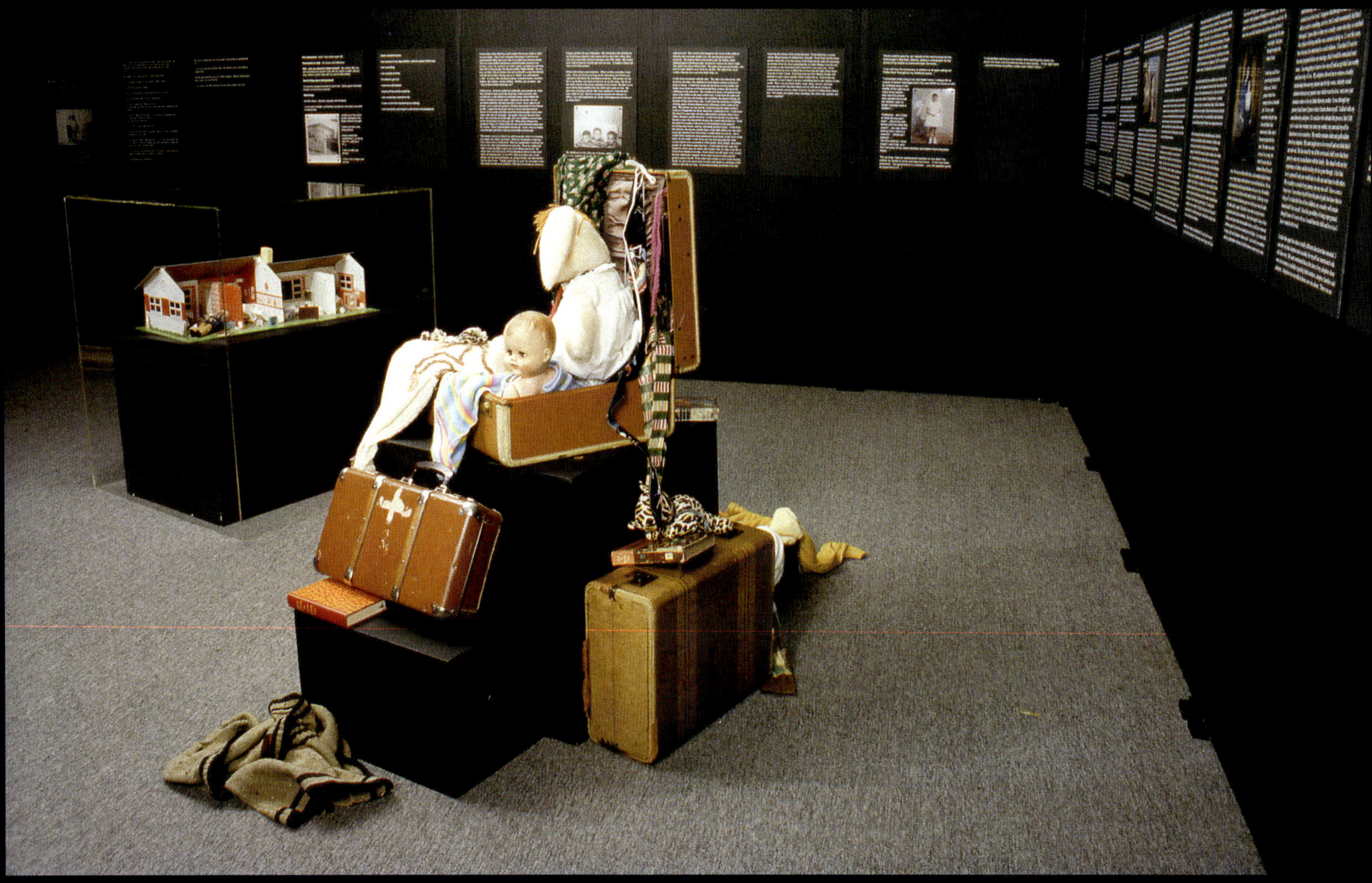

Dis-placed Indians: The Sixties Scoop multi-media installation :: 1996

In Canada during the 1960s, government agencies instituted policies whereby thousands upon thousands of First Nations children were taken away from their natural parents, families and communities, often by force. They were sent as far away as Europe and the United States. Lives were fractured and torn, and they were often abused; this era is now known as the Sixties Scoop. The loss was huge; language and cultural practices were lost due to children being raised in non–First Nations care.

As a survivor of the Sixties Scoop, I felt it was important to share that experience with the public. I interviewed five other survivors who also shared their stories. These stories and photographs, mounted on black gallery walls, surrounded a dollhouse and suitcases. Items belonging to these young children are displayed—dolls, toys, books, baby blankets and clothes. All that they owned was stuffed into a suitcase or a bag. The survivors told their memories of their apprehension by welfare workers. I created a soundtrack that accompanied the installation based on these stories: a car pulling up, footsteps as the car door shuts, a knock on the door, a child's cry, more steps, car doors, moans and sniffles as the car drives away. The child was taken to an agency for processing in order to be adopted or fostered out to non–First Nations families as their parents were deemed unfit. This installation was displayed at the Surrey Art Gallery in BC, curated by Amir Alibhai.

"Hours used to pass by, as I stared at the road turning into the Orphanage in Mundare, Alberta, waiting in anticipation for the arrival of my mother to come and take me home...."

"I can still hear the harshness of children of all ages calling me "Indian-face" throughout my childhood years...."

"I remember while living in my last foster home, I always felt so unsure of where I belonged and if this was NOW my home or will I be whisked away in the middle of the night as so many times before .. who was this person who wanted me to call her Mother; was I to forget I already have a mother?..."

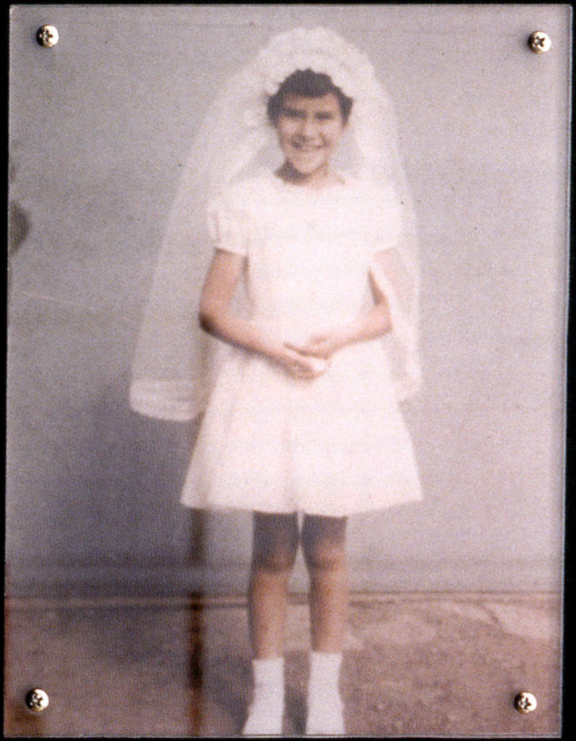

"Confusion .. am I Cree or what did you say I was? .. why is my skin brown and not white like yours? .. you say I don't belong here; what is a reserve? .. where do I belong? ...."

"As time went by, I soon forgot I was Cree, and the memories of my native brothers and sisters have long been faded....."

"For so long, I had an unanswered question of why didn't my mother try harder to come and take me home .. It now has been answered .. the government is a trickster .. your life appears good on paper but is it?...."

detail of ***Dis-placed Indians: The Sixties Scoop***

Priscilla Riel, who is my first cousin, shared her impressions about her time in foster care. She is seen wearing her first communion outfit in the photograph.

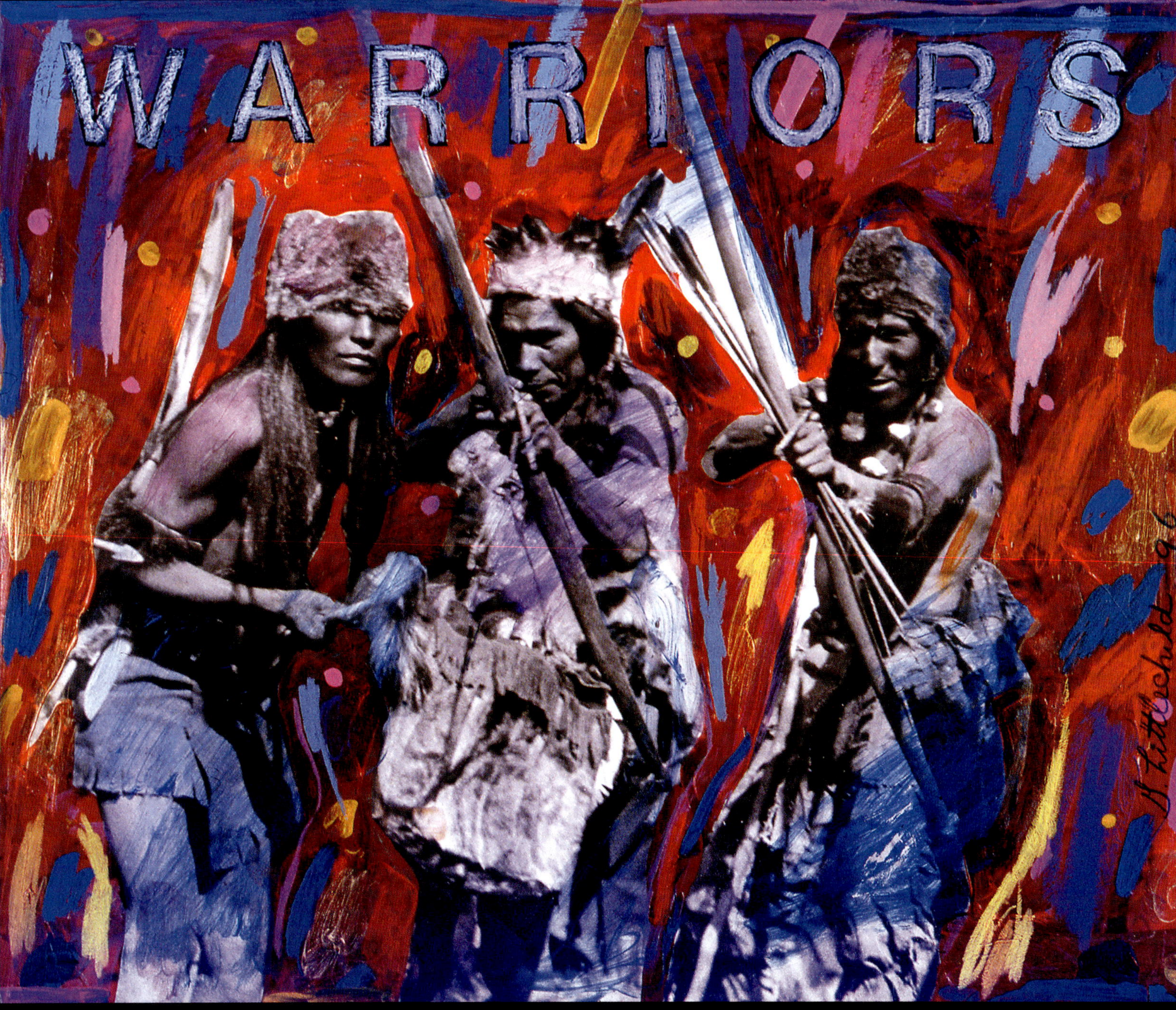

Warriors mixed media :: 22" x 30" :: 1996

A photo taken in the 1940s of Plains Cree men from Hobbema, Alberta, conveyed a scene of warrior exploits. These young men were re-enacting a traditional scene of anticipation before counting coup or hunting, reminiscent of days gone by when acts of bravery bore credence to the character of a man. The men wear the clothing their ancestors would have worn. I cropped out the people in the background of the original photo, who, dressed in '40s clothing and surrounding the men in the warrior gear, created an ironic scene.

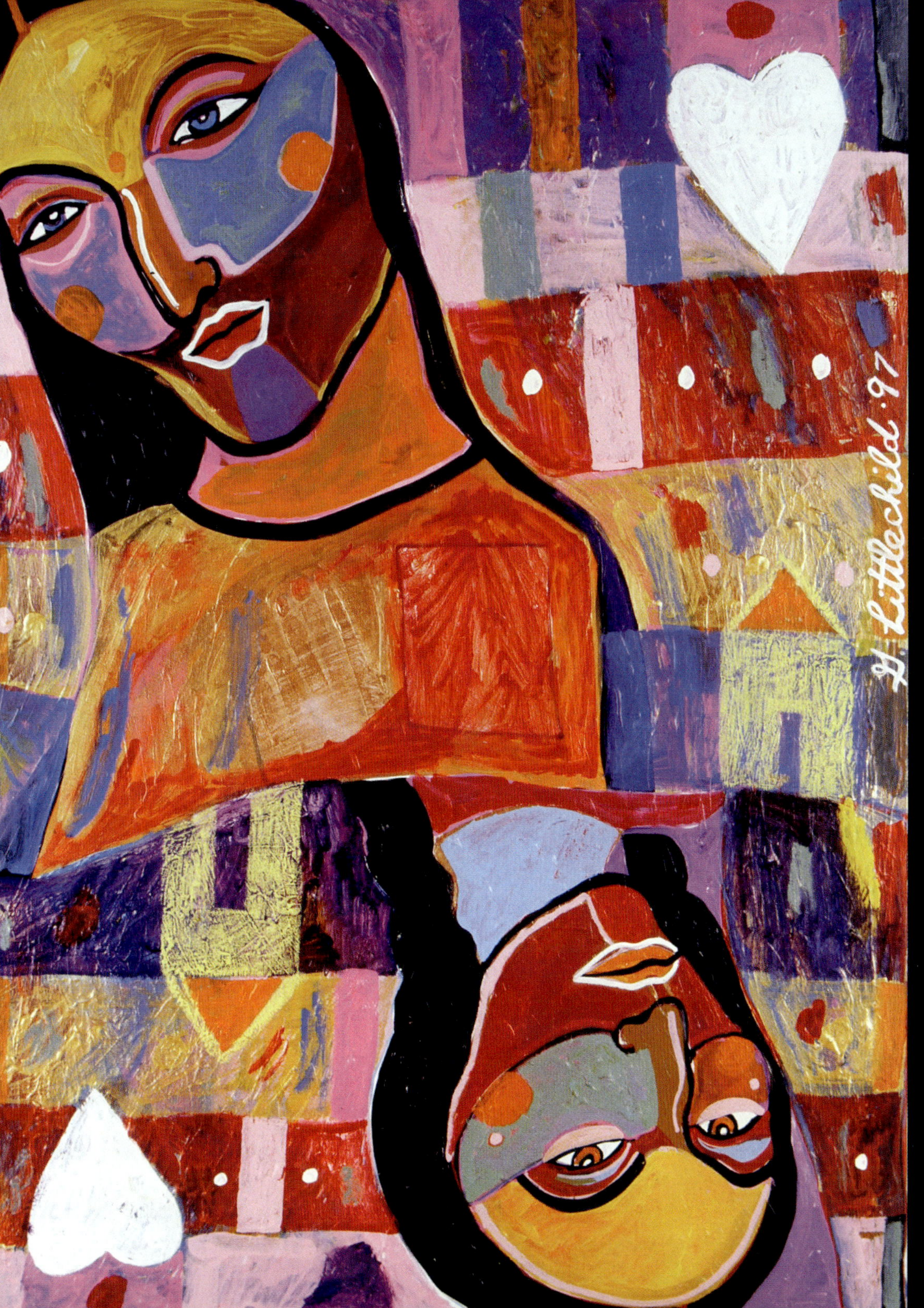

The Power of Transformation

acrylic on canvas :: 44" x 30" :: 1997

As a child, I was given a deck of colourful playing cards. I like the designs, layout and composition. I am sure at the time I was unaware of the formal design qualities, but the content captured me. The high, sweet King, Queen and Jack were magical to me, the duality of the characters, the ying, the yang. From time to time, I employ that visual aid from my youth to create certain paintings. Transformation of self, two lives equals one. One day, one moment. We see ourselves one way and others see us another way.

Healing Hands

acrylic on canvas :: 44" x 30" :: 1997

Prayer gives words to a higher power than what is in us. Healing transforms and shifts energies to help lift up those in need of the healing touch, be it mental, physical, emotional or spiritual. Here, a young man holds a smudge bowl in his hands, offering prayers to the Creator. His white hands are a symbol of the spiritual world and its necessity for all humanity, especially all First Nations and Aboriginal cultures. The ancestral energies light the way. They are represented in the top row of the painting.

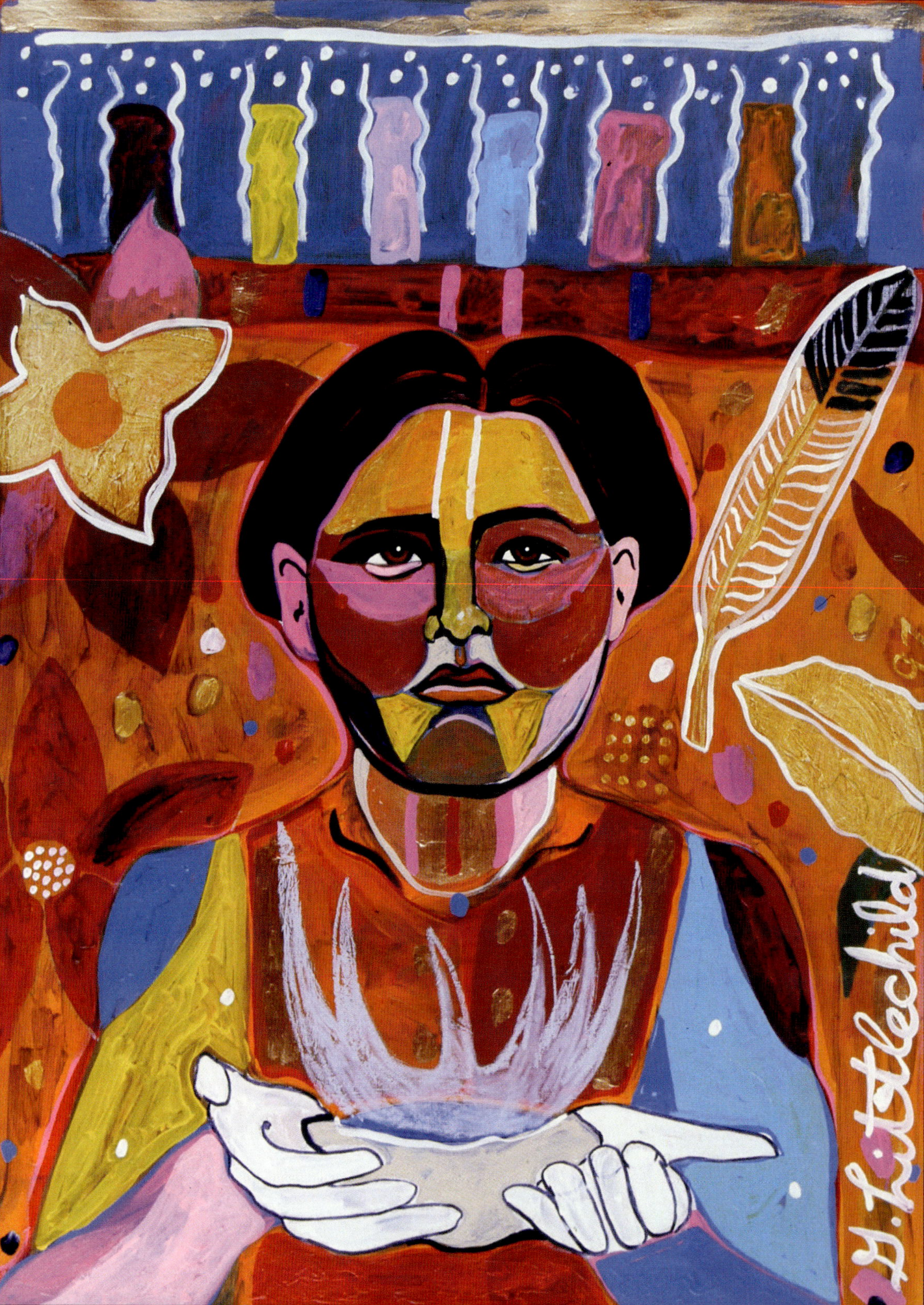

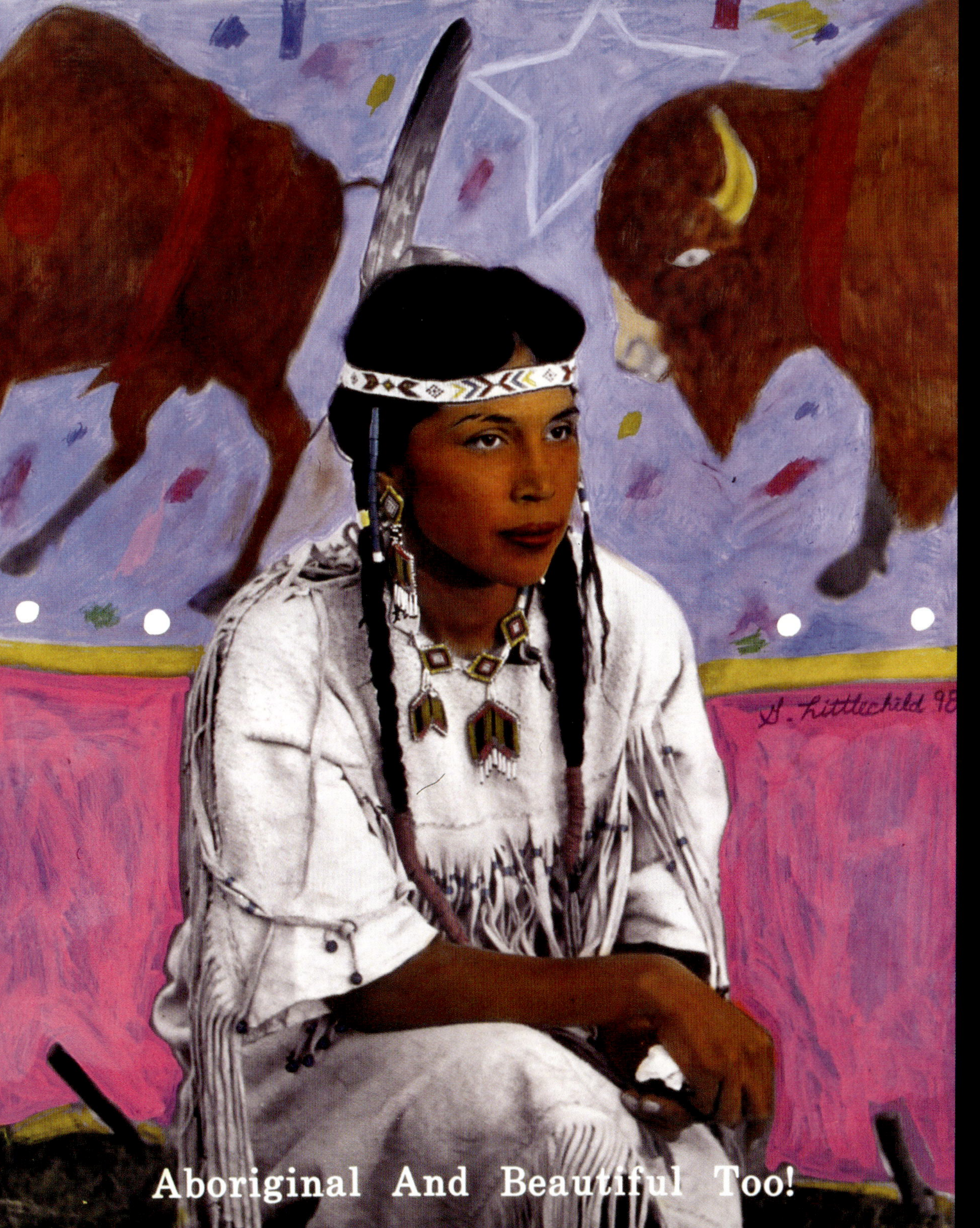

Aboriginal and Beautiful Too 2

mixed media
36" x 24" :: 1998

I used to visit my relative Tracey when she lived in Vancouver. This gorgeous photo is of her mother, Elizabeth Lightning, the daughter of James Lighting and Marie Myicat from the Samson Reserve in Hobbema. The photo haunted me, and I had to incorporate this image into my art somehow. I learned more about the photo. Elizabeth married Hans Busch, a German who had immigrated to Canada. He liked photography and took these wonderful photos. In some, she looked like Elizabeth Taylor. In this photo, she is posed in front of her late uncle, Albert Lightning, a historic Alberta visionary and orator. She is adorned in Plains Cree regalia, looking so proud. I asked Hans and Elizabeth's permission to use the photo in my art—they both agreed.

Cultural Veneration 1

mixed media :: 30" x 24" :: 1998

My great-great-great-uncle Chief Alexis Bobtail was born along the North Saskatchewan River in the Alberta Rocky Mountains. In his day, he was a prominent leader who had a large encampment of followers who believed in his council and leadership. He was allotted a reserve for his people in Hobbema. He deplored the continuing ill treatment of his people by the Canadian government and Indian reserve system. He became enfranchised, left his reserve and tried to maintain the old ways, which were dying off fast. Settlers had encroached, and the buffalo were nearly wiped out. He would return to spend his last days on the reserve of his brother, Chief Jean Baptiste Ermineskin, and died there at age 70 in 1900.

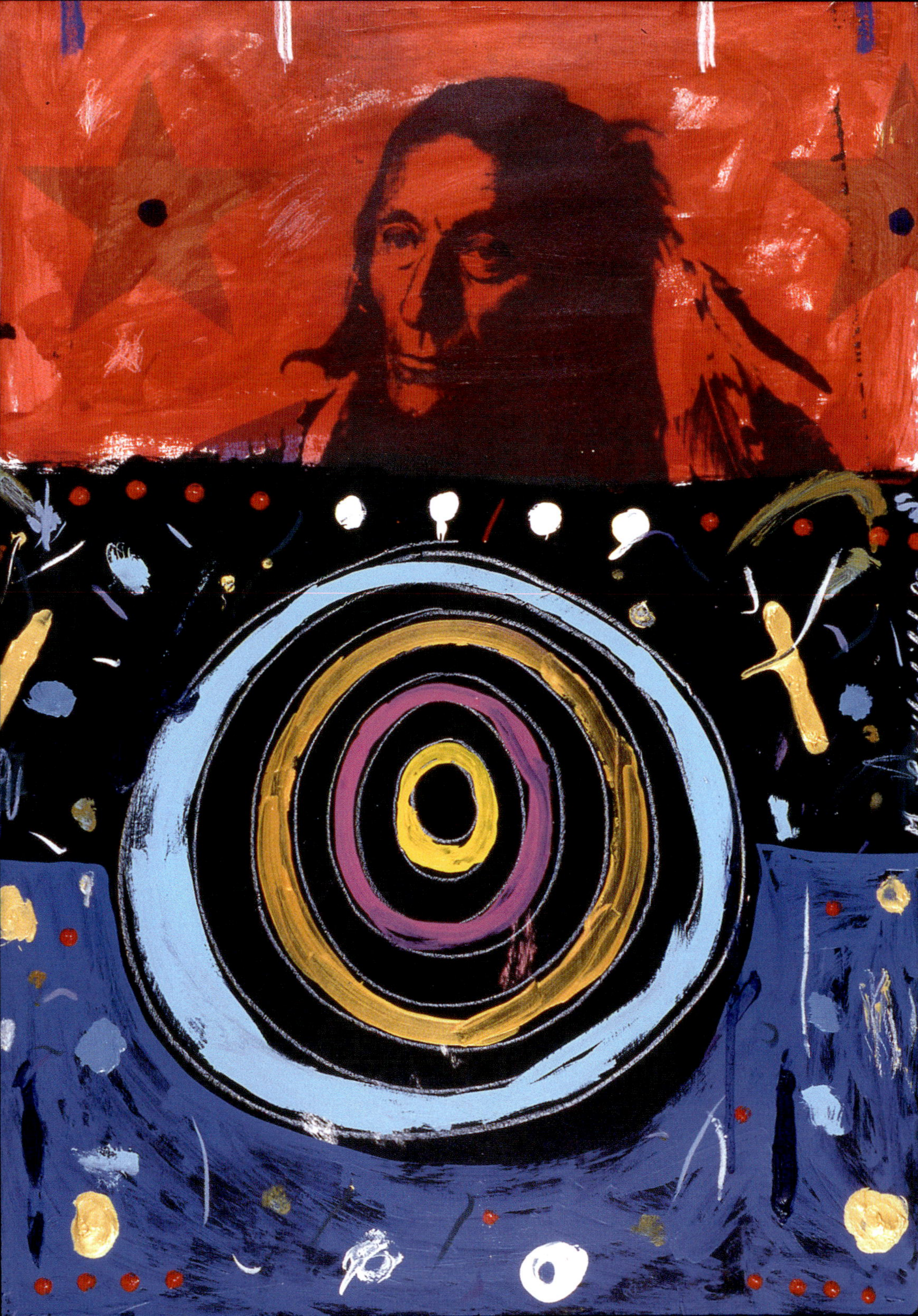

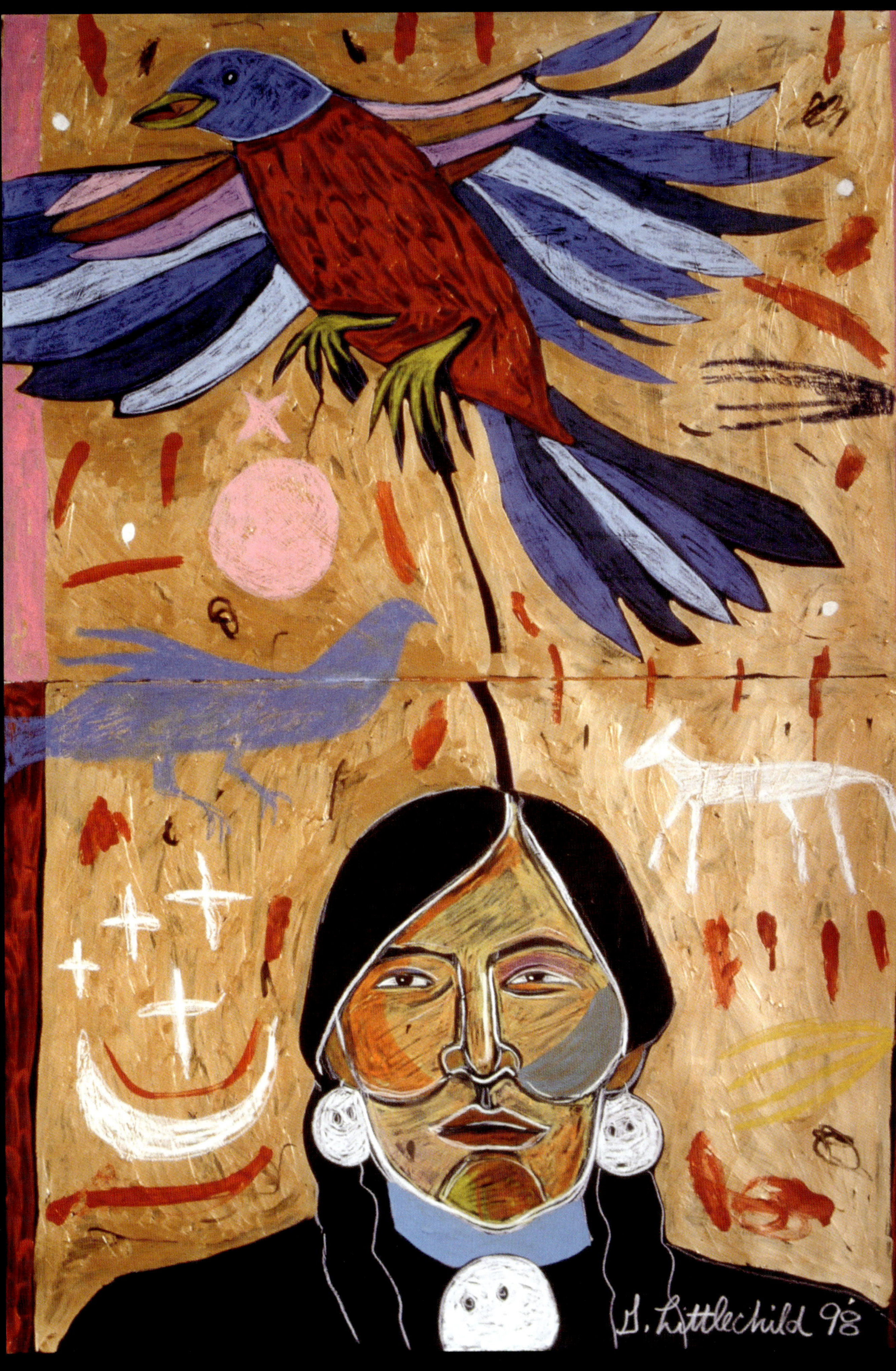

Spirit Guardian

mixed media :: 59" x 49.5" :: 1998

In my research I was fascinated with pictographs and Native American artwork drawn in ledger books, as well as traditional winter counts, which were painted on hides. The code-like winter-count drawings offered information about events, time and places and some were meant only for tribal members to understand. The art was glorious, and I responded with my own, implementing some of these motifs and ideas. Warriors would have an animal guardian image drawn above their heads to inform the viewer of their connection to their guardian. This spoke to me, and I created this piece in honour of those who created these strong works of tribal art.

Who Will Save the Salmon

mixed media :: 30" x 22" :: 1998

My art is inspired by history and events that shape, inform and sometimes peeve me. I have to speak out and address in my art some of these things that are near and dear to my heart. At times, governments and businesses do not have our best interests and those of our Mother Earth at heart when they implement laws, reforms and quick remedies to natural situations. Salmon are the coast's gold, along with all sea life. We are here to nurture and protect, to ensure these food sources feed us and future generations. Take a stand when things disturb or bother you. Speak out!

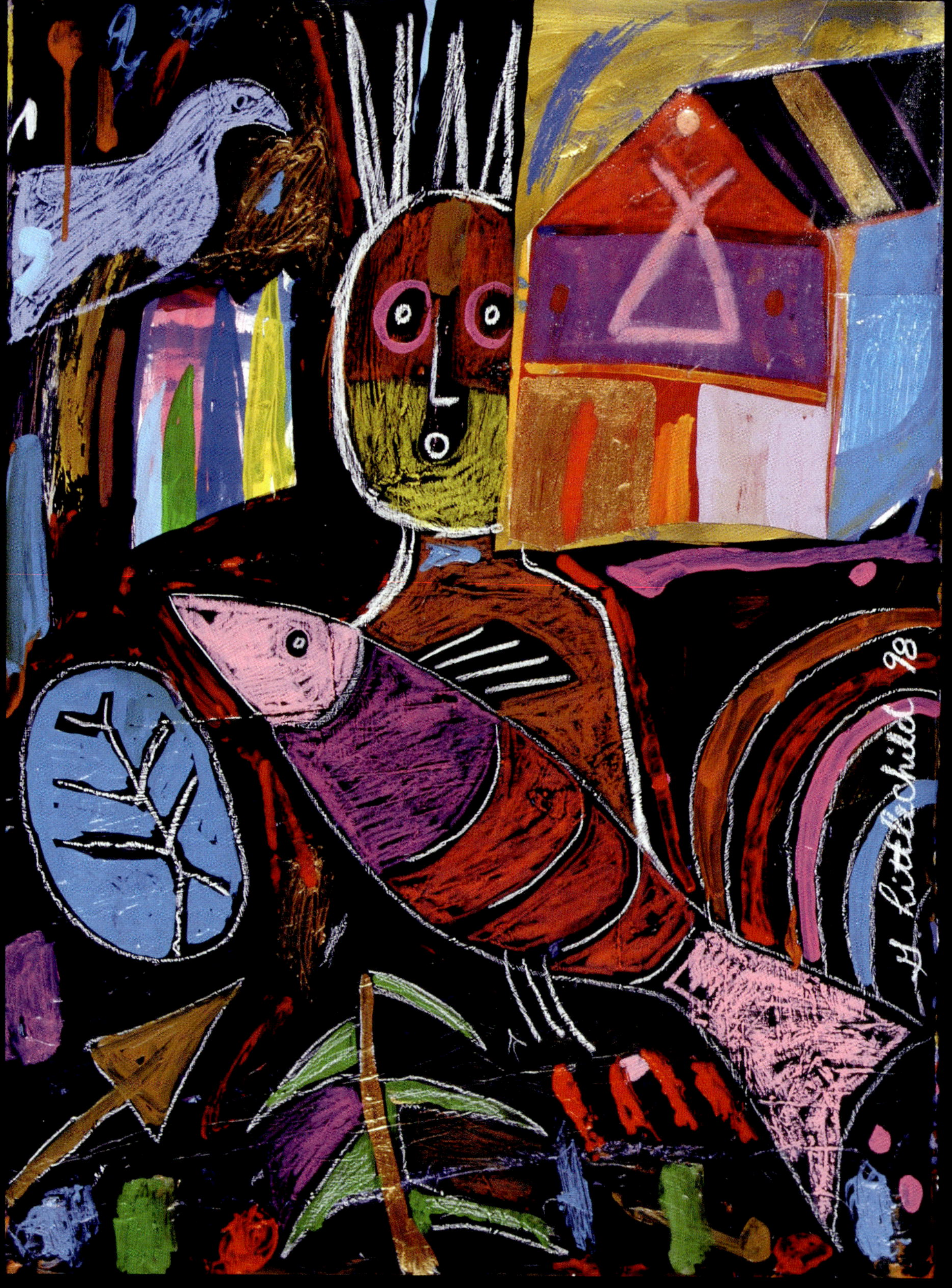

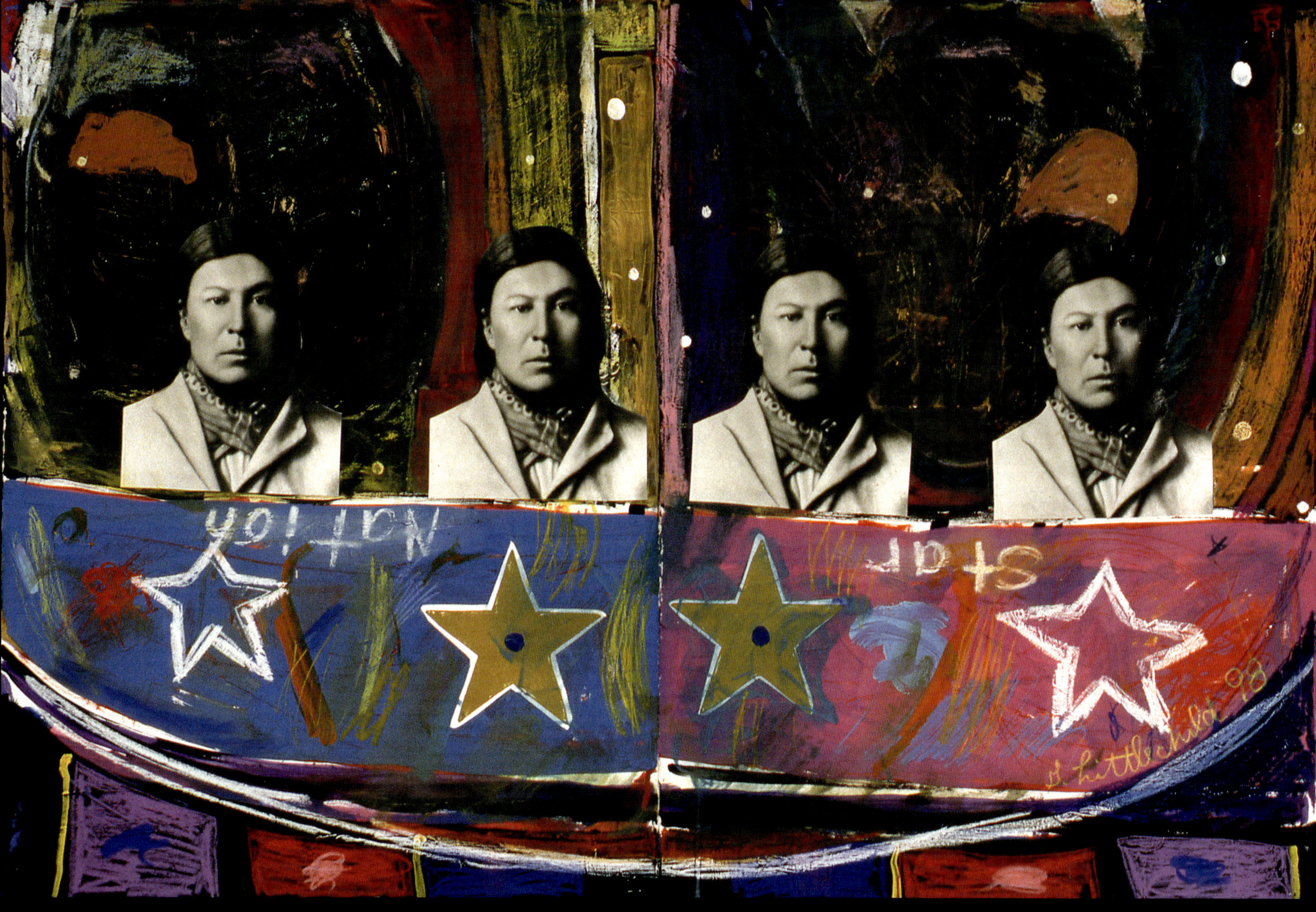

Sacred Star, Star Nation mixed media :: 30" x 44" :: 1998

The sacred number four is seen throughout this art piece: four portraits, four stars and various sections. Space and patterns are broken. The division creates a dramatic backdrop that honours the First People who are known as Star People or Star Nation. This man is my great-grandfather Chief Francis Bull.

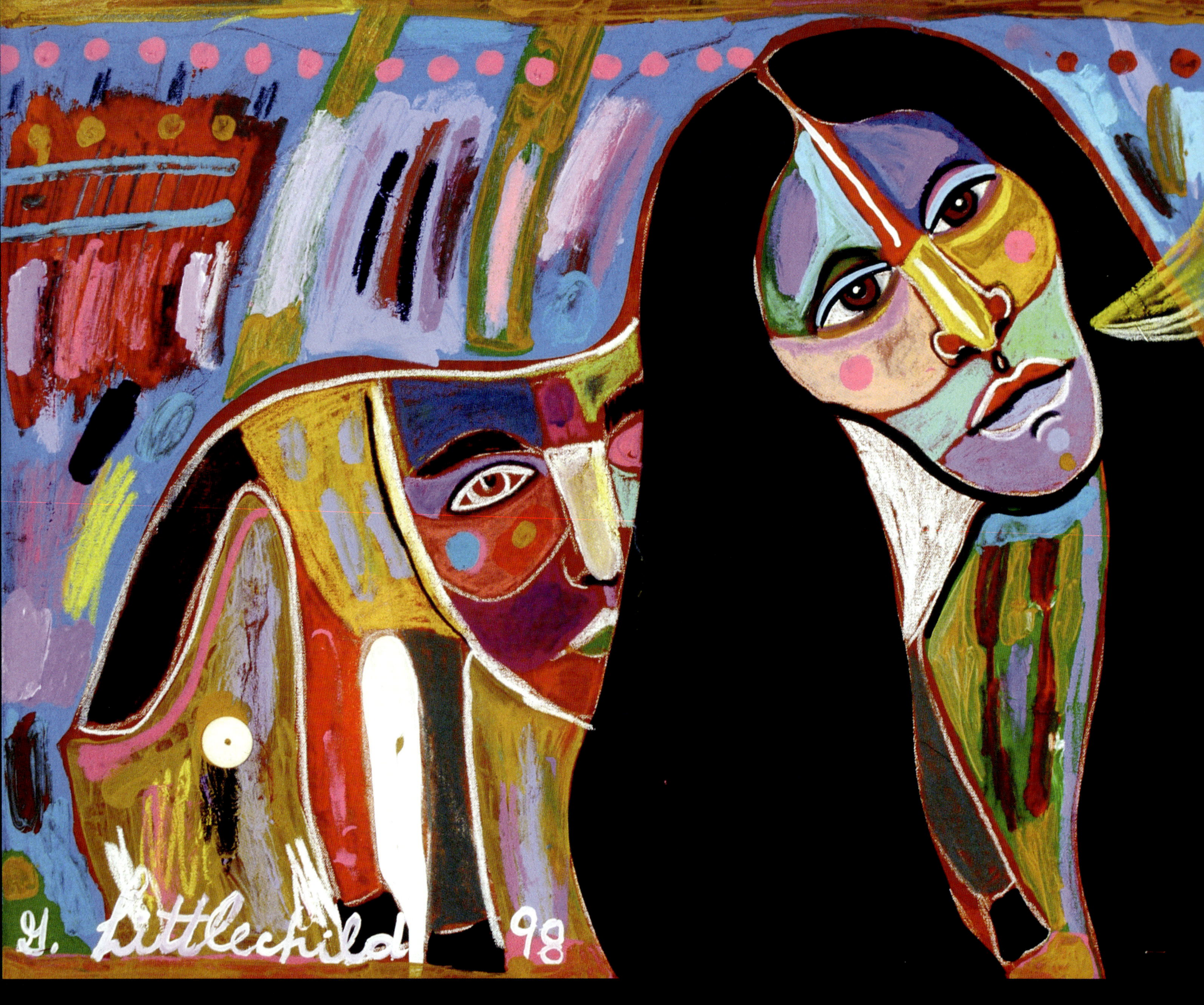

Cries for a Vision mixed media :: 22" x 30" :: 1998

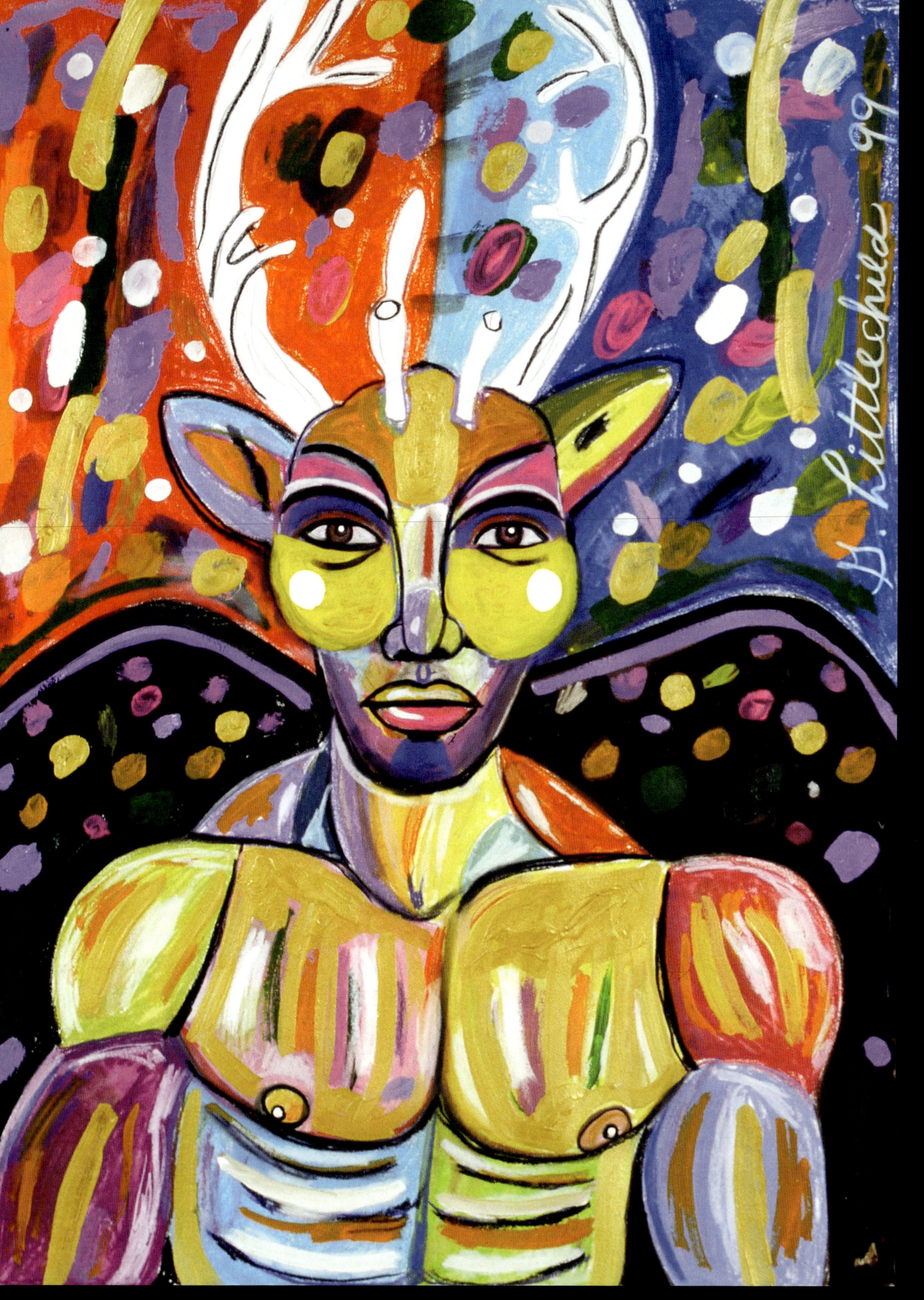

Elk Man

mixed media :: 30" x 22" :: 1999

Elk man is an ominous character, drifting in the wild with a powerful stance. He lives off the plains, forging, gathering, existing and procreating in order to preserve a species—to transform and enlighten their journey.

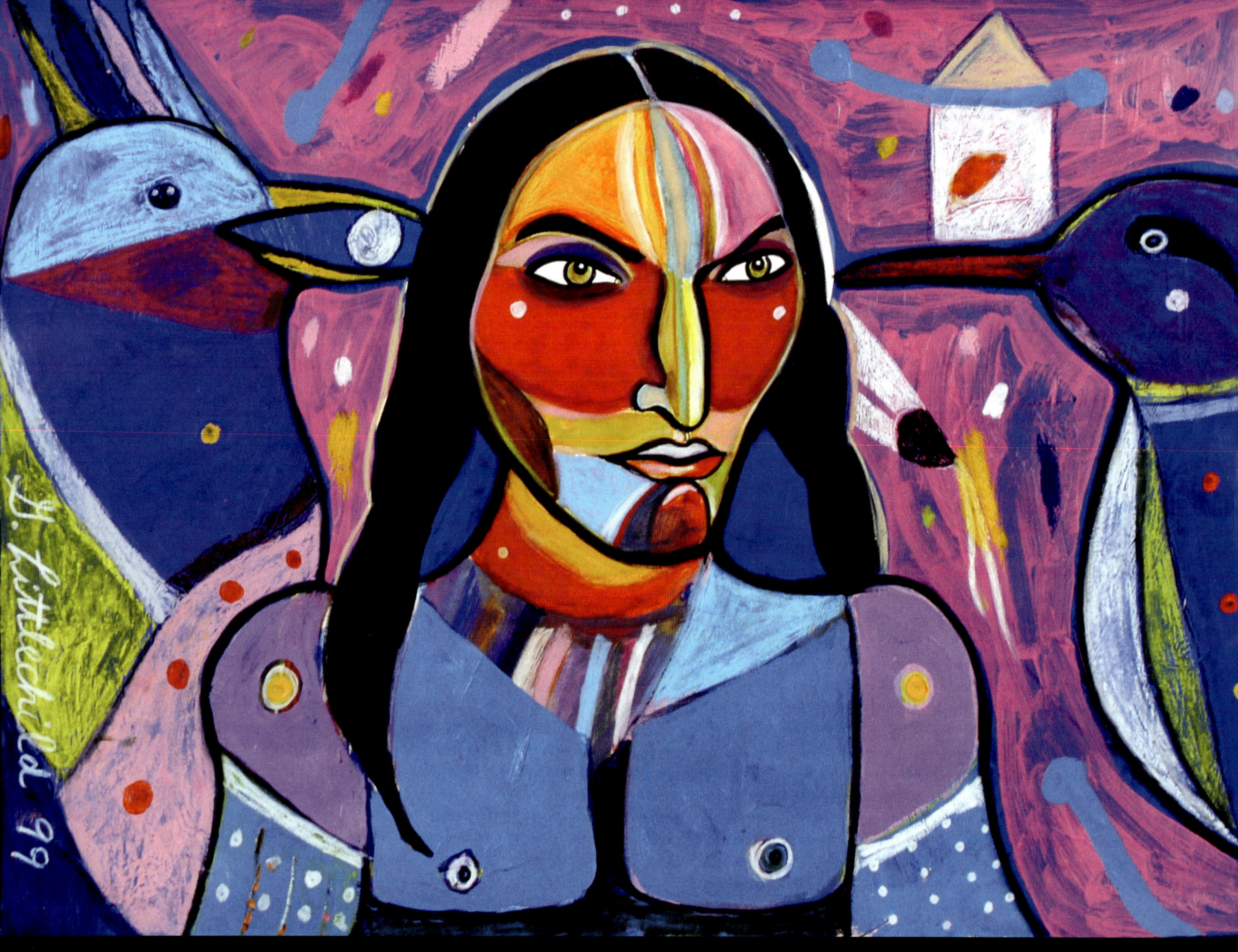

A Winged Bird Told Me So mixed media :: 22" x 30" :: 1999

Gossip, back talk, people chatting bad things about you that create fear and paranoia—is it true what the little bird told you? Have you questioned its accuracy? Do we believe everything others tell us about someone? Do we slander people after we repeat what we were told—be careful, you shouldn't

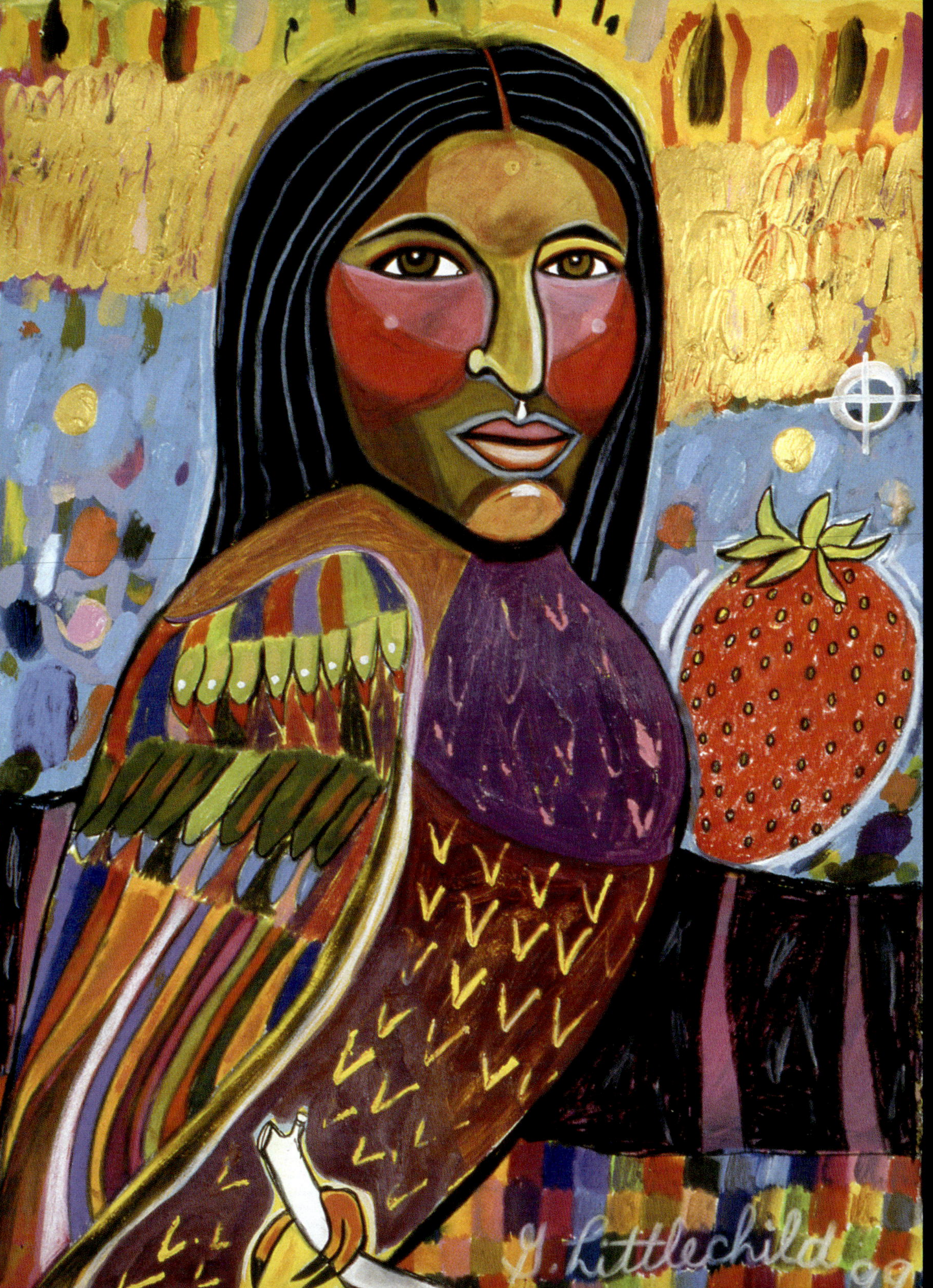

Natasha Rae Transforms into Bird Woman Who Sneaks Strawberries from Yvette's Garden

mixed media :: 30" x 22" :: 1999

I once spent my summer weekends on Mayne Island, BC. I would watch the birds mill around the garden in search of worms and food. The strawberries made a lovely little meal, and they would watch and dive in at the right moment to take the red berries. The gardener worked so hard for these berries and the birds would ruin them for human consumption! The bird woman is my niece Natasha Rae, who won the battle and the red strawberries.

PART 3 2000–2011

Biracial, Mixed Blood, Half Breed, Whole Person

mixed media :: 30" x 22" :: 2001

The idea and the realities of being mixed race do not always match others' notions of race. Often, mixed-race individuals are viewed differently, seen as the Other or incomplete. However, within the Metis nation, everyone is similar. Their duality is celebrated. I know when I'm with other mixed-race people, I feel complete.

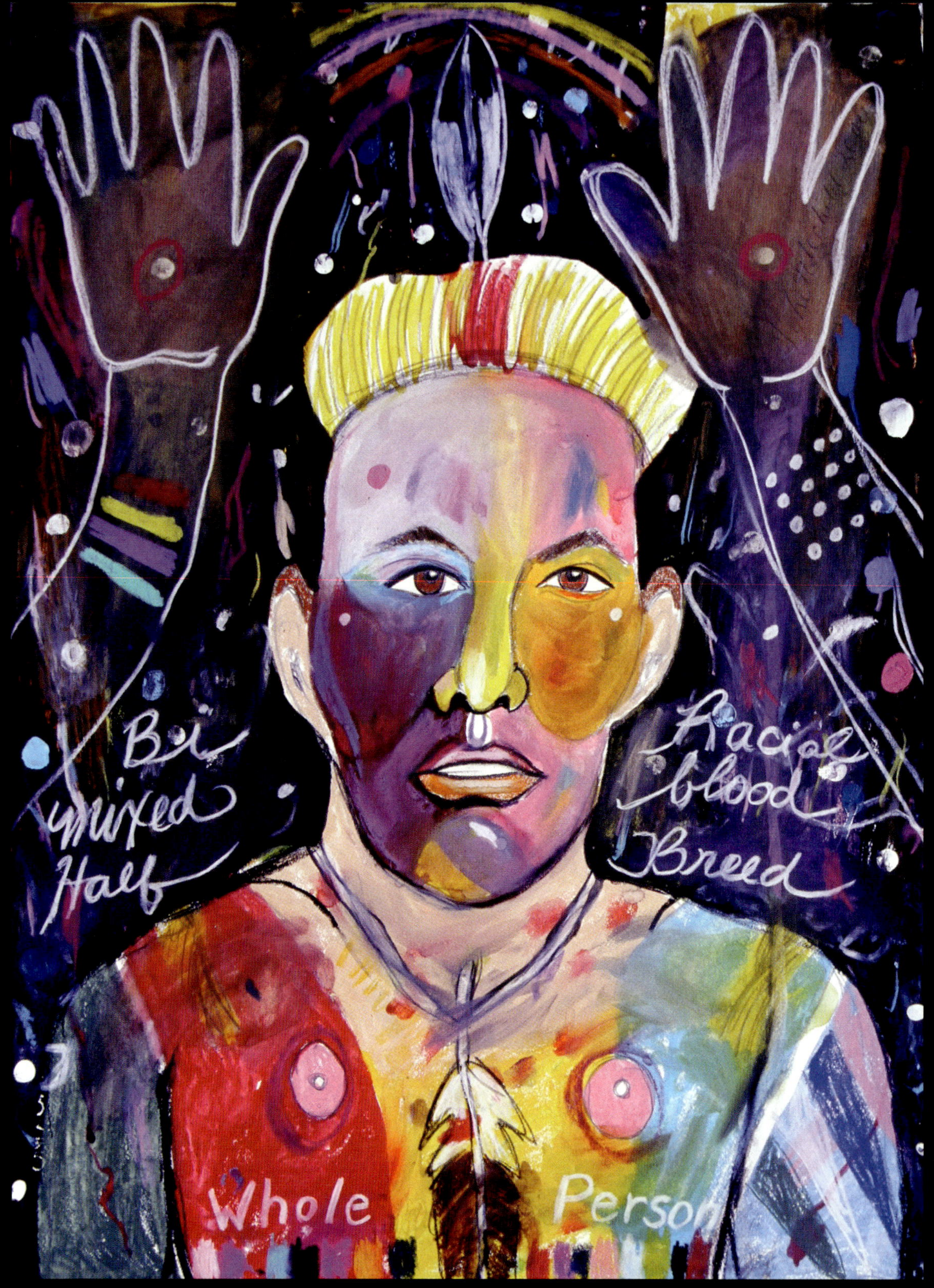

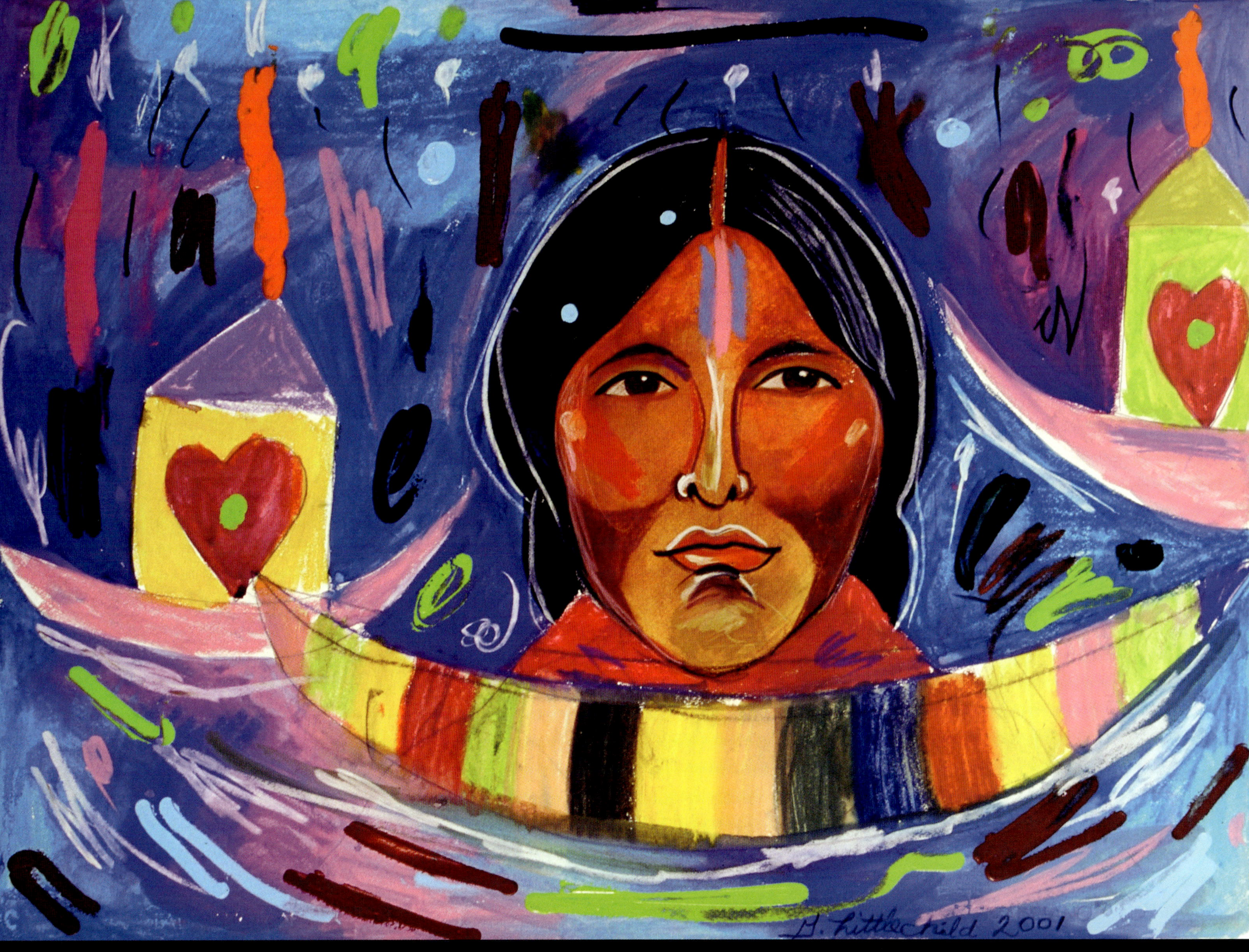

Panychat's Granddaughter mixed media :: 22" x 30" :: 2001

I see canoes as symbols of passage and change. The movement from eastern to western Canada occurred in canoes, transporting trade goods, furs and men. Here, I painted three canoes, two with love houses and another with a lovely Cree woman. Her name was Mary Okissin. She married Chief Sam Minde of the Ermineskin Reserve. I was struck by her beauty and wanted to pay her homage. She, too, is a relative.

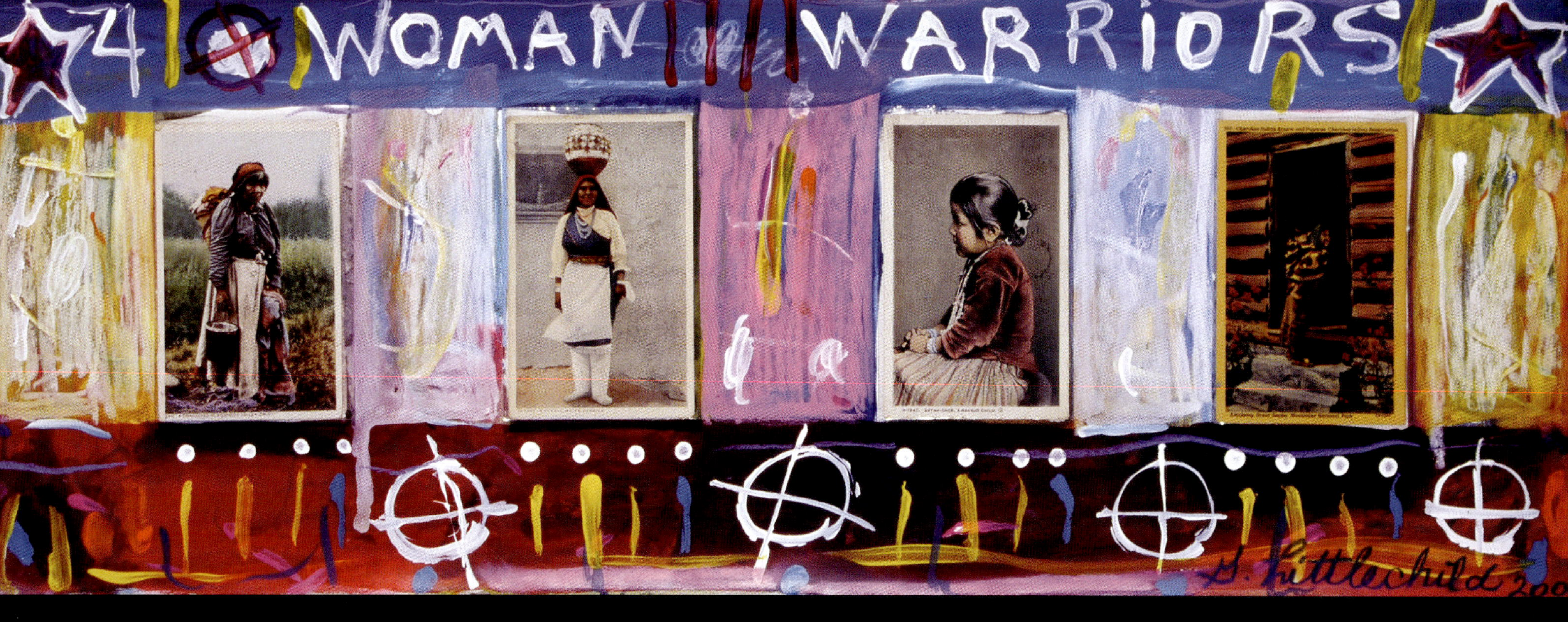

Four Women Warriors mixed media :: 11" x 30" :: 2001

Antique postcards were collaged into this mixed-media painting. The women are Native American and were photographed many years ago when their lives were being changed by reservation life and governments. They stand poised in the traditional regalia of their Nations, so dignified, so true to their culture. They are role models for their daughters and all Native women, warriors for having survived

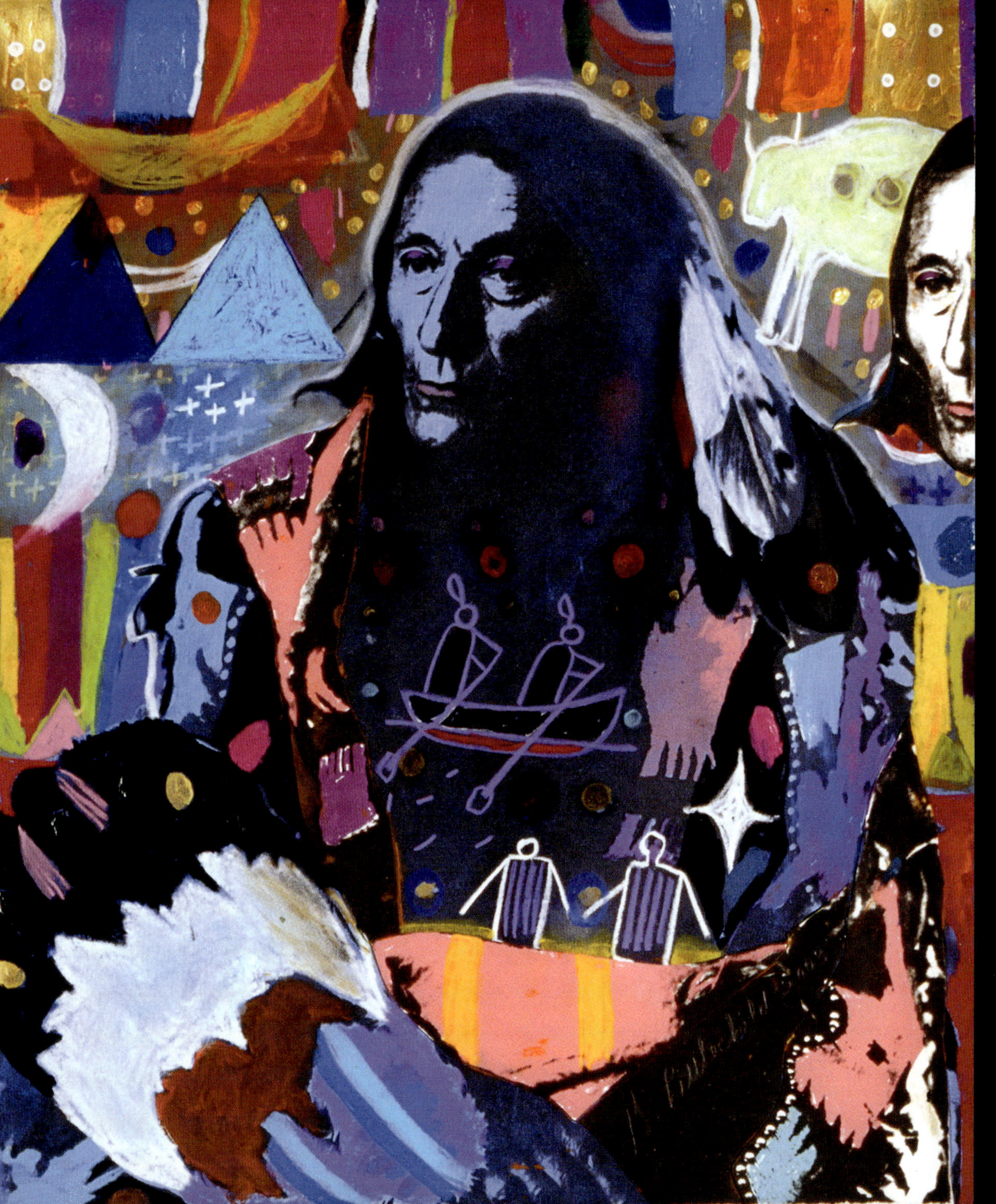

From Sacred Lineage He Came

mixed media on paper
26" x 22" :: 2001

Plains Cree chief Alexis Bobtail (also known as Alexis Piche or Kiskiyo in Plains Cree) was born in 1830 on the Saskatchewan River in the Rocky Mountains of Alberta. He believed in his culture and its continuance. He fought when drastic changes driven by the government and settlers took away sacred lands and territories. His people had roamed freely, and within his lifetime they were confined to forced living arrangements on reserves. Their traditional hunting patterns and ways of living were disrupted by new laws and practices. Kiskiyo is not only my great-great-great uncle, but my HERO.

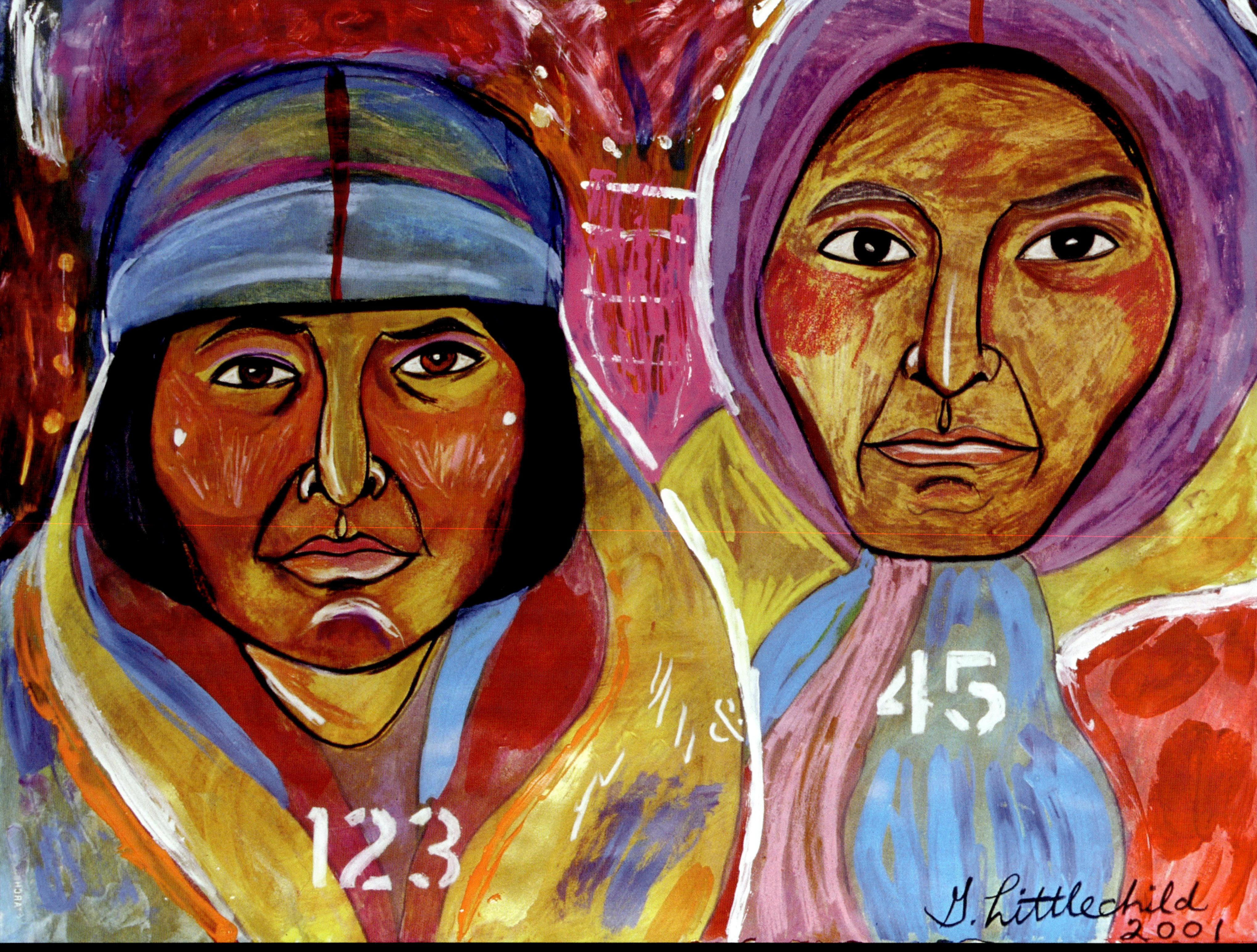

Numbers 123 and 45 mixed media :: 22" x 30" :: 2001

Indian Nations were forced like cattle to allocated land. Voices were changed, disturbed and silenced. Numbers were given to each Indian, which is how Indian agents identified them. They became wards of the government, forced to live out their lives stuck on plots of land. They couldn't even leave the reserve without permission from the agent, who gave them a ticket for the day or for the amount of time they were allowed to be away. If they did not return, they were tracked down and incarcerated. The ancestors suffered a lot.

Too Ethnic Looking to Model mixed media :: 17.5" x 29" :: 2001

When I was younger, people told me that I should try modelling, so I joined an agency for a short period of time. I had many photos taken by professional photographers; however, one of the agents said I was "too ethnic looking to model." Exotic or unusual looks were not accepted in the late 1970s and '80s. In fact, I never saw ethnic or coloured models on TV or in magazines.

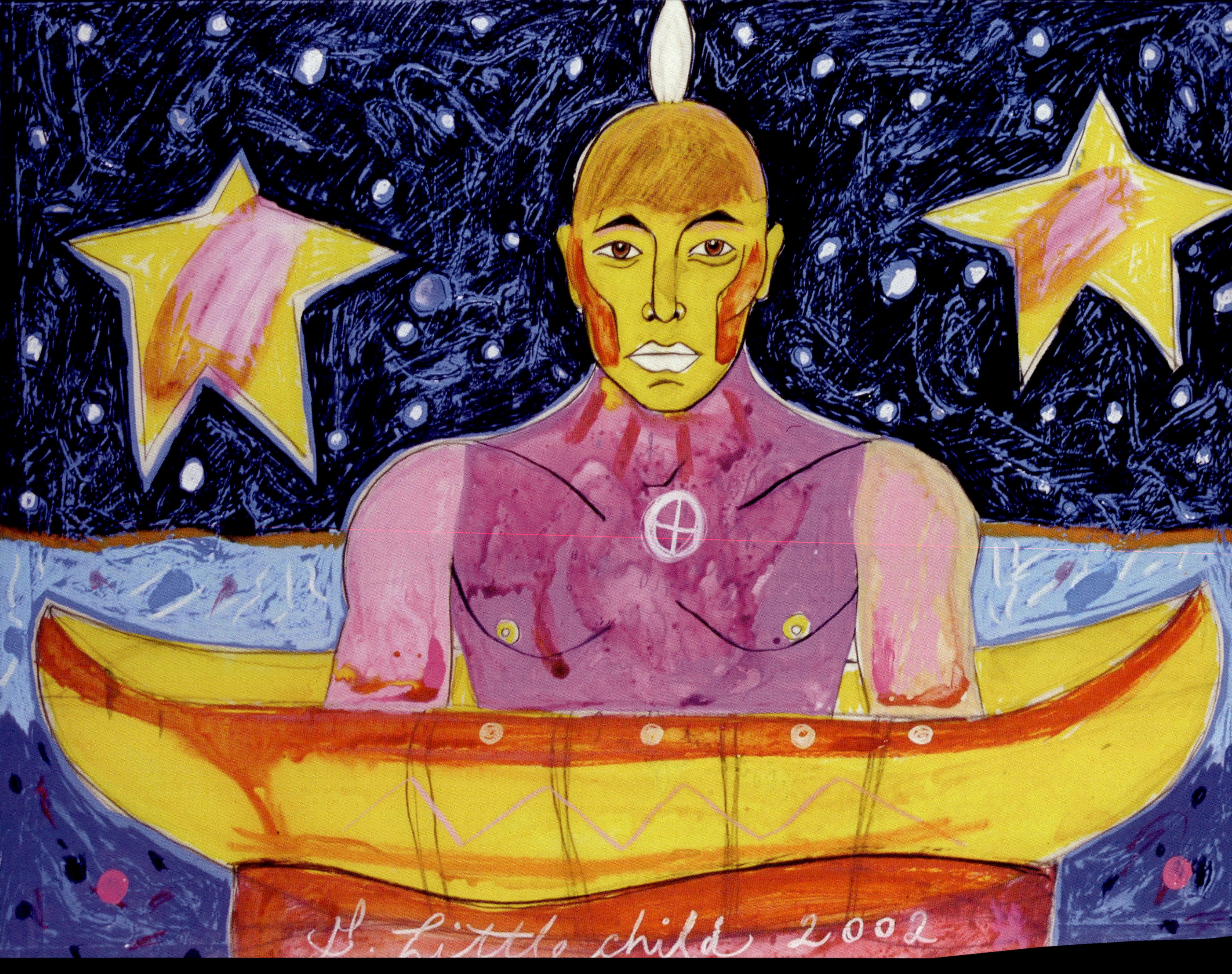

Man Who Makes the Waters Move mixed media on Mylar :: 22" x 30" :: 2002

I was part of a competition to create a sculptural piece for the Calgary airport. I proposed a large, seated figure of a man in a canoe as a welcome figure to greet passengers. However, I did not win; that honour went to the late First Nations artist Dr. Joane Cardinal-Schubert. Her horse sculpture welcomes many travellers, and her memory and legacy live on. I am proud of all she accomplished in her lifetime.

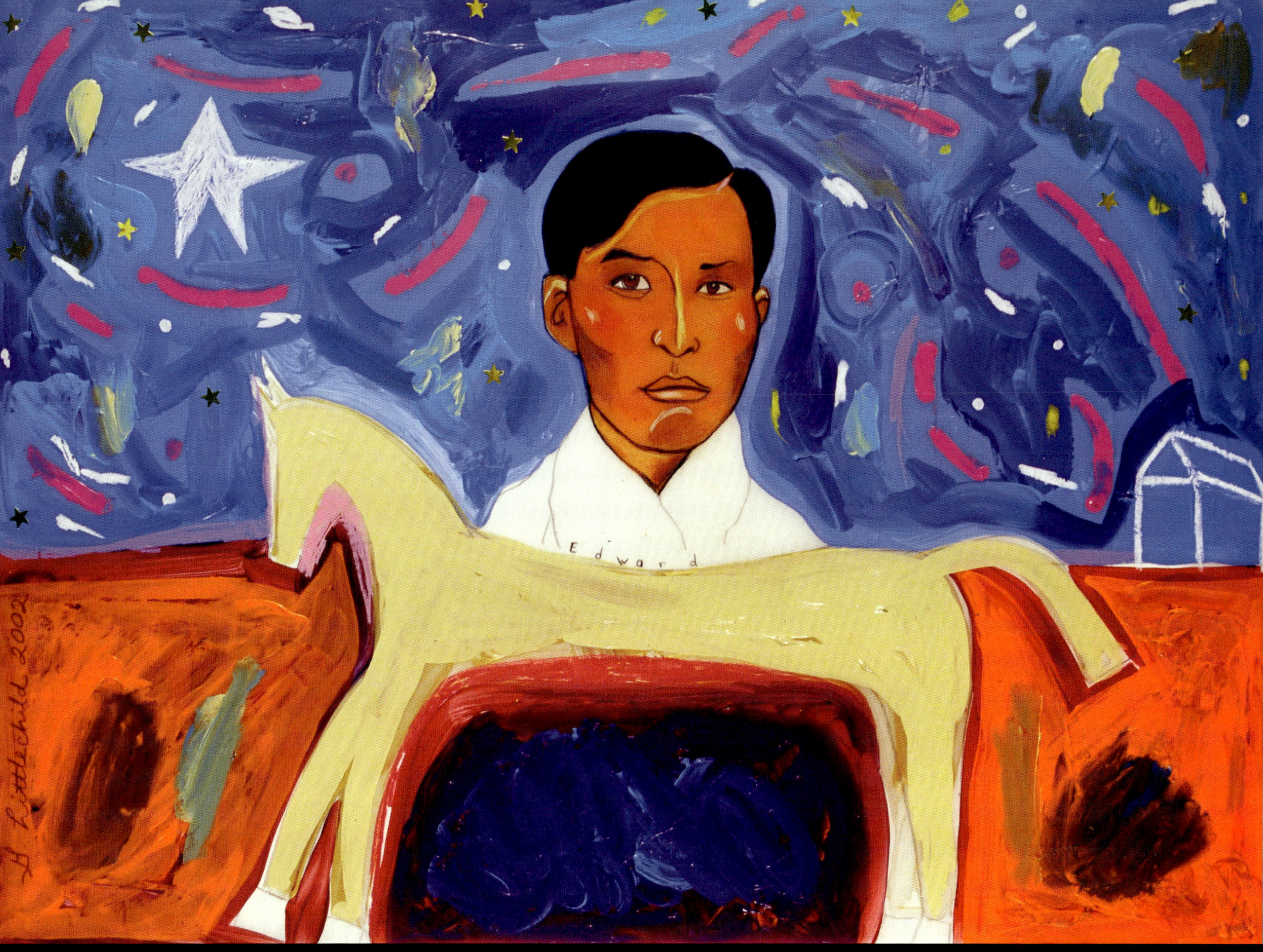

Grandfather Edward, So Handsome mixed media on Mylar :: 22" x 30" :: 2002

A dramatic sky supports this portrait of Mosom (Edward Littlechild) who rides a horse (Mistatim). His reserve home is on the horizon. His time at the Ermineskin Indian Residential School and his life on the reserve is part of his story. The other part is his love for sports; he was a natural, gifted athlete. He stood six feet tall and was drafted to play professional ball in the US but couldn't because he was a father of 12. He played on a team that won the 1913 Provincial Championships in the United Farmers' Association. He and three other Cree men from Hobbema were on the mostly white team.

I Could Do Nothing as I Was a Boy

archival digital image
24" x 24" :: 2003

This photograph of Mother and Jack, my older brother, was taken in 1956, two years before I was born. I see such joy in her face; she exudes happiness. She stands in front of her home off 96th Street in Edmonton, looking complete and content. She was in love with her husband, Joe Smith, who died that same year. After his death, her life did what we would call a 360 as she mourned his loss immensely. She met my father, James Price, and had four more children; however, she spiralled downward, dying tragically on Edmonton's skid row in 1965. R.I.P., my dear mother—I wrote you a little note in this art piece, dedicated to you with love. Your son, George.

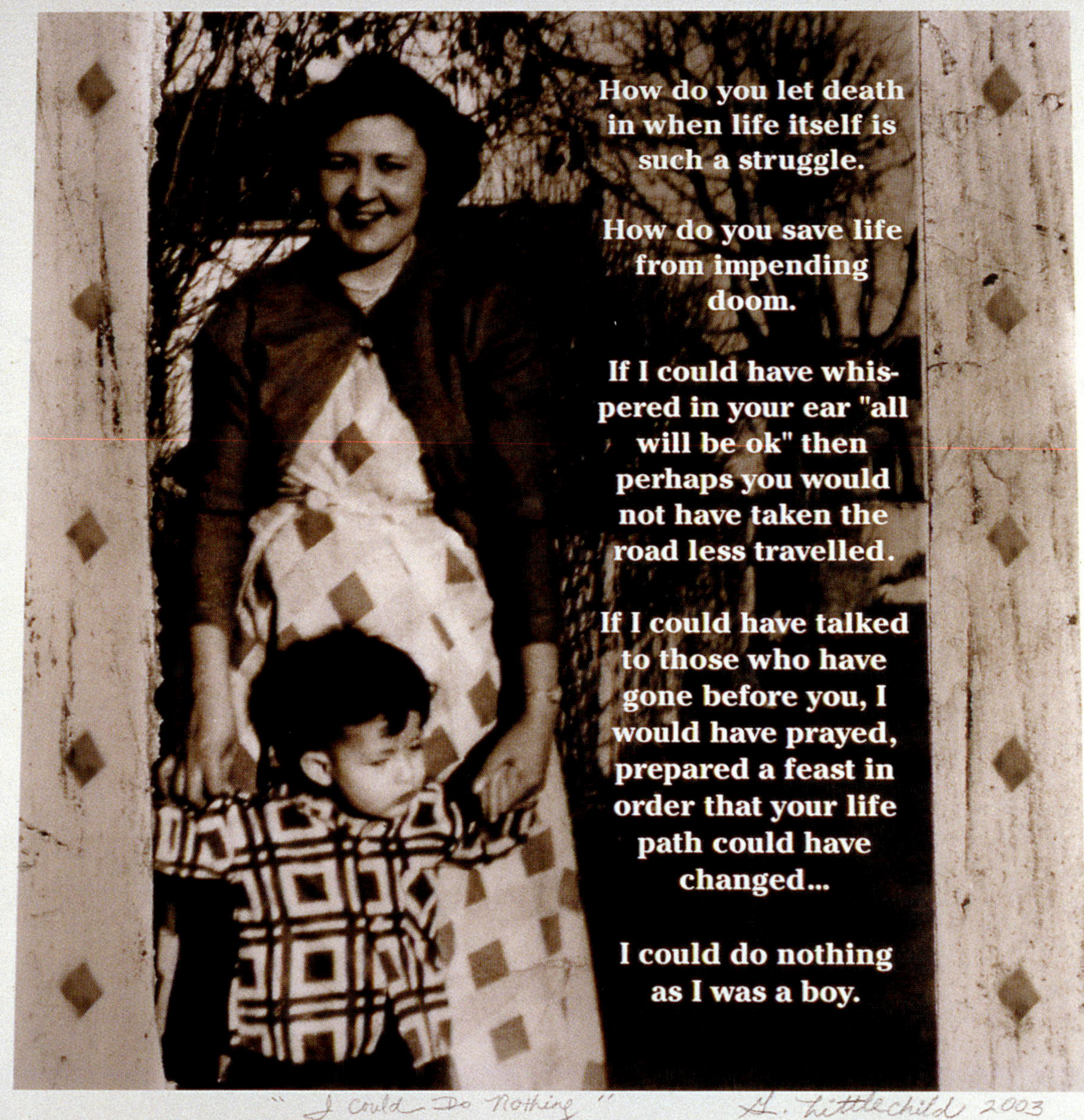

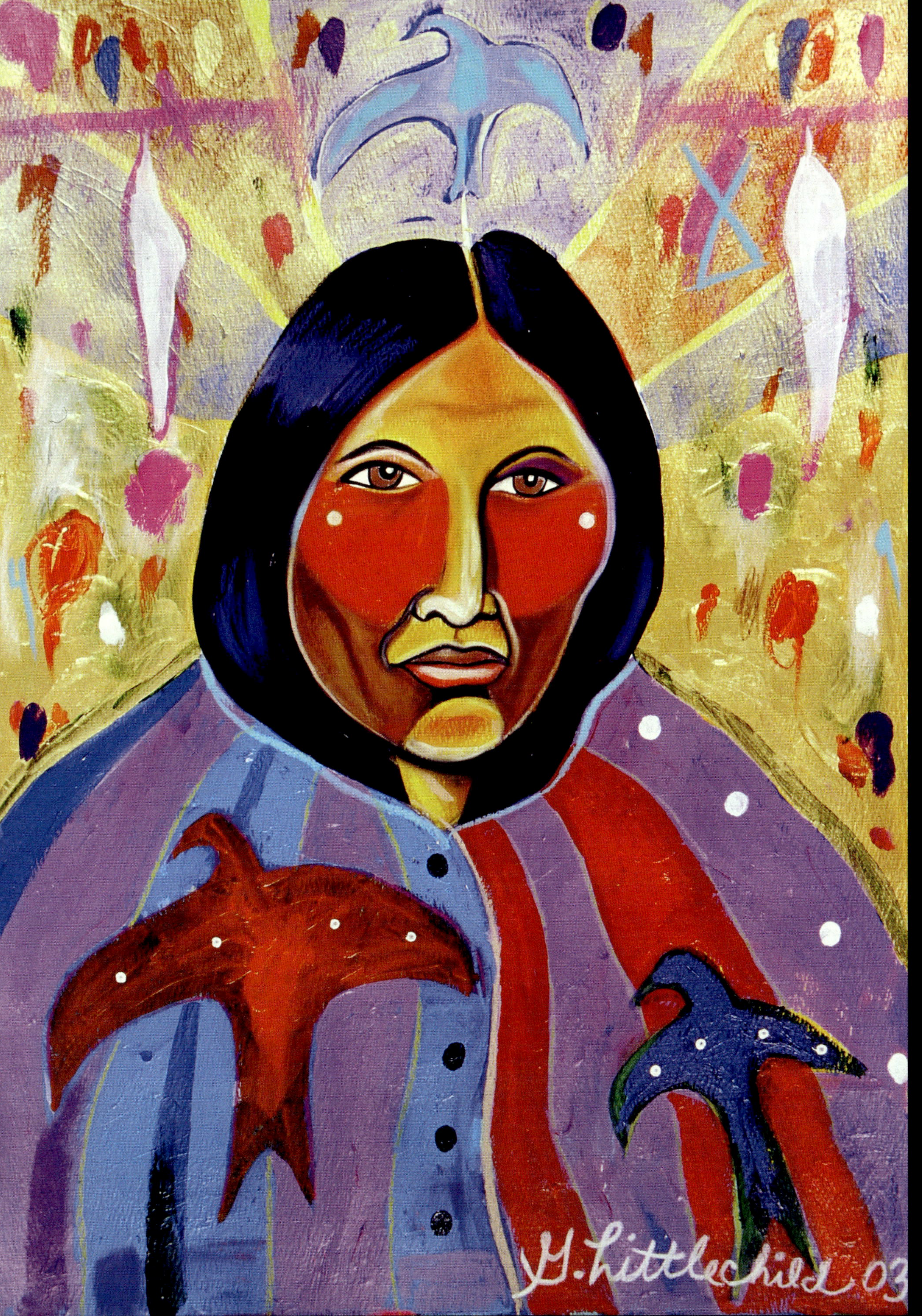

Granddaughter of Wapiskakwan

mixed media
30" x 22" :: 2003

My aunt Rachel (Ayiwastin) Littlechild's mother, Julia (Whitefog) Allard, was the granddaughter of Wapiskakwan, otherwise known as Jean Baptiste Whitefog. Julia's beauty and sculpted high cheekbones compelled me to create an homage portrait in recognition of her time on this Earth. Three of her daughters married three of my mother's brothers.

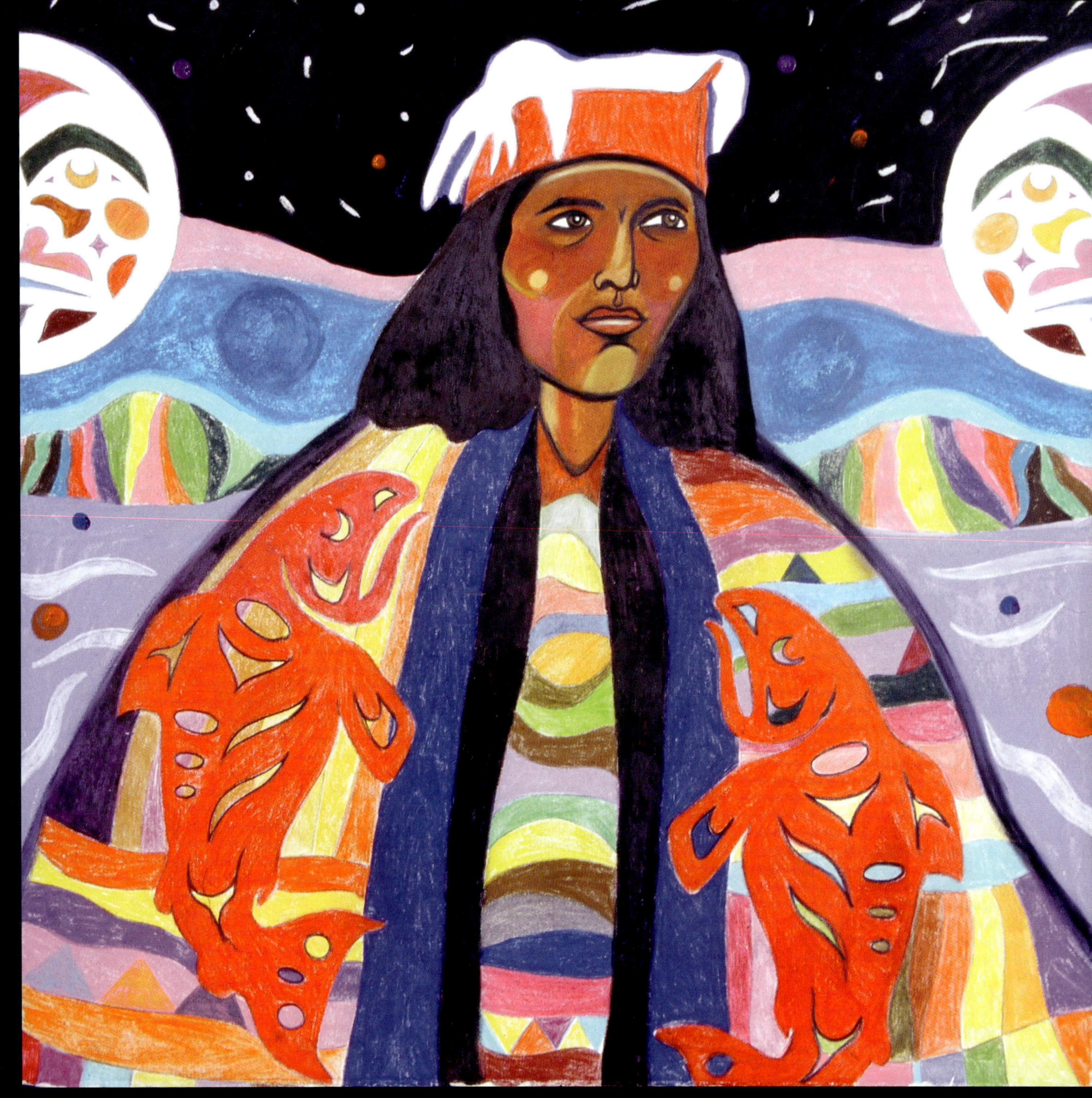

Kwagulth Autumn mixed media :: 22" x 22" :: 2004

This is a portrait of my good friend John Powell of the Kwagulth Nation. John is well versed in his culture and the ways of the potlatch. His grandparents Henry "Jumbo" and Eliza (Wallas) Bell ranked high within the tribe. John kindly lent me two of his designs for this painting, Salmon and Moon. John's oration of events, places, people and family connections are extraordinary. He is a historian, an artist and a designer and represents his nation well.

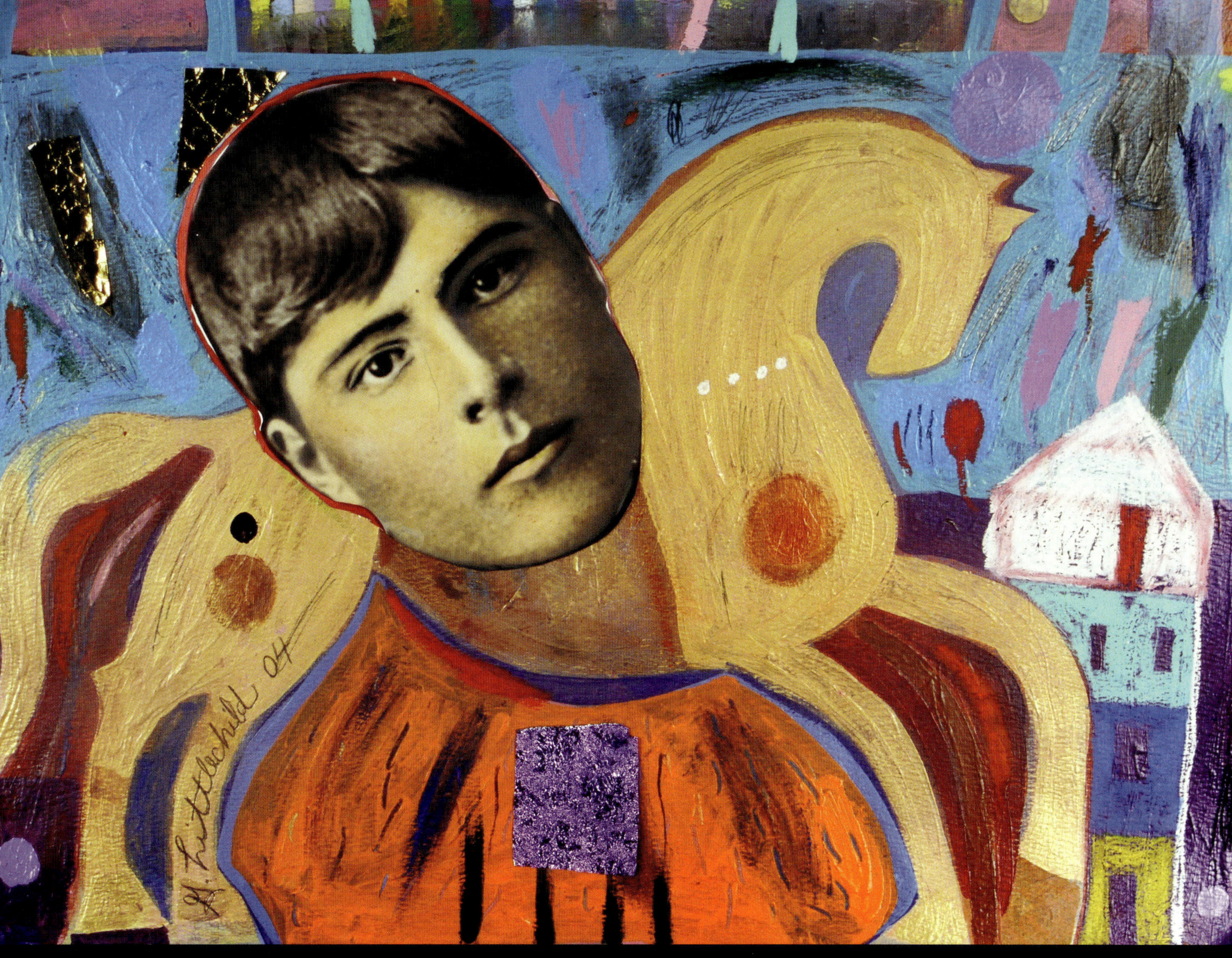

Ride the Metis Mile mixed media :: 22" x 30" :: 2004

This young, unidentified Metis man rides a horse freely among a stacked house, bits of gold and purple shiny foil and an atmosphere of positivity and hope.

Welcome Figure

mixed media :: 30″ x 22″ :: 2004

I painted a welcome figure with a little ego guy inside him. In a tiny canoe, they hold their hands up, meeting and greeting those about to enter unknown land. John Powell explained to me that welcome figures were carved by the Kwagulth tribe during times of potlatches to greet the guests. Eventually these figures would rot into the ground, at which time new ones were created.

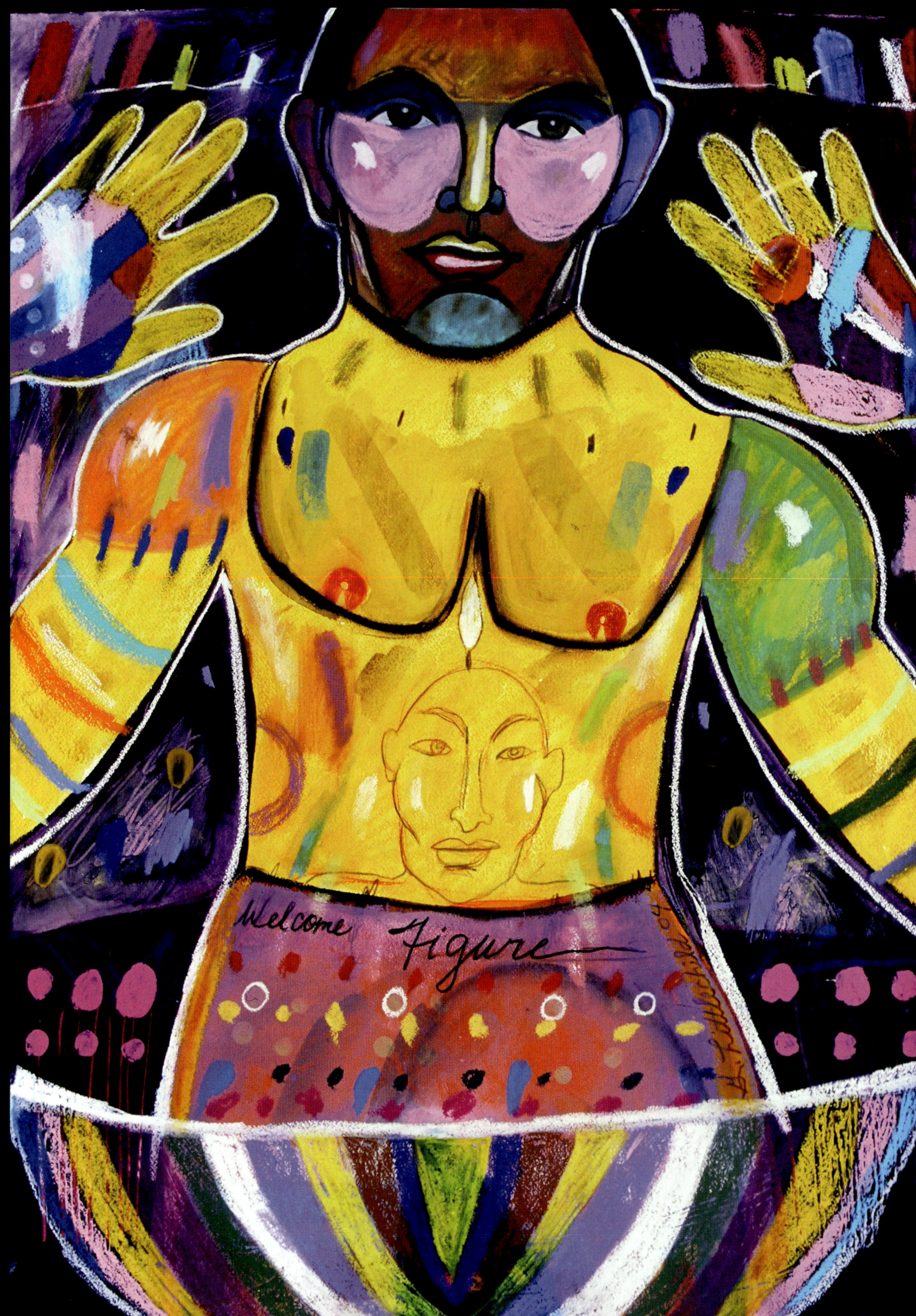

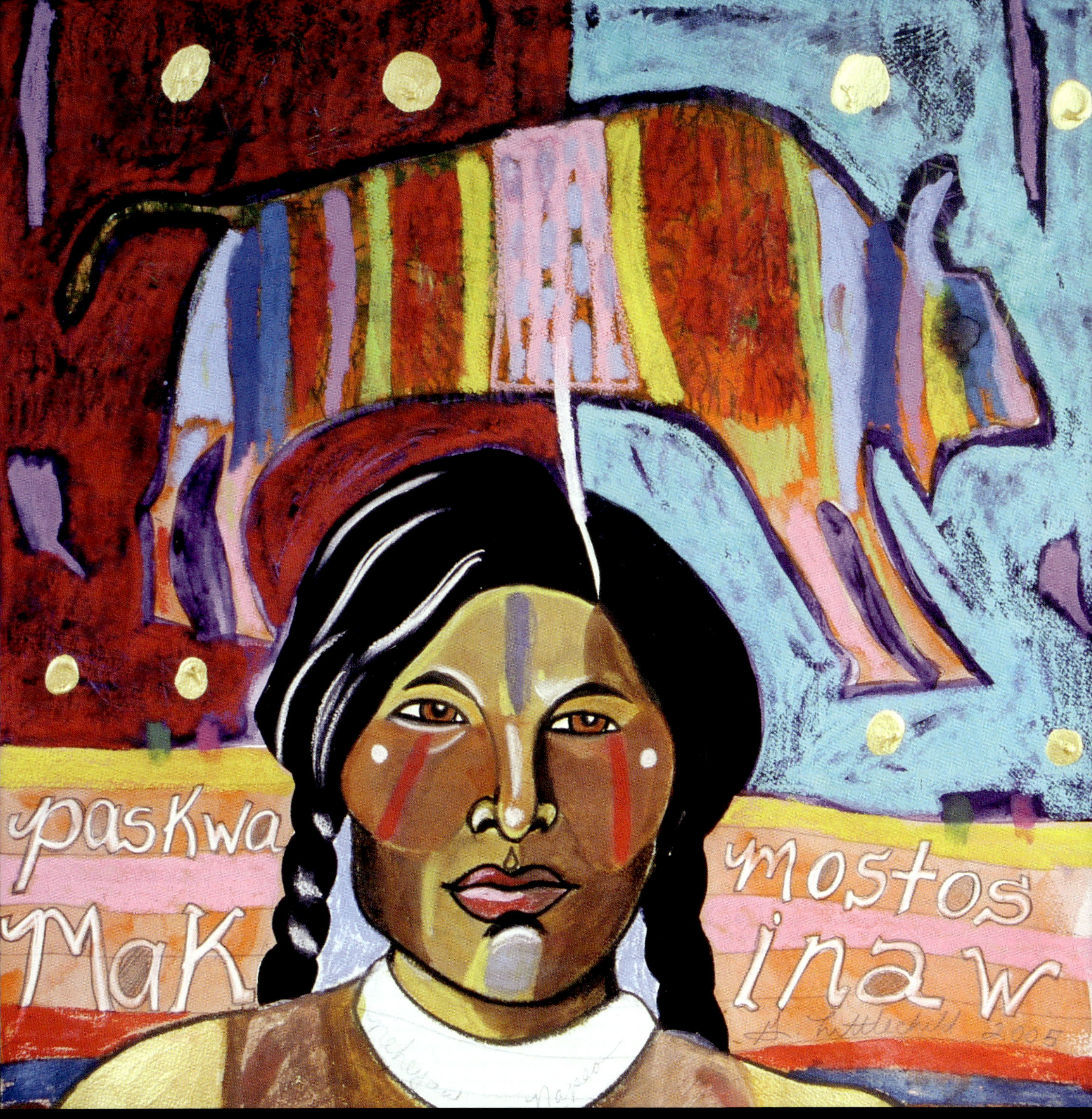

Paskwa Mostos mixed media :: 21" x 21" :: 2005

Augustin Mackinaw was the son of Antoine and Therese Sikak. Antoine died young and Therese remarried Adam Mackinaw. As a result, Augustin became Mackinaw. Augustin's uncle Louis Natuasis was Antoine's brother and my great-great-grandfather. Paskwa Mostos means plains buffalo. Augustin Mackinaw, like his ancestors before him, would have been reliant on the buffalo for food, clothing, shelter and ceremony.

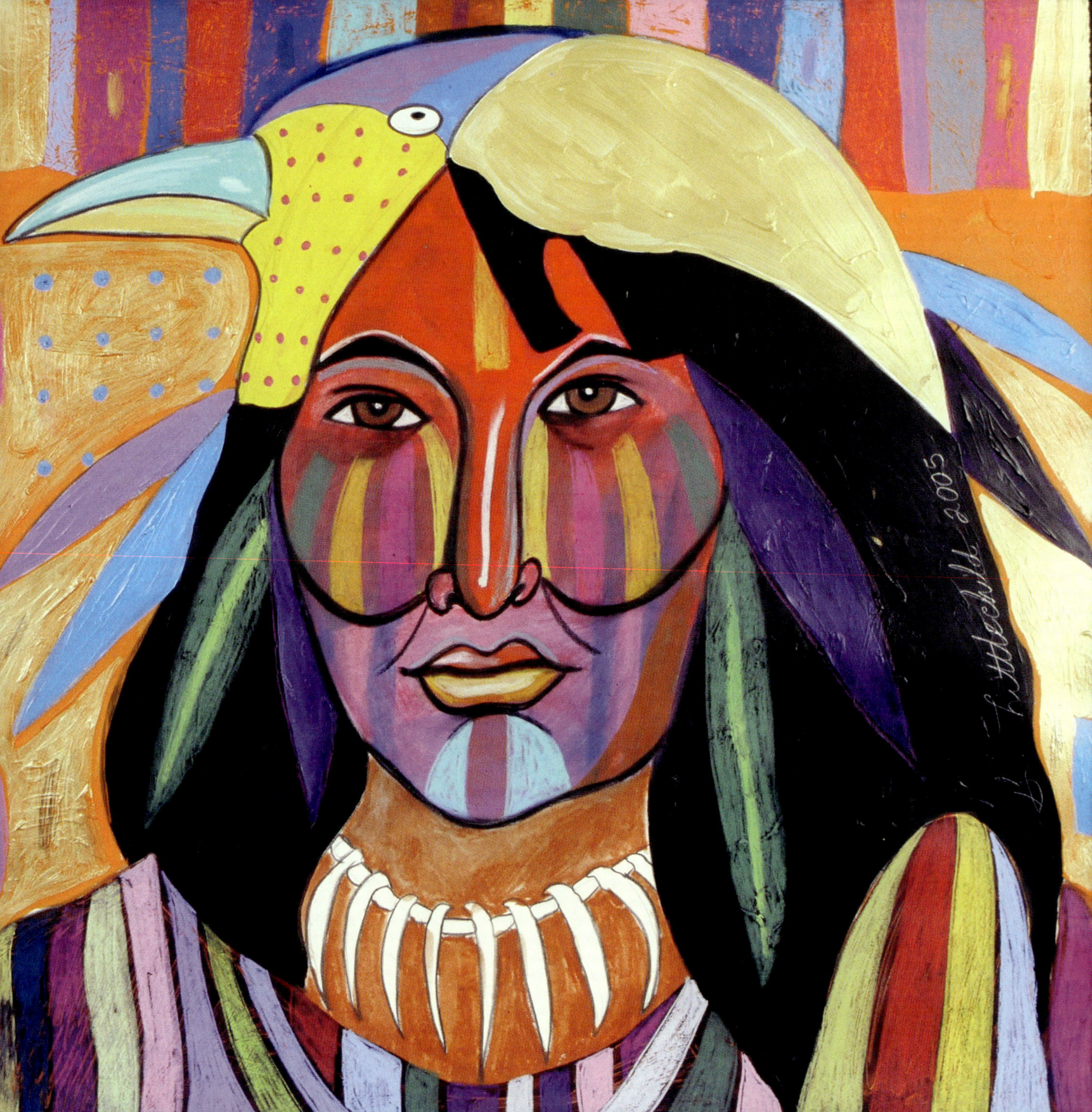

Red Willow, Mitik-âpemak mixed media :: 22" x 22" :: 2005

The Plains Cree are known as the People of the Red Willow, a tree that has important cultural and medicinal qualities. In my portrait, Red Willow has a striped face and wears a transformational bird headdress. The portrait style was influenced by artist Karl Bodmer, who painted Native American tribes in and around the Missouri River from 1832 to 1834 while accompanying Maximilian zu Wied-Neuwied on his North American expedition.

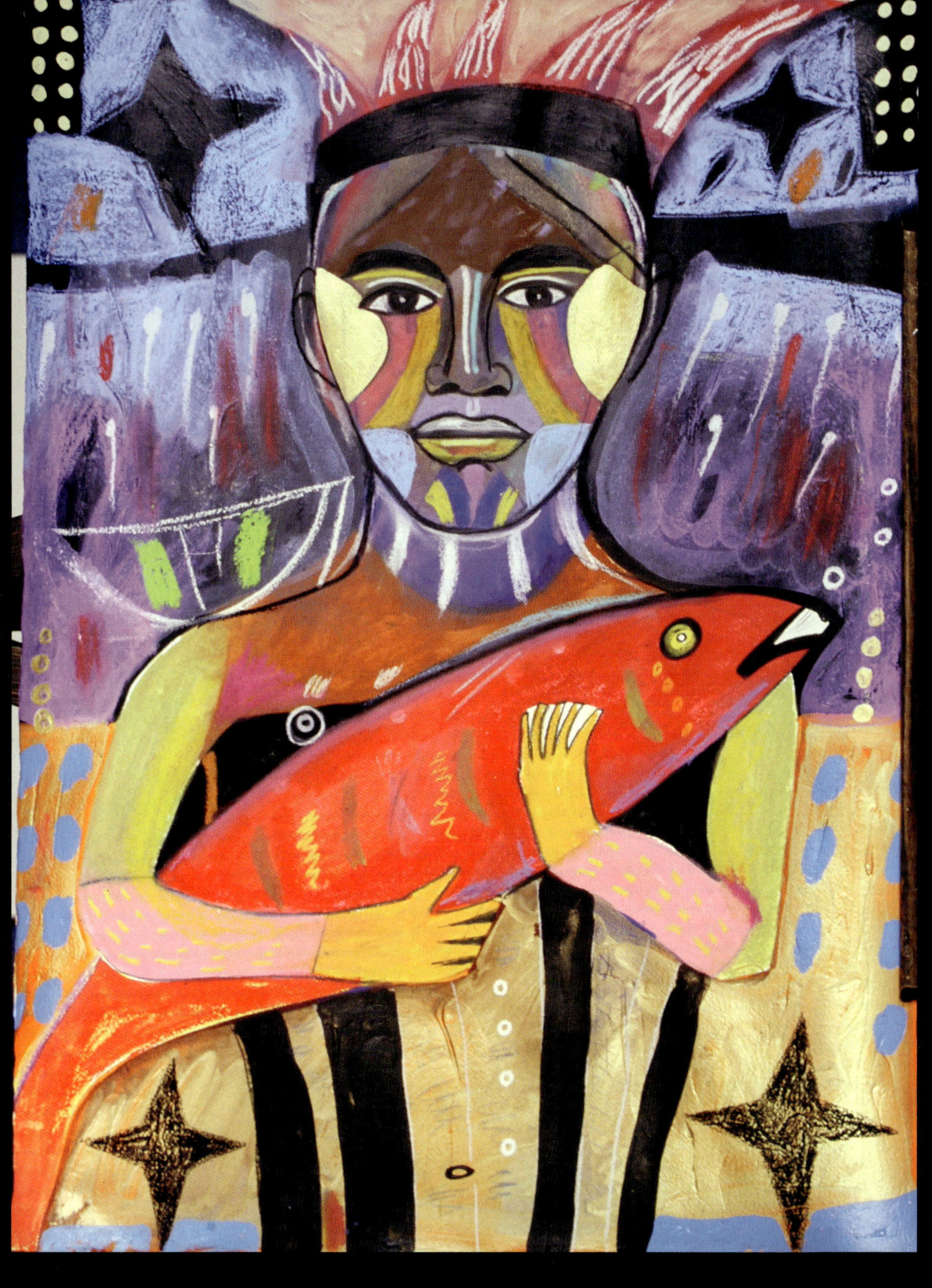

King of Salmon

mixed media :: 30" x 22" :: 2005

I have been blessed to live on the West Coast since 1990, and have been privy to many Kwagulth potlatches on the north end of Vancouver Island. I have learned many things about salmon and its importance to First Nations of British Columbia. In respect for this abundant fish, I created *King of Salmon* to honour and thank the salmon for all the meals and feasts I have been to.

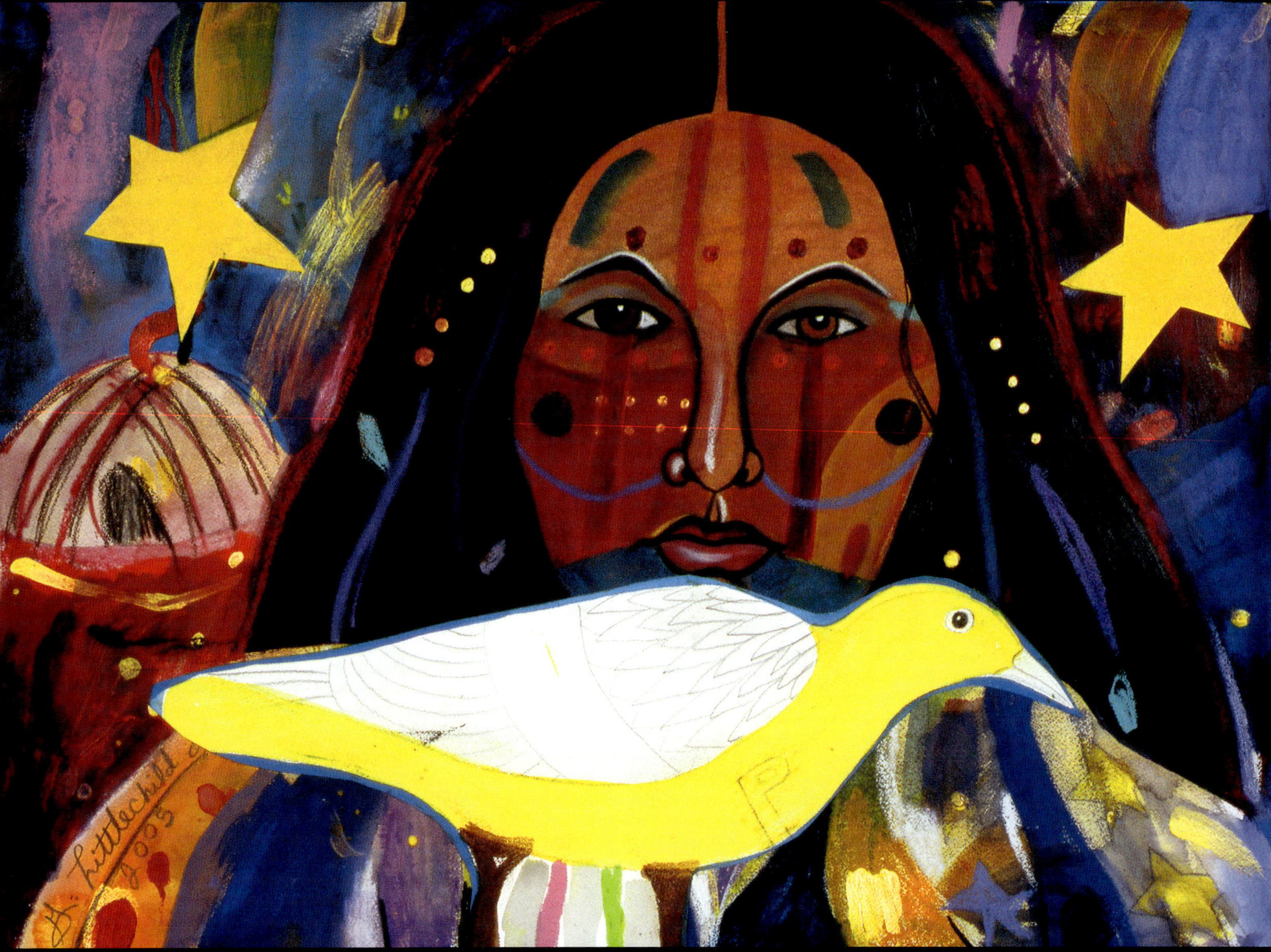

Painted on the Day Pope John Paul II Died mixed media :: 22" x 30" :: 2005

Coincidentally, this painting was made on the day that Pope John Paul II died. There is a sacred sweat lodge in the background, something that the Catholic religion tried to destroy. A sacred yellow bird and yellow stars fill the environment while my mother stares into our eyes and acts as a witness to the near-destruction of her culture by missionaries and government agencies. Had she lived, she may have benefitted richly from her Cree culture, which she lost by being forced to attend residential school.

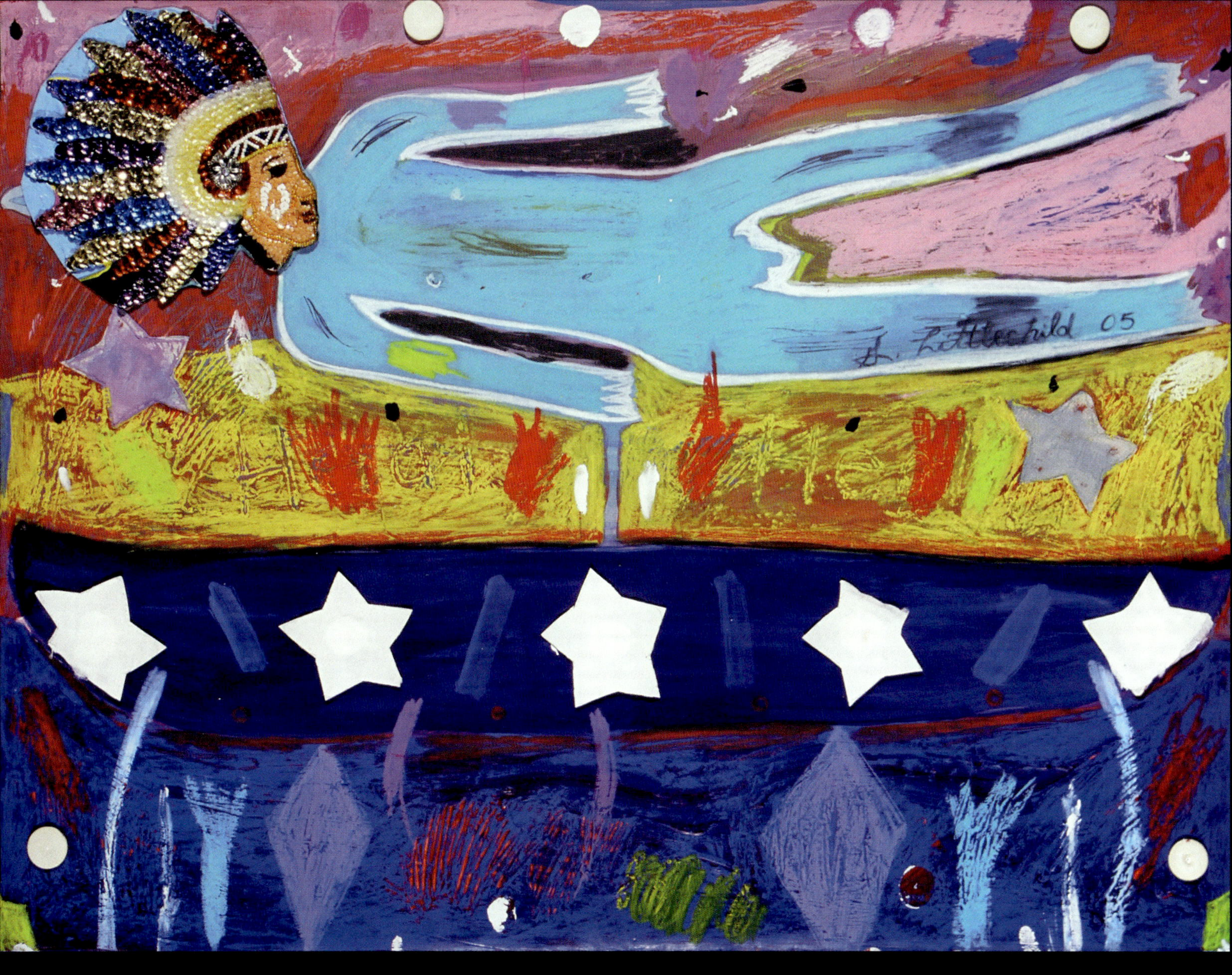

Healing the Spirit Within mixed media :: 22" x 30" :: 2005

A floating man is connected by a thin, mauve line to a blue canoe floating on a stream that carries him on his life's journey. Little red flames activate the pain of his past wounds as he heals the spirit within. "Star, bright star, sacred white, won't you help me on my healing journey?"

I Am Not a Cree Savage

mixed media :: 30" x 22" :: 2006

There is laughter and joy on this Cree man's face. Humility and prowess guide him. Some would say he was a savage. He would say, "I am not a savage."

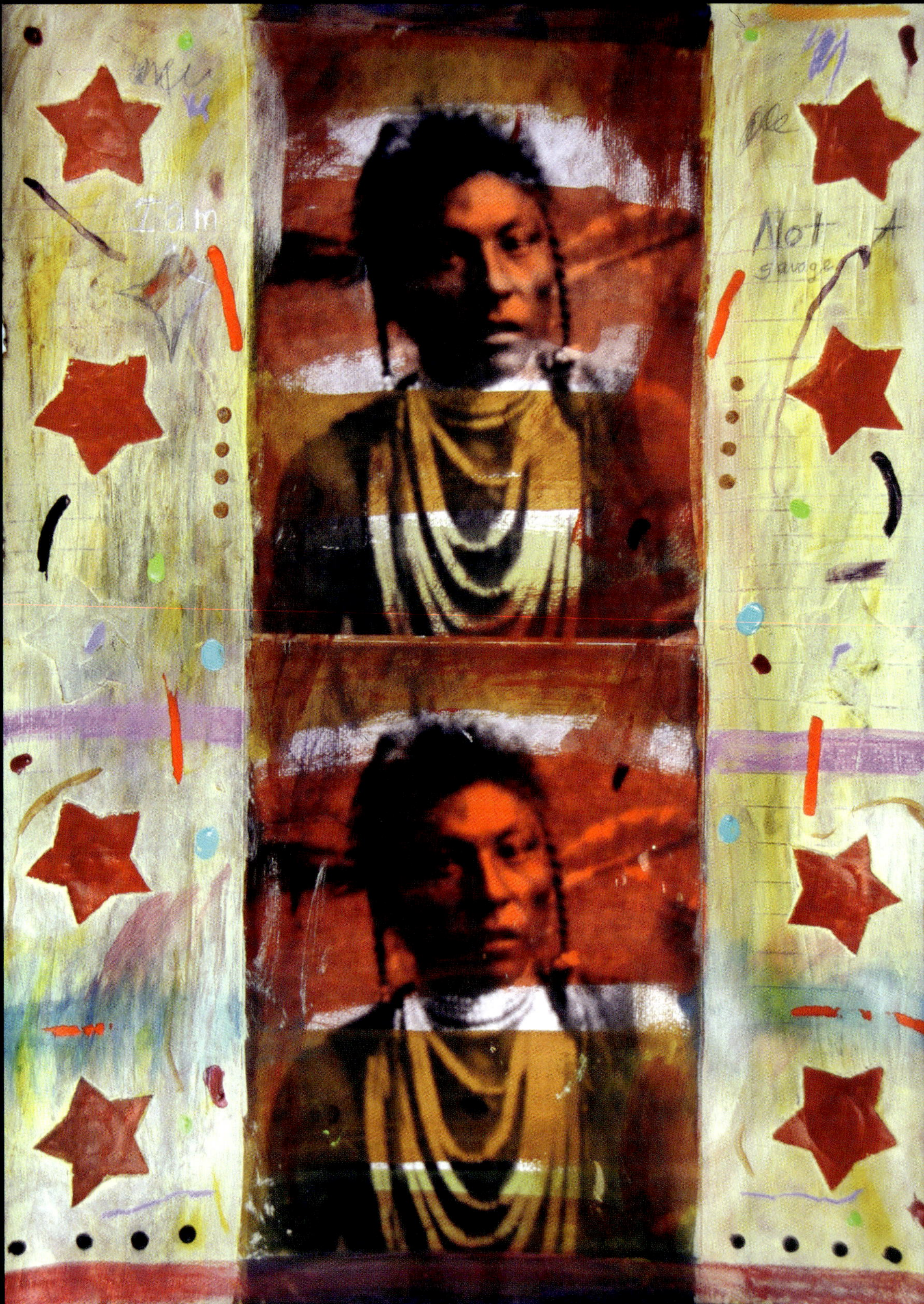

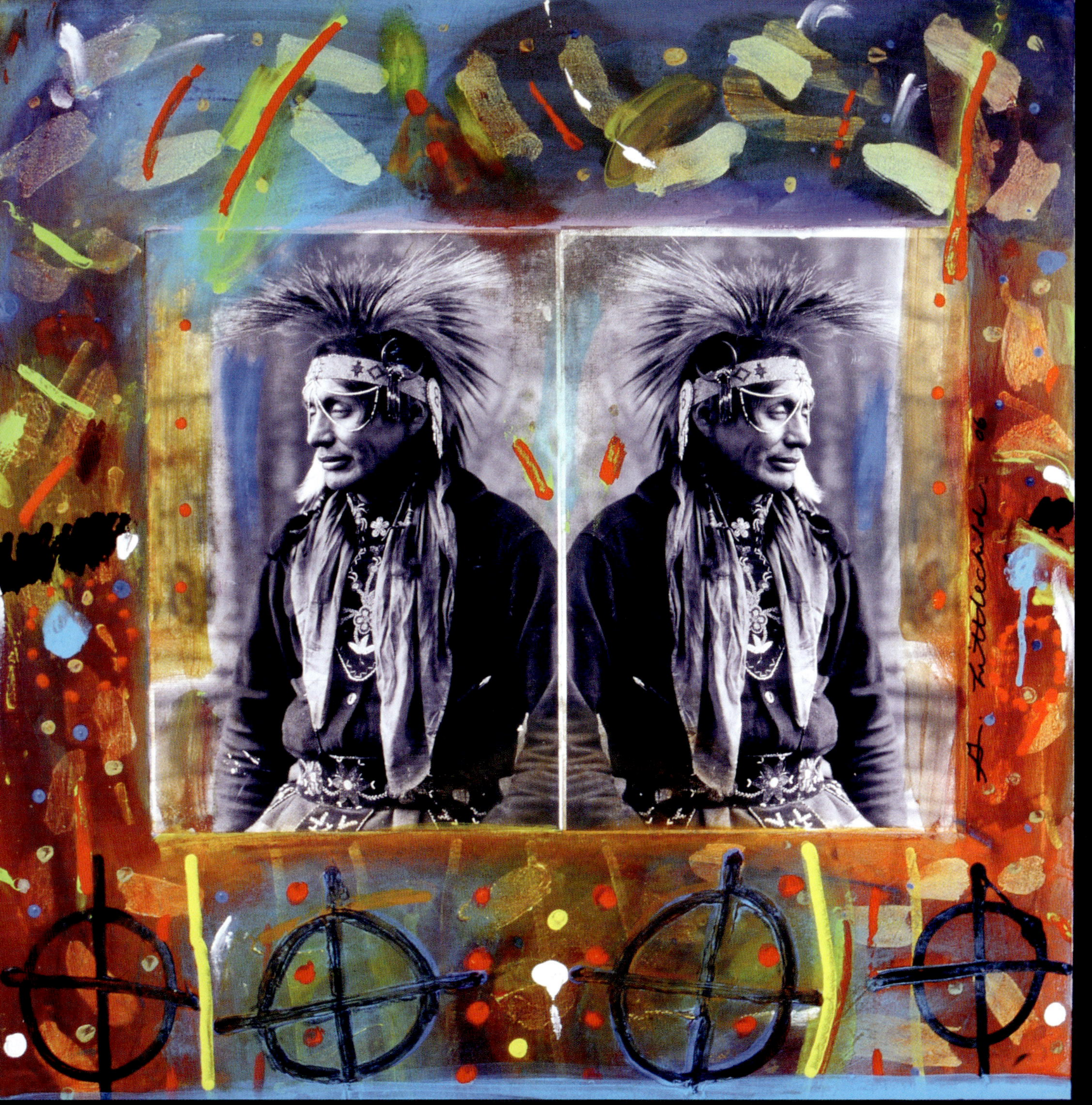

Chicken Dancer mixed media on canvas :: 30" x 30" :: 2006

Antique photography, although nostalgic, creates a portal into the past. It captured events and portraits, like this 1920s Plains Cree dancer from Hobbema, Alberta. Was he dancing at a powwow held in a town next to the reserve, or was he performing in Edmonton and photographed in a professional photographer's studio? His regalia and the roach on his head indicate that he was dancing in the Chicken Dance, which is a prestigious ceremonial dance, highly regarded in the powwow dance order.

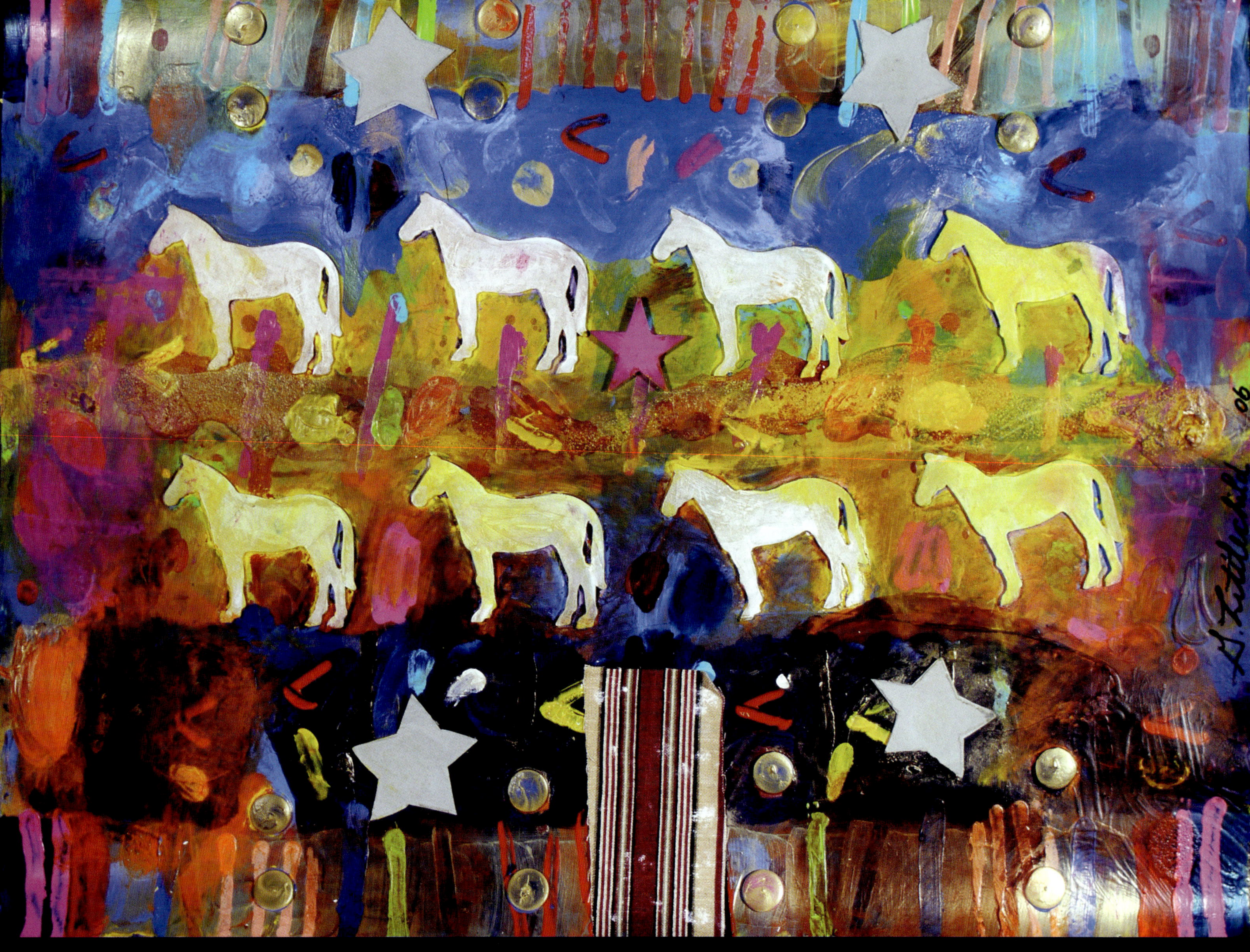

Horse Menagerie mixed media :: 22" x 30" :: 2006

Haihai Mistatim: Horse Spirit. Sacred, special and divine friend, vivid, strong, wild and free. You are always near, present and admired.

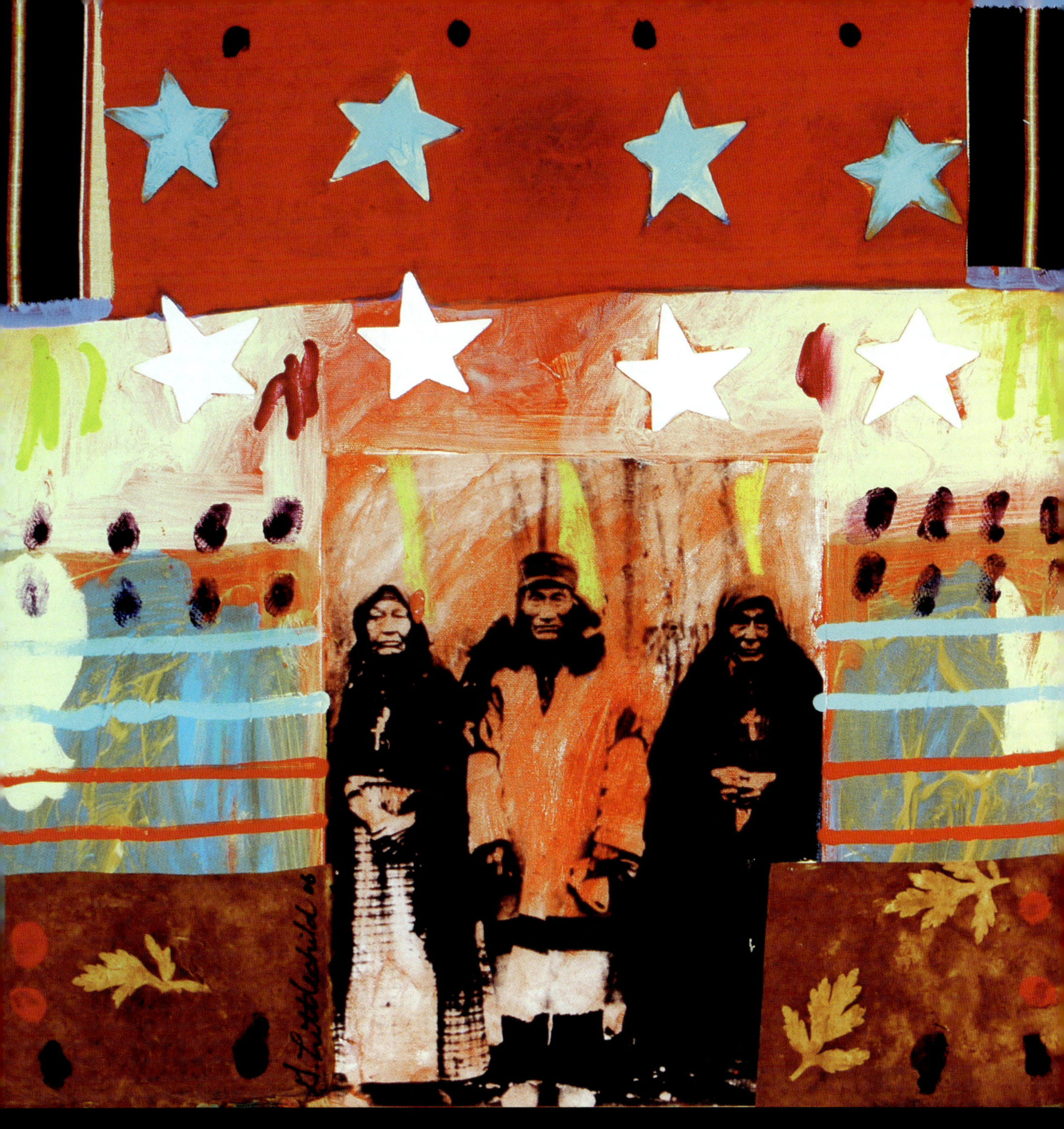

Boreal Forest Songs 1 mixed media on canvas :: 24" x 24" :: 2006

Northern tribes, ancestors of long ago, made a living off the land. Muskrat, mink and moose dwell in the woods. Lavender tea and green mint line the water's edge, and sacred medicines help heal the sick. Northern nations, so strong, you dance to drum beats of your nation's singers, who chant boreal forest songs.

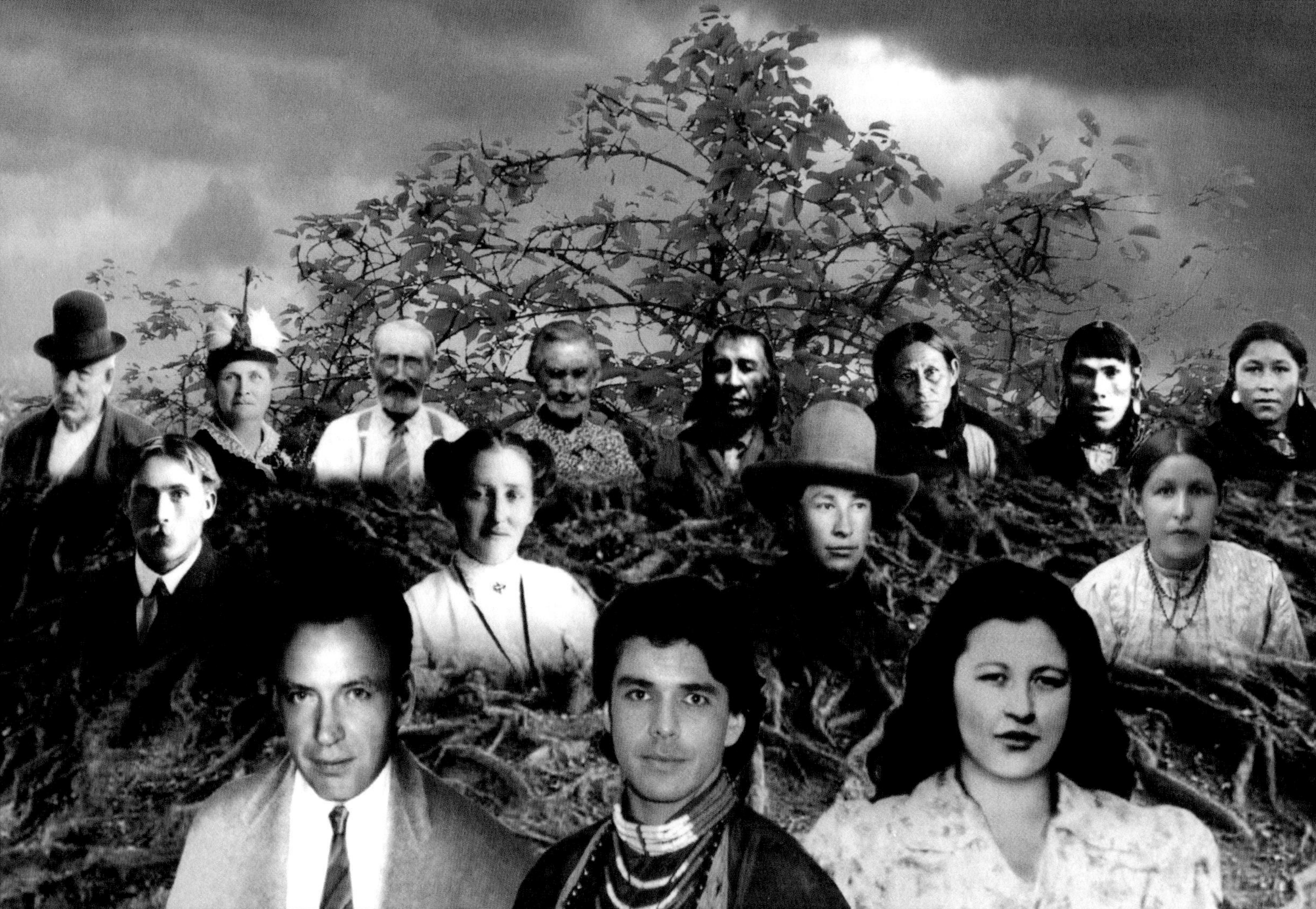

Cross-Cultural Examination: Ancestors and Descendants

archival digital image :: 24" x 36" :: 2007

Ancestral images have inspired me during the course of my career. I feel a connection to my ancestors' lives and the era in which they lived. I try to imagine their experiences, their lives, who they were and what they did. I have been gathering genealogical facts and photographs for many years. I thought it would be interesting to create a piece that shares some of the research and photographs I found. Here are some of my ancestors. I am proud of each and every one. There are four generations represented here, including me. Back row (my great-grandparents), L to R: Clairville Price, Charlotte (Graves) Price, Richard Dunn, Jessie (Armstrong) Dunn, Alexandre Littlechild, Jenny (Cardinal) Littlechild, Antoine Bruno, Peggy (Louis Natuasis) Bull. Middle row (my grandparents), L to R: John MacKenzie Price, Sarah Jane (Dunn) Price, Edward Littlechild, Bella (Bull) Littlechild. Front row (my parents and me): James E. Price, me, Rachel (Littlechild) Price.

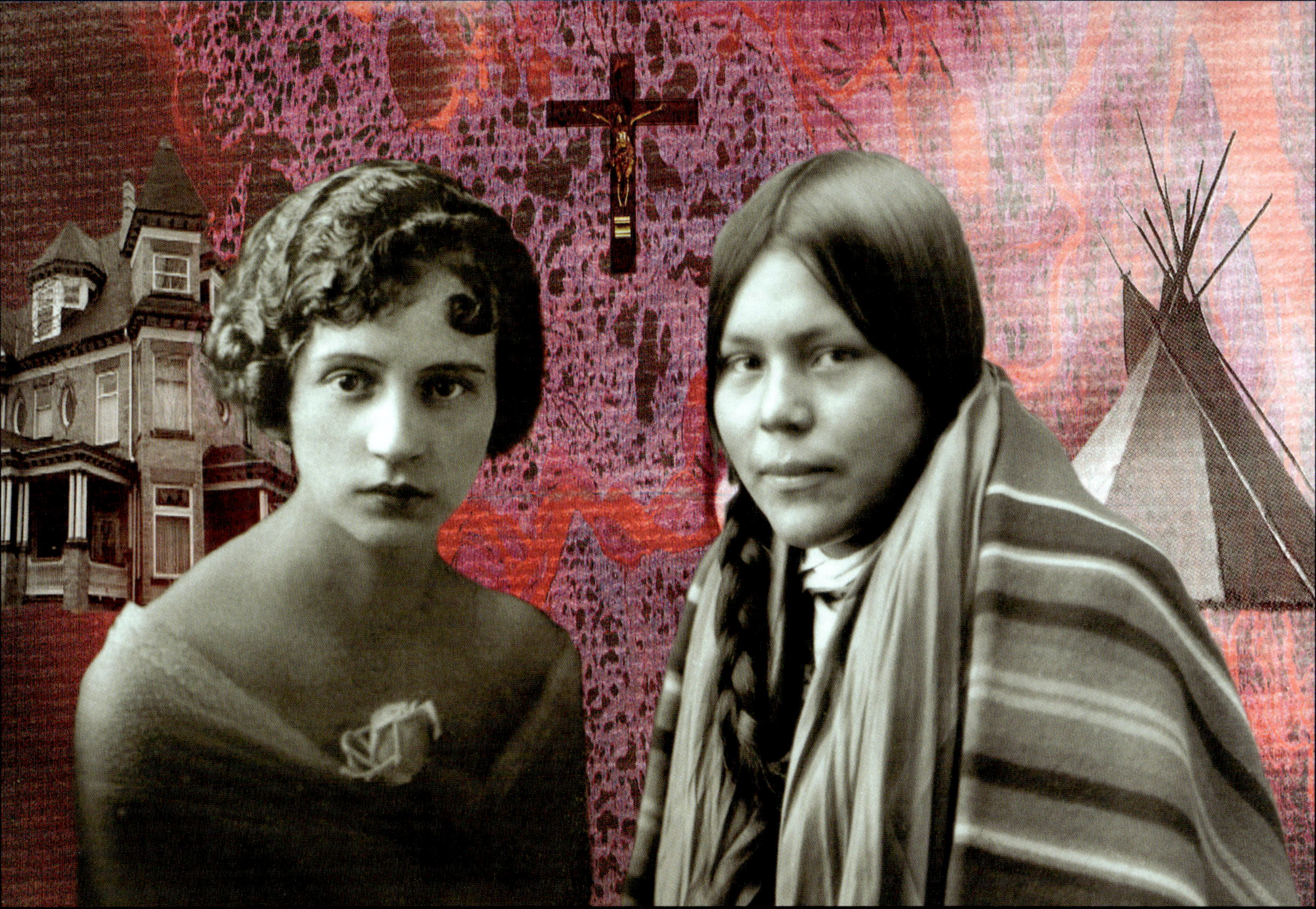

Cross-Cultural Examination: The Meeting

archival digital image/mixed media :: 24" x 36" :: 2007

Two women, two cultures. Both beautiful, poised within their own nations, meeting in modern-day digital artwork. Grace Marston of Los Angeles, California, is on the left, and Eva Cutknife of Hobbema, Alberta, is on the right. Would these two women have ever met? Probably not. If they had met, would they have talked, or judged each other because of race and language? Or perhaps they would have giggled over a nice cup of tea? Grace is the first cousin of my paternal grandfather, John MacKenzie Price, and Eva is a descendant of the famed chief Big Bear.

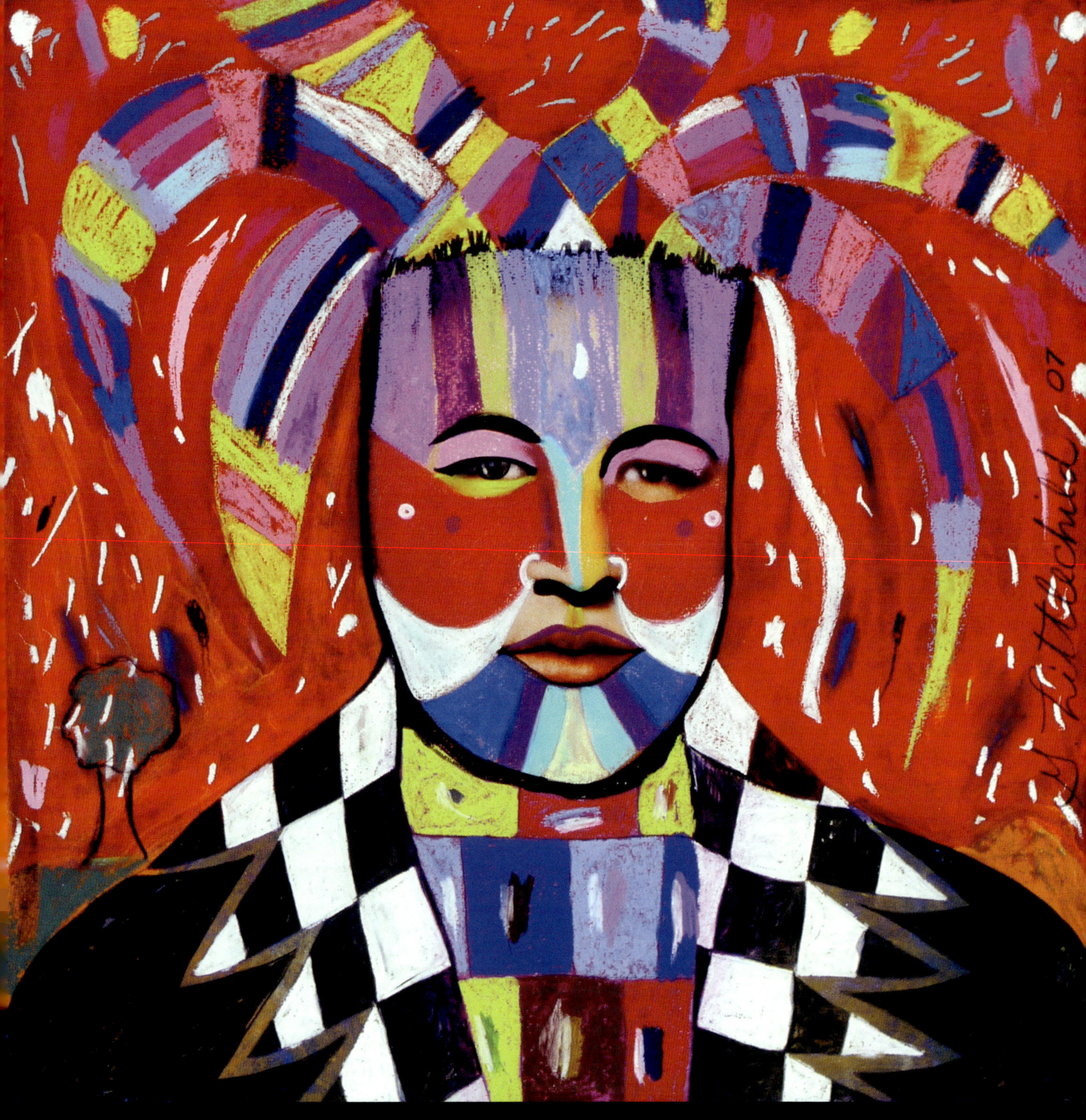

Tricksters mixed media :: 24" x 24" :: 2007

In First Nations culture, tricksters have always been important. Stories about feats and challenges, sometimes fantastical, are used to teach lessons. In the Cree culture, we have Wesakechak, the benevolent hero. He is a trickster character and his adventures are often humorous.

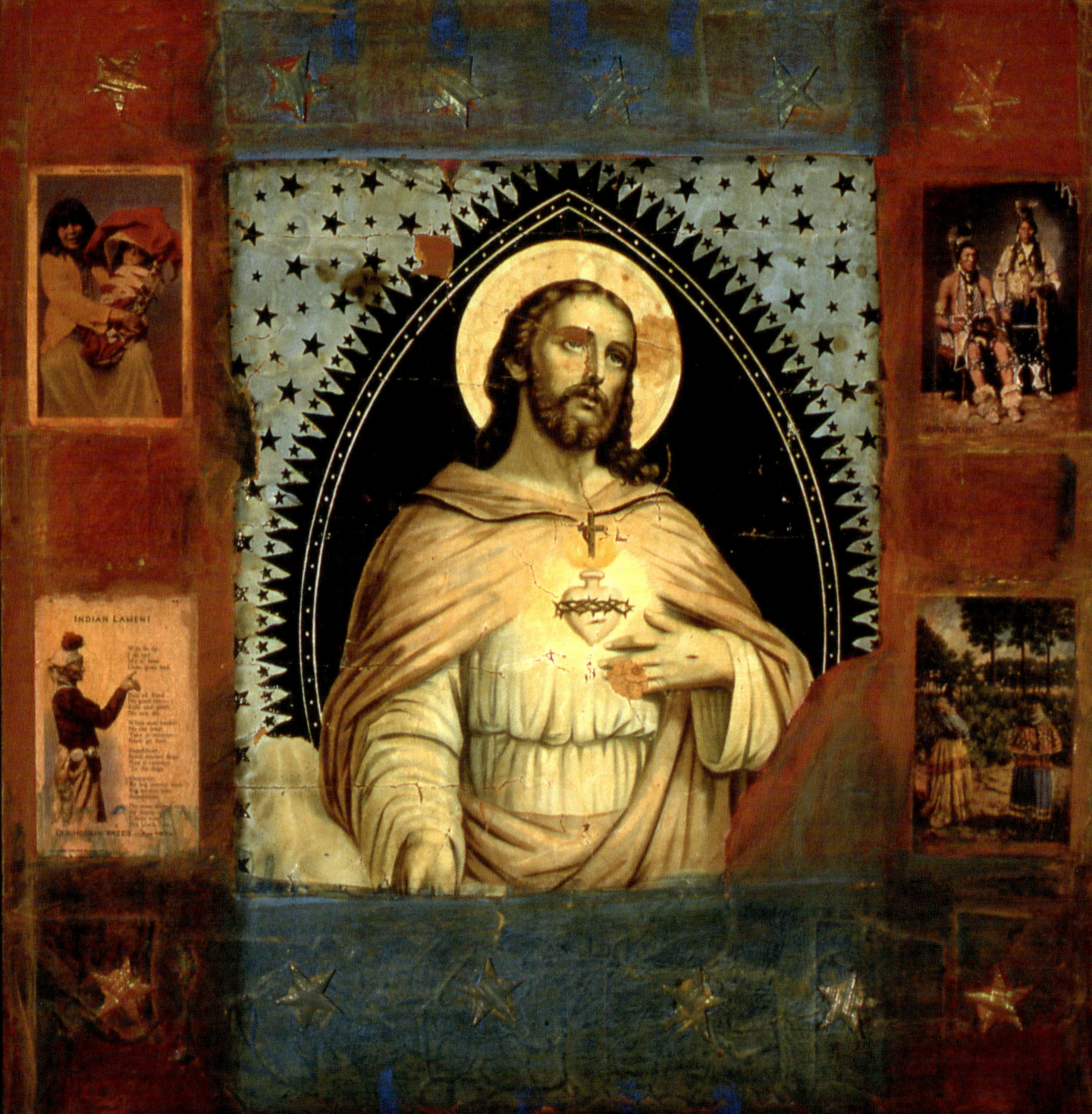

Sacrifice mixed media on canvas :: 24" x 24" :: 2007

Years ago, I found this beautiful painting of Jesus in an old, abandoned church in Saskatchewan. I stashed it away for years, along with other finds. Eventually it found its way into this painting, surrounded by antique postcards of Native Americans. I asked myself who sacrificed the most: Jesus or the indigenous peoples who suffered greatly at the hands of those who imposed religious beliefs upon them? Millions perished. Enslavement, reserve systems, residential schools and the Sixties Scoop all created huge sacrifice and loss. We are still healing.

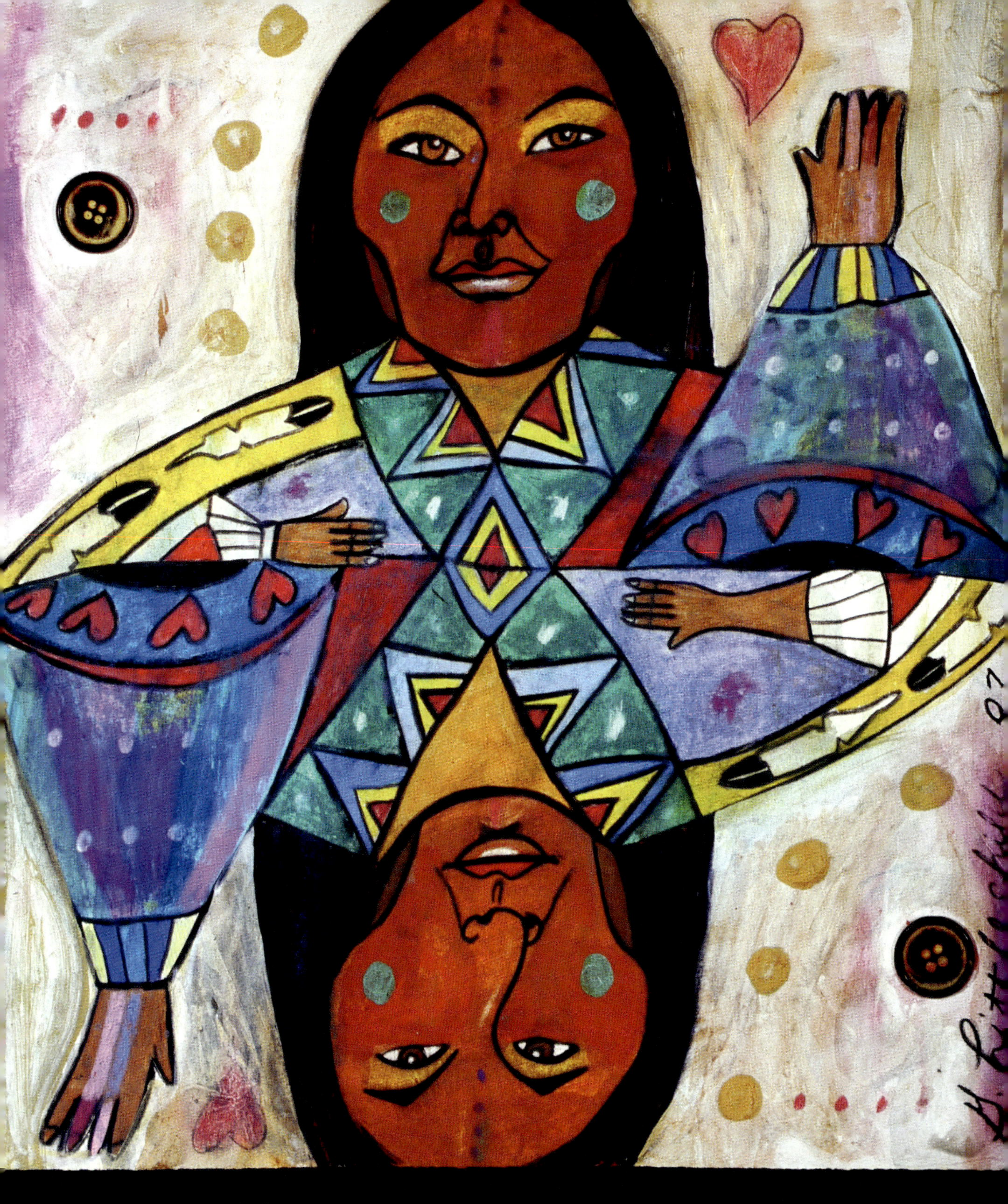

Chief of Hearts mixed media :: 16" x 14" :: 2007

I love the balance of the mirror images on playing cards. In this painting, there are two chiefs who are the same, but not the same. They are here to help and to lead the Nation, but sometimes that is not the case

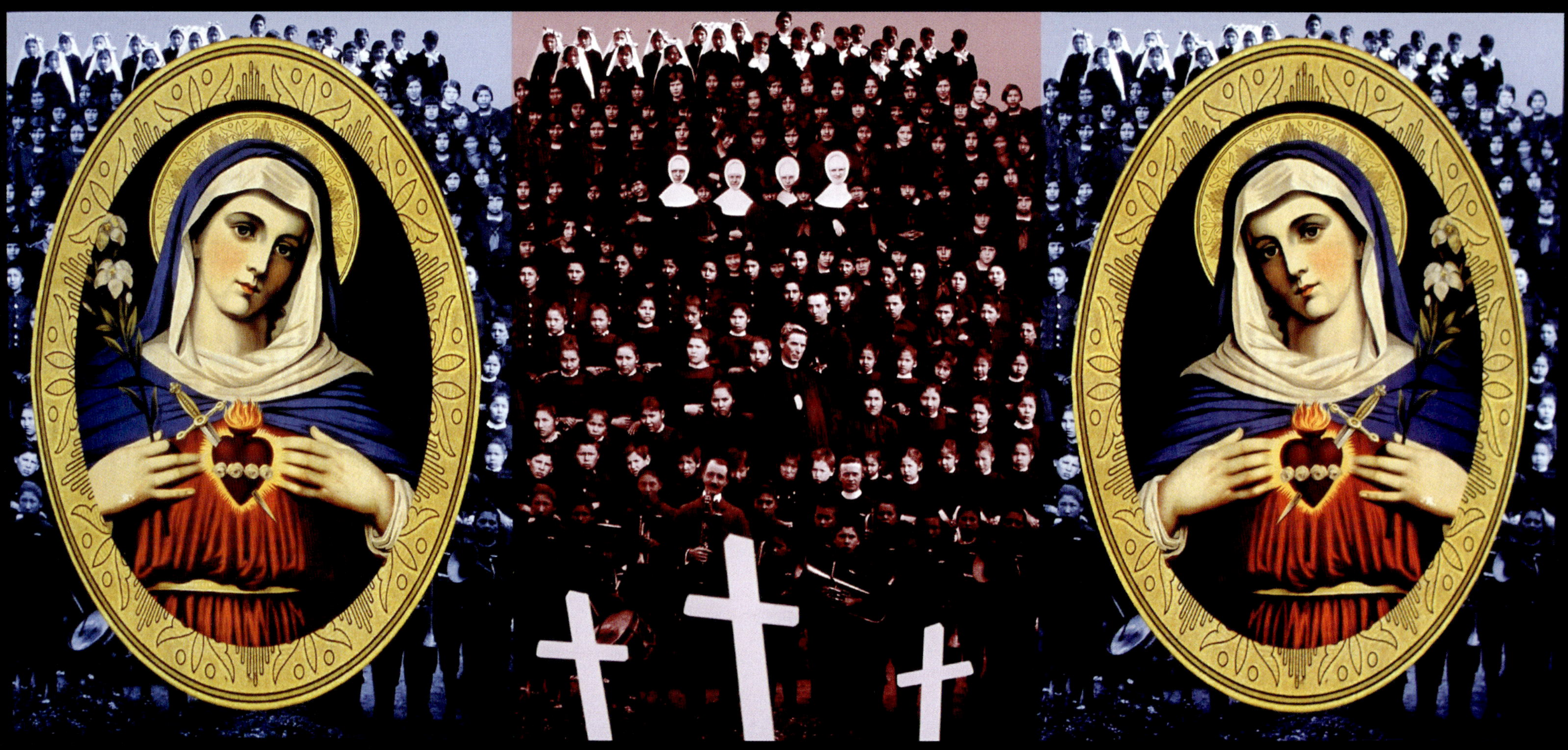

Ermineskin Residential School, Students, Priests, Nuns and the Virgin Mary

archival digital image :: 29.5" x 64" :: 2007

Hundreds of photos depict the students of the Ermineskin Indian Residential School. An Oblate brother named Gilbert took many of them; in fact, he had a little studio at the school. Elders tell me he used to say, "I'll make you look good." There are photos of my grandparents, my mother, her siblings, her cousins and extended family, and others in rows and rows, with priests and nuns. These are haunting images, telling of an era that robbed so many of their true identities and connections to their families, language and communities. These children did not get to experience their coming-of-age rites and ceremonies and learn from the Elders of their tribe—such a sad, sad era. My grandparents, the late Edward and Bella (Bull) Littlechild, are students in this photograph. The three crosses represent the crucifixion, and the flipped images of Mother Mary create a stage on which to tell a story. Did religion almost destroy a people?

What Was

archival digital image :: 36" x 24" :: 2007

My mother was born Ragene Rachel Littlechild, but she used her middle name, Rachel. Here she is in 1947 at age 18, two years after graduating from the Ermineskin Indian Residential School in Hobbema. She arrived at the school at the age of nine and spent seven years there. This affected all aspects of her life, mostly in negative ways: loss of culture, disconnection from her family and poor self-esteem.

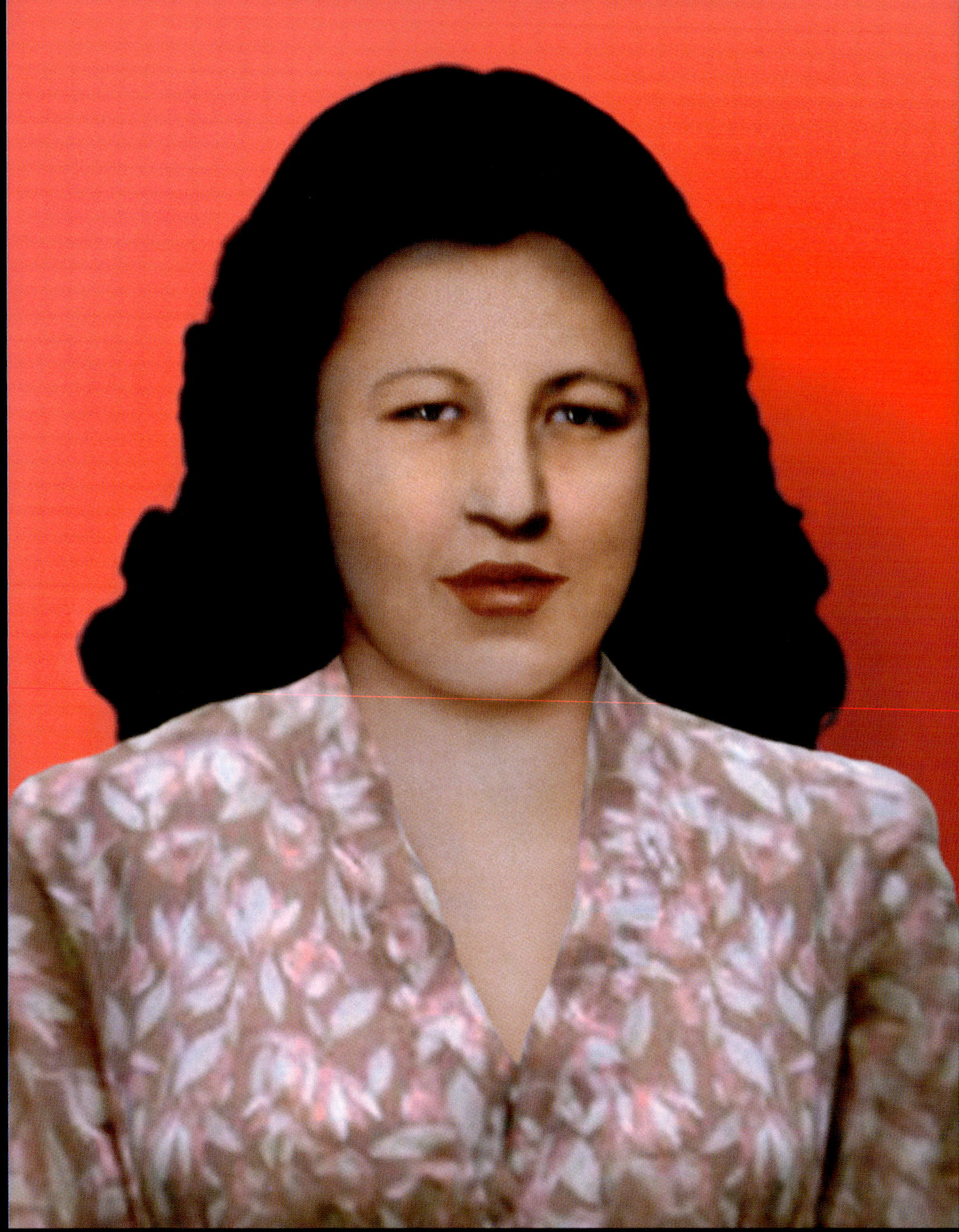

Mother
Rachel Littlechild, age 18, 1947,
two years after graduation from
the Ermineskin Indian Residential
School Hobbema, Alberta

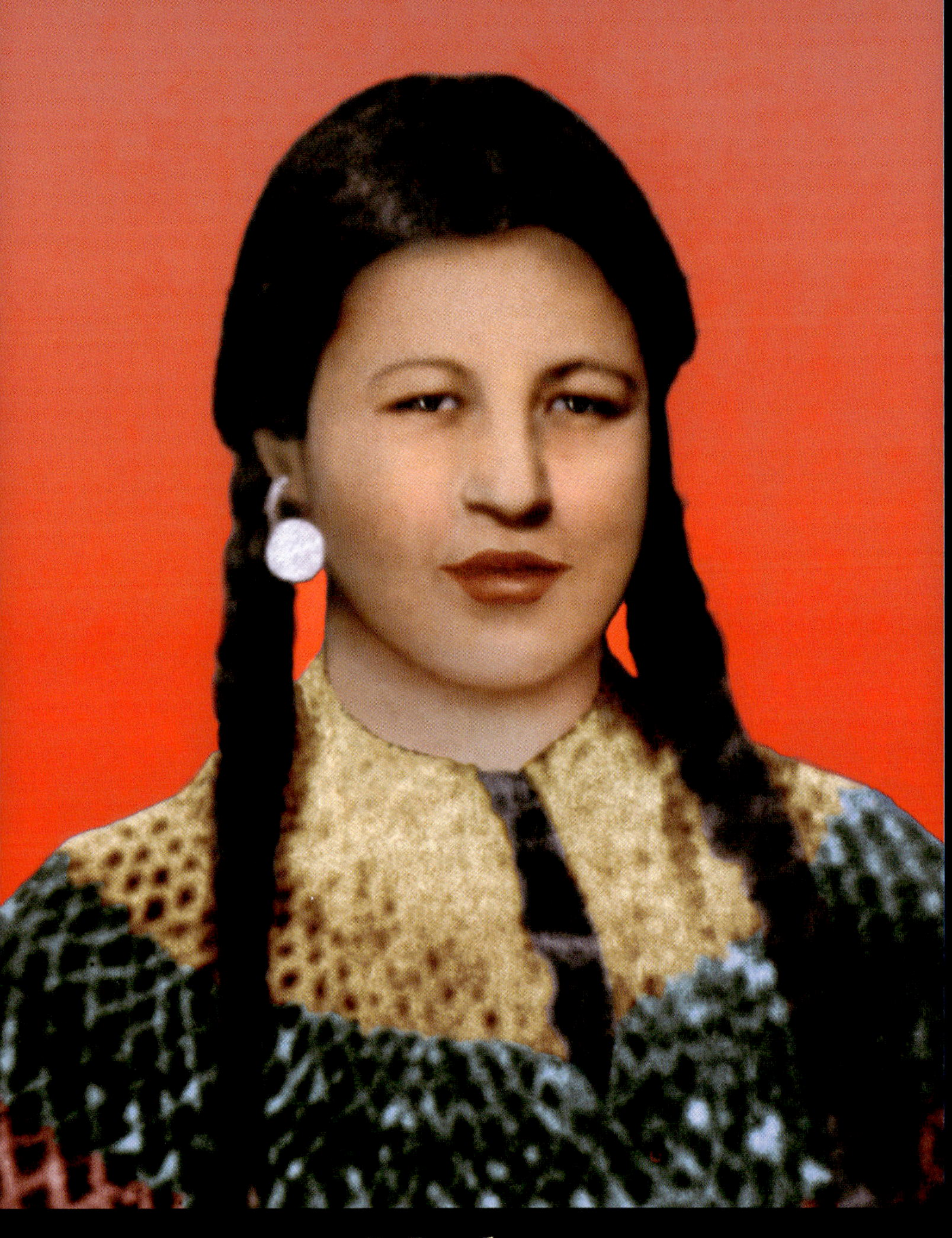

Mother
Rachel Littlechild, age 18, 1947.
Clothed in traditional attire she would have worn had she not attended Indian residential school.

What Could Have Been

archival digital image :: 36" x 24" :: 2007

The statement below this piece says it all. Had Mother not attended the residential school, she may not have died so tragically and young, and her five children would not have been raised in foster care or adopted.

First Nations Joe

archival digital image
29" x 21" :: 2007

When I was a kid, people would often refer to First Nations men as "Indian Joe on TV." Thus, I used *First Nations Joe* as the title of this piece for which I photographed a Skookum Doll. These dolls came in sets, a man, woman and child. All of their eyes looked away. Did the designers who made the dolls think Indians were shifty, or had they met Indians who always averted their eyes, which was done out of respect in some tribes?

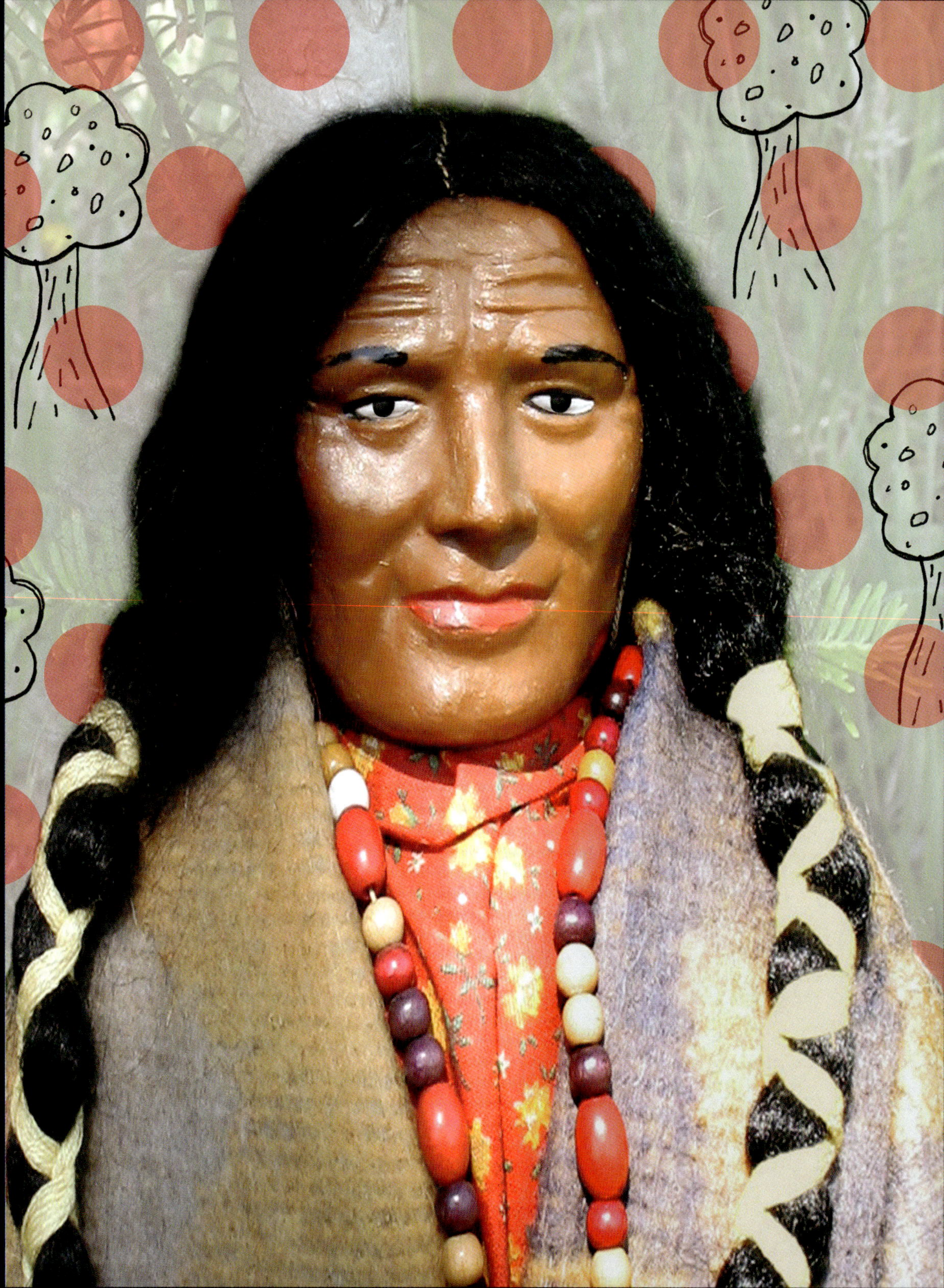

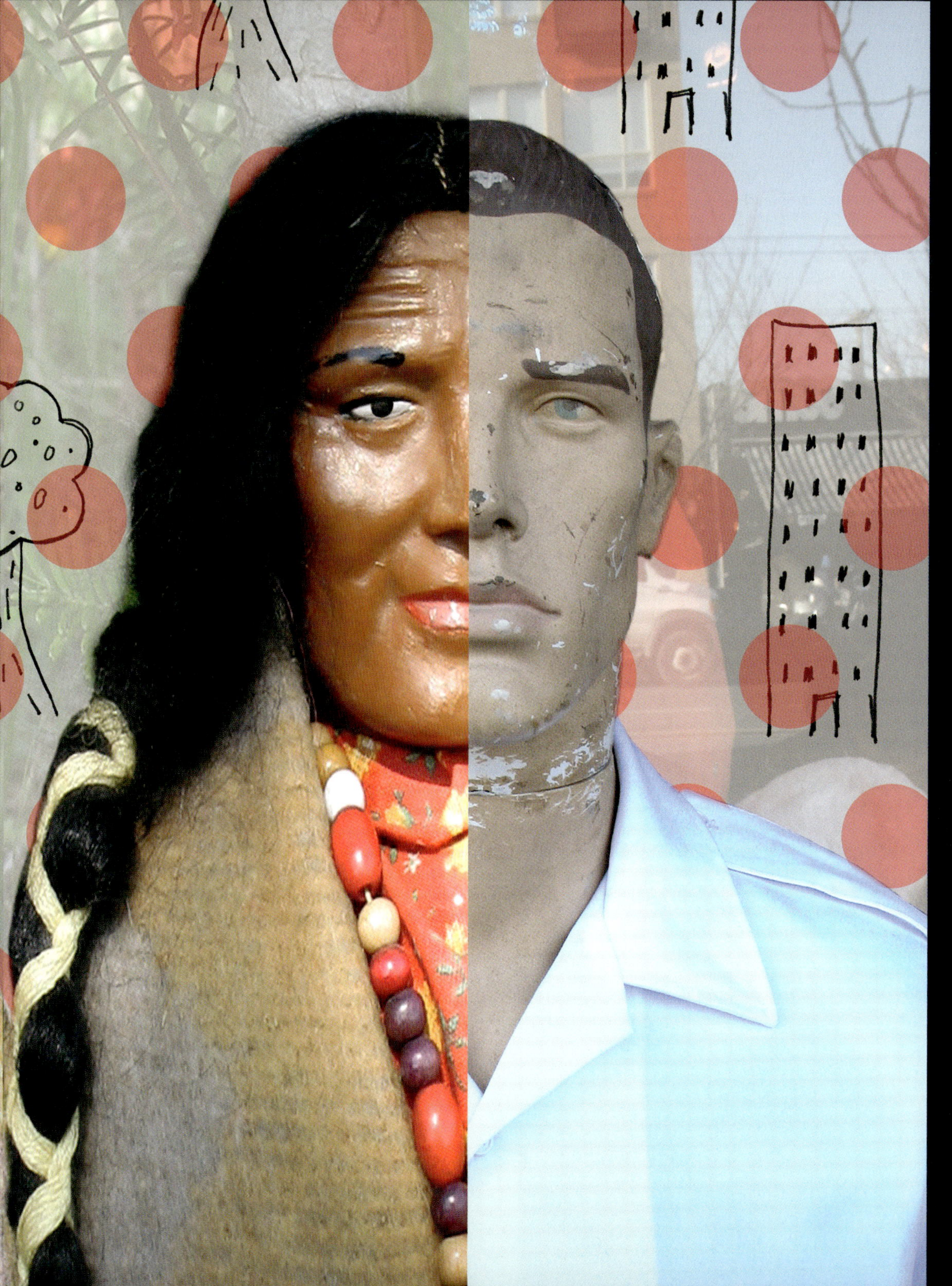

Mixed-Blood Joe

archival digital image
29" x 21" :: 2007

The mannequin wears a crisp white shirt; his lips, nose and neck blend together—the two halves, the blending of two nations.

Second Nations Joe

archival digital image
29″ x 24″ :: 2007

If the Government of Canada refers to its First Peoples as First Nations, what does that make the people who came here to settle? Second Nations? Drawn buildings and a photograph of a city scene are the backdrop for *Second Nations Joe*. Settlers dreaming of a new beginning came by the thousands, reshaping the traditional territories of the First Nations of Canada. We are still learning about each other and the ways of other peoples who come from all over the world.

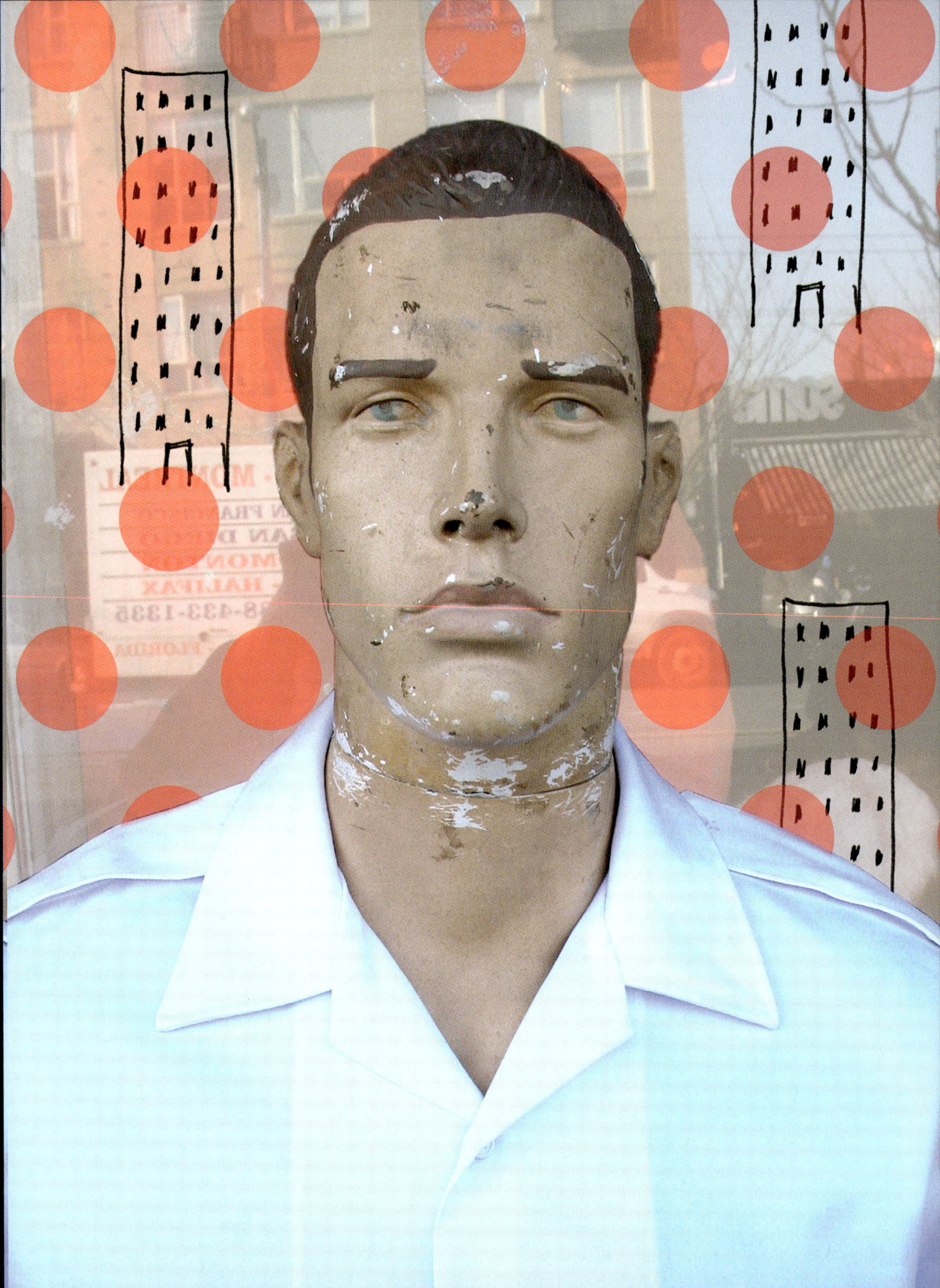

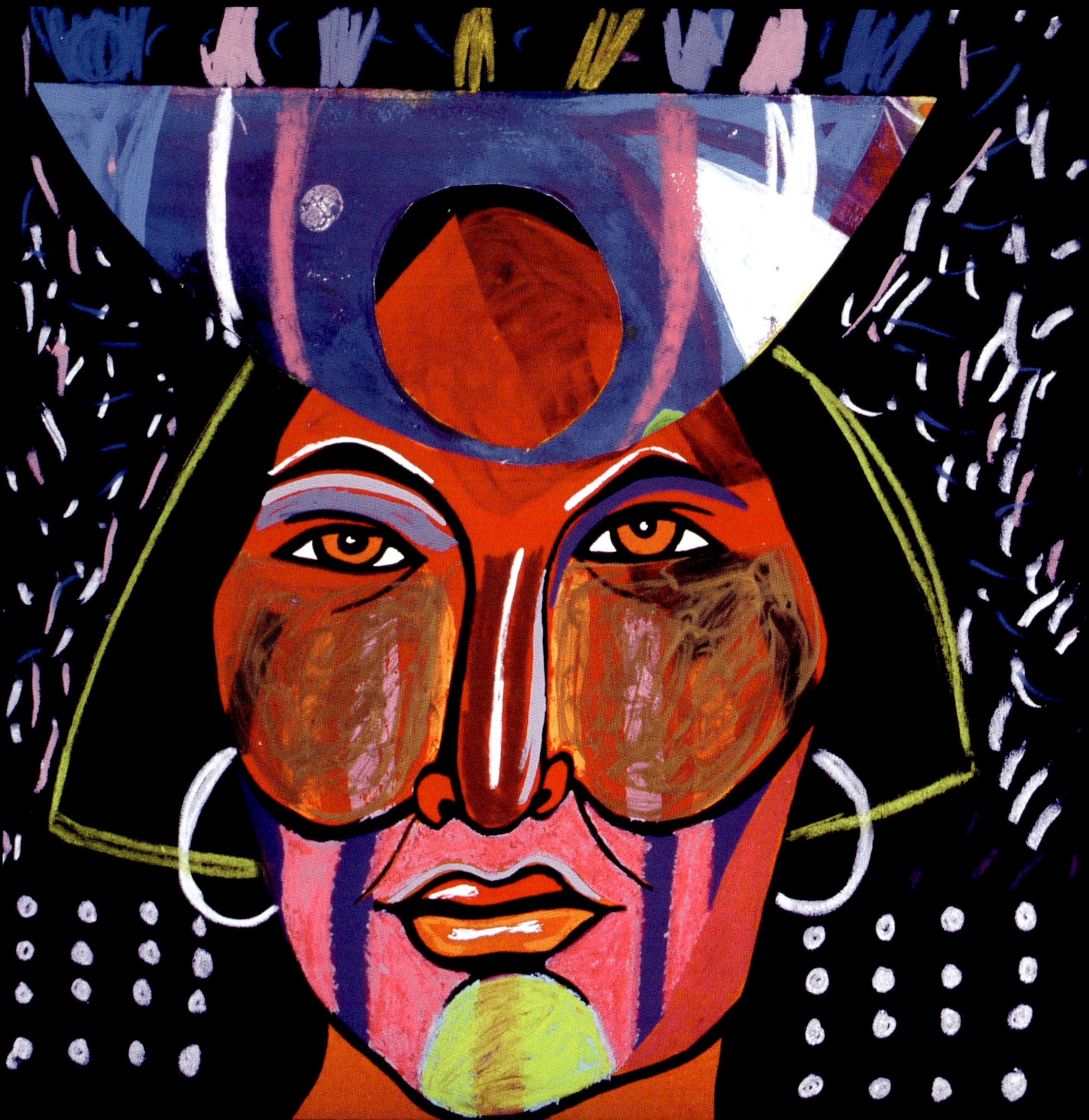

Plains Cree Oracle 1 mixed media :: 30″ x 30″ :: 2008

Those who have the ability to see and know about people's lives and the future existed (and still do exist) in all tribes and races. They were born with these gifts and acted as advisors to their people. These people played an important role and their counsel was relied on in personal affairs and warfare.

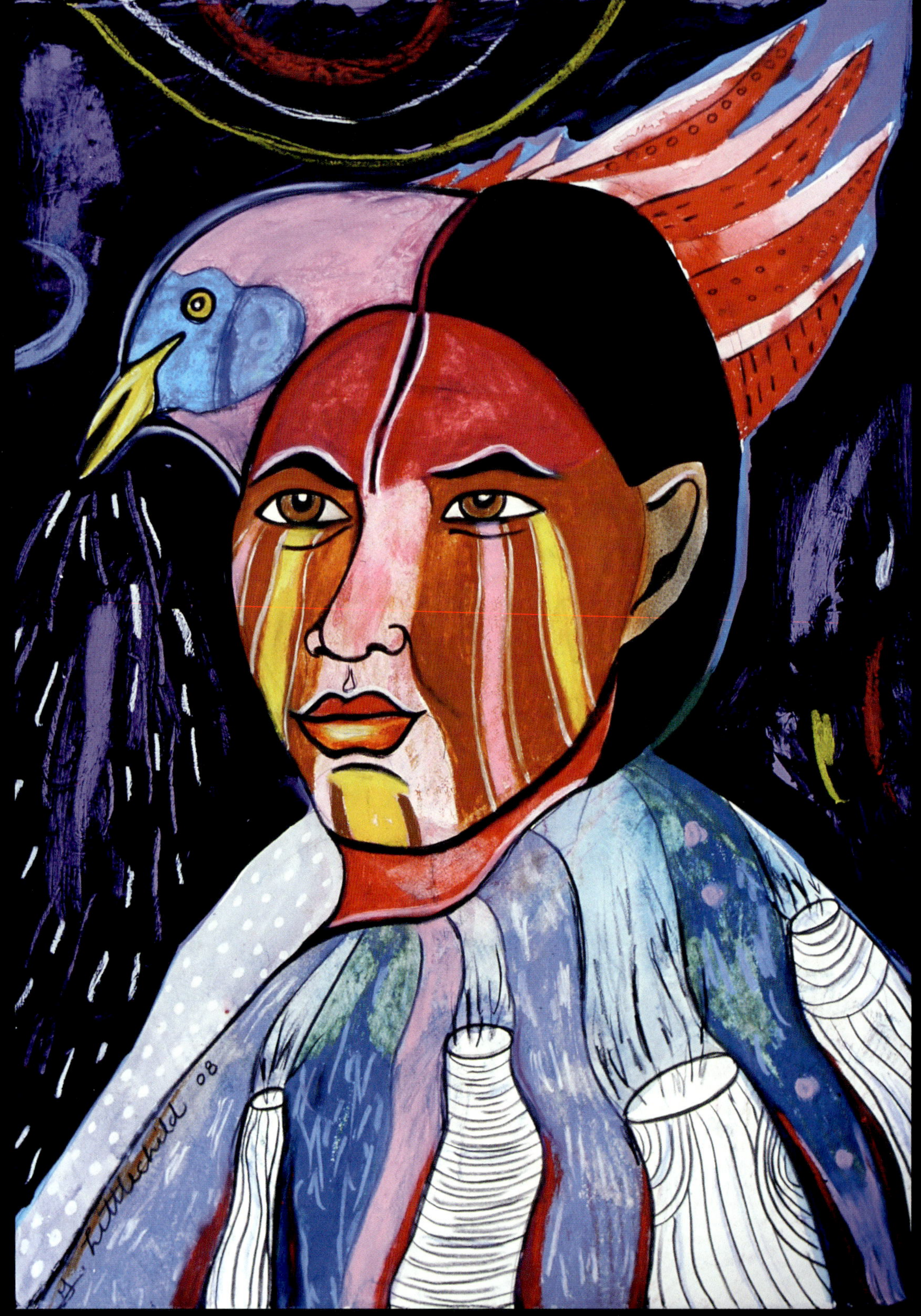

A Feeling Came over the Forest

mixed media :: 22.5" x 16.25" :: 2008

A loud, sharp noise came over the forest. Large, thick trees fell to the ground. Thuds were heard for miles around as forest creatures ran. Grizzly bear, brown bear, elk and deer fled to safer grounds. Aromas of freshly disturbed forest canopy, flora and earth rose up in dust particles. Homes, nests, places of safety were lost as greed took away natural, undisturbed habitat. Mother Nature, wearing a bird headdress, looks at the tree stumps in dismay.

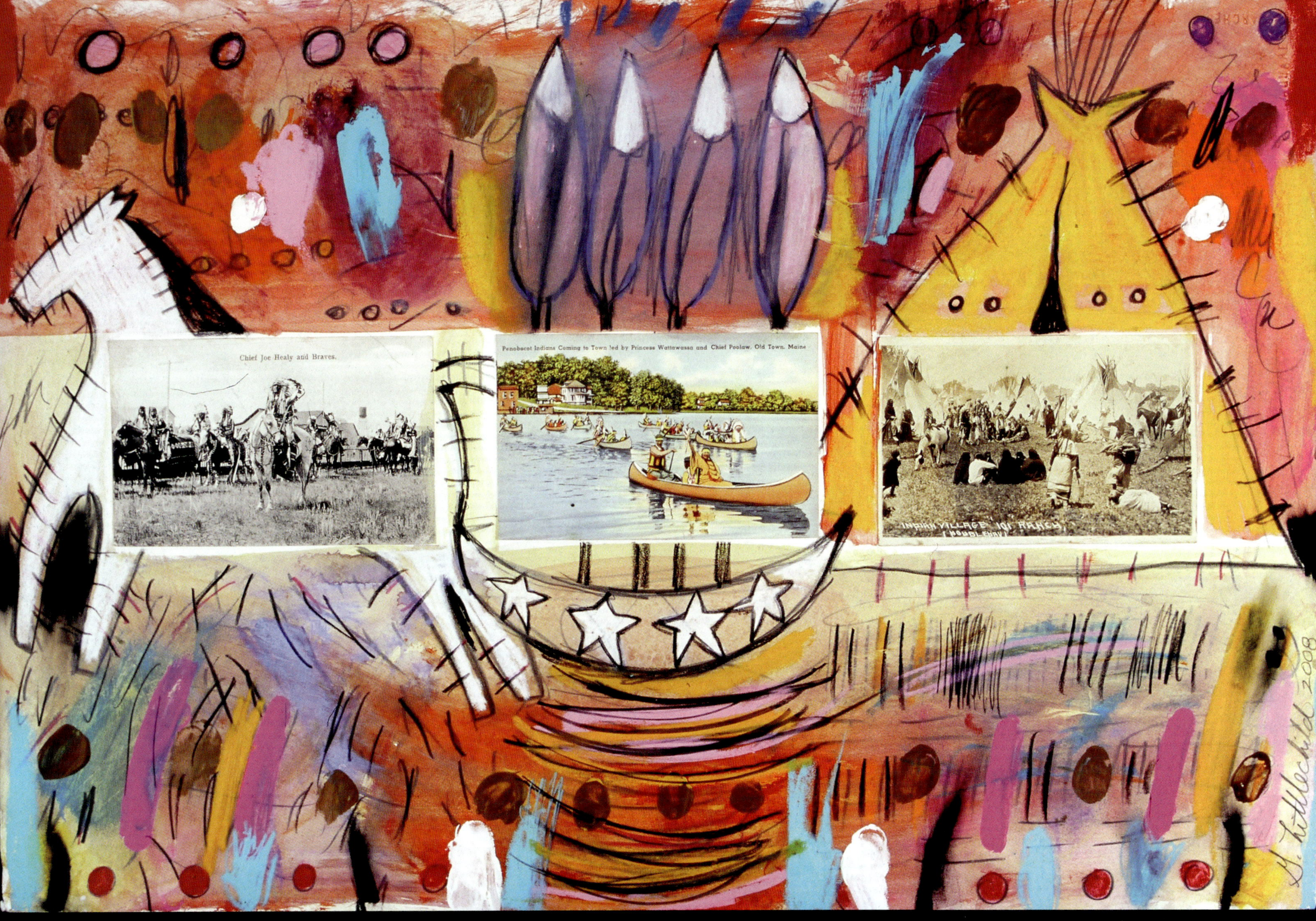

Chief, Canoe, Indian Village mixed media :: 15" x 22.5" :: 2008

Did the scenes depicted in antique postcards create stereotypes or did they capture moments in time? I believe they did both. Photographers entered situations and captured the moment. Their photos, transformed into postcards, were sent around the world, informing people about cultures of which they had little or no awareness. In 2012, people who have never met First Nations people still have these images in their mind's eye and believe we still live like this, frozen in time.

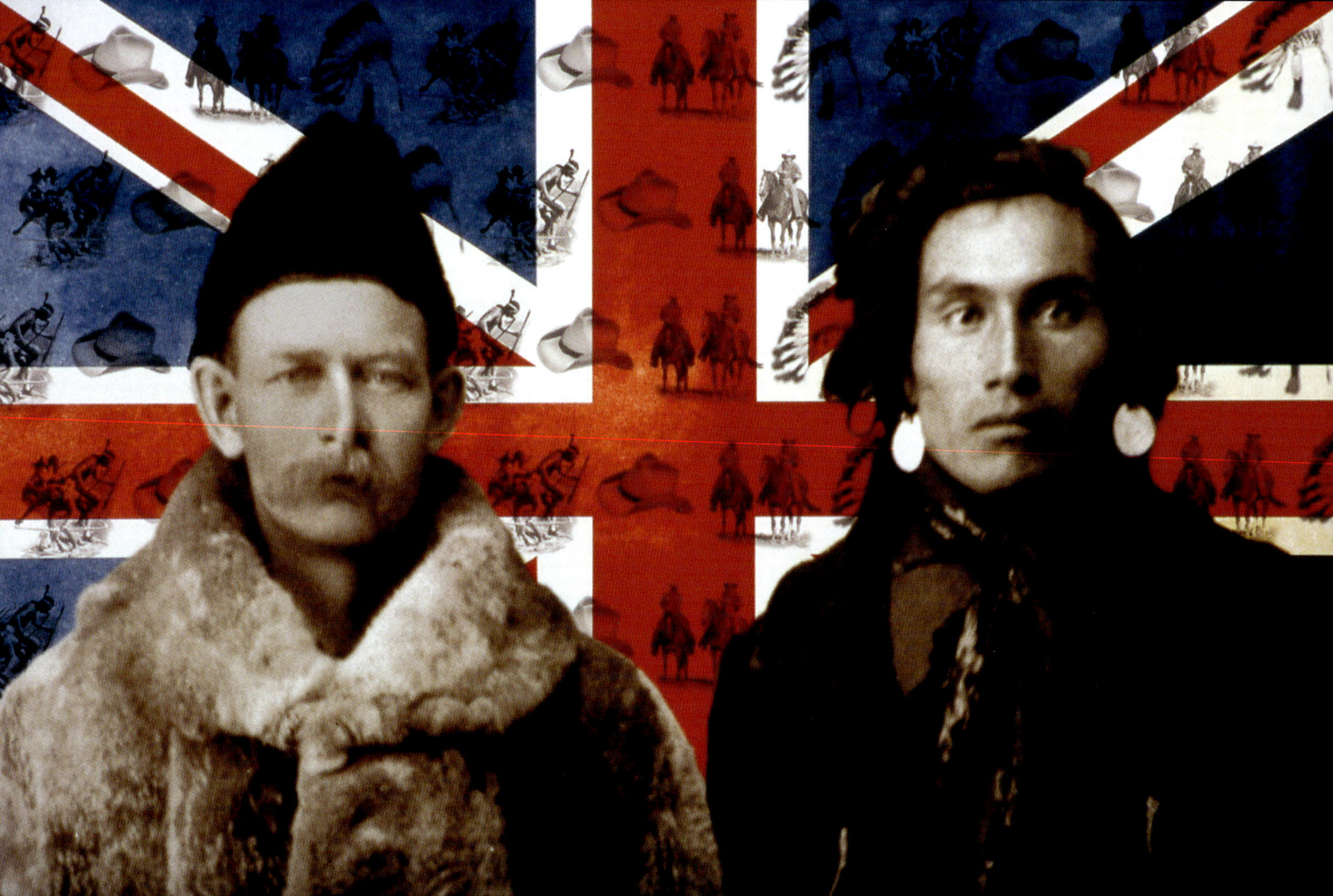

Cross-Cultural Examination: E.E. Chandler and Headman Louis Natuasis

archival digital image :: 24" x 36" :: 2008

My great-great-grandfather Louis Natuasis was a headman for Chief Joe Samson of the Samson reserve in Hobbema. E.E. Chandler was the overseer (mayor) of Wetaskiwin, Alberta. These two men were photographed in the Brown Photographic Studio in Wetaskiwin in 1898. Why were they photographed together? Because of their positions in life, or was the photographer intrigued by their differences? It must have been winter as Mr. Chandler is wearing a buffalo coat. My ancestor Louis had striking good looks. With his black long braids and shell earrings, he was so Cree, so handsome and a great ambassador for his people. I am proud and honoured to descend from this great man.

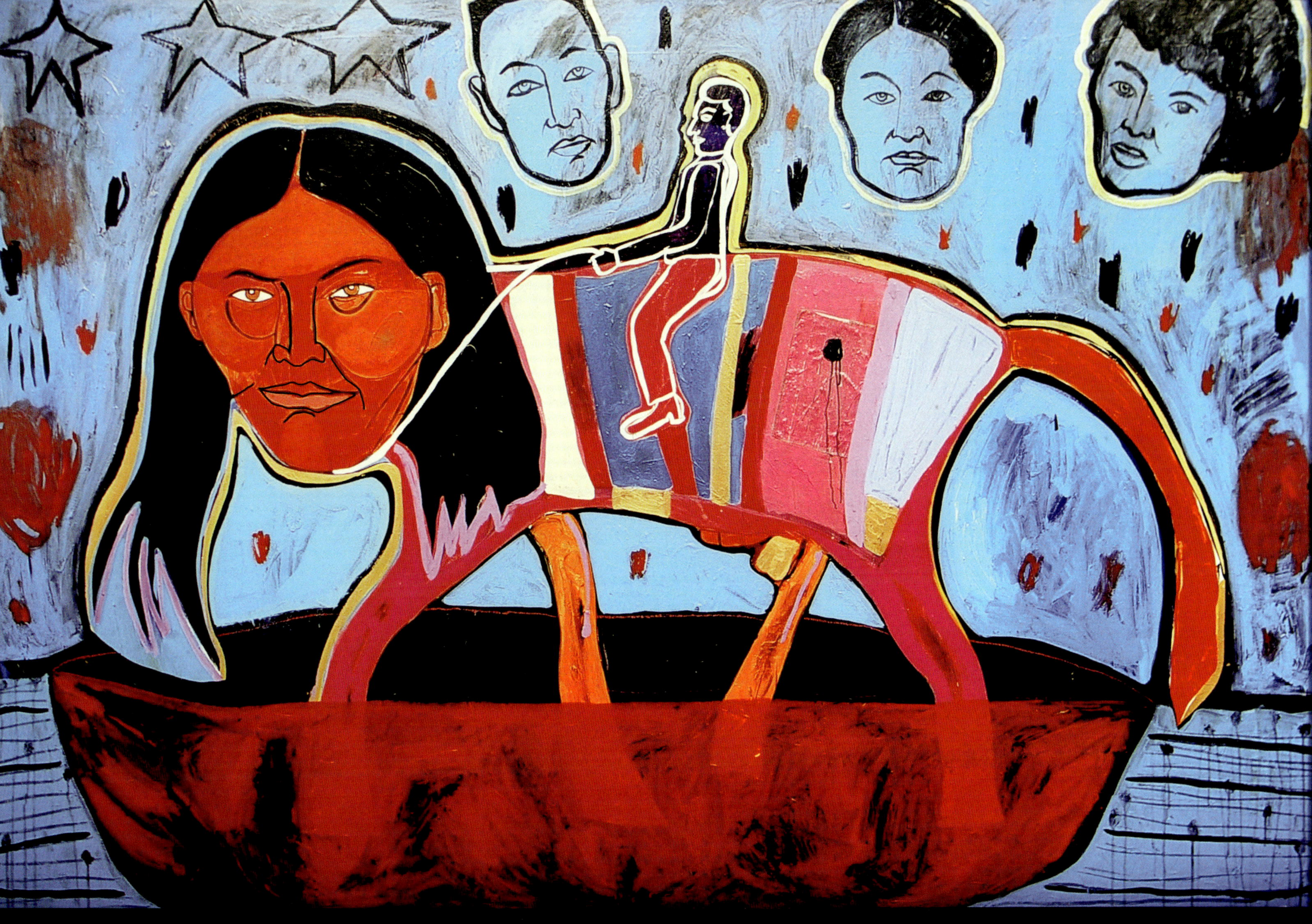

The Oppressed and the Oppressor mixed media :: 5' x 7' :: 1998, 2008

A white figure holds back a First Nations man transforming into an animal spirit. He sits on the anamorphic body with a noose in hand. He restrains, controls and censors the First Nations language. In the sky, First Nations ancestors look down, watching the drama unfold, knowing their teachings will one day overcome the restraints and limitations the First Nations' man endures. I first painted this piece in 1998 and reworked it in 2008.

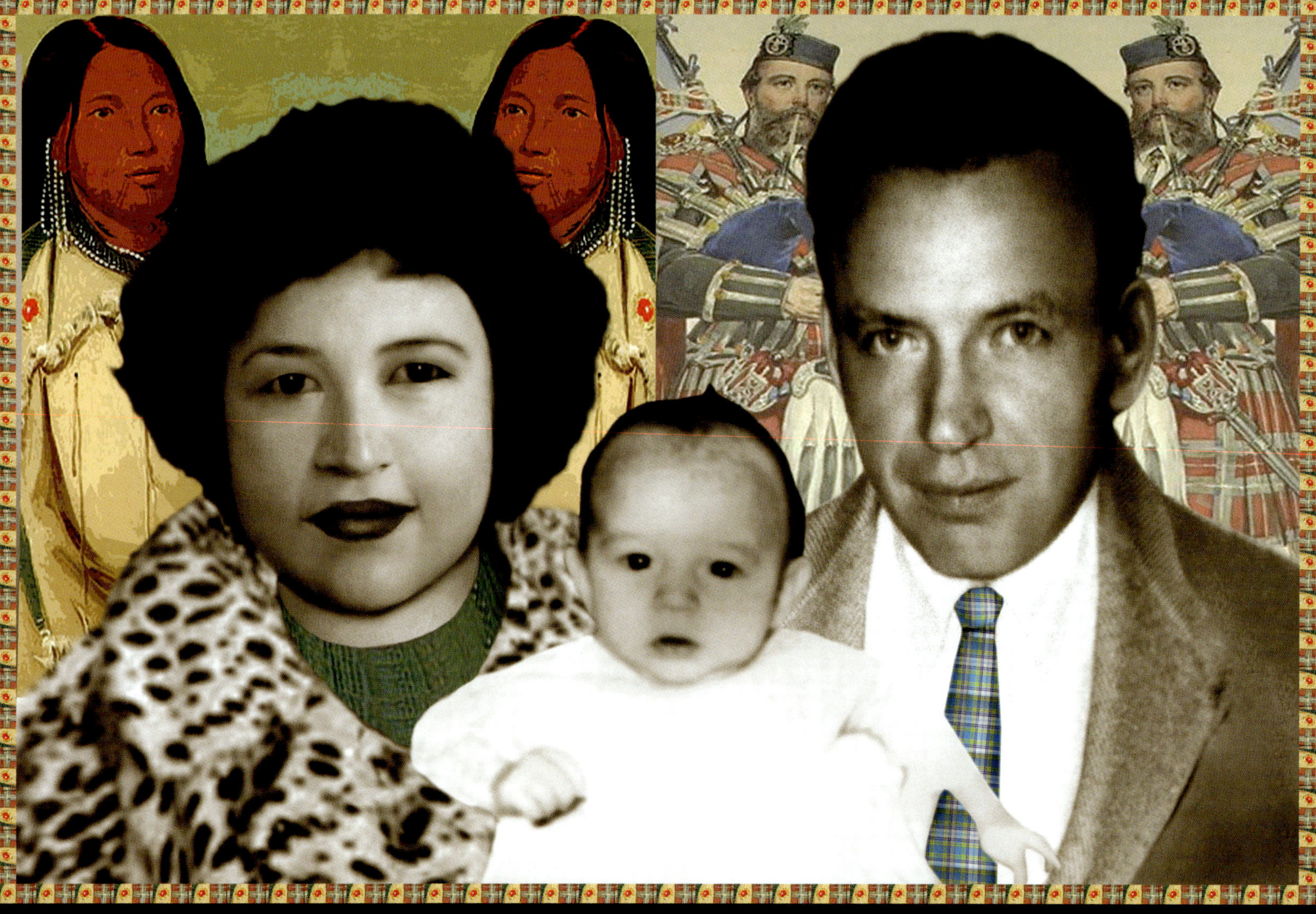

A Mixed-Race Couple and Their Child archival digital image :: 24" x 36" :: 2008

In the '50s, many people would have taken note of a mixed-race couple, one person First Nations and the other white. My parents were that couple! James Ernest Price was Celtic—a mix of Irish and Scottish. His people came from Scotland and the United States and made their home in New Brunswick. His ancestors were Dunn, Irving, Armstrong, Stitt, Graves, Mills, MacKenzie and Price. The Price family have lived in Canada since 1767 when Edmund and Jane (Webb) Price relocated from Woodbridge, New Jersey. They had 22 children and many more descendants. My mother's ancestors were Plains Cree of Alberta. She was of Saulteaux blood, which is a French name given to the Plains Anishinabe people, known as Ojibways. I am the baby, four months old. This photo was taken in Edmonton.

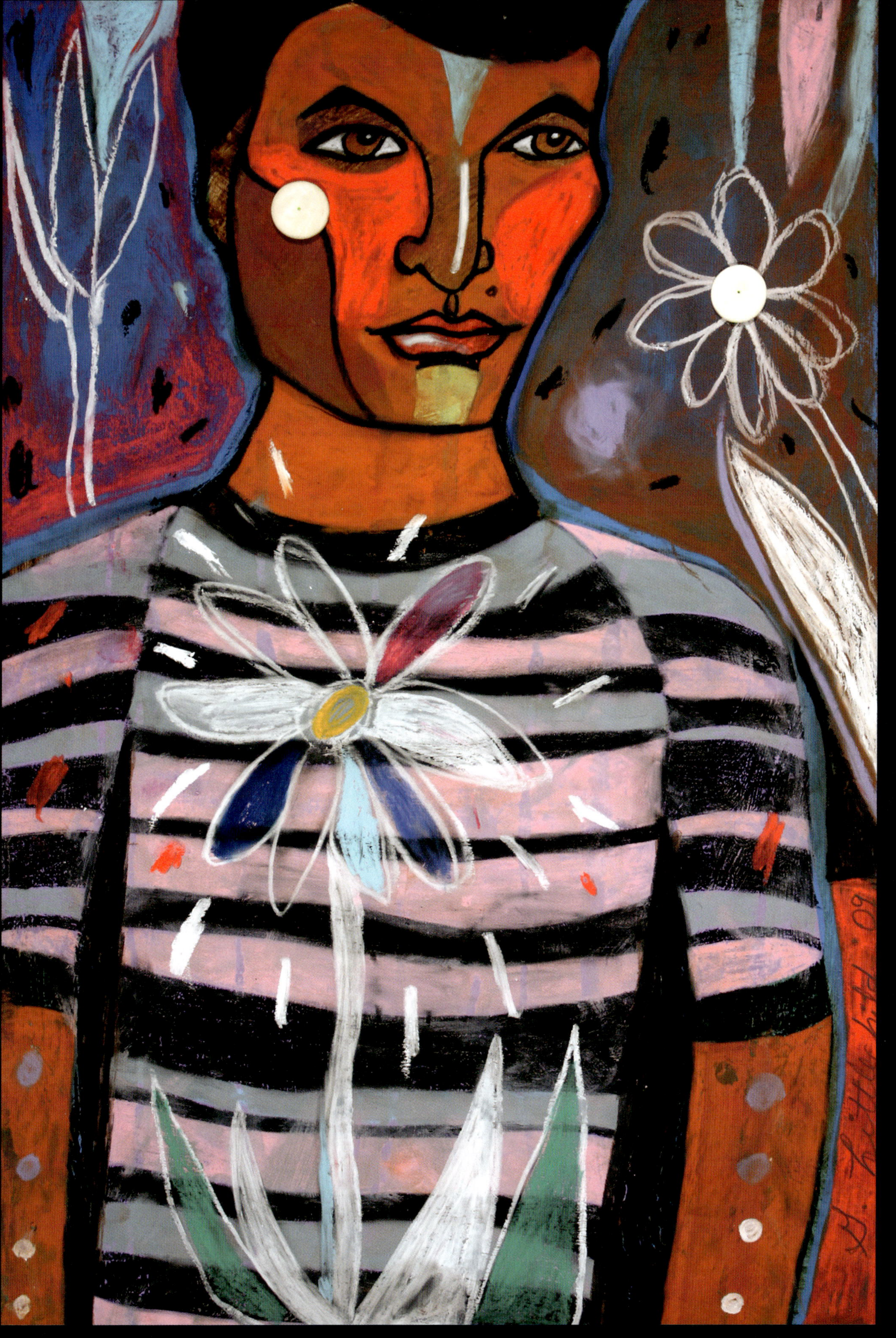

The Man in the Skinny Shirt

mixed media :: 22" x 15" :: 2009

Fashion dictates the lives of some, but others seem to dismiss it in their lackadaisical, thrown-together attire. Some thrive on dressing well; they feel good and like to be seen—a new shirt, a new look and a confident stride all combine to make them that styling man or woman about town. On some people, bold stripes accent strong shoulders, ripped abs or a barrel chest. The man in the skinny shirt is tall, regal, Aboriginal and proud.

Mixed Blood in Traditional Regalia

archival digital image :: 36" x 24" :: 2009

Years ago I photographed John Powell in traditional Kwagulth regalia, which he made by hand. His guardian spirit from his dance order of the Warrior Society is Sisiutl, the two-headed sea serpent. Sisiutl is seen coming out from behind him on each side of his body. A portion of John's button blanket is used for the background.

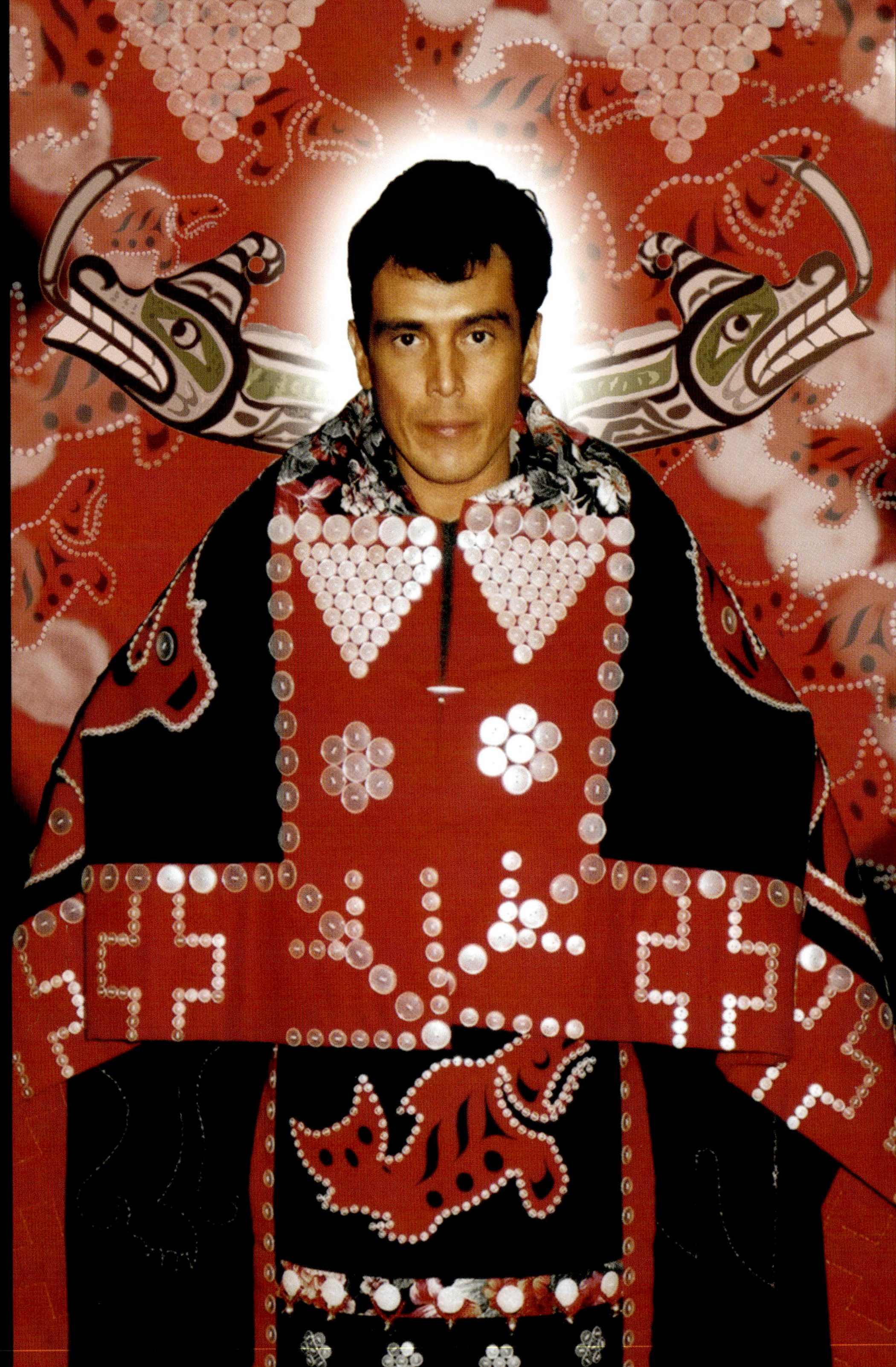

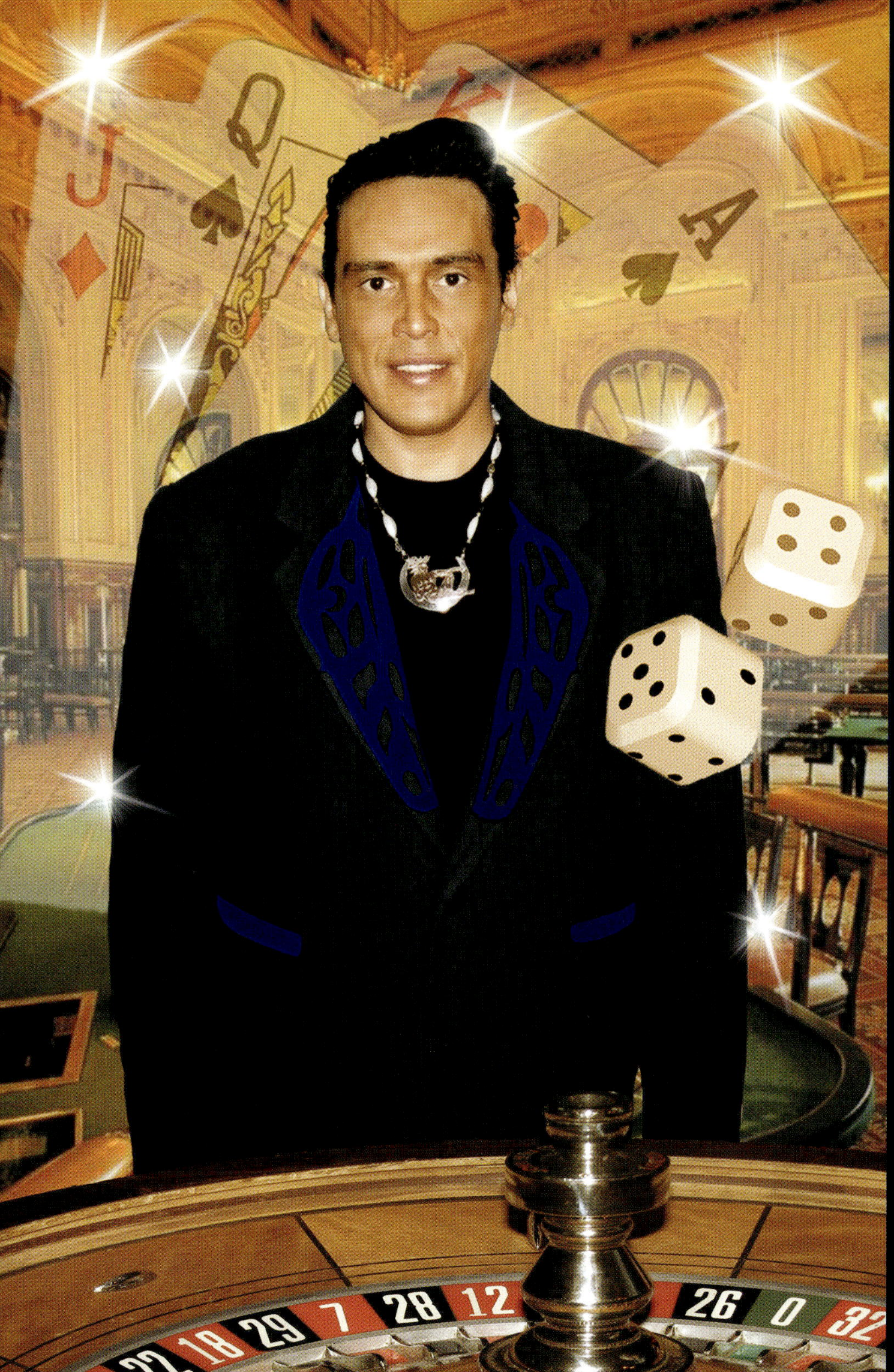

Mixed Blood as Player

archival digital image :: 36" x 24" :: 2009

I photographed John Powell wearing one of his First Nations designs. He stands by a roulette wheel in a gambling establishment. The idea behind the piece is the stereotypica notion some people have about First Nations and casinos on reserve lands, which is not true for all reserves and First Nations.

Man with Horse Energy

mixed media on paper
22" x 15" :: 2009

One of my favourite themes is transformation. I love creating anamorphic art, such as animal heads on human bodies. In *Man with Horse Energy*, a blue, flying horse comes out of the man's head, as they are spiritually connected to each other. A shift of consciousness transports one from this world to the other world and back. In Cree culture, the artist's animal spirit is the horse, as the horse is the conveyor of messages.

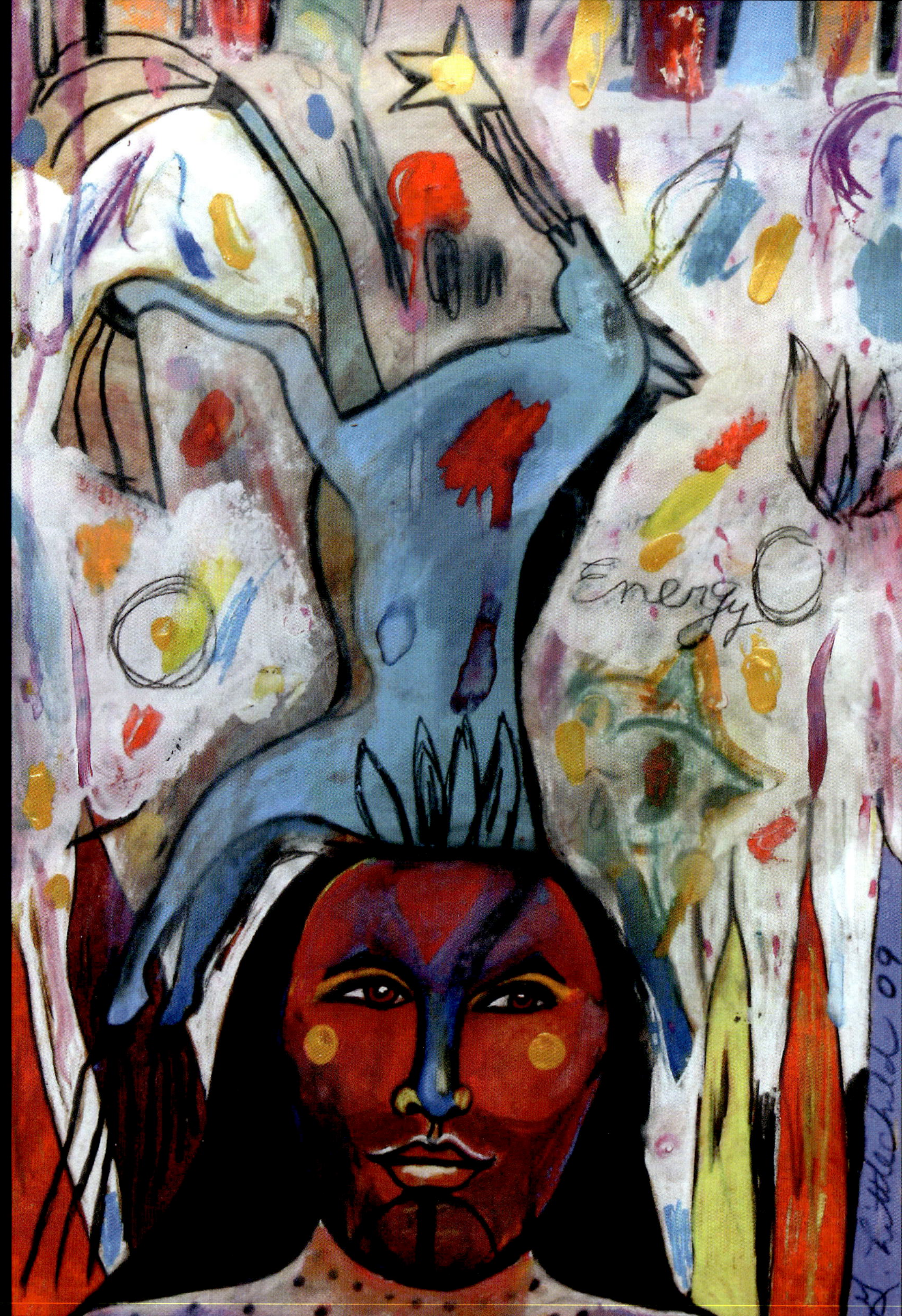

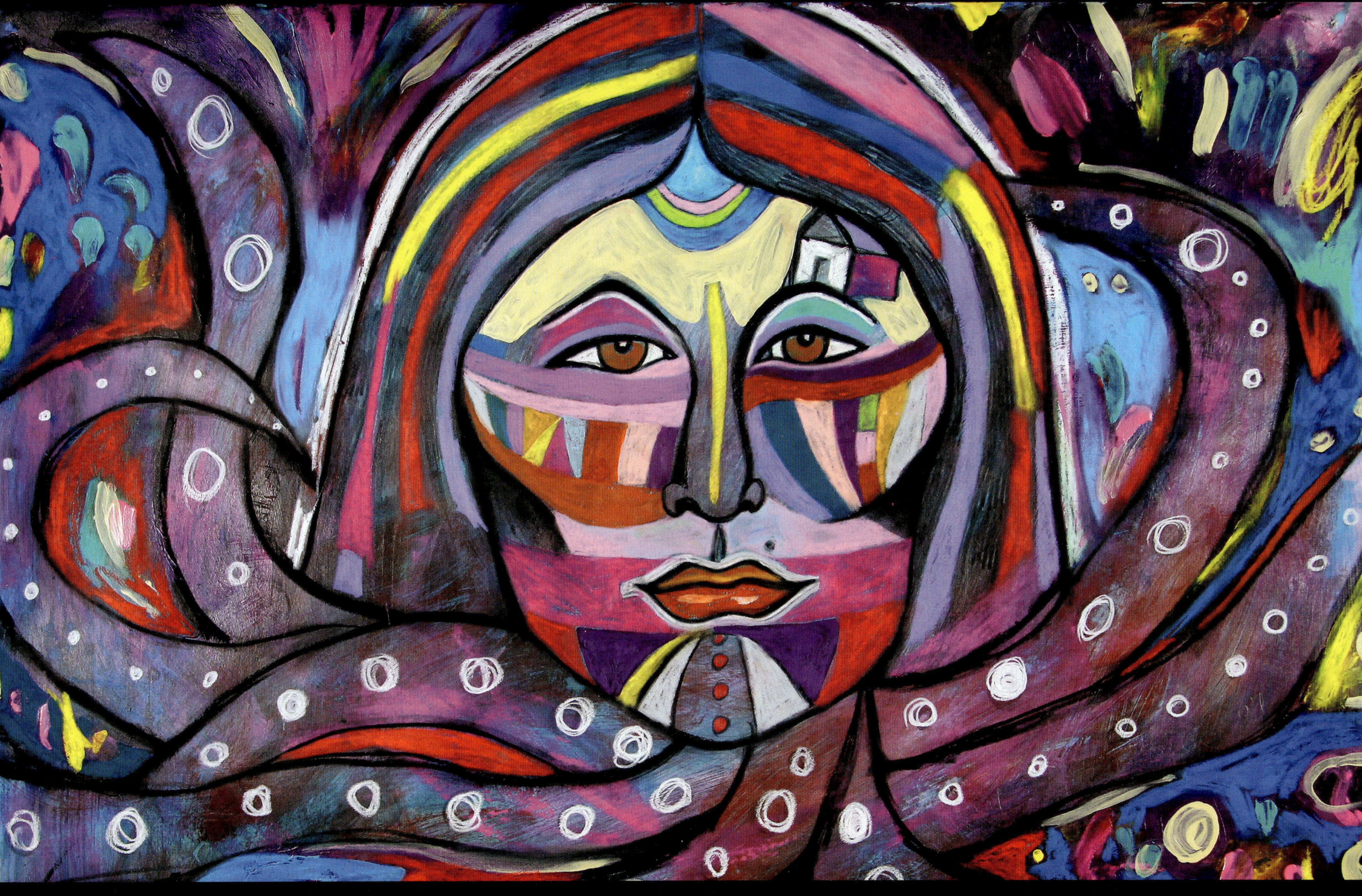

Octo-Lady mixed media on paper :: 22" x 30" :: 2009

As an artist, I live in an intuitive world. Images are born from a place of connectedness. Before this painting was created, I felt an urge to create an Octopus-transformation image to honour the ocean and territory in which I live, and to honour the sea beings. After this piece was finished, several hundred squid appeared on the east coast of Vancouver Island and Haida Gwaii, British Columbia, beaching themselves and perishing.

Red Man Descending

mixed media :: 30" x 22" :: 2009

Christianity has—in fact, all faiths and religions have—merit in each of the practitioners' lives if practised truly and from the heart. Sadly, explorers brought their religious views to the New World, and this contributed to the deaths of millions of Aboriginal people. Dominated and forced into slavery, many were murdered or died of disease, and those who survived were forced into submission by the church and colonial settlers. Greed and the desire to own land made it acceptable for colonial powers to practise genocide in the name of their religion and for the glory of their country. The destruction of culture and humanity is the legacy left behind for First Nations across the western hemisphere. We remember those who perished and suffered. Columbus will never be revered by the First Peoples.

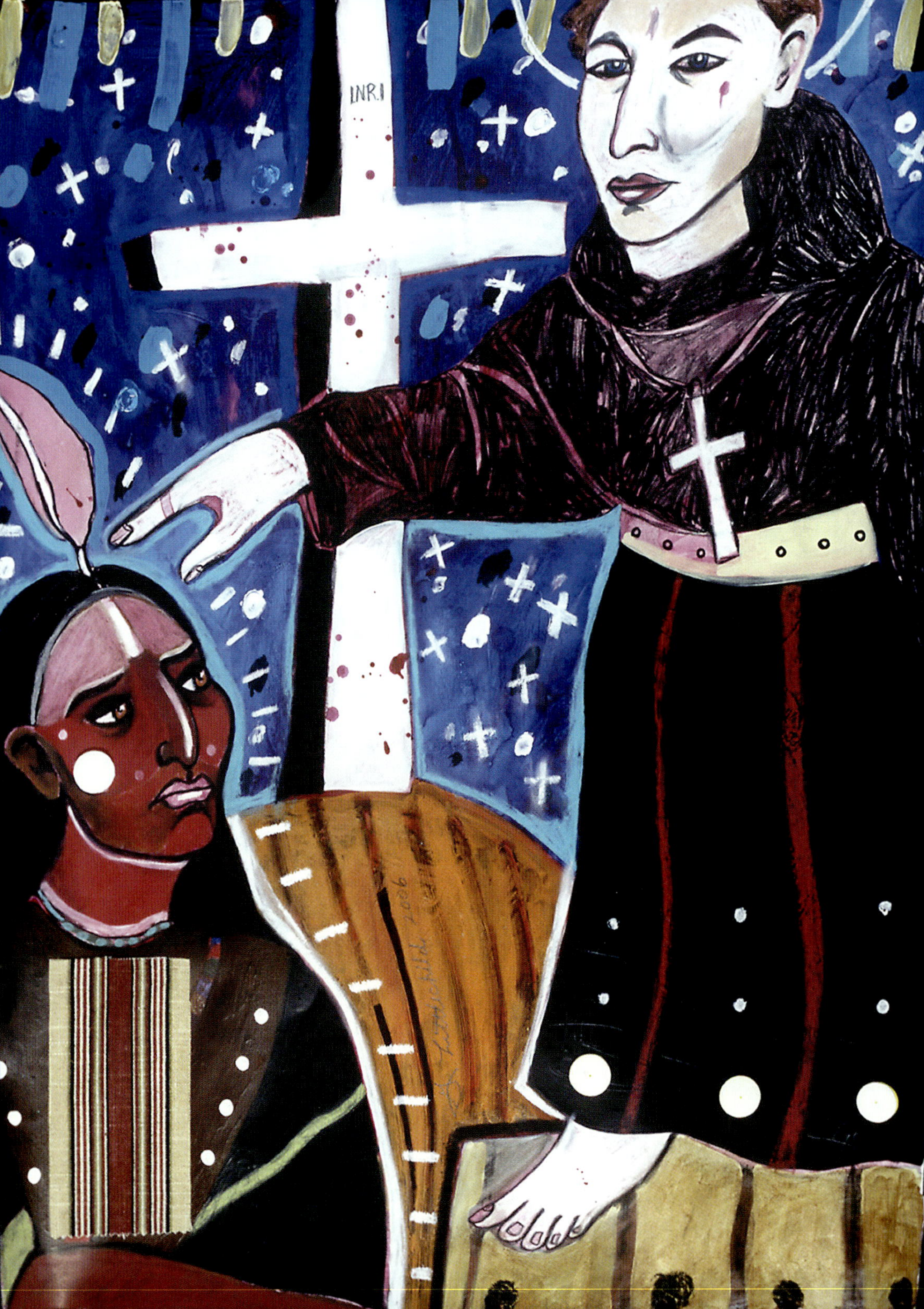

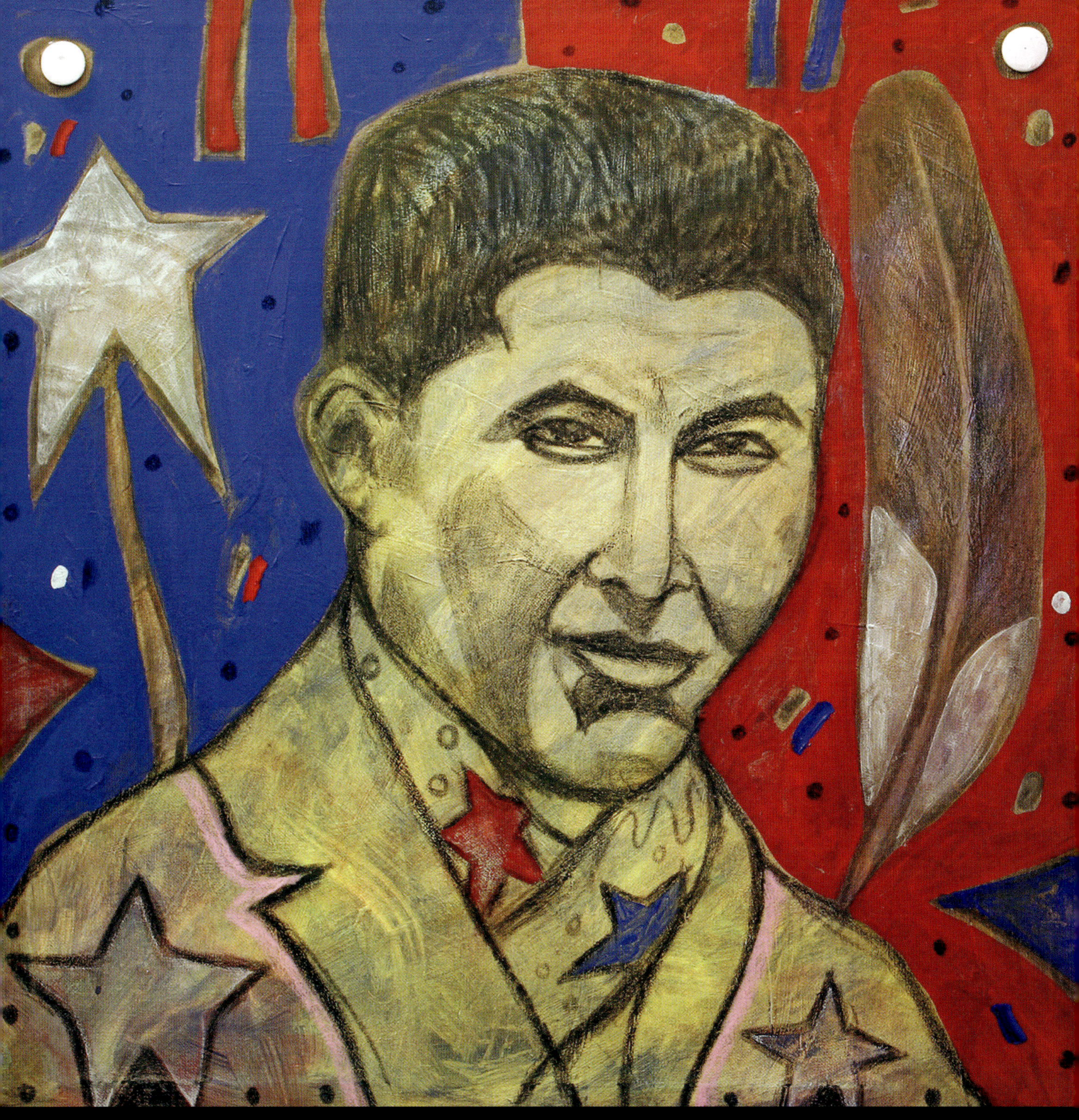

Eloquent Cree Man, So Wise mixed media :: 24" x 24" :: 2010

My great-uncle John Louis was the son of Louis Natuasis and Betsy Samson. He, like his father, was a headman or councillor for the Samson Band in Hobbema and a gifted orator. John Louis was known for his wisdom and sound advice. He had several marriages and was the father of one son and two daughters, and has several descendants. In the Cree way, he would be called Mosom, which meant grandfather

She Walked across the Stars

mixed media
49" x 39" :: 2010

She is a strong, powerful, soft, wise woman who knows her duties and her responsibilities to her culture. She makes connections to her people, her relatives. She is respected as she walks in humility and grace, a woman who could recite generations of her genealogy and tell stories of people long gone. She lived in a good way, untouched by petty behaviour. Who was she? No one I know, but someone I wish I did.

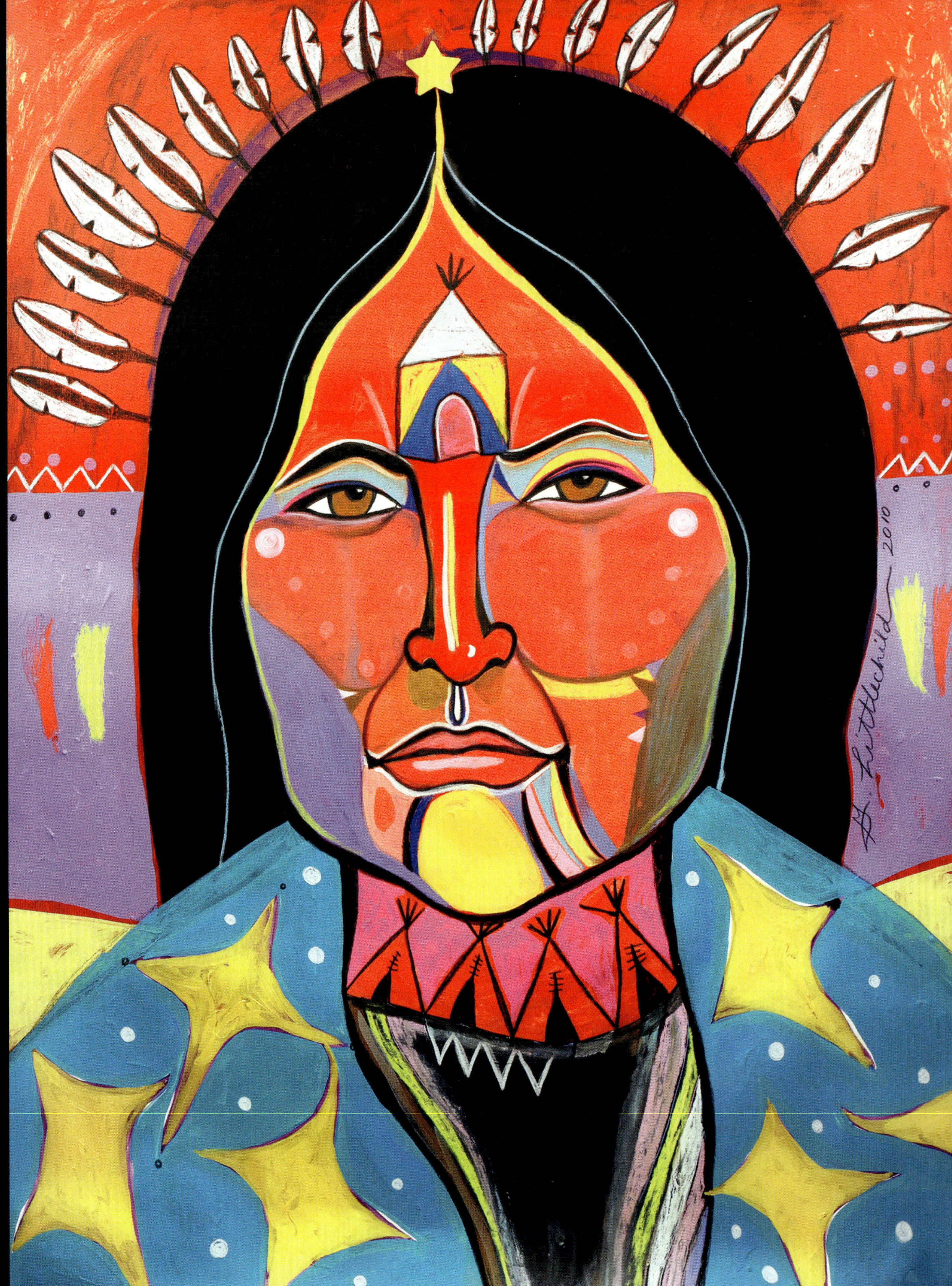

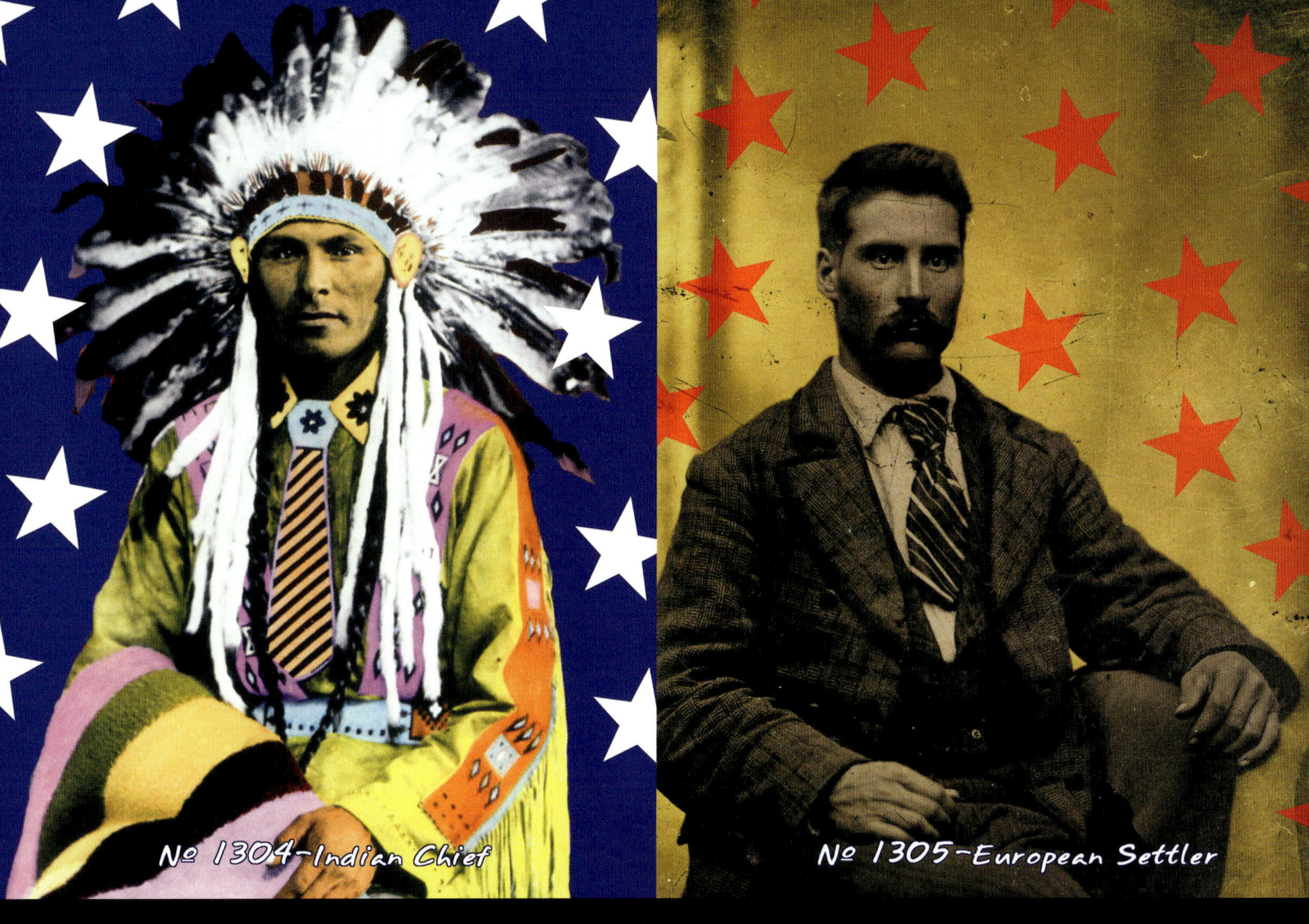

Cross-Cultural Examination: No 1304—Indian Chief, No 1305—European Settler

archival digital image :: 24" x 36" :: 2010

I hand-coloured this old photo of Chief John Bear of the Montana Reserve near Hobbema. He was a dignified Plains Cree Nation chief who married Mary Ermineskin, the daughter of Chief Panee Ermineskin and Suzanne Panychat. He wears a beaded tie, influenced by white man's fashions. The man on the right looks very European. I purchased his photo in Saskatoon. The original photo is printed on tin. He also wears a tie, and is as dashing as Chief John Bear. Would these two men ever have met, chatted or shared a pipe?

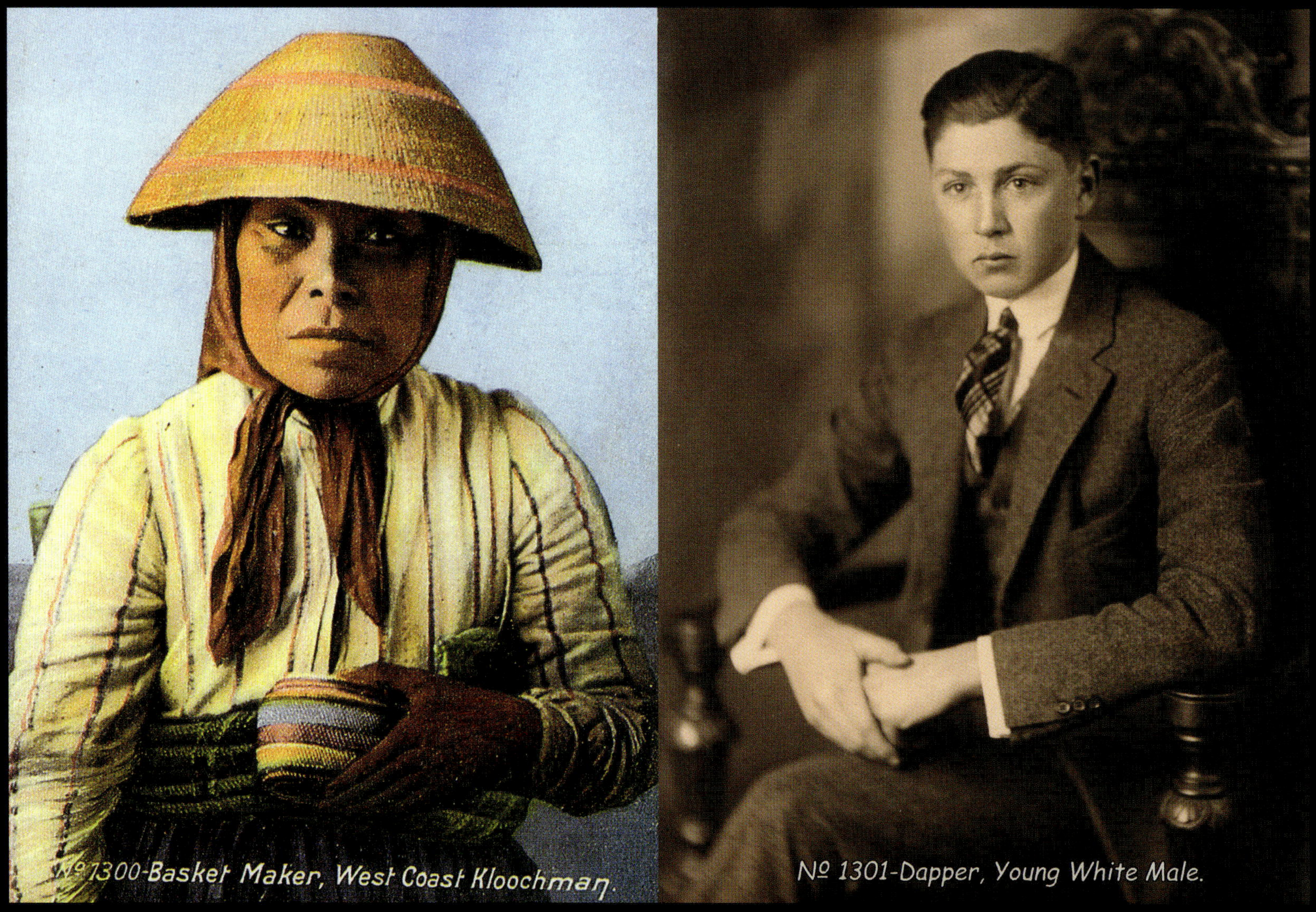

Cross-Cultural Examination: No 1300—Basket Maker, West Coast Kloochman, No 1301—Dapper, Young White Male

archival digital image :: 24" x 36" :: 2010

Around 2007, I began a series of digital images exploring First Nations and non–First Nations relationships. My research and interest in antique postcards and photographs had me shopping in many an antique shop, purchasing photos and old postcards, mainly in Vancouver and Victoria. I made some interesting finds. My purpose is to juxtapose two nations and create a relationship of sorts between them. Sometimes there was text on the images, which I included. Other times I added text that created a dialogue. For example, the image of the First Nations woman had "No 1300—Basket Maker, West Coast Kloochman" on the card, while I added "No 1301—Dapper, Young White Male" onto the other photo.

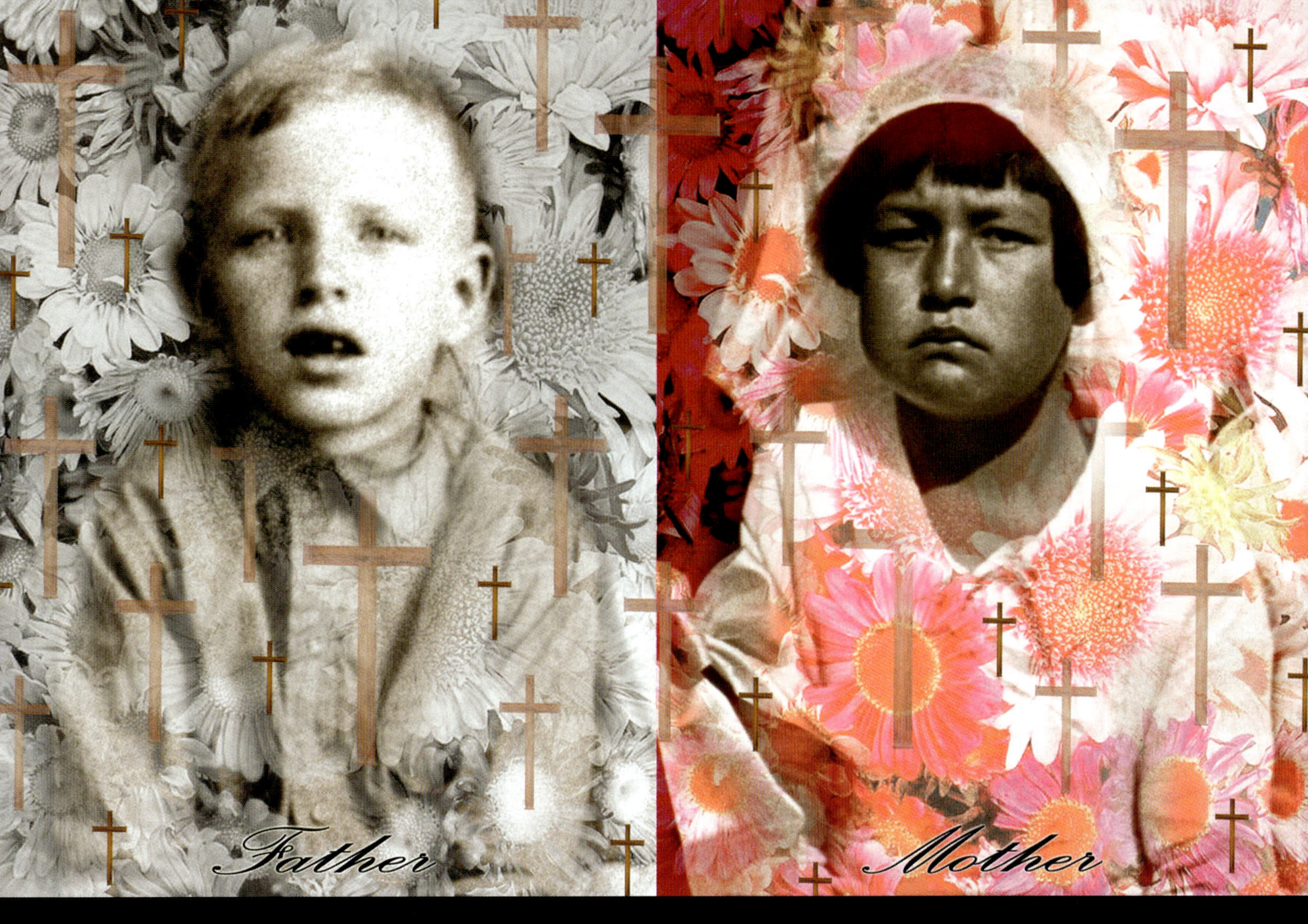

Cross-Cultural Examination: Father James E. Price, Mother Rachel Littlechild as Youth

archival digital image :: 24" x 36" :: 2010

Father was about nine in this photo, taken in 1923 at Great Falls, Montana. Mother, also about nine, was seated with others who had taken their first communion at the Catholic Mission in Hobbema on the Ermineskin Reserve. Her brother, Ross, also had his first communion that day. They were so vast, so different, my late parents, whose lives would not have touched until the day they met. I wish I

Modern Girl, Traditional Mindset

mixed media on paper
49" x 39" :: 2010

A traditional woman living in a modern world/cityscape struggles to reconcile her beliefs with those of the city around her. She maintains a traditional lifestyle that has been passed down to her through sacred ancestral teachings. She also has made a commitment to practise her culture. These teachings sustain her in an ever-changing world; she draws her strength from them.

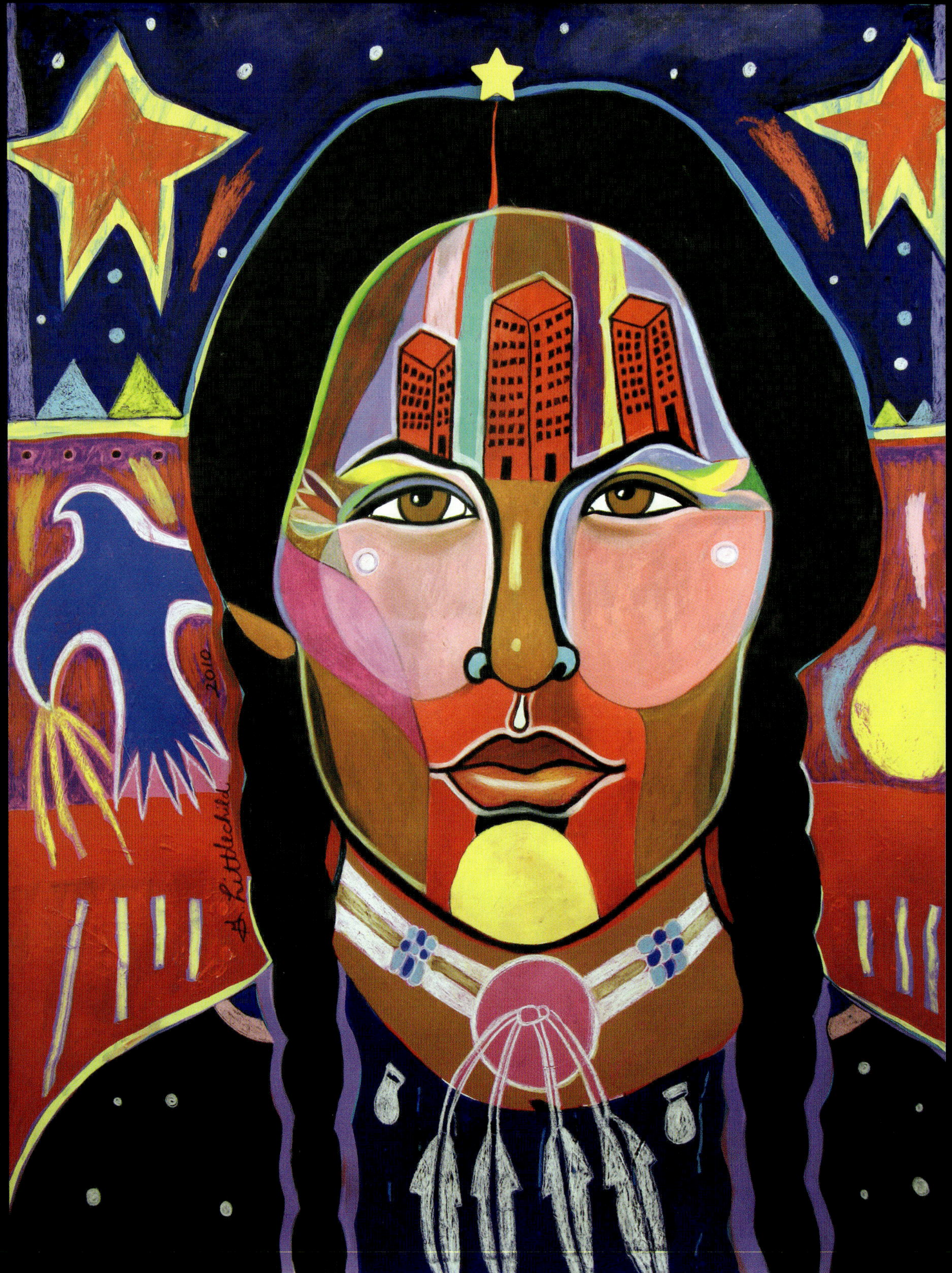

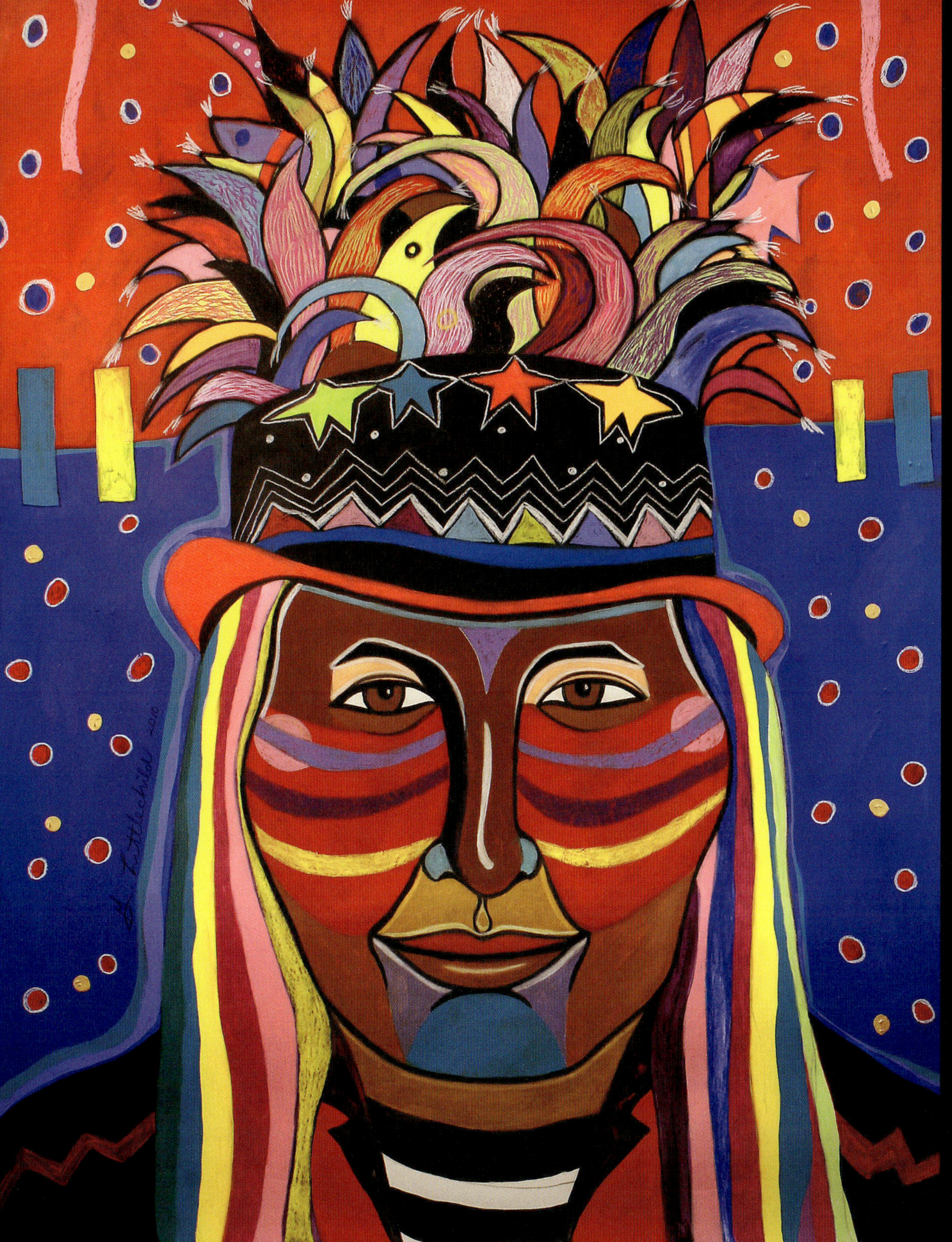

Bringer of Light, Love and Peace

mixed media on paper
49" x 39" :: 2010

I was captivated by an antique photograph of a Cree man with a smile on his face. He was seated, wearing Cree and European regalia that indicated he was a chief. He wore a chief's coat issued by the Department of Indian Affairs. I was compelled to paint this man's portrait, the man being Chief Moosomin, a Plains Cree chief from Saskatchewan. His eyes emanated humble wisdom, and his smile a depth of knowing.

Cross-Cultural Examination: Strong Is the Metis Man

archival digital image/mixed media
36" x 24" :: 2011

I wrote an homage script to honour this Metis man, as he is iconic and representative of his people and nation. I want to let people know about the struggles he and his people faced, as they were outcasts, people between worlds, belonging to neither the white nor First Nations communities. The Metis are a people unto themselves, a strong, determined nation.

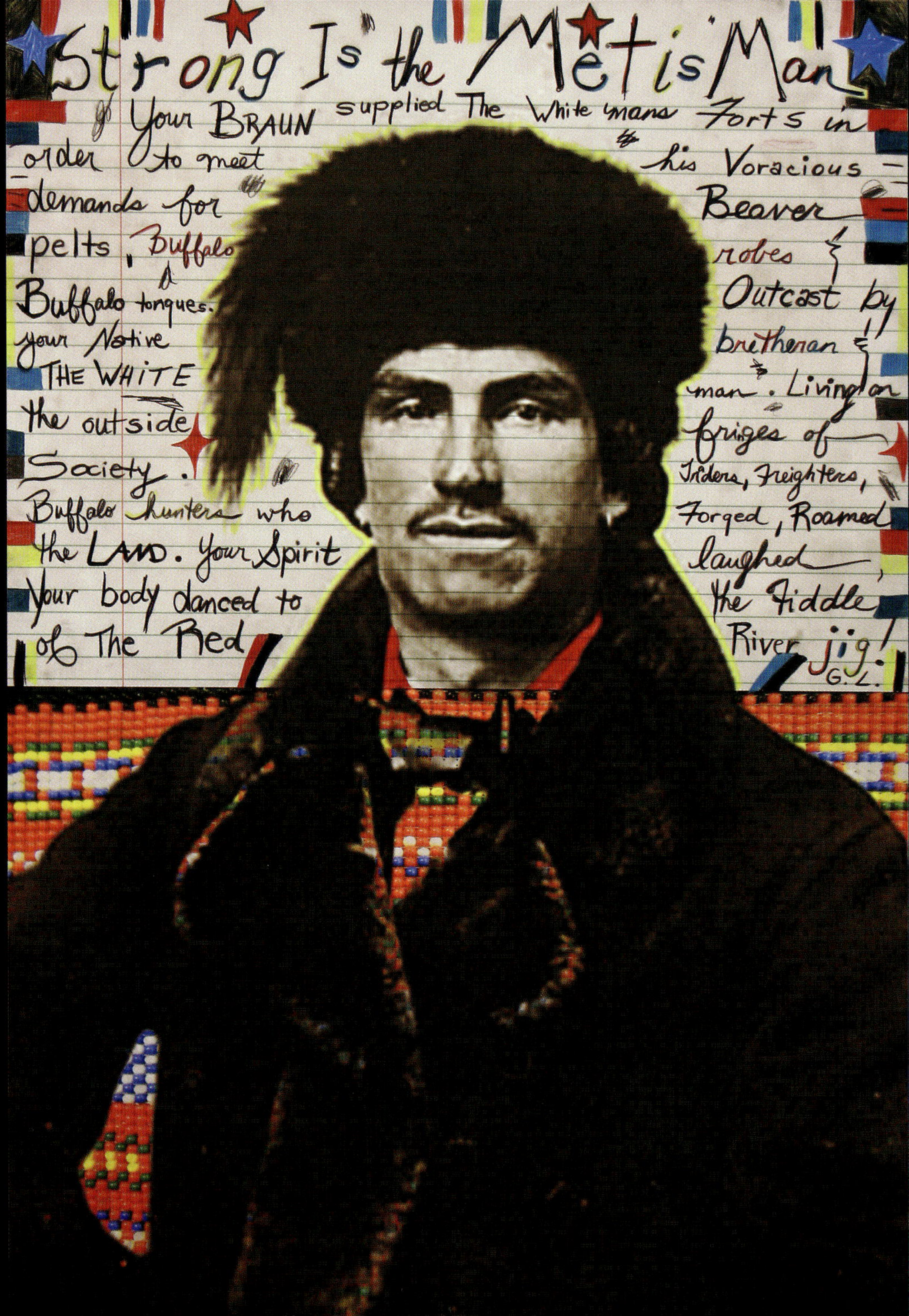

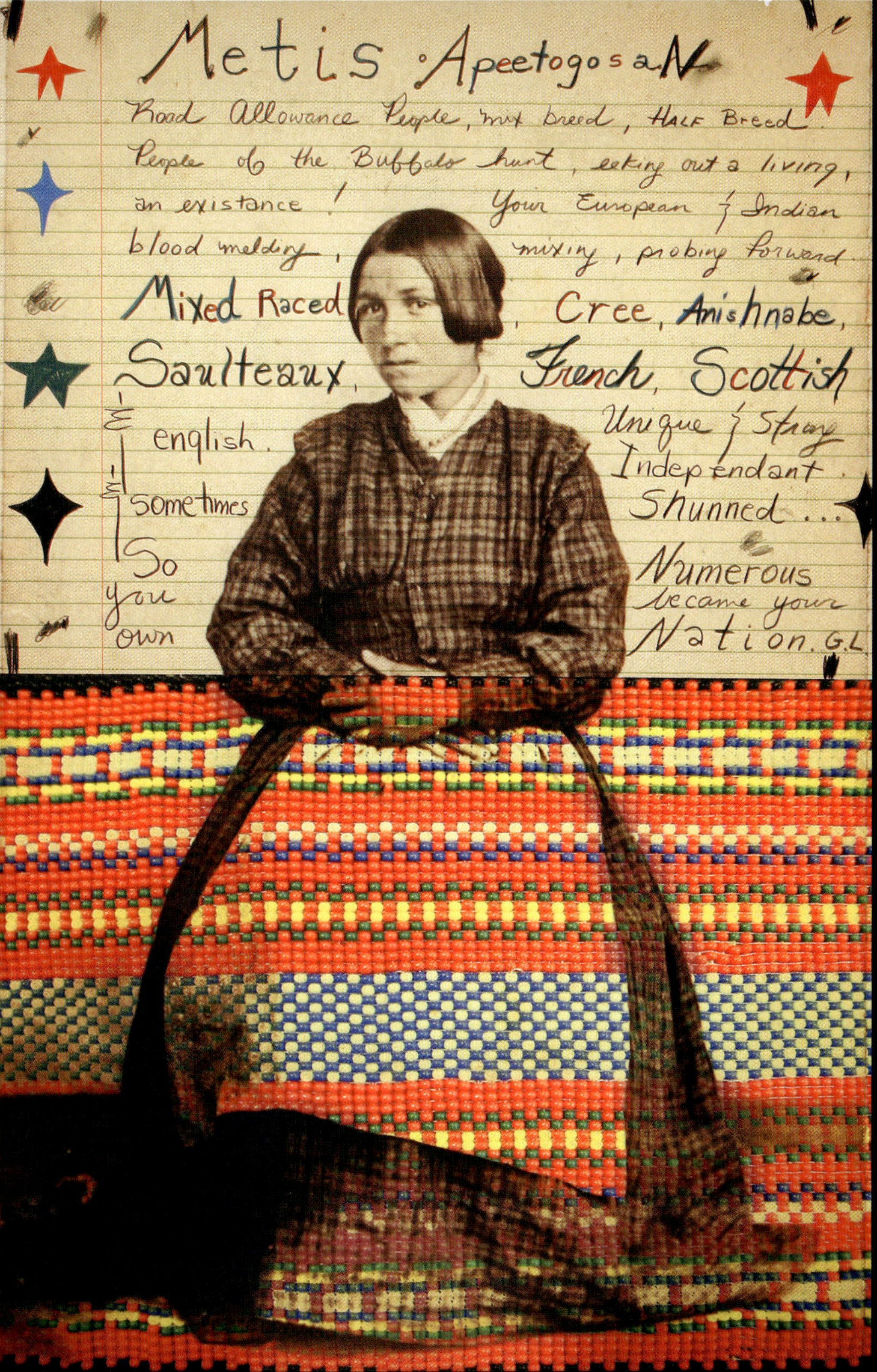

Cross-Cultural Examination: Metis Woman, Apeetogosan

archival digital image/mixed media
36" x 24" :: 2011

The Metis Nation was born from unions between Aboriginals and whites. The children of these unions carried this unique melding of two worlds, both races, which made them distinct peoples in the Canadian landscape. As I have written in the background text, "Road Allowance People . . . People of the Buffalo hunt . . . Your European & Indian blood melding, mixing, probing forward."

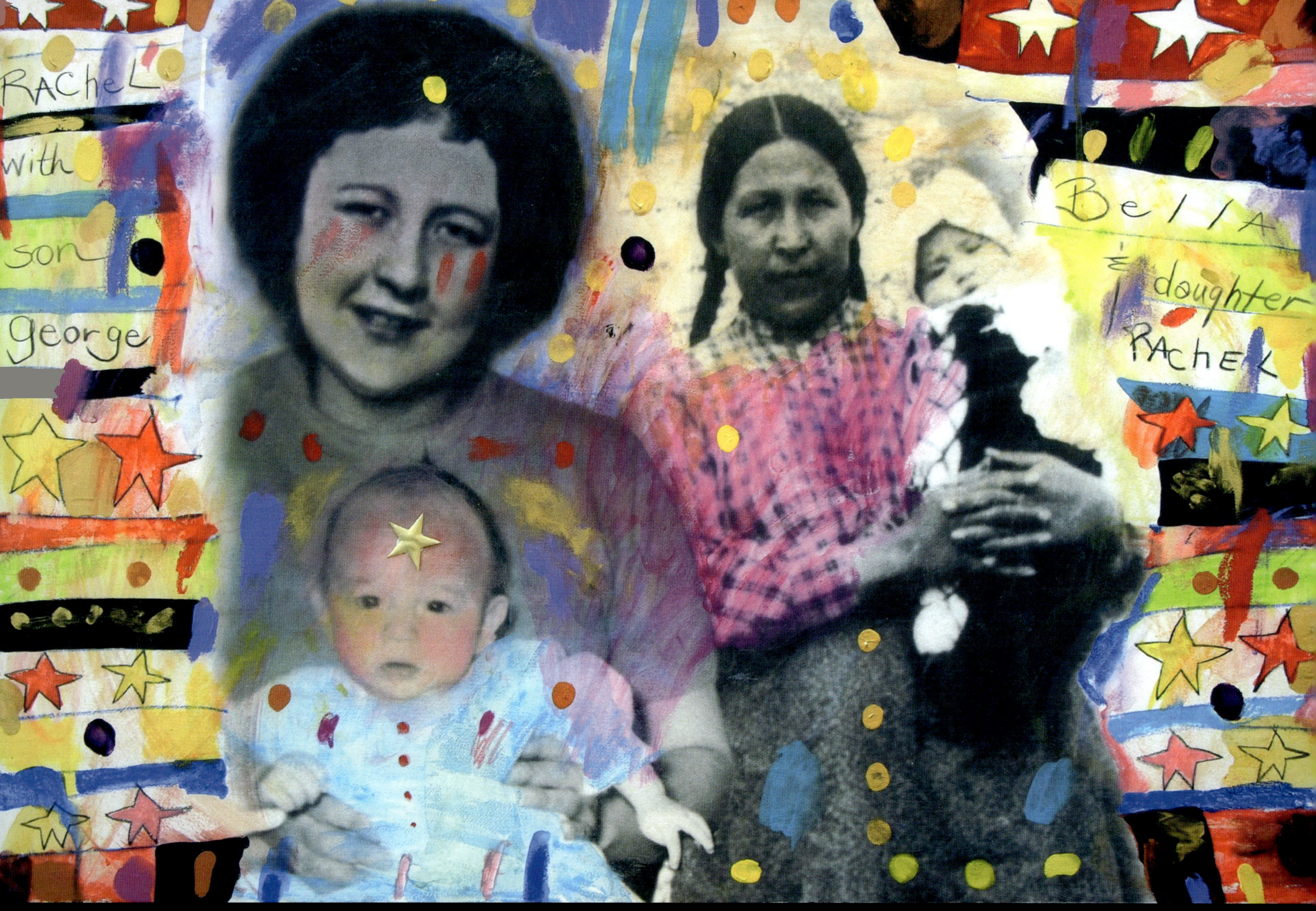

Bella and Daughter Rachel, Rachel and Son George mixed media :: 24" x 36" :: 2011

Grandmother Bella (1898–1937) holds her daughter Rachel in a moss bag in 1929 on the Ermineskin Reserve in Hobbema. She was the daughter of Chief Francis Bull and Peggy Louis of the Louis Bull Reserve in Hobbema. Bella married Edward Littlechild of the Ermineskin Reserve. They had 12 children: Helen, William Edward, Alfred, Sarah, Louis, Mary Jane, Francis Ross, Rachel, Rosalie Mable, Rene, Raymond and Marie Evelyn. Alfred and Louis died while at residential school. Louis was an artist. He was only 11 when he died. My Auntie Rosalie says he was nice looking.

My mother, Rachel, holds me in November 1958 in Edmonton. I was her second child and my father's second child. They both had one child from previous relationships. Together they had me, Marilyn, Raymond and Shirley, leaving a strong legacy behind in their children, one to be proud of. My thanks go out to all women and mothers

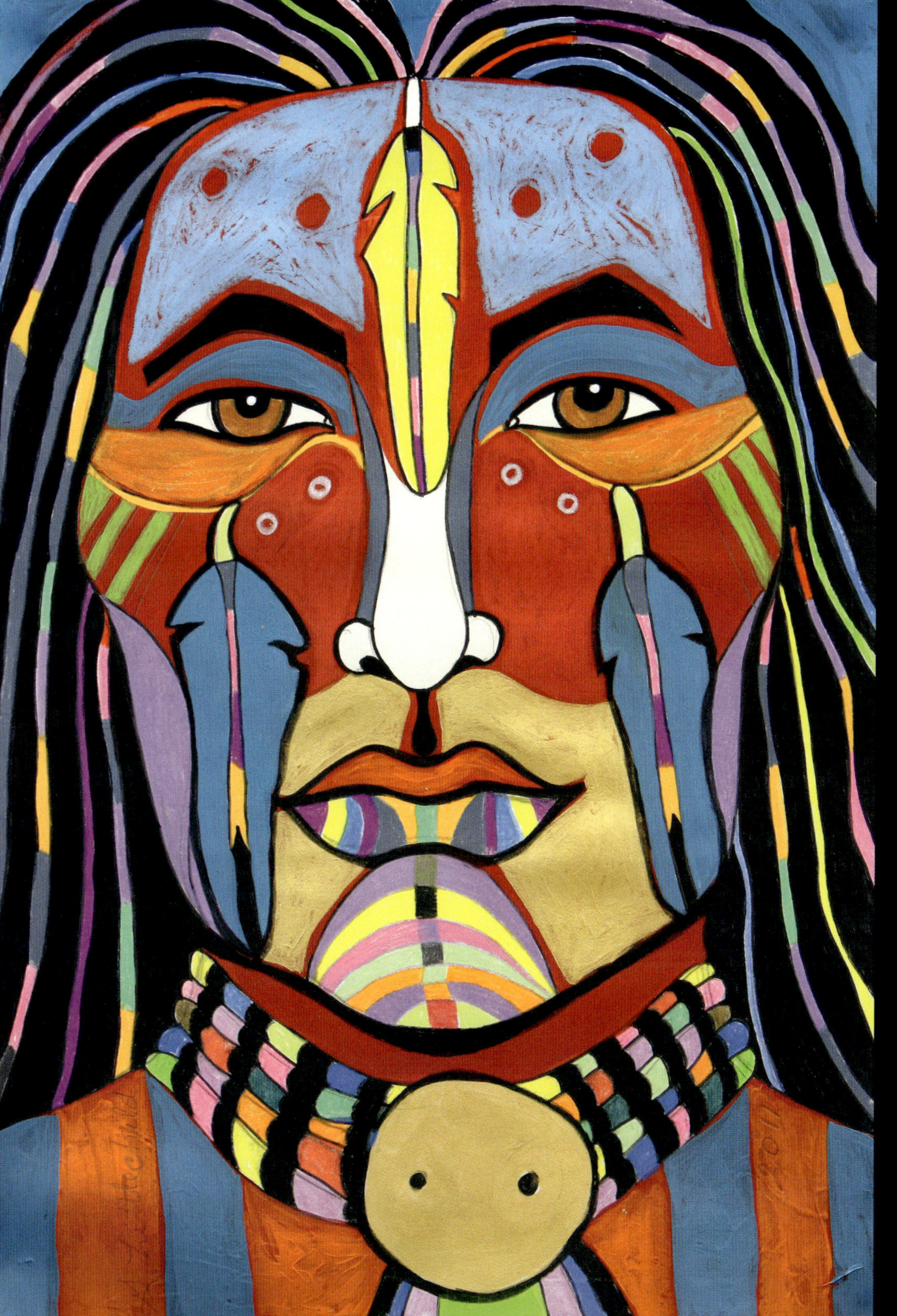

Rainbow Man Warrior

mixed media :: 22" x 15" :: 2011

Gay, lesbian, transgendered and bisexual men and women are often the targets of hate crimes and bullying. Acceptance of non-heterosexual people has gradually increased and attitudes are much more positive since the Stonewall Riots and the beginning of gay pride. Parades and festivities have become part of mainstream society. Role models of all races in gay society need to be acknowledged. Their lives and deeds should be part of school curricula—education helps people carry themselves in the world with less ignorance and greater acceptance of others. Only then can all of humanity live in true peace and harmony.

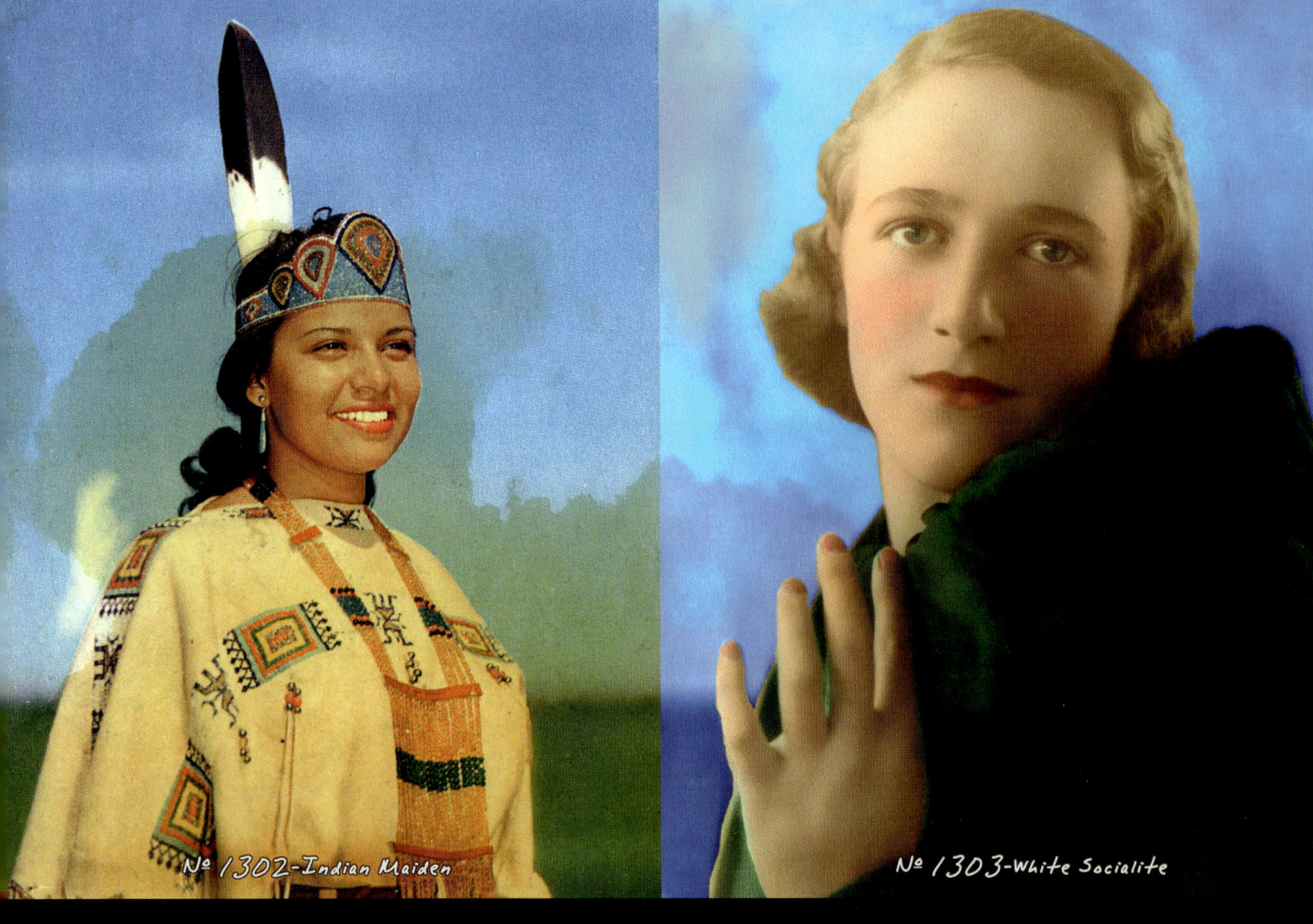

Cross-Cultural Examination: No 1302—Indian Maiden, No 1303—White Socialite

archival digital image :: 24″ x 36″ :: 2011

This photograph I found of a lovely Native woman had the caption "Indian maiden" printed on the back. She was perhaps in a princess pageant when it was taken. I found the image of another lovely woman in a stack of old photos at an antique store. I gave her the name "white socialite."

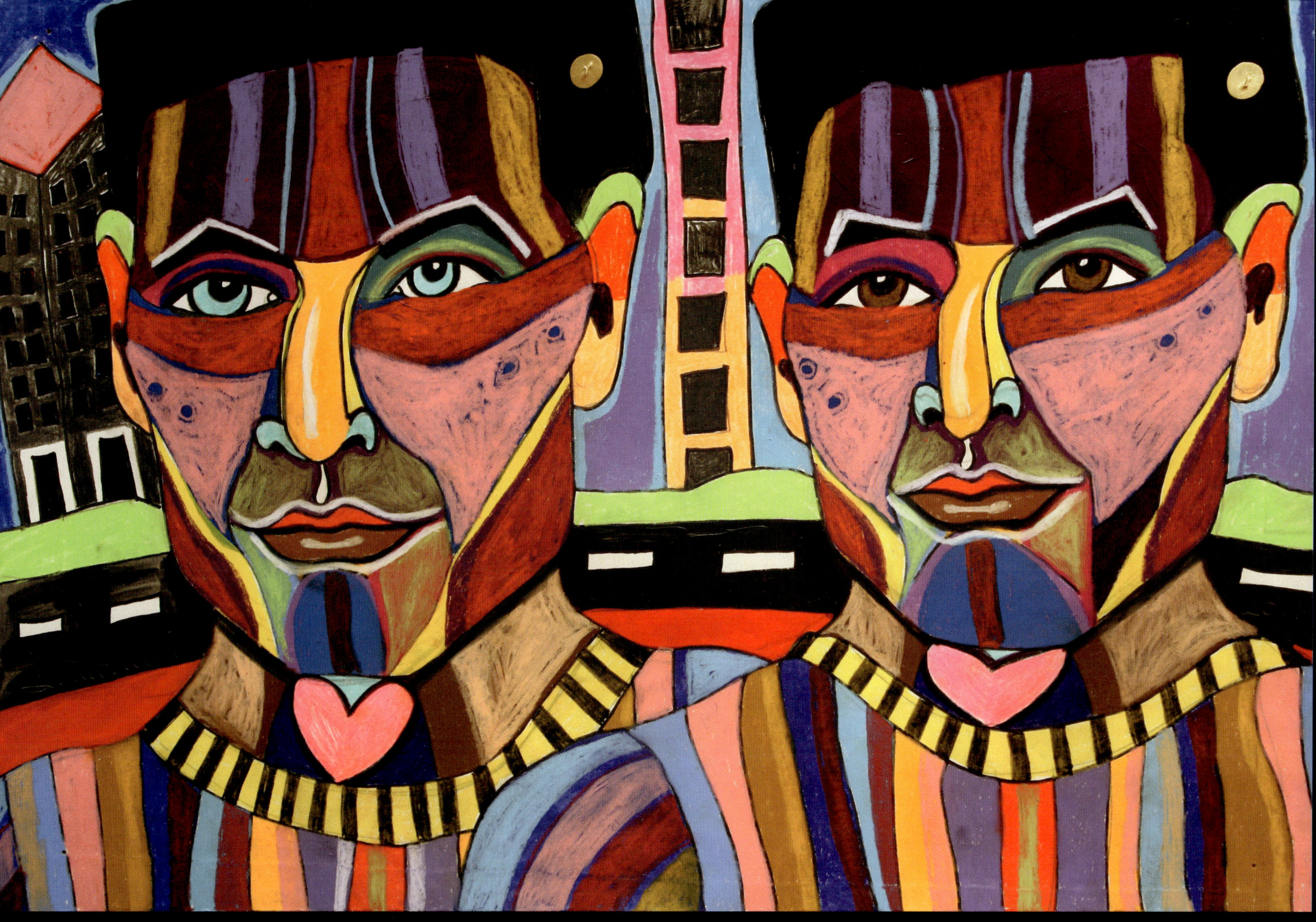

The Boys of Dual mixed media :: 15" x 22" :: 2011

This painting examines the idea of the same/similar. In our mind's eye, we have thoughts about who we are and how others view us. When we look in a mirror, we see a reverse image of ourselves. We never really see ourselves the way nature created us. Then there is the way others view and perceive us. Who we are is a fusion of many perceptions. In the end, only we truly understand our true selves, with all our quirks. This portrait of one individual painted twice represents the way a person is seen.

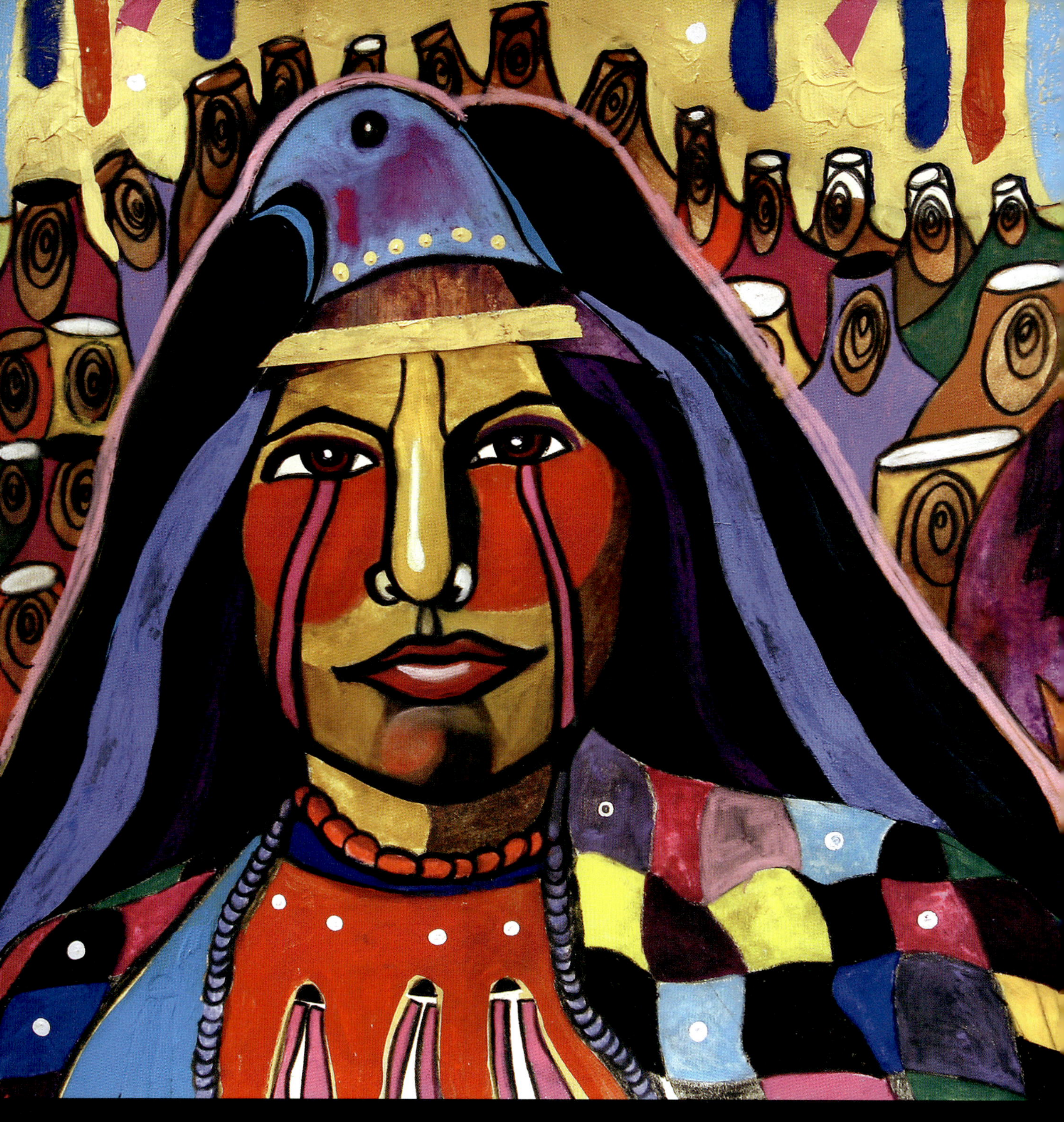

Woman, Thunder Bird, Clear-Cut mixed media on paper :: 15" x 15" :: 2011

The land is sacred to those who have knowledge of her strength, character and BEAUTY. Activist groups fight for her, "Protect our Mother Earth" and "Save our precious water" painted on banners and placards. Humanity exists merely by our connection to the Earth: without Mother Earth, we would not be here. In this piece, I painted Mother Earth as a woman with a pained face standing by a clear-cut, in hope that we will change and take only what we need and stop abusing our home, sacred Mother Earth.

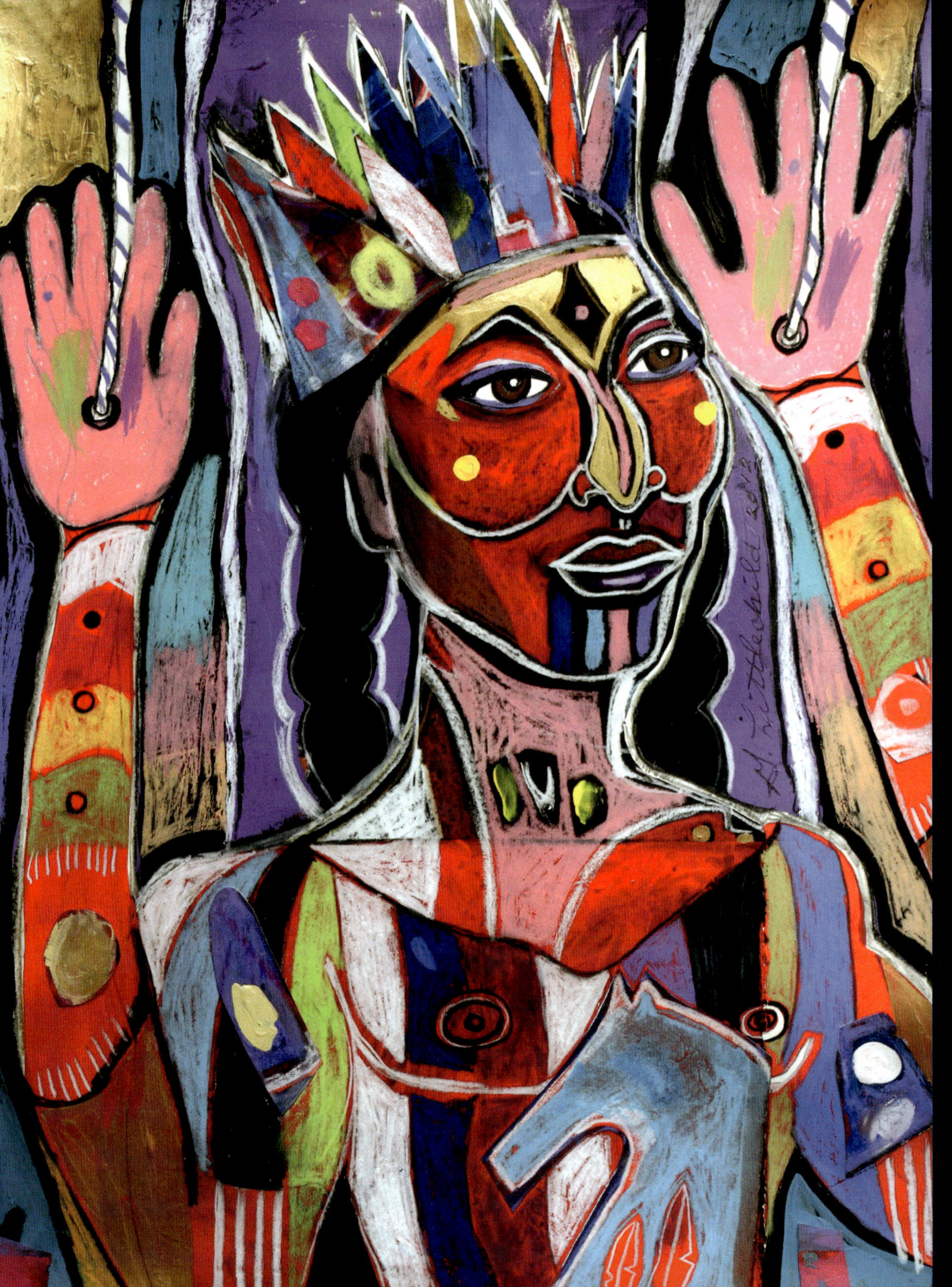

Indian Affairs Puppet

mixed media :: 30" x 22" :: 2011

This painting of a puppet, almost garish in colour, depicts First Nations peoples, chiefs and councils who are controlled by the Department of Indian Affairs and have to answer for their every move and action. The control is much more lenient now than it was prior to 1960, when First Nations people had no vote in Canada or were not allowed to leave their reserves without a permission slip or temporary pass unless they had enfranchised their Indian rights. Pull one string to move the hand, another to make the puppet walk and another to talk. First Nations peoples and communities are still on the healing path and want to maintain and operate their own affairs and lives, which I believe is a step in a positive direction.

Horse Spirit, Helper Brother

mixed media :: 22" x 15" :: 2011

Author Richard Van Kamp makes a comment in his book *What's the Most Beautiful Thing You Know About Horses?* regarding our special connection to an animal spirit and the fact there is an animal on this earth that knows your special name. First Nations culture, philosophy and teachings have always had great respect for animals and our connection to them. We are one, not separate from each other.

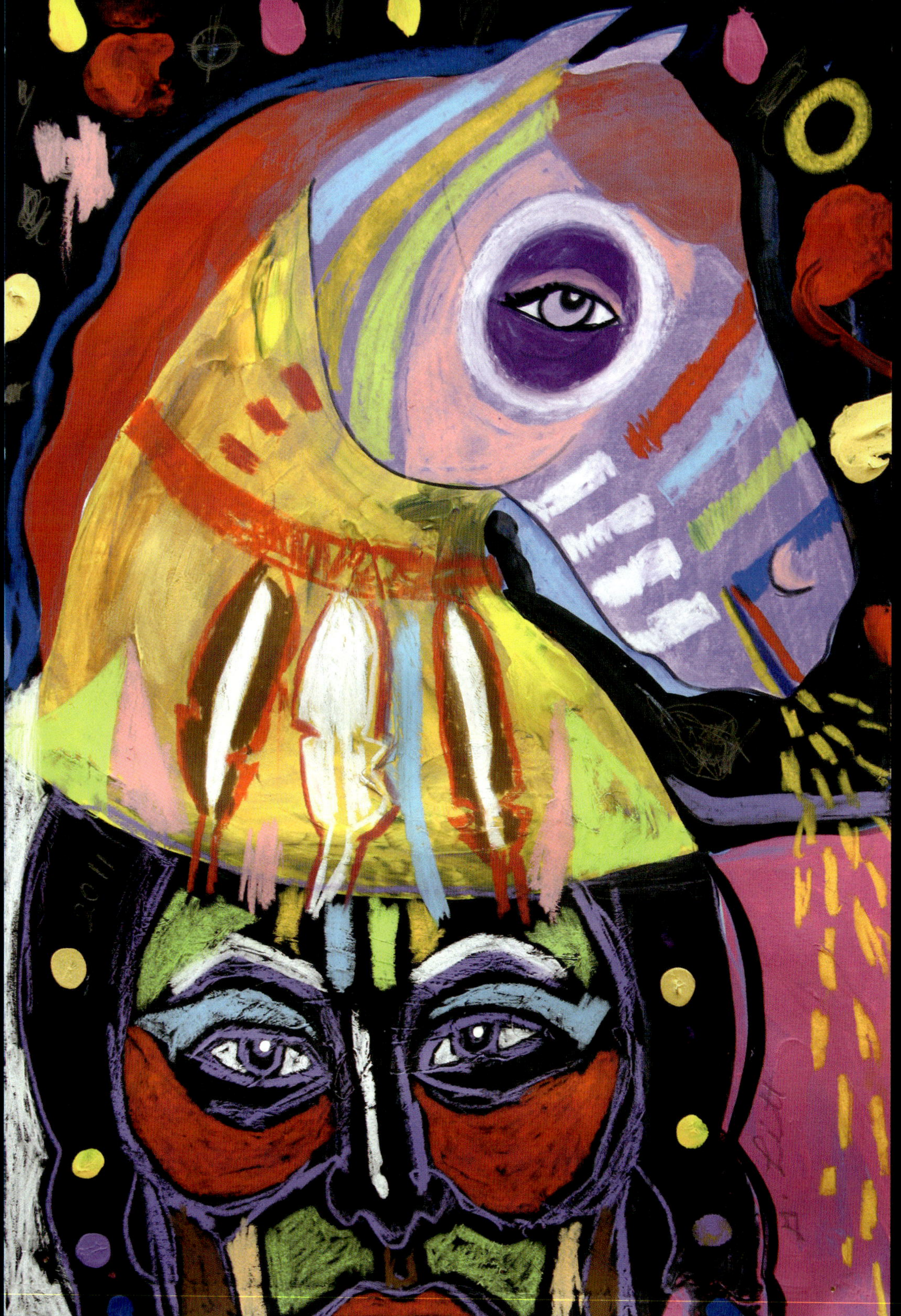

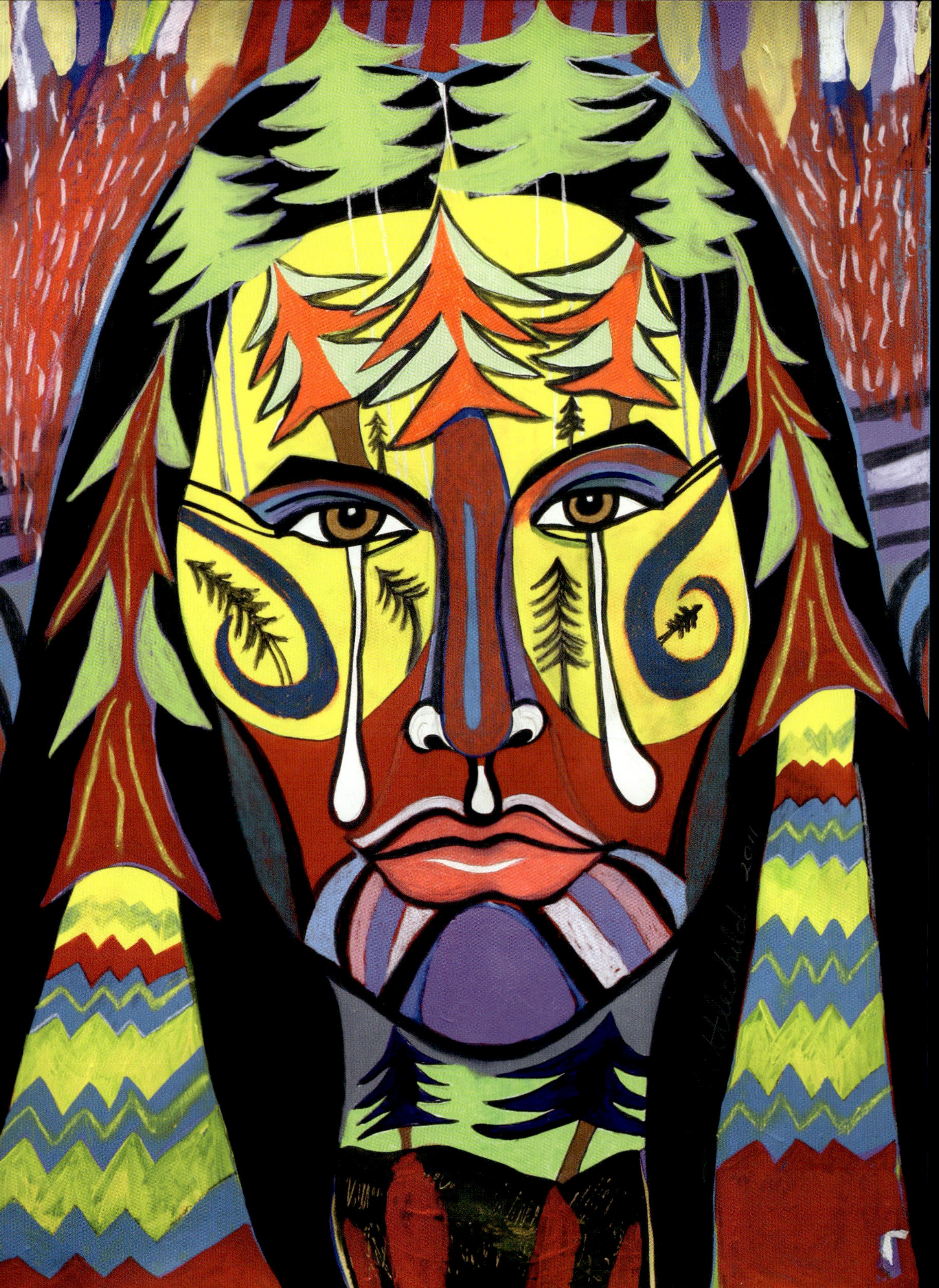

Strong Tree Spirit Becomes Strong Tree Medicine

mixed media :: 30" x 22" :: 2011

There is a fine line between protecting the forest and using it sustainably for purposes like building homes or making paper products. Our population is hugely dependent on trees and with the population exploding, that need becomes even stronger. I always find it sad when I drive the highways of Vancouver Island because I know that behind the tall stands of trees beside the road there is often a clear-cut where most of the trees and foliage have been ripped from the land. I realize reforestation does occur; however, I long to walk on virgin terrain where the sacred forest is alive and in its true element, pristine, wild and free.

Horse Man
Communicate, Communicate

mixed media :: 22" x 15" :: 2011

A figure of a man in profile (me) talks to a powerful horse spirit, represented by lines of several dashes from one mouth to another. White lines of insight and vision, coming from the eyes, create a code only the horse and the artist understand. It is their sacred, special world that becomes reality in the artwork produced.

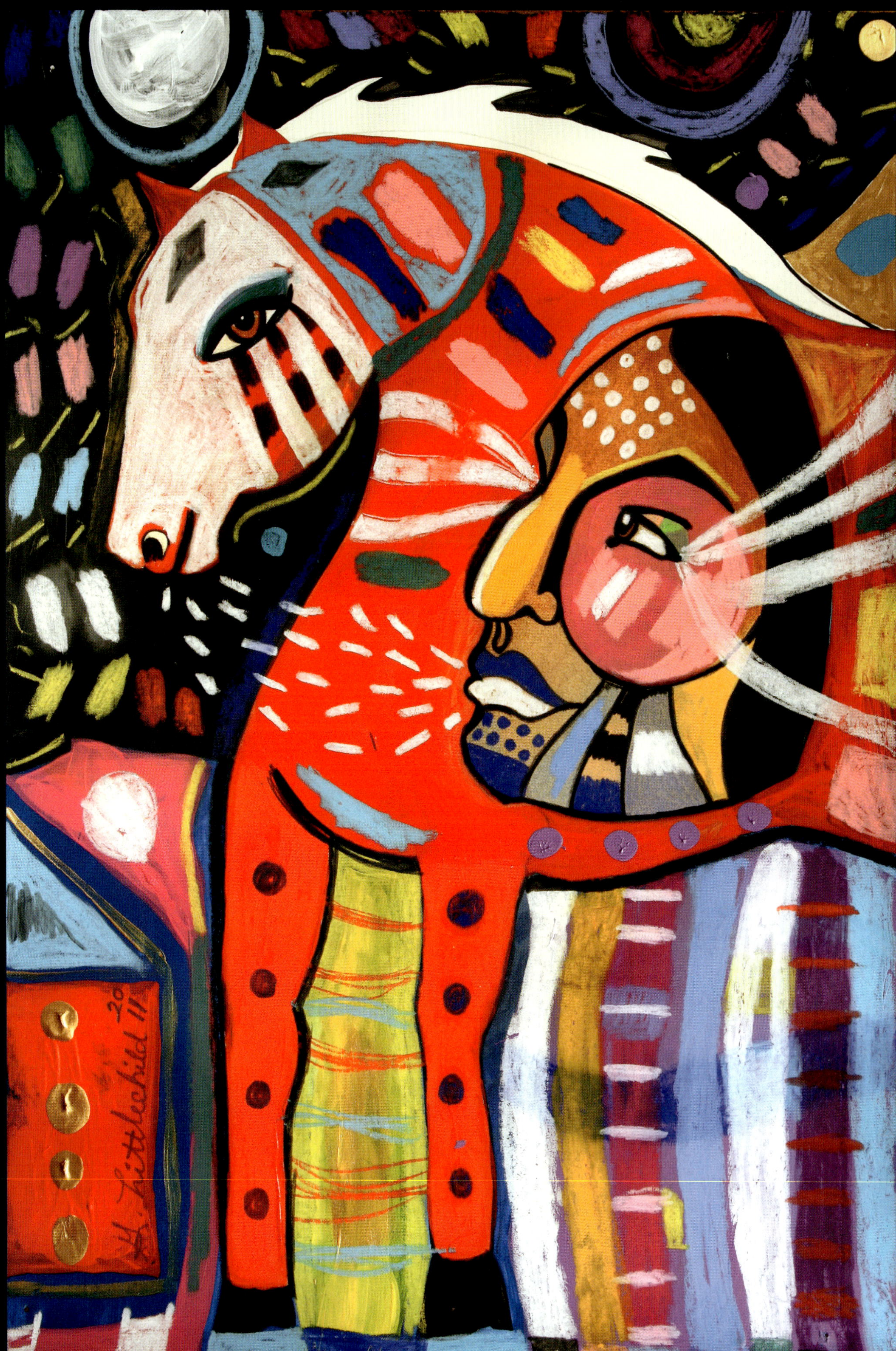

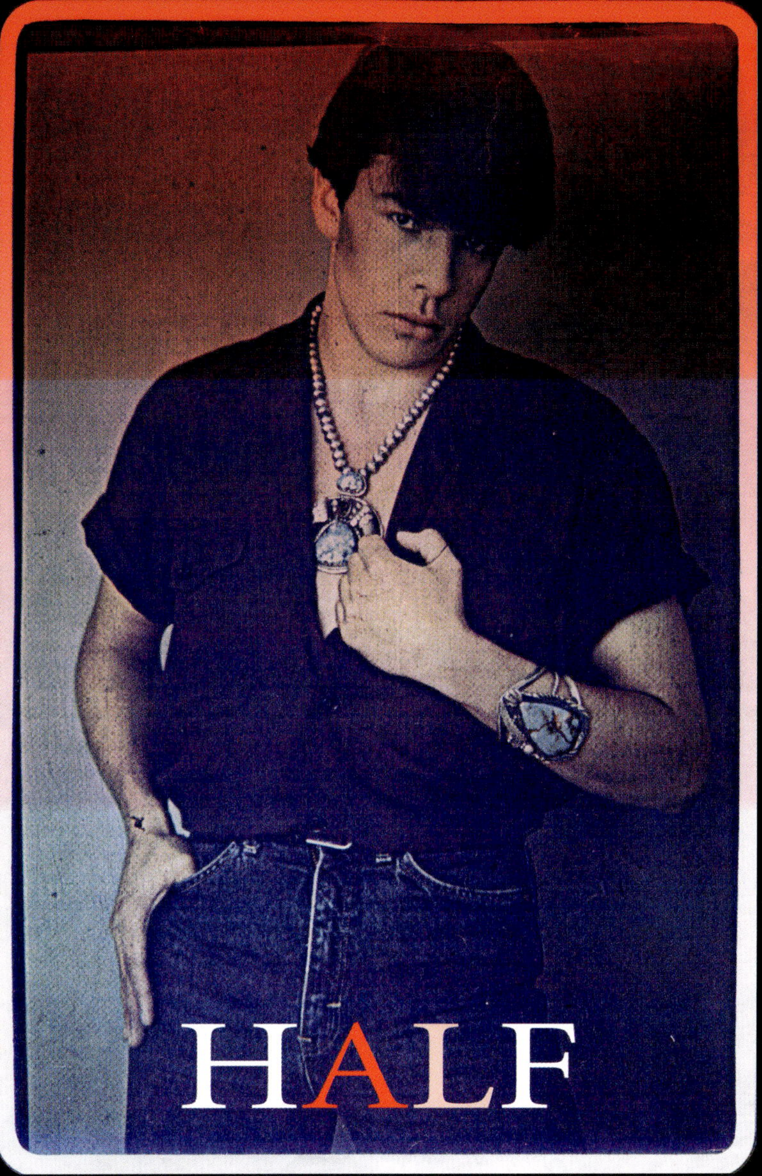

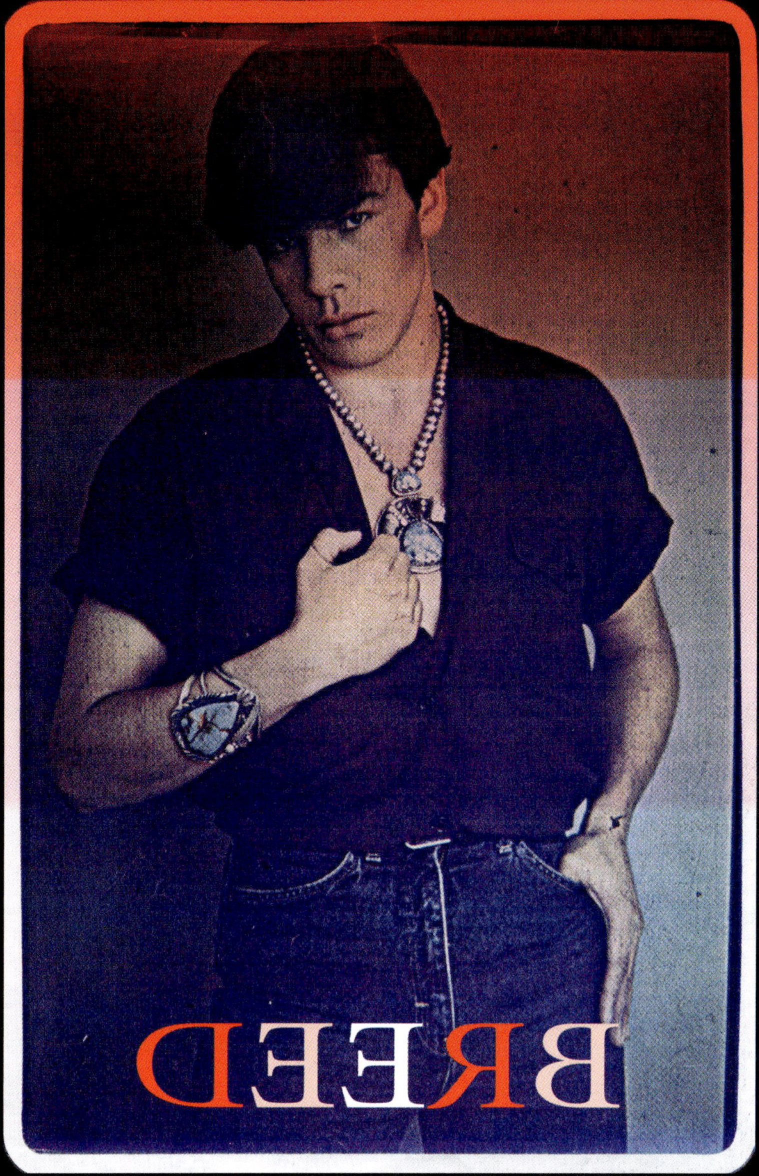

Half archival digital image :: 36" x 24" :: 2011

This is an old modelling shot of me, taken in 1978 at age 20 in Calgary, Alberta. I have several old modelling shots, and some of these have now re-entered the world through my art, such as this image with the word "half." Half is not whole. The second image, *Breed*, informs the viewer. Half Breed. How the singer Cher loved to hate the word; her famed song "Half Breed" poignantly describes some strong issues for mixed bloods born of First Nation and non–

Breed archival digital image :: 36" x 24" :: 2011

The word "half breed" is derogatory and belittling. In Cree, Apitikosan is the word for people of mixed blood; it means half a human. In the Kwagulth First Nations language, the word means 50 cents, not full, but half. No one truly understands the life of a mixed-race person except for other mixed-race people. Some try to deny one half of themselves, while other accept themselves as exactly who they are: a whole person.

INDEX OF PAINTINGS

ACKNOWLEDGEMENTS

I wish to thank all of the art institutions and educators I've had over the years: Red Deer College, Nova Scotia College of Art & Design, Banff Centre and Miss Ethel Field, my childhood art teacher.

Thanks also to the Miyo Wahkohtowin Education Authority and all the schools, colleges and universities where I have ever had residencies, taught or conducted workshops.

And thanks to all the art galleries in various parts of the world that have shown or carried my art. There are too many to name; however, there are a few people to whom special thanks are due: Lynn Fahlman at the Front Gallery, Edmonton, AB; Derek Simpkins and Isobel Proctor at Spirits of the North, Gallery of Tribal, Indian, Aboriginal and Inuit Art, Vancouver, BC; Elaine Monds and her staff at Alcheringa Gallery, Victoria, BC; Amir Ali Bhai and Leanne Davidson at the Surrey Art Gallery, Surrey, BC; Doreen Mellor and Rosie Potter and the Tandanya Aboriginal Cultural Institute, Adelaide, Australia; Reisa Schneider at the Jewish Community Centre, Vancouver, BC; Otto van de Loo at Galerie van de Loo, Munich, Germany; and Tony Martin at the Comox Valley Art Gallery, Courtenay, BC.

I would also like to thank some of the artists I admire and who have been an inspiration to me: Dr. Joane Cardinal-Schubert, Linda Frimer, Teresa Marshall, Mary Longman, Shirley Bear, Barry Ace, Ryan Rice, Liz Carter, Steve Smith, Ruth Cuthand, Lonnie Vigil, Conrad House, Adrian Stimson, Terrance Houle, Peter Morin, Faith Louis-Adams, Jack Shadbolt, Daphne Odjig, Bill Reid, Robert Davidson and printmakers Michael de Courcy, Terre Bonim, Andy MacDougall, Wolfe and Dave Johns.

Thanks to all the collectors and patrons of my art and to all the special friends, some of whom have stuck by me, and others who were there for part of my artistic journey. I appreciate you all: John Holt; Christopher Vollan; Linda Frimer and her large extended family; Gil Cardinal; Yoshimi Nishi Woolsey; Steve, Jenny and Rachel Smith; Lynn Wainwright; Derrick Sorochan; Brian and Pam Wildcat; Theresa (Minde) Wildcat; Matthew Wildcat; Leanne Franson; Rob Spooner; Jeff Fisher; Rebecca and Joshua Raphael; Marianne Bear-Palmer; Sara Potts; Mono Potts; Lydia Yellowbird; Aaron Rice; Terry Haines; Rob and Lee Everson; Verna Flanders; Tony Rogers; Rita Irwin; Mary Everson; Joyce Rice; Laurie Gates; Barb Ali Bhai; the late Montana Poole; Scott and Lasha Roche; Steve Charles; Loretta Todd; Valerie Arnault; Connie Watts; Matthew Jacobs; Gail Tremblay; Josee Tremblay; Suzanne Wilkinson; the Comox First Nation and many others.

And thanks to my amazing uncles, aunts, cousins and siblings; and to my foster and biological brothers and sisters and their families: Jack, Richard, Winnifred, Evelyn, Brian, Raymond, Shirley, Marilyn, and Marilyn and cousins; Lorna Visser; Joanne Solomons; Dot Prins; Priscilla Riel; Marvin Littlechild and family; Marcella Child-Paul; Sandy Belrose; the late Connie Omeasoo; Joan Foulston and Gloria Johal; Rick Crume; Garth, Dell and Skip Reistad; and the Powell family, to name a few. Particular thanks must go to Uncle Rene and Auntie Rachel Littlechild for all your love.

And a very special thank you to John Powell for always being there and for all your unconditional love to one and all.

Heritage House Publishing Company Ltd.
heritagehouse.ca

LIBRARY AND ARCHIVES CANADA CATALOGUING IN PUBLICATION

Littlechild, George
George Littlechild: the spirit giggles within / by George Littlechild; foreword by Ryan Rice.

Issued also in electronic format.
ISBN 978-1-927051-51-1

1. Littlechild, George. 2. Painting, Canadian. 3. Indian painting—Canada. 4. Native artists—Canada—Biography. 5. Artists' books—Canada. I. Title.

ND249.L58A2 2012 709.2 C2012-904113-0

Edited by Kate Scallion
Proofread by Lana Okerlund
Cover and book design by Jacqui Thomas
Front cover: detail of *Woman, Thunder Bird, Clear-Cut*
Back cover: *Cross-Cultural Examination: Strong Is the Metis Man*

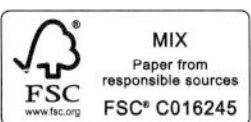

This book was produced using FSC®-certified, acid-free paper, processed chlorine free and printed with vegetable-based inks.

Heritage House acknowledges the financial support for its publishing program from the Government of Canada through the Canada Book Fund (CBF), Canada Council for the Arts and the province of British Columbia through the British Columbia Arts Council and the Book Publishing Tax Credit.

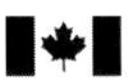
Canadian Heritage Patrimoine canadien

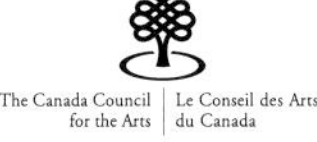

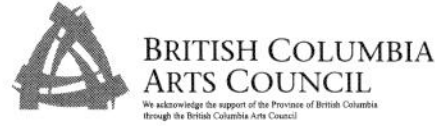

16 15 14 13 12 1 2 3 4 5

Printed in Canada